A HISTORY OF
THE KING'S AFRICAN RIFLES
AND
EAST AFRICAN FORCES

The Battle Honours of
THE KING'S AFRICAN RIFLES

Ashanti 1900
Kilimanjaro
Nyango
British Somaliland 1940
The Omo
Abyssinia 1940–1941
Mawlaik
Arakan Beaches

Somaliland 1901–1904
Narunggombe
East Africa 1914–1918
The Juba
Gondar
Madagascar 1942
Kalewa
Burma 1943–45

A HISTORY OF
THE KING'S AFRICAN RIFLES
AND
EAST AFRICAN FORCES

by

Malcolm Page

with a Foreword by
THE RIGHT HON
THE LORD ALPORT
PC TD DL

LEO COOPER
LONDON

First published in 1998 by
LEO COOPER
an imprint of
Pen & Sword Books Ltd
47 Church Street
Barnsley,
South Yorkshire
S70 2AS

© Malcolm Page, 1998

ISBN 0 85052 538 1

The right of Malcolm Page to be identified as the author of
this work has been asserted by him in accordance with the
Copyright, Design and Patents Act of 1993

A catalogue record for this book is available
from the British Library

Typeset by Phoenix Typesetting
Ilkley, West Yorkshire

Printed by Redwood Books Ltd,
Trowbridge, Wilts.

FOR
A M d'E

CONTENTS

Foreword ix
Introduction xi
Glossary xiii
Chapters
 1. How It All Began 1
 2. The "Mad Mullah" Campaign 1900–1920 10
 3. From German East Africa to Tanganyika 1914–1918 25
 4. Between the Wars 1919–1940 50
 5. Italian East African Empire – Part I 65
 6. Italian East African Empire – Part II 75
 7. Madagascar and Mauritius 115
 8. Burma 133
 9. Victory and Afterwards 176
 10. Malaya 187
 11. Kenya and Mau Mau 201
 12. Imperial Twilight 221
 13. The Kenya Regiment – by Len Weaver CBE 239
     Epilogue 253

Appendices
 A. Lt Col H Moyse-Bartlett MBE MA PhD –
    a personal tribute by Professor Anthony Allott 255
 B. "They Went Singing" – by Professor
    G. G. Shepperson CBE 257
 C. The Royal East African Navy – by
    Lt Cdr Barry Mitchell 264
 D. East African Artillery 269
 E. The Royal Wajir Yacht Club 271

Bibliography 275
Index 277

MAPS

1.	Colonial East Africa	xx
2.	The Mullah Campaign 1900–20	11
3.	The Campaign in German East Africa 1914–18	26
4.	The Ethiopian Campaign 1940–41	64
5.	The Battle of Tug Argen 1940	69
6.	The River Awash Crossing, 3 April, 1941	89
7.	The Battle of Colito, 19 May, 1941	98
8.	Madagascar and the Comoro Islands	114
9.	Burma	134
10.	Kenya: Mau Mau and after	200

FOREWORD

by The Rt Hon The Lord Alport PC TD DL

A generation has passed since the King's African Rifles and East African Forces ceased to exist. Yet for those British ranks who served with them before, during and after the Second World War the bonds of comradeship remain strong, as does the affection felt by the officers for the Ascaris whom they trained in peace and led in war.

Brigadier Malcolm Page served with one of the most attractive and volatile units of the East African Command and his experience has encouraged him to write a history of the King's African Rifles and East African Forces covering the whole span of the years when they existed.

The attraction of service in East Africa was of course also generated by the marvellous countries stretching from the Horn of Africa to the Zambesi. It is good to know that the contribution of KAR and the East African Forces have made to the success of the independent African countries which are now in existence has been immense and enabled those countries, at any rate to some extent, to avoid the disasters which have occurred elsewhere in post-colonial Africa in recent years.

It is right that, while the memory of that service is still fresh in the minds of those who served in East Africa, a comprehensive history should be published and I am delighted to think that future generations, who will not have the opportunity and advantage of serving with Her Majesty's Forces in East Africa, will be able to obtain from the following pages some idea of the history and achievements of this remarkable part of the fighting forces of the British Crown.

ACKNOWLEDGMENTS

I am indebted to the following for the loan of, and permission to reproduce, photographs in their possession: By permission of the Syndics of Cambridge University, from the Royal Commonwealth Collection, 1, 19; G.B. Lambert Esq, 2, 3; Lt-Col Peter Mulloy, 4, 7, 8, 9, 10, 11, 12; Brig Michael Biggs, 5, 6, 34; Capt John Watson-Baker, 17; Capt R.E. Vanderpump, 18; Lt-Col J.A. Gibb, 22; Col H. J. Lowles, 23, 24, 25, 26, 27; Major John Spurway, 28; Major Geoffrey Whitworth, 29; Major B.J. Lambert, 31, 32; Rhine Link, 33; Officers of the Kenya Regiment, 35, 36, 37, 38, 39; Professor George Shepperson, 41; Lt-Cdr Barry Mitchell, 42, 43. The map on p. 98 has been redrawn from a sketch kindly loaned by Brig Michael Biggs.

INTRODUCTION

The idea for this book came from my colleagues of the Rhino Link team, as we surveyed the growing quantity of material sent in by members for publication in Rhino Link, the newsletter of the KAR and EA Forces Dinner Club. With the Club approaching its fiftieth anniversary it seemed appropriate to mark the event and to capture and to put before a wider audience the experiences of our members. These are in many cases rare, sometimes unique, and almost certain never to be repeated. At the same time it was necessary to set them in a historical context; this extended to include social, economic and political considerations, as so much has changed since these events took place.

The book, as it has emerged, is an end-to-end history of the KAR and the East African Forces. It does not aspire to be another Moyse-Bartlett; it covers a longer period, until after Independence for the territories involved, and is wider in scope, as it has covered many non-KAR Corps, organizations and units which were excluded from Moyse-Bartlett's book by his terms of reference. It draws on individual experiences to a large extent, but relies heavily on published works, particularly Moyse-Bartlett, for those events which lie outside the scope of the living testimonies available to me. Versions of events sometimes vary. When there has been doubt about dates, places and other details, I have relied on Moyse-Bartlett and the Army Commander in Chiefs' Despatches, particularly those of FM Lord Wavell. For political and strategic settings I have drawn heavily on Churchill's *The Second World War*. For colonial history the two main sources were Thomas Pakenham's *The Scramble for Africa*, and Jan Morris' *Pax Britannica* trilogy. For the rest I have been wonderfully supported by members of the Club – and others – who have ransacked attics, rummaged in memories and plundered photograph albums to produce much previously unpublished material. Notes on other sources and suggested further reading are given in the Bibliography on page 275.

I would particularly like to thank Brigadier Michael Biggs, the Club President, Major General "Rowley" Mans (who also appears as "Toto" in the book), Lt Col Richard Corkran and Captain Peter Stocken of Rhino Link, Brigadier Ken Timbers of the RA Historical Trust, members of the

Kenya Regiment Association – especially Ken Weaver and Carol Gurney, Professor George Shepperson, Lt Cdr Barry Mitchell REAN, J.A.L. Hamilton Esq in respect of the West African connections in Burma, Roger Perkins, the author of *Regiments and Corps of the British Empire and Commonwealth* (an invaluable work of reference), plus all those who sent me material or submitted to being interviewed by me. Iris Norton kindly assisted with the maps, and I am most appreciative of the patience of my brother-in-law, Ronald Meacham, for his careful reading of the drafts.

With so much to cover, I have concentrated on the major campaigns: against the Mullah, German East Africa, Italian East Africa, Madagascar, Burma, Malaya and Mau Mau, with linking narrative, followed by the run-up to Independence and a little beyond, plus some specialized appendices. But this does not give the full picture. Units of the KAR were in West Africa in the early days of the century, rounding the Cape to get there. Their furthest north is probably represented by some men who were prisoners of war in Germany during World War II. Their furthest east was to reach the Irrawaddy in Burma, also in World War II. I have sought to tell a story of military prowess, initiative, fortitude, gallantry, improvisation, loyalty and heroism, together with occasional light relief. I hope that something of the spirit of the age, and of the dedication and comradeship of the KAR and EAF have come through. It has – to my regret – not been possible to be able to tell it all, and balance may be lacking in places. With so much to cover, some omissions are unavoidable. The faults are mine alone.

Malcolm Page
Henley on Thames, Jan 97

GLOSSARY

ABVAT	All Burma Veterans' Association of Japan
AD	Air Despatch
ADOS	Assistant Director of Ordnance Services
AKC	Army Kinema Corporation
AOC	Air Officer Commanding
AOP	Air Observation Post
askari	(Arabic/Swahili) literally "soldiers" (ie: plural) describes African soldiers trained by Europeans. Sometimes incorrectly pluralized as "askaris"
"Askari"	Swahili language newspaper for African soldiers
A.Supt	Assistant Superintendent of Police (equivalent to Chief Inspector in British Police Forces)
AT	Animal Transport
AOR	African Other Rank (ie; below commissioned rank)
Banda	Italian irregular Somali or Ethiopian troops
BCFG	Burma Campaign Fellowship Group
Bde	Brigade
Bn	Battalion
Brig	Brigadier
Brig Gen	Brigadier General
BEM	British Empire Medal
Bhang	(Arabic/Swahili) Cannabis
BNCO	British Non-Commissioned Officer (ie; excluding warrant officers)
BOR	British Other Rank (ie; below commissioned rank)
BURCORPS	1 Burmese Corps
Burma	Myanmar
Bwana	(Swahili) Sir
BWO	British Warrant Officer
Capt	Captain, RN or Army
CCF	Combined Cadet Force
CDRC	Coast(al) Defence Rifle Company
Ceylon	Sri Lanka
CF	Chaplain to the Forces (eg; a padre)
chai	(Urdu/Swahili) tea

chaung	Burmese waterway
CIGS	Chief of the Imperial General Staff
CO	Commanding Officer (usually a Lt-Col)
Cpl	Corporal
CPO	Chief Petty Officer
CQMS	Company Quartermaster Sergeant
CRA	Commander, Royal Artillery
CT	Communist Terrorist (in Malaya)
DC	District Commissioner
DCM	Distinguished Conduct Medal
DDT	An insecticide
DIMCOL	An ad hoc column of 28 (EA) Bde, formed for its advance to the Irrawaddy, commanded by Brig WA Dimoline
DO	District Officer
DOS MELF	Director of Ordnance Services, Middle East Land Forces
DRAFORCE	5 KAR Companies grouped under the 2ic, Maj WD Draffan, to cross the Chindwin
Dubas	(Somali – "red fire"), tribal police in the NFD, so called because of their red pagris (turbans)
DZ	Dropping Zone
EA	East Africa(n)
EAA	East African Artillery
EAAC	East African Armoured Corps
EAAEC	East African Army Education Corps
EAAMC	East African Army Medical Corps
EAASC	East African Army Service Corps
EAAEME	East African Army Electrical and Mechanical Engineers
EAMR	East African Mounted Rifles
Effendi	(Arabic/Swahili) Sir. Respectful form of address, Egyptian title, rank of junior African officer
ENSA	A Services entertainment organization
FANY	Female Auxiliary Nursing Yeomanry
FARELF	Far East Land Forces
FG	Fighting Group
Field Company	Basic unit of the *Schutztruppen* and of SA and EA Engineers
FOO	Forward Observation Officer, for artillery or mortars

FOWCOL	Fowkes' Column, 22 (EA) Brigade, reinforced and tasked for specific operations
French IndoChina	Laos
GC	Gold Coast
German East Africa	Tanganyika, now part of Tanzania
GHQ	General Headquarters
GOC	General Officer Commanding
GOCinC	General Officer Commanding in Chief
goose-necks	Portable airfield landing lights
Gp Capt	Group Captain (RAF)
GR	Gurkha Rifles (eg; 10 GR)
G(R) Force	Formation from Aden which re-occupied Berbera
habash	(Somali/Swahili) Ethiopian (not a popular term with Ethiopians)
habari	(Swahili) News
Haji	Title of a man who has made the haj (pilgrimage) to Mecca
HA-GO	(Japanese) Plan Z
HMEAS	Her Majesty's East African Ship
HMT	His/Her Majesty's Troop Ship
HQ	Headquarters
IBEAC	Imperial British East African Company
Ind	(In unit/formation designation) Indian
I Force	An ad hoc company of the Kenya Regiment, with KAR askari, tracker dogs and de-oathed Mau Mau
India	pre-1947 India, including India, Pakistan and Bangladesh
Inf	Infantry
Illalo(s)	(Somali) literally "watcher", armed tribal police
IO	Intelligence Officer
IS	Internal Security
K	(In unit designation) Kenya, eg; 11(K) Bn KAR
Kanzu	(Swahili) Long white gown worn by mess waiters
KARMI	KAR Mounted Infantry
KARRO	KAR Reserve of Officers
KARSTAFF	HQ for KAR regimental affairs in 1914/1918 war. Disbanded in July 1920
KDF	Kenya Defence Force
KG	Kikuyu (Home) Guard
KPR	Kenya Police Reserve

KRRC	King's Royal Rifle Corps
LAA	Light Anti-Aircraft (unit or gun)
Lcpl	Lance Corporal
Lt	Lieutenant (RN or army)
Lt Col	Lieutenant Colonel
Lt Gen	Lieutenant General
Malaya	Western Malaysia
Malgash	Indigenes of Madagascar, particularly those in French service
MILCOL	Ad hoc column of 28(EA) Brigade, formed for their advance to the Irrawaddy, commanded by Lt Col D Campbell-Miles
MO	Medical Officer
MRS	Medical Reception Station
MTO	Motor (or Mechanical) Transport Officer
murram	(Urdu/Swahili) unmetalled road surface, usually red, corrugated and dusty
N	(In unit designation) Nyasaland, eg; 2(N) Bn KAR
NAAFI	Navy, Army and Air Force Institutes, ie; canteen service
Netherlands East Indies	Indonesia
NFD	Northern Frontier District of Kenya
ngoma	(Swahili) dance and party, also the title of the Regimental March of 6 KAR
NRR	Northern Rhodesia Regiment, eg; 1 NRR
ngombe	(Swahili) cattle, but used by Mau Mau to refer to aircraft
Northern Rhodesia	Zambia
Nyasaland	Malawi
OCS	Officer Cadet School
OCTU	Officer Cadet Training Unit
Ogaden	Fifth (Somali) Region of Ethiopia, also a Somali clan who live there
ORQMS	Orderly Room Quartermaster Sergeant (warrant officer class II)
padre	Chaplain, usually an officer in the Royal Army Chaplain's Department
panjis	(Urdu) Improvised field defences, with spikes of fire-

	hardened bamboo; usually concealed in pits or trenches
para	parachute, eg; para-illuminating mortar bomb with a parachute and an illuminating flare
Portuguese East Africa	Mozambique
posho	(Swahili) Maize meal, a staple in African diet
poncho	A water-proof cape
PoW(s)	Prisoner(s) of War
PSI	Permanent Staff Instructor
PSM	Platoon Sergeant Major, (African warrant officer class III)
PT	Physical Training
QL	3-ton Bedford truck with 4x4 drive
QM	Quarter Master
QMG	Quarter Master General
Q Staff	Staff of the QMG at various HQs
RAAF	Royal Australian Air Force
RAEC	Royal Army Education Corps
Rangoon	Yangon, Burma
1 RAR	1 Bn Rhodesian African Rifles
RASC	Royal Army Service Corps
RAVC	Royal Army Veterinary Corps
RAY FORCE	Three groups of police posts, reinforced with Kenya Regiment and Kikuyu (Home) Guard
RB	Rifle Brigade
REAN	Royal East African Navy
REME	Royal Electrical and Mechanical Engineers
recce	Reconnaissance
RMO	Regimental Medical Officer
RMS	Royal Mail Ship
RNR	Royal Navy Reserve
RNSA	Royal Navy Sailing Association
RPC	Royal Pioneer Corps
RSM	Regimental Sergeant Major (warrant officer class 1)
RSPCA	Royal Society for the Prevention of Cruelty to Animals
S or Som	Somali in a unit designation, eg; 71 (Som) Bn KAR
SAAF	South African Air Force
SAEC	South African Engineer Corps

Sapper	Junior rank in the Royal Engineers, and a collective name for all Royal Engineers
Salisbury	now Harari, Zimbabwe
Schutztruppen	(German) literally guard troops; German/African units raised in German East Africa
SEAC	South East Asia Command (and, unofficially, called by its American members "save England's Asian Colonies)
SS	Steam Ship
shifta	(Somali) bandits
shamba	(Swahili) garden or small farm
shauri	(Swahili) responsibility, problem, dispute, business
shenzi	(Swahili) poor, untidy, indifferent quality
Siam	Thailand
simba	(Swahili) lion
simi	(Swahili) knife, panga
SITREP	Situation Report
SKEECOL	Ad hoc column, commanded by Lt Col THS Galletley, formed to take Indainggyi
S & T	Supplies and transport
Southern Rhodesia	Zimbabwe
Ssgt	Staff Sergeant
Supremo (Mountbatten)	Supreme Allied Commander, South East Asia
Tanganyika	Former German East Africa, now part of Tanzania
TT	Tanganyika Territory, eg; 36 (TT) Bn KAR
talata	(Arabic) Figure 3, badge of 3 KAR
tarboosh	(Arabic/Swahili) tall fez worn by KAR on ceremonial occasions and by mess waiters
TICKYFORCE	Ad hoc column of 13 KAR, commanded by Major EC Spurr
TP	Tribal Police
toto	(Swahili) small boy
tug	Dried up riverbed
U	Uganda in unit designation, eg; 36 (U) Bn KAR
U-GO	(Japanese) Plan C
uhuru	(Swahili) freedom, independence
VC	Victoria Cross
Waganda	People of the kingdom of Buganda
W/T	Wireless telegraphy

WOPC	Warrant Officer Platoon Commander (warrant officer class 3)
Yunnan	Chinese Province, also describes Chinese armies based there
Zanzibar	Former British protectorate, now part of Tanzania
zariba	(Somali) field defence or cattle pen made of thorn bush

Colonial East Africa

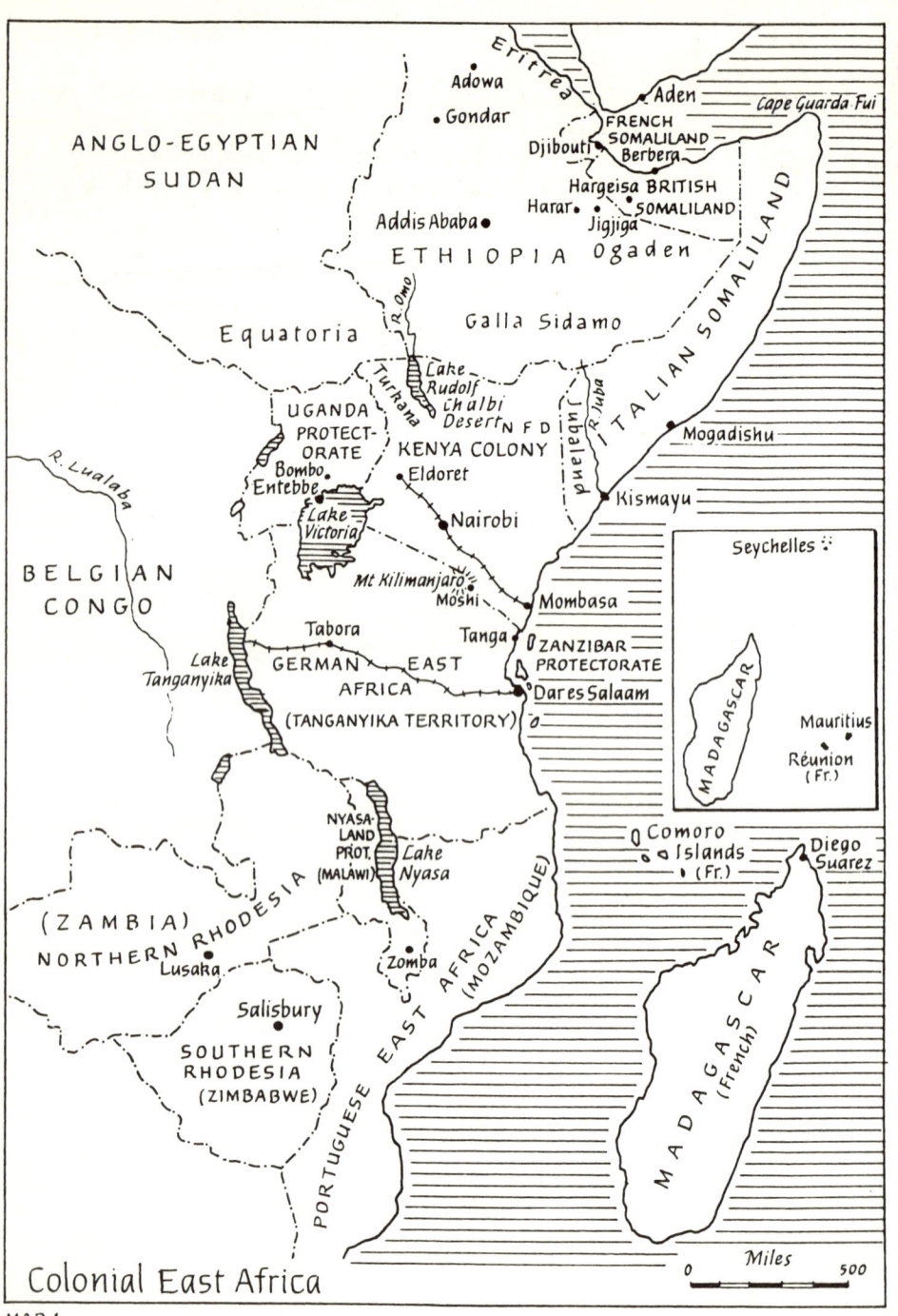

MAP 1

Chapter 1

HOW IT ALL BEGAN

"Giving up what one has is always a bad thing".
Queen Victoria to Lord Salisbury, 1890

The Scramble for Africa in the late 19th Century led to the formation of the King's African Rifles on 1 January, 1902. The original six battalions came from units established as the situation had demanded in the various territories where British rule was being introduced. Before 1 January, 1902, there had been the Central African Regiment (previously the Central African Rifles), the Uganda Rifles, the East African Rifles and various levies and units in Somaliland. There were also several Indian Contingents, and the remnants of Emin Pasha's Sudanese in Uganda. The original six battalions did not include the 6 KAR that was formed during the closing stages of the 1914/18 war, in what became Tanganyika; the first unit called 6 KAR was a mixed Indian/Somali battalion.

British, French, German, Italian, Portuguese and Belgian interests were in conflict in Africa. Britain was concerned for the security of the Nile headwaters and the southern exit to the Red Sea. The discovery of quinine and other medicines for tropical use, the development of the steam ship and the railway, and the opportunities to expand trade that they provided, all stimulated the rapid development of colonial empires in East Africa. Some European countries also wanted to export their surplus populations, while others wished to suppress the slave trade – the source of Arab prosperity on the coast and the scourge of the peoples living inland.

The first East Africans to be trained on European lines were Zanzibaris. In 1877, when the Sultan of Zanzibar agreed to the Royal Navy engaging local men, Lt Mathews of HMS *London* recruited and trained 300 Zanzibari Arabs. This number eventually increased to 1,300 all ranks, and Mathews, with Admiralty permission, became a Brigadier-General in the Sultan of Zanzibar's army.

Livingstone's activities focused interest on the horrors of slavery and the opportunities for Europeans in Africa. He discovered Lake Nyasa in 1858 and his reports included news of the great Lualaba River that ran north from somewhere west of Lake Tanganyika. Other missionaries followed

Livingstone and trade followed the missionaries; later came administration and settlement. Settlement progressed in various degrees, according to the nature of the territory and as opportunities for cash crops and minerals were detected. When administrations developed, law and order had to be enforced. The Arab slave traders were particularly dangerous as their business was disrupted. Against this background young and comparatively junior officers raised and led some very ad hoc bodies of men. The archetype was Captain F.D. (later Lord) Lugard of the Norfolk Regiment, who went to East Africa in 1888 to shoot elephant. He also considered joining the Italians in their war against Ethiopia and rescuing Emin Pasha, the German-born Governor/scientist isolated in the Equatorial province of Sudan, whom many considered to be a "second Gordon".

First, his attention focused on an incident involving the African Lakes Company. A coastal Arab (ie: half-caste) slaver named Mlozi was persecuting the Ankonde people and the potentially important town of Karonga at the head of Lake Nyasa, which controlled the road from Lake Nyasa to Lake Tanganyika. The British had attacked Mlozi with the support of the Ankonde and another tribe, after he had forced them out of Karonga. The attack was successful, but the "allies" disappeared with their ivory and other plunder. Karonga was rebuilt, but Mlozi's power was still intact and had to be destroyed if the area was to be pacified. Lugard offered his services to the British Acting Consul and was appointed to lead the expedition. With a nucleus of some twenty British and South Africans he went to Blantyre and then on to Bandawe on the lake, where, with the aid of the Free Church Mission, he selected his allies. He decided against the Angoni, but recruited among the Atonga, who had lost many of their villages. In an assault on the slavers' stockade Lugard was shot in both arms and the attack was abandoned.

After Lugard recovered from his wounds and when the gun he had sent for had arrived, the attack was renewed. The force had been reorganized into three separate tribal companies and the adjacent countryside was under better control. The 7-pounder gun had been bought by the Nyasa Anti-Slavery and Defence Committee and reached Lugard in January, 1889. The forts were bombarded three times with little effect, by which time Lugard had left the scene and smallpox was rife in the slavers' camp. Lugard recommended setting up a military headquarters on the plateau between the two lakes, with garrisons at both ends, to be provided by a force of 1,000 men, with officers and NCOs from the Indian Army.

This proposal was implemented shortly after Nyasaland became a Protectorate. Capt C.M. Maguire of the 2 Hyderabad Lancers raised the force, beginning with forty Sikhs and thirty Muslim cavalrymen from his own regiment. Their first objective was a Yao slaver named Chikumbu, who had attacked two British coffee planters at the end of 1891. By 1894 the force was 350, a mixture of Sikhs and locally enlisted men. In 1896 they were called the British South African Rifles, but this was changed to 1 Bn Central African Rifles two years later. In 1897 and 1898 they were in action under the officer who later became Sir William Manning, against the Angoni and the Anguru peoples, and three companies were detached to north-east Rhodesia, where they remained until 1901. These commitments led to the formation of a second battalion in 1899. They co-operated with the Portuguese against the Yao chief Mataka and in the same year 100 men took part in a punitive expedition in north-east Rhodesia, during which they marched 1,000 miles in two months.

2 CAR was sent to Mauritius to replace the Mauritius Regiment, but were unpopular with the Creole people. The battalion arrived on 29 June, 1899; seven officers, thirty-two Sikhs and 878 Africans, with 220 wives and seventy-seven children. The unit was unarmed and poorly equipped, as most of their kit was shipped later. The men were allowed out of barracks only in groups of ten or more, for self-protection. The battalion was reinforced by eleven officers and a sergeant major, and gained a good report at their annual inspection in November. But because of constant Creole hostility they were moved to Flat Island, an inhospitable place without adequate water. They were then ordered to British Somaliland to operate against the Mullah. Some of the troops were cooped up on a ship for five weeks, pending adequate arrangements being made for the move. In Berbera they were armed and equipped for operations and took over from an Indian battalion which returned to Aden.

In the same year shortages of British military manpower led to the CAR being sent to the Gold Coast, where a dispute with the Ashanti over the Golden Stool, their symbol of royal authority, had got beyond the control of the local garrison. On 19 June, 1900, four officers, seventy-three Sikhs, 276 African askari and a machine-gun detachment, plus a medical officer and a hospital, left Zomba for Ashanti, under the command of Major A.S. Cobbe, with half of 2 CAR to follow from Berbera. Cobbe and his men were in action in August, but they suffered heavy casualties in thick bush, with Cobbe among the wounded. Lt Col Brake, Headquarters and four companies of 2 CAR arrived on 13 August and were in the operational area a week later. They fought several actions in conjunction with the West African Frontier Force; Brake was invalided home in September and Major A.F. Gordon took over. The campaign ended in an operation in which two companies from each of 1 and 2 CAR took part, when they earned praise from the commandant of the West African Frontier Force (Willcocks) and

Manning for their discipline, drill and shooting. They returned to Nyasaland via the Mediterranean, (having gone out round the Cape), so they circumnavigated Africa.

The other half battalion of 2 CAR moved to the Gambia following the murder of two commissioners and their police escort in June 1900. They travelled to Bathurst by the SS *Dwarka*; Brake rejoined them when the ship called at Gibraltar. At Bathurst the women and children, together with H Company, were disembarked and Brake advanced at once. With the rest of the field force, including four companies of 3 Battalion, West Indian Regiment, they sailed up the river and eventually landed at Tendaba. Their objective was the stockaded town of Dumbutu, which they reached after a three-hour advance through long grass. Two companies of 2 CAR, under Major Plunkett, moved round to the left flank to get between the village and the French border. Surprise was complete and when the defenders finally surrendered more than forty men were dead and over 200 men and women were captured. Losses on the British side were one carrier killed and four men wounded. There were some sweeping-up operations, including tax collection and the capture of over 200 rifles.

The British and French administrations mounted a joint operation against Fodi Kabba, who was a problem to them both. The West Indians went back to Sierra Leone, apart from one company. The French guns pounded the walls of Fodi's main town, Madina, until it capitulated; Fodi was among the killed. 2 CAR was not directly involved in the fighting. Afterwards they destroyed some of the remaining towns belonging to Fodi's followers. Due to a shortage of officers, 2 CAR had "borrowed" three RN officers when they first arrived at Bathurst, who did well in command of troops.

Brake and his men went to the Gold Coast next, to put down a mutiny in the West Indian Regiment, which took them two weeks. The majority of 1 and 2 CAR returned to Zomba in January, 1901, but representative detachments of both battalions went to England. On 26 June King Edward VII inspected them at Marlborough House and presented medals for both the Ashanti and the Gambia campaigns. They were also inspected by Lord Roberts, saw the Royal Tournament, a military exhibition and a review of the Household troops, before returning to Nyasaland in July.

In what became Kenya the Imperial British East Africa Company (IBEAC) received a Royal Charter in 1888, to exploit the region of the Great Lakes and take over the British concessions negotiated with the Sultan of Zanzibar earlier. Britain also occupied Kismayu. The British wanted a Cape to Cairo route, while France sought west to east suzerainty. IBEAC did not have the kind of backing that Cecil Rhodes gave to the Africa Lakes Company; by

1892 it was nearly out of money and ready to pull out of Uganda. The company collapsed in 1895 and the British East Africa Protectorate was declared – with the support of missionary and humanitarian interests. It covered present-day Kenya and the land west of the Juba River. Italy gained control of the Jubaland east of the river from the Sultan of Zanzibar.

The new Protectorate's soldiers were formed as the East African Rifles, and consisted of Sudanese, Swahili (ie: coastal Africans), Punjabis and locally recruited tribesmen in equal numbers. They were based on the Company's own body of armed guards which had been formed earlier from Sudanese, Somalis and Swahilis. The Inspector-General wrote fifteen years later that they were "ready made but really untrained troops". The first Commandant was Major G.P. Hatch, with headquarters at Fort Jesus, Mombasa. The establishment authorized in 1895 allowed for 300 Punjabis, 100 Sudanese – but this was increased to 250 soon afterwards – 300 Swahilis and 200 "mixed" men. India was asked to send fifteen trained gunners and some hospital attendants.

Their first sortie, in 1896, was against the Wakamba, who had burned some police posts set up to prevent slave trading. The operation was successful, with the help of 800 Masai. A large collective fine was imposed, villages were burned and a barracks was constructed in the heart of Wakamba territory to discourage recurrence. Jubaland had a garrison of 300; mixed Sudanese, Somalis and Wagosha. Pay and conditions were better than in Uganda, where a mutiny was put down by Kenyan troops in late 1897/early 1898. Harrison marched eighty men 360 miles in nineteen days to get to the scene, and the railway line, although incomplete, was pressed into service to transport the remainder of the force, including numbers of carriers.

After the Ugandan mutiny the battalion was reorganized into five Sudanese and three Swahili companies. The Indian Contingent remained until their contracts expired in October, 1900, when they were replaced by a fourth Swahili company. There were a punitive raid against the Kikuyu in 1901, and a campaign into Jubaland in 1899/90, which led to a proposal for the battalion to be increased to 1,500, but it was not approved in full. Attempts to raise a company of fifty Masai failed. A Camel Corps was formed in the Jubaland, which was very effective locally but could not be used elsewhere. Kenya was soon a colony in all but name. The priority became economic development and the highlands gained importance over the coastal belt.

Emin Pasha had been governor of Equatoria, and Henry Morton Stanley (then employed by King Leopold of the Belgians) was commissioned to rescue him in 1887 as a byproduct of his west to east exploration of the Congo. Mackinnon, the Chairman of a major shipping company, signed treaties with the Sultan of Zanzibar and some up-country tribes, and established the headquarters of the British East Africa Company at Mombasa. Apart from Stanley, a German named Peters was looking for Emin Pasha. The German Government claimed that Peters was on a private mission, but by May, 1890, he was reported to have signed a treaty with Mwanga that gave Germany a Protectorate over Uganda. Lord Salisbury played his master-stroke before the Kaiser could ratify the Protectorate proposal. Britain owned the three-square-mile rock of Heligoland which had, by 1890, become the key to the Kiel Canal. Salisbury stressed its importance to the German Ambassador and proposed an exchange. In July Salisbury explained his plan to the Queen; in return for tiny Heligoland she would gain at least 100,000 square miles of Africa – Zanzibar, Uganda and Equatoria. The Queen grumbled a little and made the remark at the head of this chapter; but the deal was done and the Nile headwaters were almost secure. A month later Salisbury agreed with the French Government their sphere of influence, including several million square miles of the Sahara. Uganda was now firmly British.

Lugard had taken service with the IBEAC in 1890 and had gone to Uganda with a force of fifty Sudanese and Somalis, and 270 armed porters. The country was on the brink of civil war and many expected that the recent murder of Bishop Hannington would be avenged. After extensive negotiations with King Mwanga, Lugard signed a treaty that gave him a recognized status in Uganda for two years. Lugard was then reinforced by Capt W.H. Williams, seventy-five Sudanese, a hundred Swahilis and a second Maxim gun; the better armed porters were formed into two companies and given extensive training. A further group arrived from the coast, to increase the force to 650, of whom 300 were reasonably well trained. Lugard was opposed by the Moslem party in Uganda and the Bunyoro. In their first battle Lugard was successful, but his Bagandan allies did not pursue the defeated enemy and the victory was incomplete. By this time Stanley's deputy, A.J. Mounteney-Jephson, had reached Emin and taken him to Zanzibar. Behind him Emin had left his Sudanese soldiers, which Lugard had heard were the best military material in Africa. Lugard set up Forts George and Edward during his search for them, then found them at Lake Albert, with their commander, Selim Bey. Selim had declined to enter German service, saying he was still the servant of the Khedive. He used the same argument to Lugard, but agreed to serve in alliance with the British pending the Khedive's agreement. Pay was to be four rupees per man per month (Selim received 420 per month). This compared with sixteen rupees per African soldier and eighteen to each Indian soldier in the East African Rifles. The agreement with Selim is the basis of the 4 KAR claim to be the senior battalion in the KAR.

Lugard engaged about 600 rifle-armed men; most of them locally enlisted, only the officers and NCOs remained from the original force. They had large households and lived on the land. Lugard was short of Europeans and realized that the Sudanese had become very self-sufficient in their exile. They amounted to 8,200 men, women and children, including 1,153 unarmed men. He set up five forts and garrisoned them with over half the men, calling them 1st and part of the 2nd battalions. The remainder, with Selim Bey, went to Kampala, where he integrated them as three companies, No 1: Old Sudanese, No 2: New Sudanese and No 3: Zanzibari.

Controversially, Lugard resolved a civil war by arming Anglicans against French-tutored Roman Catholics and Muslims, and divided the country into six provinces; two to the Anglicans, three to the Muslims and one to the Catholics. Lugard returned to the coast in June, 1892, with a railway survey party under Capt J.R.L. Macdonald and an Indian escort. But Macdonald was ordered back to Uganda to investigate complaints about Lugard and his methods, which the British Government had learned about from claims for compensation made by the French missionaries. His report criticized Lugard and his methods.

There were now serious problems with the Sudanese, who were split between "enlisted" and "unenlisted" men. Selim Bey would not agree to more men being converted to "enlisted" status. Eventually Macdonald ordered the Sudanese to take an oath of allegiance to the Queen. Although they insisted that they were loyal to her, this was not good enough for Macdonald. With the aid of his Swahili reinforcements and two Maxims crewed by British officers, the Sudanese were disarmed. Selim was tried for mutinous conduct (among other things) and was sentenced to degradation and deportation, but he died of heart disease at Nyvasha. After the civil war broke out again, Macdonald defeated the Moslems on 18 July. He then reorganized Lugard's line of forts, closing some and establishing a few new ones.

When the Protectorate was declared in 1894, the local forces (all nationalities) were 600 regulars and 200 reservists. They were in action in December under Lt Col H. Colvile against Kabaranga, who had taken Owen's closure of the southern forts as a sign of British weakness. Colvile took 420 Sudanese and 1,000 Buganda spearmen into Bunyoro, but they failed to reach Kabaranga in the foodless forest, despite stories of a hoard of ivory. Later Kabaranga was caught in the open by the Buganda spearmen, who took his cattle and some weapons. He fled across the Nile, but Colvile did not follow. Other expeditions against him became more difficult when he received supplies of modern weapons; he seriously defeated one in February, 1895. Another, commanded by Major Ternan, crossed the Nile a few months later, but it took a further expedition in August to break his power.

The Uganda Rifles Ordinance was enacted, providing for a Commandant, chief officers ("wing commanders"), native officers and under-officers. The men were to serve on twelve-year engagements. There was then a series of operations, mainly against the Nandi, followed by the mutiny in 1897. The causes were obvious; the men were exhausted by continuous campaigning, their pay was six months in arrears (apart from being far less than for askari in East Africa), their clothing was in rags and many of the British officers did not know their language or customs. Discipline was slack and the Sudanese thought that they – as the only effective troops to hand – were in a strong position. Macdonald (now a major) had returned for more survey work in the north of the Protectorate, with an escort of three Sudanese companies. These assembled reluctantly in September; but when arrangements for families to travel with the column were rescinded by Mabruk Effendi, most of the men deserted. They joined the disaffected Muslims in Buganda, located several forts and occupied the fort at Lubwa's, where three British officers were held prisoner. Macdonald reached Lubwa's with 350 Swahilis plus some British and Sikhs, positioning them on a hill nearby. The mutineers attacked in a series of well-mounted assaults, but were driven back into the fort; Macdonald lost forty-six killed and wounded. The mutineers executed their three hostages, Thruston, Wilson and Scott. The fort was besieged twice more before the end of the year, the second time by the East African Rifles, but the situation remained unaltered.

As the mutiny had involved only three companies (Nos 4, 7 and 9) and fears of a general anti-British revolt had receded, it was hoped to retain the services of the remainder. But there were undercurrents of restlessness which led to a major overhaul of the military organization. The plan was for 400 Indian troops to be enlisted in India, 700 Sudanese were to be retained and 700 Swahilis were to be recruited. The Viceroy of India would not spare the Indians and thought was given to recruiting Zulus. Formed Indian units eventually arrived as reinforcements and the mutineers were pursued by a variety of forces. Rewards were offered for the capture of the murderers of the three hostages at Lubwa's. Events moved quickly in the final quarter of 1898, when one of the mutineers was shot and two others were exiled.

A review of events surrounding the mutiny led to the establishment of a police force so that the Army could concentrate on military duties, the Administration was considerably strengthened and a new Military Ordnance was published in February, 1899. This introduced four-year terms of service, as standard, with the prospect of re-engagement, and authorized the attachment of British NCOs as instructors. By 1900 the Uganda Rifles consisted of thirty-six officers, twenty-one British NCOs and 1,952 men, organized into sixteen companies; there was an Indian contingent of 402 Indians with British officers, known as 1 Bn Uganda Rifles. Pay for the Sudanese was improved, but as the Sudanese soldiers' wives were great looters and a continual source of difficulty, it was decided to waste out the Sudanese. Pay was still often in arrears, clothing supply remained inadequate and discipline was poor. In April, 1901, a final thrust was made against the mutineers and their Muslim allies by the Lango Field Force (four companies of the Uganda Rifles plus levies of men from a variety of tribes). The operation lasted until August and the column returned with 1,485 prisoners, hosts of animals, weapons and seven tusks of ivory. The Government lost twenty-one killed and sixteen wounded, including their allies and porters.

In 1902 the battalion was designated 4 KAR and the Indian contingent became 5 KAR. The Indian battalion was disbanded in 1904 and most of the Indians returned home when their engagements ended. In 1906 4 KAR (still with an Indian element) occupied their barracks at Bombo. The battalion had many relatively minor operations until the outbreak of war with Germany in 1914, including Lumbwa, Budama, Nandi, Lake Kivi, Somaliland and Turkana. In 1913 the battalion was operational against the Dodinga and in 1914 were in Jubaland until they were redeployed closer to German East Africa. 5 KAR was reformed to garrison Jubaland and the NFD in 1916, but disbanded again on 31 December, 1925, when Jubaland was ceded to Italy. It reformed in 1930.

6 KAR formed first in Somaliland to operate against the Mullah. It varied from all Somali to a mixed Somali/Indian unit, and it was also reconstituted with all Punjabis in 1905. In 1910, when the administration withdrew to the coast, they were disbanded. 6 KAR re-emerged in 1917, when two battalions were raised in the liberated areas of what was then still German East Africa.

7 (Zanzibar) KAR were formed on 1 May, 1917, absorbing the Zanzibar African Rifles. They moved from Zanzibar to Voi in August, 1917 for lines of communication duties. At the end of World War I they were reduced in strength and became No 1 Company in 6 (TT) KAR. The title 7 KAR was revived again in May, 1939, for 7 (Uganda Territory) Bn.

Other KAR and East African Units appear in the context of the events which led to their formation in subsequent chapters of this book.

Chapter 2

THE "MAD MULLAH" CAMPAIGN

(SEYED MOHAMED ABDULLAHI HASSAN)

1900–1920

"A land of dust and poverty . . . a wilderness of dust and stone . . . peopled by rifle-wielding zealots with more than their share of 'Wadads'." (itinerant religious teachers).
W.S. Churchill, 1907.

"He was a God-send to officers with an urge to fight and a shaky or non-existent bank balance".
Lt Gen Sir Adrian Carton de Wiart.

The campaign against the Mullah was the longest and most varied in the KAR's history. The Empires of the Khedive of Egypt and the Sultan of Zanzibar had met at the tip of Cape Guarda Fui, but with both regimes collapsing, the European powers exploited the situation. France negotiated a rail corridor to Addis Ababa in return for modern weapons, with which the Ethiopians defeated an Italian invasion at Adowa in 1896. Italy developed Assab and Massawa and parts of the Somali Indian Ocean coast. Britain had negotiated a series of treaties with coastal Somalis, mainly from the Issaq clan, from 1822 onwards, culminating in the Protectorate treaties in the 1880s. The boundary with Ethiopia was agreed first in 1894, but after the battle of Adowa it was renegotiated; half the Protectorate was ceded to Ethiopia when the Rodd Line became the boundary. Britain's objectives were to secure British Somaliland as an adjunct to Aden, in particular as a source of fresh meat for the garrison there, and to keep the French, Ethiopians and Italians out. The Somali people were split between five administrations in this struggle. Italy, France, Ethiopia and Britain twice, in Somaliland and in Kenya and the Jubaland west of the River Juba.

Major H.G.C. Swayne RE (later Col H.G.C. Swayne CMG FRGS FRZS) first went to Somaliland in January, 1885, to shoot game. He made seventeen visits in all and was with the British mission to Emperor Menelik

The Mullah Campaign, 1900-20

MAP 2

in 1897 when the Rodd Line was agreed. Egypt had vacated the coast a few months before Swayne arrived and a British Assistant Resident from Aden controlled Berbera and Bulhar with a few Aden policemen, while Zeila was in the hands of both British and French consuls. In August, 1885, the Government of India sent Swayne on a reconnaissance of the coast and the interior, which lasted until February, 1887. At first he had an escort of Indian cavalry, but they caused friction with Somalis, so he replaced them with thirty Somalis, whom he trained and who helped him with his survey work. His book and sketch maps were invaluable during the campaigns.

Not all Somalis welcomed the intrusions into their territory. Most British contacts had been along the coast. The Dolbahanta and the Ogaden both belong to the Darod group of clans, and extend far inland. Seyed Mohamed Abdullahi Hassan was of mixed Ogaden and Dolbahanta origin and lived with the Dolbahanta. In childhood an operation on his head left a scar on his forehead which he later claimed was God's thumb print. He was very religious and by the age of thirty had made the Haj to Mecca seven times. He decided to free his land of Christians, including the Ethiopians. Because of his threat to British interests, several campaigns were mounted against him between 1900 and 1920, initially under the Indian Government; then until 1905 it was a War Office problem. Thereafter the Colonial Office was concerned but made two attempts to pass responsibility back to the India Office. In 1899 the Mullah reached Sheikh, about forty miles from Berbera, with armed followers. He raided the Issaq clans, who were under British protection, and sent what was virtually an ultimatum to the British Consul-General in Berbera. The Consul-General declared the Mullah an outlaw and tried to arrest him, but he moved rapidly southwards into Ethiopia, where he built up his strength. His assets included the excellent ponies and horsemanship of the Dolbahanta and the religious fervour of his followers, who became known as Dervishes (holy men) in imitation of the Mahdi's supporters in Sudan.

Deterred by a Royal Navy presence from attacking Berbera, the Mullah struck Jigjiga fiercely, losing over 1,000 men and badly shaking the Ethiopians. He looted stock and recruited from the Ogaden clans who resented Ethiopian rule. With modern weapons obtained from Djibouti, he raided the British-protected clans grazing their flocks and herds in the parts of Ethiopia they use after the rains (ie; south of the Rodd Line), then threatened Hargeisa, provoking Britain to commit 2 CAR (from Mauritius) against him and to attempt to act in conjunction with Ethiopia forces. The Mullah was just inside the Ethiopian border in September, 1900, with 2 CAR opposite him to the north, in British-protected territory, to cover Hargeisa. 2 CAR planned to strike across the border to take the Mullah by surprise, but political considerations prevented this. The opportunity was lost and Major A.W.V. Plunkett withdrew his troops towards Hargeisa. During the next few months 2 CAR marched and counter-marched to head off the Mullah, but they were then called away and left Berbera in December 1900.

Britain undertook four expeditions against the Mullah. The first was in 1901, using local levies in conjunction with Ethiopian troops. The Ethiopian units were to block the Mullah in the west, while a Somali force took care of the east. The Ethiopians were back in Harar within a few months, having looted the Ogaden without encountering the Mullah. In early 1901, Capt J.E. (Eric) Swayne, Harald's younger brother, with the aid of twenty British officers and fifty Punjabi instructors, raised, trained and took into the field a force of 1,000 infantry and some 160 mounted men (fewer than he needed, because of a shortage of ponies). Their equipment included Martini-Enfield rifles and Maxim guns, but training was delayed until sufficient rifles arrived. Against them the Mullah had a force of 5,000 riflemen and spearmen, backed by 20,000 less well trained and less dedicated spearmen. Estimates vary; Moyse-Bartlett puts the Mullah's strength at this time as being 1,200 horsemen and 300 foot, with 300 rifles. The Mullah's force fluctuated constantly in strength, and he became particularly harsh when dealing with deserters.

Swayne left Burao on 22 May, 1901, when the rains had replenished the wells, to defeat the Mullah and to punish the Dolbahanta for having supported him. There were two columns; the combat element was under Swayne's direct command, while his transport animals, stores and provisions, plus any wounded, with an escort of troops, were commanded by Capt M. McNeill. Swayne had been watched by the Mullah's scouts from the outset, and the Mullah was waiting at Yahel. Swayne left McNeill at Samala on 31 May, as it had a good water supply, and pushed on. McNeill's camp was surrounded by two zaribas [thorn fences] supported by barbed wire. They had one Maxim gun well sited, about 350 riflemen and some ancillaries, plus a small mounted force. McNeill narrowly avoided being taken by surprise when the Mullah's main force of about 3,000 men fell on his camp. They nearly surrounded it and almost broke in, but could not progress against the heavy fire. They attacked again next day, after reinforcements arrived, but were beaten off, leaving some 600 dead. The Mullah led the Dervishes away rapidly, straight into the arms of the Levies' main body. Swayne attacked and the Mullah's force dispersed into small groups, moving in all directions. The Mullah and his bodyguard took refuge in Italian-protected territory, where Swayne was not allowed to follow him. Swayne punished the Dolbahanta he could reach by taking most of their stock. The Mullah had to return to British Somaliland when the Sultan of Obbia became hostile, and Swayne moved out of Bohotleh to engage him again. By 16 July he had located the Dervishes in strength at Fer-Diddin. Swayne left his less mobile elements in a protected camp about fourteen miles from his objective.

He and his force were then recalled, but he decided to attack first. They were advancing to contact when a burst of gunfire swept the column. Some of the auxiliaries began to panic and desert, and some of the camels carrying the Maxims were killed, but the Levies disentangled the guns and got them into action. Swayne attacked frontally with his mounted troops and sent his infantry left and right flanking, then sent his infantry reserve after the mounted men. The Dervish camp was burned and over sixty Dervishes were left dead when the Mullah retreated, but most of his force got away to Italian protected territory. They left a trail of discarded kit, some dead and some chained prisoners. Although the Levies then withdrew, Swayne's scouts followed up the Mullah for a considerable distance and almost succeeded in shooting him and one of his sons. The Mullah and his bodyguard were reduced to drinking water from the stomachs of dead camels during their retreat. Swayne's casualties were one officer and nine men killed, and one officer and sixteen men wounded.

In these two actions, known together as the First Expedition, over 1,000 of the Dervishes were killed, for forty of the Levies dead and wounded, including Captain Friederichs, who was shot when helping a wounded man. A great deal of stock had been captured, but the Mullah had great powers of recuperation and the core of his force (the men in the white turbans) were powerfully motivated. He became aggressive again in early 1902, when a second expedition was launched. Swayne was now Commissioner, with authority over both civil and military matters, and the Italian Government allowed him to enter their territory. The Levy were hastily restored to 1,500 strong again, and by May, 1902, there were two companies of KAR, a Sikh detachment with two Maxim gun sections, heliographs, and the Levy available. The Mullah had about 12,000 mounted men and between 600 and 1,500 riflemen. Swayne hoped, with the Sultan's support, to land a force at Obbia and to attack the Mullah in the rear. Despite a joint British/Italian naval blockade, there was an extensive coastwise trade in rifles from Djibouti, mainly French Le Gras 1874 pattern. Swayne had Cordeaux as Vice Consul and Cobbe as his Chief of Staff for military affairs. To neutralize the Warsangeli clan he marched through their territory towards Las Koreh in April, 1902, and seized stock, while Cordeaux visited the port in HMS *Cossack*. Under pressure the Sultan of the Warsangeli made a formal submission at Berbera.

With his rear secure, the flow of weapons disrupted and major towns garrisoned, Swayne took with him 1,200 rifle-armed infantry, fifty pony-mounted infantry, twenty camelry, two seven-pounder guns, three Maxims and a vast array of camels carrying water and rations. Moving via the Nogal Valley, they located the Dervishes on 4 October and on the morning of 6 October a scout detected an ambush. Swayne formed square in dense bush and was immediately attacked on three sides. The recently recruited Somalis on the left flank panicked and some fled. The fear spread, but the Yaos from Nyasaland stood firm and saved the day. Despite their efforts, one Maxim gun was lost. (It was recovered in 1920.) Swayne restored order and gained the initiative but Capt J.N. Angus RA was killed while serving the 7-pounders. Lt Col Cobbe manned one of the Maxims himself with a Somali sergeant as his number 2. and later saved the life of a wounded man, for which he was awarded the Victoria Cross. Swayne attacked in the centre once the flanks were secure, with two companies of Yaos and two of the Levies. Following up the retiring enemy, Swayne recovered most of the burden camels and their precious loads of water. Large quantities of stock were taken, as well as several prisoners. Apart from Capt Angus, Major G.E. Phillips was killed and Lt Everett was badly wounded. Swayne buried fifty-six of the Levies and forty-three spearmen, then withdrew to Bohotleh, reaching there by 17 October.

The Mullah regarded this battle as a defeat, because of his heavy losses, but Manning (Inspector-General KAR) thought Swayne had relied too much on the Levies. After a major review of policy in London it was decided to defeat the Mullah totally, using extensive reinforcements. Manning had already recommended drafts from 1 KAR, the other half of 2 KAR, 100 Sudanese from 3 KAR and 100 sepoys of 5 KAR. The Indian Government offered a battalion, but Manning wanted to rely on African troops. With the Boer War over, there was less need to depend on the half-trained Levies. Regular soldiers were drafted in as Manning proposed, orders reaching Nyasaland on 21 October. Elements of 1 and 2 KAR force-marched to Chiromo and embarked at Chinde on 8 November, leaving in Nyasaland only thirty-five Sikhs and 375 askari of 1 KAR. Two officers and 103 askari of 3 KAR reached Berbera on 9 November, on the *Bincoora*. Manning accepted the Bombay Grenadiers, who were en route by the end of October. When Swayne was in London for discussions, a converging attack on the Dervishes was agreed and the Third Expedition was authorized.

Obbia was unsuited for a landing, and 1 KAR had to build a breakwater. The camels that had been arranged failed to arrive and the move inland was severely delayed. It was intended to form 6 KAR from the best of the Levies and some Indian troops, but events prevented this being done quickly. B, C and D Companies of 2 KAR joined the "flying column", as the Bohotleh-based strike force was called. A detachment of Sikhs took over the two 7-pdrs from Somali gun crews and became the KAR Camel Battery. Other reinforcements included a Pioneer Regiment to work on the lines of communication and a telegraph section from the Royal Engineers. The force landed at Obbia on 26 December were three companies of 1 KAR, one company of 3 KAR and one company of 5 KAR, plus 150 of the Punjab Mounted Infantry, together with all their equipment and requirements for six months. From India, shipped direct to Obbia, were 2 Sikh Regiment, 200 men of the Bikineer Camel Corps, Sappers and Miners and a section of mountain guns. From South Africa came one company of British Infantry and one of Burgher Mounted Infantry.

They operated in two columns, under Cobbe and Fasken. Cobbe (now commanding 1 KAR) pushed forward cautiously once he had some camels, with men from 3 KAR, 5 KAR and 2 Sikhs, the last with five Maxim guns. There were some minor skirmishes, in one of them Lt Chester of 6 KAR was killed, one Burgher and two Somalis were wounded. A patrol led by Capt H.E. Olivey met the advancing Dervishes and called for reinforcements. Major A.W.V. Plunkett set out with one company of 2 KAR, forty-eight Sikhs and two Maxims, to bring in Olivey and his men, while Cobbe reinforced his zariba and recalled the second patrol.

The Mullah laid a successful trap and Plunkett was surrounded by a force of horsemen and spearmen. On 17 April, 1903, in a battle lasting two and a half hours, his force was cut to ribbons. With their ammunition exhausted and the Maxims damaged, a bayonet charge by the survivors added to the dead on both sides. The Mullah lost over 2,000 men; the dead were in piles around the remains of the square. Only forty-seven Yaos of 2 KAR survived, and all but seven of them were wounded. Apart from Plunkett, Capts J. Johnson-Stewart, H.E. Olivey, H.H. de B. Morris and L. McKinnon, and Lts J.A. Gaynor and E.W. Bell, all of 2 KAR, were killed, plus one officer of the Sikhs and one medical officer. This virtually ended the Third Expedition; the total awards for gallantry were three Victoria Crosses, one African DCM and one Indian Order of Merit.

Lord Roberts authorized the Fourth Expedition, under Maj Gen Sir Charles Egerton. It was largely an Indian Army affair, as Egerton considered the units in Somaliland to be exhausted; forces raised locally included the Gadabursi and Tribal Horse and irregular mounted scouts ("illalos", literally "watchers"). The camelry of 6 KAR were disbanded in June and a second pony company raised instead; the battalion then consisted of four companies of Somalis and two of Indians. The final plan was for a three-pronged approach, with Fasken's 2 Brigade (Punjabis, Sikhs, a half-battalion of the Hampshire Regiment and a Mountain Battery) in the north, moving on Halin, and Manning's 1 Brigade (half of 1 KAR, 2 KAR, companies of 3 and 5 KAR, the Central Africa Indian Contingent and the KAR Camel Battery) was feinting towards Mudug. 6 KAR and the Bombay Grenadiers were on lines of communication duty, and an Ethiopian force was supposed to prevent the Mullah getting into the Ogaden. Egerton concentrated his two Brigades twenty miles east of the Mullah's force and advanced towards them at Jidbali in two columns on 10 January.

He fought a bloody battle at Jidbali after his square was attacked. Eventually the weight of fire and enormous casualties made the Mullah break off the action and flee. He was pursued for two days, but Egerton had no cavalry to press home his advantage. There were over 1,000 Dervish dead, hundreds of prisoners and masses of weapons. Egerton had lost twenty-seven killed, including three British officers, and had inflicted a severe defeat. The Mullah moved towards the north-east of the Protectorate, plagued by large-scale desertions, and then to his garrison at Illig. A joint British/Italian flotilla landed marines and seamen north of the port and forced its evacuation. Dervishes streamed down the coast, harassed by naval gunfire, and the Mullah moved to Garoe. The Fourth Expedition ended on 2 May, 1904. Britain considered the Mullah had become an Italian problem and withdrew practically all troops from the eastern parts of the Protectorate. The Treaty of Illig was negotiated with the Mullah by Italy, with British concurrence, but it was not accepted by Ethiopia or the Sultans of Mijurtein and Obbia. On 1 April the Colonial Office assumed responsibility for the Somaliland Protectorate and decided to set up an administration in the interior, backed by a tribal militia.

The militia scheme did not get off to a good start, but when Cordeaux told a group of elders at Sheikh that regular troops were going to be withdrawn from the interior, they requested weapons and ammunition, so that by the end of the month the militia was in being and 33 Punjab Regiment withdrew. It was a compromise between a tribal militia to protect the grazing areas and a standing militia, but it was not a success and, despite many changes, it never attained Swayne's concept of a fleet desert force of Somalis led by a Lawrence-type figure. The Treaty did not last long, and in late April, 1906, the Mullah was raiding and occupying wells outside the area allotted to him under it. He expelled an Italian consular agent, who was rescued by a British ship. His raids continued into the following year and Italy and Britain were finding it difficult to co-operate.

Churchill, then Under-Secretary at the Colonial Office, visited Berbera and made a short journey inland. In his Minute on the Somaliland Protectorate dated 28 October, 1907, he wrote that the territory was unviable financially, the military situation weak and the troops vulnerable to attack. There were 6 KAR (400 Indians, although there were plans to raise some Somali companies to serve with the Indians), the Somali Standing Militia with 350 mounted men and 100 infantry, 180 police and 100 camel-mounted illalos. Churchill saw only two options, to occupy the country and join forces with the Italians to destroy the Mullah, or to withdraw to the coast apart from small garrisons at Burao and Sheikh. Instead of sending messages by camel to Djibouti and then by French telegraph to Aden, Churchill wanted a direct telegraph cable from Berbera, at a cost of only a few hundred pounds, to bring reinforcements over quickly. There would be considerable savings by "using the paring knife upon those smart companies of Somalis mounted on their wiry active little ponies or perched on their camels", which he proposed with regret.

Churchill's report was rejected. As it was not practical to hold the coast without control of the interior, it would mean abandoning the "friendly tribes" and it might lead to the collapse of the regime in Ethiopia, setting off a fresh "scramble for Africa". However, it was adopted later and was described by *The Times* on 8 April, 1910. as ". . . one of the most deplorable acts ever committed by a British Government". The telegraph to Aden had not been constructed and the arms trade along the coast continued virtually unchecked. The withdrawal began on 6 March and took three weeks. The Indian soldiers of 6 KAR made the long trek to Berbera as the rains broke, then the battalion was disbanded. Within months the whole country was in uproar and trade in Berbera was at a halt. The Mullah then changed his strategy. With advancing age and increasing corpulence he could not ride long distances, so he built a series of stone forts. A raid on Berbera in February, 1912, and the chaos in the interior prompted the new Commissioner to raise a Camel Corps for use as a striking force. It was intended to operate only within a fifty-mile radius of Berbera, and was authorized in June, 1912. Its initial strength was 150 Somalis, backed by 350 troops from Aden and 200 Indians from the disbanded 6 KAR.

The Camel Corps was raised rapidly, but obtaining suitable camels and saddlery from India took time. The corps was organized into two companies, each of four sections of eighteen men. The leader was Richard Corfield, a political officer, as the Corps had the status of a constabulary. By December, 1912, the Corps was based at Mandera, to guard the main trade route between Hargeisa and Berbera. Then, on 24 January, 1913, their radius of action was extended to 100 miles from Berbera. Corfield moved to Burao and so successfully established peace and recovered looted stock that the Indian troops were returned to Aden. When the Commissioner went on leave in June, Archer (Acting Commissioner) visited Corfield at Burao in early August, at a time of considerable Dervish activity, accompanied by Capt G.H. Summers, who commanded the Somaliland Indian Contingent.

Archer was pressed to authorize action against the Dervish raiders in the area south-east of Burao, towards Ber, but he thought the reports were over-coloured to provoke British involvement. He agreed to a reconnaissance and sent Summers along as a restraining influence. The Camel Corps set out on 8 August, 120 men mounted on camels or ponies, armed with rifles and a Maxim. There were about 150 followers, some with rifles; on the way they were joined by 600 spearmen and 2,000 riflemen from pro-British clans. Two forces of Dervishes were located and Corfield halted for the night and built a zariba. 300 Dolbahanta joined them, to recover their looted stock.

Corfield proposed a night attack, but Summers advised against it as the Corps was not trained for night fighting. Corfield decided to attack and at dawn the Corps advanced, having been stood to for an hour. After one false alarm, they made a genuine sighting, but were attacked when in thick bush at 6.30 a.m. before they could form square. The Dolbahanta decamped, leaving an exposed flank. The Maxim was damaged by a bullet and Corfield was killed while trying to get it back into action. The Dervishes struck in waves; Summers organized the Corps into a smaller defensive position, using the dead bodies of camels and ponies for cover, but he was wounded three times (the last time seriously) and command devolved on Dunn, one of Corfield's assistants. Just when all seemed lost, the Dervishes called off the attack and withdrew. The Camel Corps had suffered thirty-five killed in action, ten had fallen out on the way, twenty-four had deserted and some forty survived, most of whom had been wounded. The Dervish casualties, even without the Maxim, were 600 dead and 200 seriously wounded and abandoned on the battlefield. The Camel Corps dead, including Corfield, were buried in shallow graves and the survivors withdrew from Dul Madobe ("Black Hill") towards Burao and then Sheikh. Later, when a burial party returned to Dul Madobe, they found the shallow graves intact. The Dervishes were in such awe of the defenders that they had not desecrated the graves or mutilated the bodies, although that was their normal practice.

With no Camel Corps to restrain him, the Mullah extended his influence, built more forts and strengthened others. Archer drew reinforcements of Indian troops from Aden and reformed the Camel Corps at a strength of 300. The possible use of aircraft was considered in mid-1914, but not progressed. A letter from the Mullah stung the Government into making a change in policy, which was announced on 24 February, 1914. This involved increasing the Camel Corps and garrisoning Burao, Sheikh and Shimber Beris. There was no limit to the Camel Corps' radius of action, and it became a military unit. Efforts to attract men from the Sudan, Nyasaland, Arabia and Ethiopia to serve in it were unsuccessful, and the Corps was established as 500 Somalis, with a reserve of 150 of the Indian Contingent, while a further 400 sepoys formed the Somaliland Indian Contingent; the Indians were from 6 KAR. There were 400 more Indian troops in reserve, detached from Aden. The Camel Corps was not under the Inspector-General KAR, who had not been consulted about its organization and who regarded the control of the force by the civil authority as unmilitary.

Eighteen officers of exceptionable ability from Britain and India were selected to serve in the Camel Corps. The Commanding Officer was Lt Col T. Ashley Cubitt, Royal Field Artillery. Among the captains were A. Carton de Wiart (later Lt Gen Sir Adrian Carton de Wiart VC KBE CB CMG DSO) and Hastings Ismay (later Gen Lord Ismay), who became Cubitt's staff officer and 2ic. Eager to see Somaliland and ready for adventure, they arrived at Berbera in July, but soon realized that greater events were taking place elsewhere. By October the Camel Corps was ready to re-occupy Burao and move on to Shimber Beris. Burao and Las Dureh were occupied by 7 November, the Headquarters were set up and training began for the attack on Shimber Beris. The Camel Corps moved out on 17 November, reaching their objective two days later. The fort was in a strong natural position high up in rocky terrain; it had three large blockhouses and three smaller ones, and several caves. The walls were loop-holed and the small doors were set three feet above the ground.

The Camel Corps were within three miles of the fort before they were detected. The Dervishes opened fire at about 500 yards range, but much of it was ineffectual. The Camel Corps charged up to the walls repeatedly, firing through the loopholes into the blockhouses. At one stage Carton de Wiart, Ismay and three other officers, on de Wiart's initiative, rushed up to one of the doors while machine guns gave covering fire, but they failed to break in. Attention then switched to the other two blockhouses, which were attacked simultaneously. The Indian Contingent secured one and de Wiart's Somali Company made three charges up to the walls of another. Captain Symons was killed and de Wiart was seriously wounded (he lost an eye and was later shot in the arm) while trying to climb a wall near the door. The successive charges continued until 3 p.m., when the Dervishes scornfully rejected Cubitt's invitation to surrender. Cubitt broke off the action and withdrew, which made the Dervishes suspect a trap so they abandoned the first blockhouse that night. On 23 November the one elderly field piece available, a 7-pdr, arrived from Burao. Capt Dobbs fired three rounds at a range of 200 yards; the effect was more psychological than physical, but the Dervishes evacuated the rest of the fort. Cubitt now possessed a mass of masonry he could neither destroy nor garrison. Reluctantly it was abandoned and the Camel Corps withdrew to Burao; two weeks later the Dervishes reoccupied Shimber Beris. They were expected to defend it stoutly, as the Mullah was reported to have castrated their predecessors.

Archer obtained explosives, field guns and machine guns from Aden, plus a platoon of twenty-three Sikh Pioneers who were trained in the use of explosives, but no more infantry. The next advance on Shimber Beris began on 3 February, 1915, when a force of almost 600 Indians and Somalis, with British officers, set out with two 7-pdrs towed by mules and six machine guns carried on mules. Some new forts and the most southerly of the Shimber Beris forts were unoccupied and were blown up. On the following day the other two forts that commanded the ravine were attacked, after an approach from the north. The forts were taken quickly, but the defenders got away to a third fort lower down the ravine and to some caves. The field guns and the machine guns engaged at close range and more Dervishes moved into the caves. The Pioneers laid charges at the foot of the wall and the resulting explosion destroyed both the fort and its remaining occupants. Later Ismay recorded: "All our efforts to dig out the defenders were in vain. I was sorry. They had fought well". Those who had fled to the caves were dealt with by hand grenades.

Cubitt counted seventy-two Dervish dead, while his own casualties were five British officers wounded, four men killed and eighteen wounded. He left a tribal post at Shimber Beris and returned to Burao, arriving there on 8 February. The Mullah withdrew towards his major fort at Taleh and Archer consolidated the political situation in the areas he vacated, but the war in Europe then claimed many of the officers and a holding policy became necessary. Archer improved his control of the west of the Protectorate, while the Camel Corps became increasingly effective against the Dervishes, as they could advance rapidly and strike hard. They were helped by several hundred scouts strung out across the terrritory on the line of the de facto frontier with the Mullah, while the towns were garrisoned by infantry. To suit their modified role, the Camel Corps was reorganized into three camel-mounted companies (two Somali and one Indian), a Pony Company and an Indian contingent of 400 men. Its name was changed to the Somaliland Camel Corps and it was formalized by the publication of the Camel Corps Ordnance.

At one stage it looked as if the Mullah might join an alliance with Turkey and the (temporary) Moslem ruler of Ethiopia, who might have married one of the Mullah's daughters. The Mullah flew a Turkish flag over his fort at Heis for a while, but the political situation changed again in Ethiopia under the influence of the Coptic Church. Early in 1916 the Mullah lost the port of Las Koreh when HMS *Northbrook* shelled the town and a company of Indian infantry occupied it. The Mullah remained active inland for a while, then moved to the south-west. The effects of drought and an epidemic of dysentery reduced him to desperate measures in attempts to restore his fortune and reputation, and he raided close to Burao and then against the Dolbahanta, but with little success.

The Camel Corps made a major sortie on 5 October, after 500 men raided the area of Eil Dur Elan. Ismay pursued the Dervishes to the north-east, and trapped them in two narrow passes. He used tribal levies to hold one pass while he attacked the other group. Six machine guns were very effective against the 300 Dervishes on the crests and in the caves, and forced them to withdraw. Ismay was reduced to two days' rations, far from base and his men and animals were exhausted after seventy hours of riding and fighting, so the pursuit was called off. The Mullah's casualties were very heavy, but only a few of Ismay's men were wounded. The Mullah had lost eighty per cent of his force since Dul Madobe, and he withdrew into his last redoubt of forts, Taleh, Jilib, Baran and Wardair; then the 1914–18 war ended.

Ismay believed he could finish the Mullah off with just a few reinforcements, but Maj Gen Sir A.R. Hoskins, who surveyed the situation, went to the other extreme. His report was rejected by the War Office as being too expensive. The Air Staff considered that the Mullah could be dealt with by a small force of aircraft, and were allowed to try. The Mullah, for no apparent reason, moved his headquarters and 1,000 men out of Taleh to Medishe, where they presented a far less attractive target for the RAF, but were more vulnerable to the Camel Corps.

All three Services were involved. The Royal Navy was represented by HMSs *Odin* and *Clio*. The ground troops, commanded by Col G.H. Summers, were the Somaliland Camel Corps, the "new" 6 KAR, a half battalion of Indian Infantry, about 300 illalos and a tribal levy of some 1,500 commanded by Capt A. Gibb. 6 KAR had three companies from Tanganyika and a company of 2 KAR attached, commanded by Lt Col J.S. Wilkinson. The RAF component was known as Z Force and was led by Gp Capt G. Gordon. He had six DH9 single-engine two-seater day bombers and six reserve aircraft. Each plane had a bomb load of 460 pounds and two Lewis guns. They had a duration of four and a half hours and a maximum speed of 110 mph. Airfields had been prepared under the guise of oil prospecting.

In Ismay's words "the plan was simple though not very sensible". The Camel Corps and the Indian Infantry prepared a landing ground and set up a forward supply base. On 21 January, 1920, an air attack was to be made on Medishe and air operations were to be continued against this and other targets until the Air Ministry (who retained direct operational command) gave permission for them to co-operate with the other forces. The Camel Corps were to be prepared to strike in any direction except eastwards, as it was feared the Mullah might leave prematurely. The need to follow up the air strikes with rapid ground action was not accepted. 6 KAR were to attack the fort at Baran and prevent the Mullah escaping to the east, the two HM ships were to put landing parties ashore to attack another small fort, the tribal levies were to occupy any wells the Mullah might use if he tried to escape into Ethiopia, and the illalos were in reserve.

The air attack on Medishe suffered from a series of misfortunes; one plane had a mechanical failure and four others did not locate the target. The one that got through dropped eight Coopers twenty-pound bombs; the first killed the Mullah's uncle and scorched the Mullah's robe. The bombing continued for the next three days but the Dervishes sheltered in the deep caves. The use of fifty-pound incendiary bombs was more effective and forced the Mullah to move back to Taleh, although this was not known immediately. On 25 January the Air Minstry agreed to let the other components take a hand. Ismay was near the fort when the bombers arrived on 27 January. In his view they were "neither lucky or accurate". The defenders were not shaken but were still "full of fight", but left in the night.

6 KAR got to Las Koreh and started towards their objective of Baran with twenty-four British officers, seven BORs and 700 askari, armed with Vickers and Lewis machine guns and Stokes mortars; they had 800 camels. On 21 January they started to advance, sent an illalo patrol to establish a listening post and a platoon to seize a water point. The fort at Baran was a square building about forty feet high, with four towers linked by a twelve-foot wall. It was held by between eighty and 100 men. The battalion surrounded the fort and opened fire with the Stokes, with very disappointing results. The attack was broken off and the battalion withdrew, leaving the illalos on watch.

On 23 January they tried again, but the Stokes still did not have much effect and it was decided to blow up one of the towers with explosives. Lt G. Godfrey, CQMS Wood and four askari reached the wall in darkness, under cover of machine-gun fire, to position and explode 100 pounds of gun-cotton against the eastern tower. Early next morning a patrol led by Lt J. Minnery arrived in time to see about a dozen Dervishes escaping from the main fort. Rushing forward with his platoon, he got inside the gate and occupied three of the towers without resistance. A sniper in the remaining tower gave some trouble for a while; attempts to bomb him out were unsuccessful, and Minnery climbed a ladder inside the tower to shoot him with his revolver. The fort was then occupied without further difficulty; the bodies of eighteen men and three women were found, plus many dead animals. For their gallantry Minnery received the MC and Wood the DCM.

On 9 February Ismay learned that the Mullah was in Taleh, but intended to move out. Calling in Gibb and his levies, Ismay moved to Taleh, but the Mullah left in the dark before they could reach the fort, and there were no tracks that could be seen in the moonlight. A hard ride followed next day; by the end the animals were distressed and the men were not much better. Ismay found the remains of a sandwich that had been in his haversack for some days. He was about to eat the unappetising piece of fat when he felt obliged to offer some of it to his adjutant. "He was as grateful as if I had given him a five-course champagne dinner." Then they located some men, women and children in a dried-up watercourse just ahead. The men, who were escorting the Mullah's extended family, died fighting. Next morning Ismay caught up with a second group of Dervishes and captured most of them, including the Mullah's favourite wife. Then some other tracks were seen, a single horseman and about a dozen on foot. He pressed ahead with the twenty ponies that were still fit, and caught up with the party after more than two hours, to find that it was not the Mullah, but an Ethiopian who had been with the Dervishes for several years and was returning to his own country. This was not discovered until he and most of the escort had been killed. The condition of the animals then compelled Ismay to give up the chase. The captives, including five of the Mullah's wives, were taken to Burao slowly, as the animals were incapable of any speed. Rounding up his followers in the Protectorate continued for some time. Ismay wrote his report and left in April, 1920.

The Mullah had lost most of his followers and possessions. He made his way, despite the betrayal of his plans by his relatives, to Gor'ah, in Ethiopia. He could not be followed by soldiers, but the veteran Haji "Warabi" and some Issaq men tracked him down, and he moved to Imi. He died there in December, 1920, after six days of illness, – probably influenza.

Chapter 3

FROM GERMAN EAST AFRICA TO TANGANYIKA, 1914–1918

"The best men to rely on in bush fighting were those who invented it."

Charles Miller 1974

This was not said about the KAR, but about their opponents during the 1914–18 war, the *Schutztruppen*, who defied the Allies until after all other German troops had surrendered. They fought on after 11 November, 1918, and the last German askari laid down their arms on 25 November, 1918. During the 1914–18 war in East Africa the KAR increased to twenty-two battalions, with 1,193 officers, 1,497 BNCOs and 30,658 askari, including two battalions of 6 KAR formed from the *Schutztruppen*. However, this rapid growth did not take place until the second half of the war.

German control of their East African territory developed in three stages. The first was expansionist and commercial, through the German East Africa Company. The second was repressive, when African uprisings were put down forcefully. The third was more enlightened, so that by 1914 there were many thousands of German settlers, two railways and a prosperous economy based on cotton, coffee, rubber, tobacco and cereals; Dar es Salaam was a major port and a city of substantial buildings, while African education and research in tropical medicine both thrived.

During the repressive phase 600 askari were recruited in Sudan and employed under German officers and NCOs in German East Africa, but after 1906 they were replaced by local men organized, trained and led in ways suited to the country and the potential opposition – both internal and external. The result was the *Schutztruppen*, men who knew and understood bush warfare, with good terms of service, high standards of training and considerable prestige. They were recruited from the tribes that had fought hardest earlier; the Wahehe, the Angoni, the Wanyamwezi and others with martial traditions. While recruits understood bush tactics, the weapons and the ethos of a European army were taught intensively. Their one weakness was the 1871 model rifle, which used black powder and had a slow rate of fire, needed constant cleaning to keep firing and disclosed the firer's position

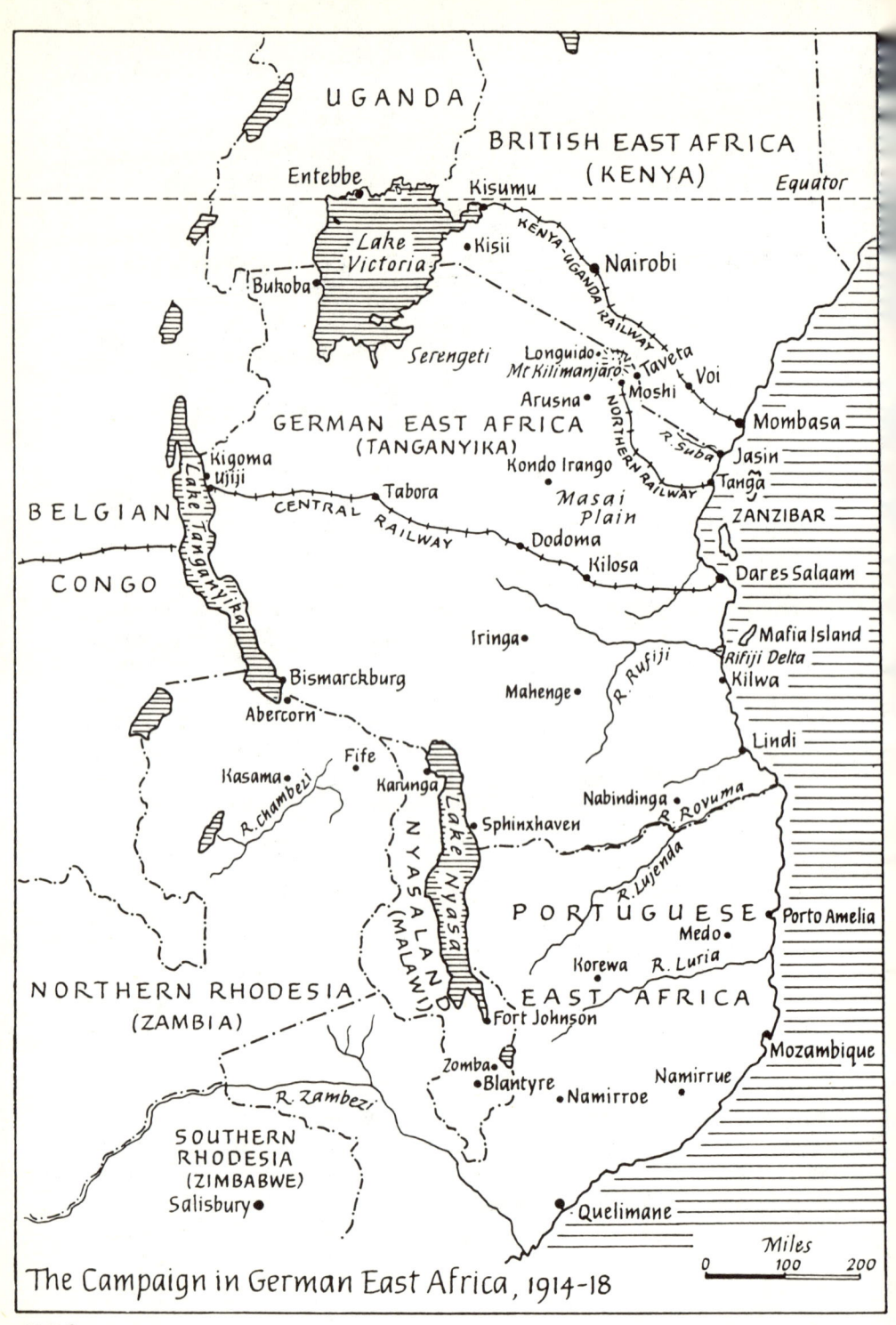

The Campaign in German East Africa, 1914-18

MAP 3

by clouds of smoke. Volley firing was taught, as being more effective than firing at will.

They wore a distinctive uniform, did no menial tasks and were paid twice as much as askari in adjacent territories. This led to some cross-border movement, particularly when 2 KAR was disbanded in 1911. There was a tribal balance in each unit and sub-unit, to ensure impartiality and reliability in an internal security situation. The officers were carefully selected and time spent in East Africa counted double when qualifying for pensions. Training was essentially practical, with a great deal of patrol work, ambush drills, making secure camp sites quickly using local materials and march discipline. Instead of the standard German army field organization, the basic unit was the Field Company of between 150 and 200 askari, seven or eight German officers and NCOs and two machine guns (sometimes even four; the KAR had one per company). It had two collapsible boats for river crossings, its own surgeon and cobbler, and a column of porters to carry rations, ammunition and other needs to make it self-sufficient for extensive periods; but they had little artillery.

The Governors of German East Africa (Schnee) and Kenya (Belfield) preferred their territories to remain neutral in the event of war, as Europe was the decisive theatre of operations and the Act of Berlin enjoined neutrality in their part of Africa. There were two countervailing factors. One was the newly arrived Commander of the *Schutztruppen*, Lt Col von Lettow Vorbeck, who wanted to make the Allies divert substantial effort to East Africa, to weaken them in Europe. The other factor was the powerful light cruiser SMS *Königsberg*, 3,400 tons, 375 feet long, 13,500 horsepower engines, ten 4.1 inch guns and two torpedo tubes. She was faster than any British warship in the area and was to become a commerce raider on the outbreak of war. On 6 June, 1914, she entered Dar es Salaam harbour and made a great impression on the German and African populations.

On the British side of the border, in Kenya, the situation had many parallels. The railway to Uganda had been built and a coastal strip ten miles wide leased from the Sultan of Zanzibar. Construction of the railway had put an end to slave trading; slaves were freed, but without them the Arabs could not work their large estates and many of them sold land to Indian and European planters. The Imperial British East Africa Company was replaced by a Protectorate administration in 1895, to keep out other European nations and to ensure the security of the Nile headwaters. The new railway, with access to the cool, relatively unpopulated highlands gave a further boost to immigration.

The KAR had been reduced and 2 KAR disbanded. In July 1907, the Committee of Imperial Defence decided that "native levies" would not be used in any defence plans for African Colonies in the early phases of any war, although they might be brought in at a late stage if necessary. In May, 1911, the role of local forces was defined as being internal security and to deal with "risings of the native population". As a result the KAR was run down to three battalions, a total of seventeen companies. In 3 KAR the effects were almost disastrous, as few men re-engaged at the end of their terms of service. In early 1912 the battalion had sixty Ethiopians in A Company, who were to be replaced as they were considered unreliable, and forty Meru who were being discharged as they were not satisfactory soldiers. B and C Companies (Sudanese) were below strength, D (mixed) and E (Nandi) were judged to be efficient, while F Company, being camel-mounted, had a limited radius of action, and G Company was new and inexperienced. The Inspector-General, Col G.H. Thesiger, warned that the situation was serious, as 3 KAR was fully committed and there was no reserve. His report was passed to the Colonial Office endorsed by the Governor "No remarks". Thesiger estimated the requirement as three companies ready in Nairobi and five committed to operations in the Jubaland, which was then still part of Kenya and where the Marihan people were causing trouble.

Thesiger submitted a fresh report when Belfield became Governor, and the new Commanding Officer 3 KAR, Lt Col B.R. Graham, found that the only striking force available in Nairobi was seventy-five strong, including instructors, the band and Headquarters staff. Belfield recommended to the Colonial Office that two more companies should be raised in Nyasaland. The conditions of service were unsatisfactory, and half of D Company 1 KAR mutinied in April, 1913, having been on extended duty, mainly on tax collection, for eighteen months away from their families, as compared with the six months originally stated. The ring leaders were tried by court martial.

Zanzibar raised the Zanzibar Armed Constabulary, including a company of infantry which was later absorbed into the KAR on Thesiger's re-commendation. The pendulum now began to swing and 1 KAR was increased by the addition of E and F Companies, recruited mainly from reservists. There were two establishments; companies for service in Nyasaland had eighty-five men and those for "foreign service" were 100 strong. G Company was added in September, when C Company moved to Nairobi. In Uganda 4 KAR were well established at Bombo, "a model station", and Thesiger compared the running of the unit with that of "a good English battalion", although he criticized their fire discipline. The Indian contingents were withdrawn because they were too expensive; the last left Uganda on 24 February, 1914.

With war imminent, the new Inspector-General, Colonel A.R. Hoskins, proposed substantial increases, but by August, 1914, the actual strengths were 1 KAR (eight companies), 3 KAR (six companies) and 4 KAR (seven companies). Apart from the problem of limited numbers, the companies were widely dispersed on internal security duties and little battalion-level training had been attempted.

The *Königsberg* put to sea from Dar es Salaam on 31 July, evaded a British squadron of three elderly cruisers and prepared to raid Allied shipping. She diverted some German ships to Dar es Salaam, providing von Lettow with 100 marine reinforcements who were returning from the Far East, but she clogged her boilers by using some inferior coal taken from a British ship and had to hide in the Rufiji delta, as Dar es Salaam was blocked by sunken ships. She made on sortie on 19/20 September, when she limped 150 miles to Zanzibar to sink HMS *Pegasus*, which was undergoing repair. She was eventually sunk by two six-inch gun monitors (HMSs *Mercury* and *Severn*) on 4 July, 1915. Her guns were removed and mounted on trolleys to give von Lettow the artillery he badly needed; some of the crew joined his land forces, while others escaped by dhow to Arabia and back to Germany via Turkey.

The relative strengths of the German and British land forces at the outbreak of war were:-

German – 216 Europeans and 2,540 askari in the *Schutztruppen*, a police force of forty Europeans and 2,154 askari; during the war 3,000 Europeans and 11,000 askari were enlisted, plus some of the *Königsberg*'s crew.

British – twenty-one companies of KAR and 3,000 Europeans of military age in Kenya and Uganda who could be utilized fairly quickly, and who could bring numbers of Africans, in some cases their own employees, with them, particularly to assist in patrolling the frontier. Lord Delamere was particularly active and formed his own troop of Masai Scouts. India and Britain and the Belgian Congo could also be drawn upon.

The positions of the railways on both sides of the border, the vulnerability of Mombasa to attack by both land and sea, and the watery west flank of the lakes were the main tactical features, apart from the dominance of Mount Kilimanjaro, the dense bush, the coastal swamps and the prevalence of the tsetse fly, which prevented the use of horses in many areas. Roads were scarce and unsuitable for heavy traffic. The Kenya-Uganda Railway ran roughly parallel to the border, as near as forty miles at one point; cutting it would do much to isolate Uganda and disrupt trade. The German Northern Railway terminated at Moshi, on the lower slopes of Kilimanjaro, and ran west of the Parc range of mountains for its first 200 miles towards Tanga. The pass between the northern end of the Parc Range and the southern slopes of Kilimanjaro was some twenty miles wide, with the British post of Taveta in the centre. The Taveta Gap was the most likely route for a British thrust from the north, as troops could be moved by rail to Voi, sixty miles north of the border. The other possible axis of advance from Voi was round the northern side of the volcano to approach Moshi from the west. Because of these two potential routes into German territory, von Lettow wanted to concentrate the *Schutztruppen* at Moshi. Governor Schnee opposed this until mid-August, when the *Schutztruppen* marched to the Central Railway and across to the Northern one, as coastwise movement from Dar es Salaam to Tanga was denied by the British blockade. A road was made across the 150 miles of mountainous country between the two railways.

Von Lettow took over the police post at Taveta on 15 August. Although the Taveta salient was known to be indefensible, its loss was a shock to the British and a morale boost for von Lettow and his men. He wanted to take Mombasa and reached to within forty miles of it at one stage. A bonus to his organization was Maj Gen Kurt Wahle, who had been in the territory to visit his son, but could not return to Germany. He became von Lettow's commander of lines of communication, effected the move to Moshi and organized the logistic support of the force, so that it became almost completely self-sufficient. Later he became an effective field command subordinate to von Lettow.

F Company 4 KAR and No 1 Reserve Company 3 KAR were on internal security duties in the River Sabaki area, but the Germans had begun to attack the railway, and detachments of both 1 and 3 KAR were deployed to track and deal with small groups of intruders. A typical incident was near Maungu on 3 September, when a patrol of B Company 1 KAR charged an enemy patrol with fixed bayonets; one of the *Schutztruppen* was killed and two were captured, while the rest dispersed. The German commander of the party surrendered at Bura after five days of wandering alone in the bush.

The European community reacted imaginatively to the threat to Kenya and formed units like Bowkeer's Horse, Wessel's Scouts, the Lancer Squadron (Lady Monica's Own) and the East African Mounted Rifles, a band of particularly staunch individualists. They did not take much to wearing uniform and, as one historian remarked "enjoyed their training to the hilt by disregarding it". The EAMR first saw action on Lake Victoria. Kisumu is a lakeside port and the western terminal of the Uganda Railway. A German armed tug-boat (*Muansa*) was on the Lake. Early in September a party of between 400 and 600 *Schutztruppen*, including porters, advanced to the village of Kisii, forty miles west of Kisumu. The plan was for three companies of 4 KAR, G in the lead, C and D following from Kisumu, to approach Kisii from the landward side, while the EAMR moved to Kisumu by rail from Nairobi, embarked on the *Winifred*, with their horses and mules in a separate vessel, to land at Karunga and launch a flank attack. They were intercepted by *Muansa*, which shelled and machine-gunned them, then withdrew into the reeds. By the time the EAMR reached the shore near their objective, they were not needed, as the KAR had surprised the *Schutztruppen* on 12 September. Capt E.G.M. Thornycroft led the attack from the right flank and was killed almost immediately. The enemy gun and machine guns made successful inroads and, low in ammunition, the KAR broke off the action and started to withdraw towards the end of the day. The enemy commander, with a substantial proportion of his Germans killed (reports vary between 25% and 50%), retired from Kisii and went back over the border. The EAMR returned to Nairobi.

The first major offensive against von Lettow was made mainly by Indian troops, in Forces B and C. C was deployed inland, to the Tsavo Valley area where half a battalion of 29 Punjab Regiment joined elements of 1 KAR (part of B Company) and 3 KAR (half of D Company). Their arrival coincided with the appearance of a *Schutztruppen* force of about 200 men, with four machine guns, who were possibly intending to attack the railway. An elaborate trap was set, but communications were not good enough to control it and the enemy withdrew rapidly. The KAR Mounted Company just caught up with them, but were not strong enough to be decisive. Sgt George Williams, an African signals NCO in 3 KAR, was awarded the DCM for his valuable reconnaissance work. Some ground was recovered by the Mounted Infantry and 4 KAR, and a chain of small forts was set up, both to steady African opinion in the area and to be supply bases for raids into German territory. "Frost's Castle" was the first of these, garrisoned by B Company 4 KAR, a section of Mounted Infantry and some Somali scouts.

The plan was for the Indian/KAR Force C under Brig-Gen Stewart to advance to Moshi, while Force B was to land at Tanga and advance up the railway to trap von Lettow and his men between them. There was no surprise, and the first companies of *Schutztruppen* moved by rail from Moshi and were in position along a railway embankment between Tanga and the beach-head before dawn on 3 November, 1914, and before the invaders started to advance. Although the Union flag flew over the Deutcher Kaiser Hotel for a short while, the rate of build-up of the *Schutztruppen* far exceeded that of the invaders, and their machine guns were very effective. Force B withdrew, accelerated by swarms of wild bees of a particularly aggressive kind. (They were impartial; 13 Field Company had to stop firing because of them.) Force B left Tanga on 5 November, speeded by von Lettow's bluff that his field guns would soon be arriving. Force B left behind sufficient modern rifles to equip three field companies, sixteen new machine guns, 500,000 rounds of ammunition, field telephones, enough uniforms to last the *Schutztruppen* for a year and other stores.

North-west of Kilimanjaro, Stewart had dispersed his troops too widely and they were scattered even further by three Field Companies and a mounted detachment. Combined with the disaster of Tanga, German East Africa was secure for a while longer.

From December, 1914, to February, 1916, the British in East Africa were, in the main, on the defensive, even though von Lettow could not launch a major offensive. The Cabinet then transferred operational control to the War Office. Maj Gen R. Wapshare assumed command, the military headquarters moved to Nairobi and two military areas were established, one based at Nairobi under Stewart and the other at Mombasa under Tighe. Forces "B" and "C" were merged and many of the logistic problems were addressed. The German objective was usually the overloaded Uganda railway, which was patrolled by British, African and Indian troops, but they held the small coastal fishing village of Jasin, on the border. In early January, 1915, Wapshire decided to reoccupy the area, which he thought was lightly defended, using B and D companies of 3 KAR, four companies of 4 KAR, some of the 101 Grenadiers, the 2nd Kashmiri Rifles, a half-battalion of Jhind infantry, an Arab Company, some scouts and two machine-gun sections – a total of 1,800 soldiers, supported by 5,000 carriers.

They set off on 17 December, mainly by the coast road, with the 3 KAR companies leading. Apart from meeting some German patrols they occupied Jasin without difficulty. The Germans retook it and were counter-attacked on the morning of Christmas Day by one company of 3 KAR and one of 101 Grenadiers; by 8.30 a.m. Capt T.O. Fitzgerald had secured the bonus of the Germans' Christmas dinner. Two German attacks were beaten off, the second on 12 January. While this was happening, 1 KAR were occupying Mafia Island, off the Rufiji Delta, at the request of the Navy. Lt Col L.E.S. Ward had A, B, C, and E Companies plus one company of 101 Grenadiers; they reached Mafia on 10 January and occupied it successfully. Major L.H. Soames, who commanded the four KAR companies, was wounded and Capt G.J. Giffard replaced him. After the island surrendered, Giffard and his men relieved the two 3 KAR companies at Jasin. While they were disembarking, von Lettow struck with nine Field Companies against the stone fort and plantation buildings occupied by the Kashmiri Rifles and some Grenadiers, commanded by Col Rajbir Singh. They attacked in three columns through sisal plantations and suffered heavy casualties at first; then two Field Companies surrounded the fort and gained a commanding position over the River Suba, which separated Giffard from Rajbir Singh. The KAR companies made three unsuccessful attempts to cross the river, and Sgt Juma Gubanda of 3 KAR was awarded the DCM for swimming it several times on reconnaisances. By the time von Lettow brought up two 75 mm field guns the defenders were in despair from thirst, von Lettow had bullets through his hat and arm, Rajbir Singh was dead and ammunition was low. The guns did little structural damage, but had considerable concussive effect. Early on 19 January, with their ammunition exhausted, Capt Hanson, Rajbir's 2ic, surrendered the fort.

Kitchener criticized Wapshare's conduct of the Jasin action and confirmed the defensive policy. Fifteen per cent of von Lettow's trained regular Germans were killed and 200,000 rounds of ammunition were expended at Jasin, so von Lettow concentrated on guerrilla warfare, particularly raids along the railway. In the following year he destroyed about twenty trains and severely disrupted railway traffic. Often his horsemen rode alongside the trains to shoot the drivers and stokers, who were held to a speed limit of fifteen miles per hour. Soon all night movement was stopped; the railway was under siege for a year.

Reinforcements arrived, including 2 Rhodesian Regiment and 25 Bn Royal Fusiliers (The Frontiersmen). The latter included the legendary, sixty-four year old Lt Frederick Courteney Selous, who had been a shooting partner of President Theodore Roosevelt. (It was Roosevelt who suggested "Marching through Georgia" as the 4 KAR Regimental March.) Stewart raided the port of Bukoba, on Lake Victoria, with a force 2,000 strong, including three companies of 3 KAR. They moved from Kisumu in four old lake steamers for a night landing three miles north of the town, then a direct assault on it. They were seen approaching and warning rockets went up at 1 a.m. on 22 June. Stewart changed his plan a little, but also delayed landing, so the opposition was much stronger when the troops eventually went ashore. By chance the beach where the British battalions landed was at the base of a steep, 300-foot-high cliff. After a stiff climb they achieved surprise by their unexpected appearance. The KAR had also landed on a wrong beach to the left of the British units. By dusk the situation had bogged down and all troops were tired and hungry.

The town was captured during the morning of 23 June, despite shelling and sniper fire. The ships gave fire support; the Fusiliers attacked frontally, while the Loyals made a flanking move; the KAR and the Punjabis were in reserve. There were eight British dead, but by 1 p.m. the Germans had withdrawn and the sappers were blowing up the radio station and arsenal. Stewart agreed to the town being looted, although naively stipulated that there should be no drinking or violence. There were both. A substantial strategic benefit was that it became easier to co-operate with the Belgians on the other side of the lake.

In Nyasaland John Chilembwe and his Watch Tower movement of rebels were dispersed by Capt L.E.L. Triscott and 100 recruits from the Zomba depot, supported by forty European volunteers. F and H Companies of 1 KAR were hurried to the scene under command of Capt H.G. Collins by lake steamer and by forced marches. They arrived to find Chilembwe dead and only a little mopping to be done. Before they returned they dealt with a German ship repair organization at Sphinxhaven on the morning of 30 May, when they captured a German flag and 7,000 rounds. At Myuyuni, ten miles east of Taveta, the German garrison was forty-five Europeans and 600 askari, with six machine guns. The plan was to attack in mid-July in two columns, one frontally, with a Punjabi battalion, two companies of 1 KAR and a troop of the KAR Mounted Rifles; the other was to attack from the rear, after a flank march. The flanking column included two companies of 4 KAR, a Baluchi detachment and some of Cole's (Somali) Scouts. Enemy machine guns stopped the main column and, although the flanking column got into position, they were withdrawn in the afternoon with two companies of 1 KAR providing the rearguard.

The railway was extended west from Voi to the border. Von Lettow was recruiting and had 10,000 officers and men under command by the end of 1915. He had received weapons, ammunition and other equipment from a blockade runner, the SS *Reubens*. Von Lettow thought that letting the *Reubens* through was the biggest single British mistake of the campaign. Food production in German East Africa was increased, particularly the output of African farms, while spinning and weaving were taught to African women. Boots, candles, a form of petrol, palm wine, "whisky" and rubber, were all obtained through imaginative improvisation. Warned by the German recruiting drive, reinforcements and machine guns were sought from Britain or India, but without success. In March, 1916, Kenya was the first country in the Empire to have conscription.

At the end of 1915 and early in 1916 South Africa raised 20,000 troops for service in East Africa. The commander of the enlarged force was Gen Sir Horace Smith-Dorrien, but he became ill with pneumonia, so forty-six-year-old Jan Christian Smuts became a Lieutenant General (the youngest in the British Army) and took over in Nairobi on 23 February, 1916. His specialities as a Boer commander had been speed and manoeuvre, but in the open veldt and not in the bush. Von Lettow was determined not to allow himself to be enveloped, and relied on speed to extricate himself from any trap that Smuts might set.

The KAR now overhauled itself, getting rid of time-expired men and recruiting fresh ones, but without any significant increase in overall numbers. It was expected that the South Africans and some better-trained Indian reinforcements would prove decisive, particularly with the support of artillery units from Britain and a detachment of the Royal Navy Air Service. The combatant troops increased to 27,000, with seventy-one guns and over 120 machine guns. The KAR were in a minority, with 1 KAR (four companies) in the Longido area, 3 KAR (five companies) at Voi – but moving to the Serengeti in mid-February, and 4 KAR (five companies) in the Tsavo-Mzima area. An attack down both sides of Kilimanjaro was planned, and the command structure was changed to control it, with 1 Division to the west of the volcano, 2 Division to its east, and a separate command for the Lake Victoria area.

    Smuts' plan was for 2 Division (including five companies of 3 KAR) to fight the main battle. The flanking move round the German position was commanded by Stewart, with 4,000 men of 1 Division, including the KAR Mounted Infantry and four companies of 1 KAR under Giffard. A third, subsidiary thrust was made by a South African column under Maj Gen J.L. van Deventer. Stewart had the longest approach, sixty miles to reach Moshi, initially across dusty, waterless lava, where movement stirred up great dust clouds that choked men and animals, and disclosed them to the watching enemy. Later came rain, difficult bush country, the ineffectiveness of mounted troops in the bush (they had to be withdrawn) and German opposition. With the cavalry gone, 1 KAR led for the rest of the advance. Three days had been allotted for them to get into position behind von Lettow before Tighe advanced on Taveta. Van Deventer's advance was successful; von Lettow saw him coming, but pulled back as he did not have enough artillery to break up the attack. 2 Division advanced to Salaita and then to Taveta two days later, restoring it to British control.

    Smuts mounted a frontal attack on the new German defensive position five miles west of Taveta, between and astride two small hills, using 1,500 men. Tighe commanded 1 East African Brigade, consisting of 2 Rhodesia Regiment, 13 Baluch and 3 KAR (Lt Col B.R. Graham). 3 KAR were on the left, the Baluchis on the right and the Rhodesians in reserve. This was 3 KAR's first engagement as a battalion. B and G Companies were forward and A and D Companies in reserve; E Company was at Taveta on garrison duty. They advanced through open country, then entered the bush at the base of the hills, where they were halted by heavy artillery and machine-gun fire. When artillery support was available and dusk approached, the Rhodesians and 3 KAR stormed up the steep slope to the crest of the ridge. Graham died at the head of his battalion, his body riddled with machine-gun bullets. The crest was reached, but the Germans counter-attacked quickly; two battalions of South African infantry eventually regained it and the enemy retired. The 3 KAR casualties at the Battle of Latema Nek were three officers (including the Medical Officer) killed – plus one officer who died later of wounds, eleven askari killed and sixty-six wounded or missing. Major T.O. Fitzgerald took over command of 3 KAR. Van Deventer found Moshi deserted.

A gun from the *Königsberg* caused distress to some of van Deventer's horses and engaged in counter-battery fire against Smuts' howitzers. 1 KAR moved forward to the south bank of the River Rufi and 3 KAR withdrew for rest and retraining. The Rhodesians reached Kahe where the *Königsberg* gun had been abandoned, and the rains began. A second blockade runner had unloaded in the southern part of the coast, it had brought much-needed equipment and clothing, together with Iron Crosses for von Lettow and Looff, captain of the *Königsberg*.

In the first phase the Germans had been forced out of one of the most settled and prosperous parts of their colony and Smuts was astride the Northern Railway. Kenya was safe from attack through the Taveta Gap, the Uganda railway was secure and the spur line from Voi was extended rapidly to Taveta. Some of the weaker commanders left and Smuts re-organized his force into three Divisions; 1 Division was commanded by Maj Gen A.R. Hoskins – newly arrived from France – and consisted of 1 EA Brigade (Shepperd) and 2 EA Brigade (Hannyngton). 2 Division (van Deventer) and 3 Division (Brits) each had one mounted brigade and one infantry brigade, all South African. More South African troops arrived and the Gold Coast and Nigerian Units (who had been in the Cameroons) were rested and then moved to East Africa. The KAR was expanded considerably. Hoskins held a meeting of senior KAR officers at Nairobi on 6 April; their plan was put to the Governor and the Commander in Chief. It was endorsed and sent to the Colonial Secretary, who accepted it and agreed that the KAR would be regarded as Imperial Troops for the remainder of the campaign. The immediate effect was that, after some recruiting, 2 KAR was reconstituted on 1 April, 1916. Recruiting among the Wakamba, Meru and Kipsikis was successful and more men came from Rhodesia and Nyasaland, so that 1/2 and 2/2 KAR were in being by August of the same year. The Nandi Scouts and the Baganda Rifles took over guard and patrol duties around Lake Victoria, and in Zanzibar the Zanzibar African Rifles and the Armed Constabulary relieved the KAR and Gwalior Rifles garrison on the island.

Smuts planned to make two separate thrusts at the Central Railway; van Deventer would cross the Masai plains, and the main body, under Smuts, would go down the Northern Railway towards Tanga and then turn south to advance parallel with van Deventer. Van Deventer started in March, in the pouring rain. Many of the horses died, and although they defeated two groups of the enemy, two weeks after leaving Kilimanjaro van Deventer's mounted brigade was down to 800 men, with the infantry brigade toiling in their rear along waterlogged tracks littered with the corpses of horses and mules. Vehicles were no good, motor cyclists could not get through, the radio broke down and mounted messengers were the only remaining means of communication; rations were halved and men and animals continued to fall by the wayside. After a further week, on 19 April, they reached the town of Kondoa-Irangi, which German forces had partly burned before evacuating it. Van Deventer had only 600 men left and the infantry did not catch up for eleven days, to bring his force to 3,000, all badly in need of rest. Behind them the roads were barely passable, but work on the railway from Voi, via Taveta to Moshi, had gone well and the first train from Kenya reached Moshi on 25 April.

Van Deventer's force was counter-attacked at Kondoa-Irangi on 8 May by some 4,000 *Schutztruppen*, one of the few times when they had concentrated in greater strength than the British. The *Königsberg*'s ensign, which had been carried by some of her crew, was captured, and about half the Germans in the company were killed. The heaviest rains in living memory ended in late May but van Deventer's force had lost its mobility as less than half its horses remained. On 22 May Smuts began his push down the Northern Railway with two parallel columns, delayed by destruction of the railway. By the time Smuts turned south into the bush his units were well below strength. On the coast Tanga and then Dar es Salaam were captured with little difficulty in July, which eased the supply position.

Von Lettow fell back to the line of the Central Railway, which served as his lateral route. Van Deventer's column recuperated and pushed south again with motor cycles leading, reached the railway at Dodoma and moved down it towards Kraut's detachment. An attempt at encirclement failed as Smuts' column was too far away and the going was difficult. Van Deventer reached Kilosa on 22 August to find it deserted. Smuts had a hard struggle for the last thirty miles to the railway, hampered by great heat and grass fires, but on 26 August 2 Rhodesia Regiment and two companies of Baluchis entered Morogoro, where (for the first time) they found German civilians and wounded left behind. Von Lettow had escaped and his force (now bigger than at the start of the war) moved through the mountain passes to the bush, swamp and wilderness that reached as far as the border with Portuguese East Africa. Smuts attempted to reach the enemy at Kisaki, on the far side of the Uluguru Mountains.

The Autumn rains had started and the tracks were muddy, slippery and almost impassable for vehicles. Von Lettow was behind a natural barrier of hills and woods sixty miles wide (east to west) and fifty miles deep. The attackers were short of rations; troops were reduced to chewing sugar cane, eating trek oxen and any game they could shoot. Smuts decided on a flanking attack on Kisaki, but the combined effects of narrow, slippery paths impassable to guns, poor maps, indifferent communications, the rain and a shortage of porters caused the columns to converge on Kisaki ignorant of each other's whereabouts and unco-ordinated. One column attacked on 7 September and the other on the next day, both unsuccessfully. Then the enemy slipped away to the southern bank of the River Mgeta, leaving behind all the European women except for some nurses, and prepared to defend the new position with the aid of some of *Königsberg*'s guns. Kraut's detachment was out of touch with von Lettow. On 26 September Smuts called off the offensive for medical and military reasons.

Smuts did not want to operate in the Rufiji Delta, particularly because the rains had damaged the army's supply lines. Motor transport was ineffective and 58,000 animals had died, mainly due to tsetse fly. The supply chain from Mombasa was 500 miles long and food was always scarce, so the health of the force was poor. Between October and December, 1916, 15,000 British troops were invalided home. The two British battalions were at half strength or less, and 2 Rhodesians had only seventy fit men. 2 West Indian Regiment and the Gold Coast Regiment were operational, the 3,200-strong Nigerian Brigade had arrived, and the build-up of the KAR began to prove effective.

Von Lettow established himself in the middle and lower reaches of the Rufiji in October. Smuts had a base at the old slave port of Kilwa, 120 miles south of Dar es Salaam, and wanted to destroy the maize crops in the Liwale area. To protect his flank he had to take the fort at Kibata first. It was fifty miles from Kilwa, through some of the most difficult country encountered in the campaign, with malaria, tsetse fly (600 mules died in two weeks), lion that killed thirteen men, black cotton soil that could swallow a wagon and its team of mules, rats, poor rations, thirst and dust. They found the fort abandoned. The air was good and there was plenty of fresh water in the mountain streams. Hannyngton, the column commander, sent back half the force, retaining 1/2 KAR (now commanded by Lt Col G.J. Giffard) and 2/2 KAR plus others for patrol work. Von Lettow concentrated at least five *Schutztruppen* Field Companies and moved them towards Kibata with artillery, including one of the *Königsberg*'s guns. The 1 Division force dug and wired field defences, and cleared fields of fire around the fort, ready for the siege to begin, but they had no guns. On 7 December, 1916, what was probably the heaviest artillery concentration of the campaign fell on the fort and its outer defences, then the three-week seige began. There were shortages of medicines, dressings and drugs, and just one doctor with six medical orderlies. Scores of amputations were carried out daily, on an old door that was both the operating table and a dining table for officers.

They were reinforced by two guns of 27 Mountain Battery and by 2/2 KAR (Lt Col H.S. Fissell), who force-marched the thirty-six miles over difficult country in thirty-four hours. After a few days of low-intensity fighting, Brig-Gen H.deC. O'Grady arrived to take over, with the Gold Coast Regiment, 40th Pathans, more mountain guns, stocks of ammunition and – particularly welcome – Mills 36 hand grenades. These proved effective when the Baluchis used them on 15 December to clear some enemy trenches. A Company 1/2 KAR took over the trenches from the Baluchis and were shelled throughout the following day. Within two days of his arrival, O'Grady counter-attacked with the Gold Coast Regiment, to get round von Lettow's right flank and relieve the pressure on Kibata. They were caught in the open by artillery and machine-gun fire for six hours, then withdrew at night having lost fifteen per cent of their men and fifty per cent of their officers. There was then another period of shelling and desultory patrol work. Christmas came; the Germans cheered when they saw a British plane apparently bombing the fort, but it was dropping cartons of cigarettes. Von Lettow's Christmas present from the Kaiser was Pour le Mérite; Smuts sent him congratulations.

At the end of December 1 Division concentrated at Kilwa to deal with Capt Ernst Otto's detachment of 1,000 men before striking at the besiegers of Kibata. Otto withdrew steadily for five days, with counter-attacks by his rearguards and a variety of booby traps left by *Königsberg*'s ordnance specialists. Sheppard almost managed to prevent further retreat, but in a brisk fire-fight the legendary Selous was killed by a sniper. Otto's men escaped the trap by dispersing, to reassemble at the River Rufiji, which they crossed and then blew up the bridge. The river was in flood and running rapidly. Boats were assembled with difficulty and the river was crossed, but the troops met sustained fire on the far bank before Otto and his men disappeared into the bush.

3 KAR had been organized into two battalions and 1/3 KAR reached Kibata on 18 December, ten days after the reorganization, while 2/3 KAR was in reserve at Mitole. Following reconnaissances and patrols, on 1 January two companies of 1/3 KAR and some mountain guns moved six miles to Pungutini and evicted a small German force as a prelude to clearing the Mtumbei Hills. Giffard led a flank attack via Mbirikia, Platform Hill and Coconut Village. He set off on the night of 6/7 January with A and B Companies, 1/2 KAR and four machine guns, to reach the top of Mbirikia

Hill in the dark, from where they commanded Platform Hill. At dawn A Company drove off the enemy and signalled with smoke bombs to the watching gunners at Kibata. They followed up the ensuing bombardment and quickly took Observation Hill. Meanwhile, 1/3 KAR and the Baluchis secured Coconut Hill. On 8 January, after another company of 1/2 KAR, 100 Baluchis, some machine guns from the Loyals and a detachment of mountain guns had joined Giffard, they advanced, took Single Palm Hill, handed it over to 1/3 KAR and moved on to clear Ambush Hill. Next day they assaulted Kommando Berg, but the Germans had gone. On 13 January 1/2 KAR made a flanking move against the German rearguard, while the Baluchis attacked frontally. This was the end of the Kibata operation; 1/2 KAR lost three officers killed and died of wounds, two officers wounded, seventeen askari killed, forty-six wounded and one missing, plus casualties among the porters.

Northey and van Deventer were also attempting to round up groups of *Schutztruppen*. Northey had some 2,000 combatants (including 1 KAR), covering a front of 200 miles, plus 500 recruits under training at the depot. Wahle and his Tabora Force, estimated to be 1,200 strong in combatants but in fact twice that number, moved eastwards in three columns, but van Deventer's 2 Division was in no condition to close with them. In late October Wahle overran a supply depot after a stubborn defence, invested Iringa, and attacked 1 KAR detachments under Hawthorn and Murray. In bitter weather Northey took the offensive, attempting to outflank Wahle's defences, but the enemy slipped away. Van Deventer was similarly unsuccessful, (his "composite mounted brigade" was totally dismounted), and the enemy escaped southwards through the cordon; it seemed that they could join von Lettow's main body whenever they chose.

Smuts had occupied three-quarters of German East Africa and the enemy appeared to be on the run, which contrasted with the general situations elsewhere, particularly at Verdun and on the Somme. To attend the Imperial Conference in London, he handed over to Hoskins of 1 Division on 20 January, 1917.

The year began badly for the new Commander in Chief, with exceptionally heavy rain which started five days after Smuts left and continued until May. The Empire troops were strung out along a 400-mile front, with indifferent supply lines behind them. The Nigerian Brigade were in the front line, which was mainly swampland. Patrols often went out in canoes or waded in water up to their necks. Rations were meagre and were supplemented by whatever could be shot, mules that had died from tsetse, even the leather lashings of a bridge were stolen (to the detriment of the bridge) and boiled to make soup. The Rufiji River continued to rise and became uncrossable, so that supplies remained on the northern bank. The Germans suffered similarly; their rations were running low, as all the locally grown maize had been consumed and the fields further south would not be ready for months. Von Lettow cut rations and evacuated all the "useless" mouths, including most of the African women and officers' servants, and abandoned his sick and wounded. Hippopotamus and elephant were shot for meat, and a method of artificially ripening maize allowed an increase in the flour ration. Smuts told the Imperial Conference that the East African campaign would now be no more than a police action, so Hoskins' requests for weapons, ammunition and medical supplies were received with incredulity and were not met for a long time.

He asked the Governor of British East Africa for a big increase in the numbers of carriers to support his force in the almost roadless country of the Rufiji Delta. An East Africa Carrier Corps had been formed at the start of the war and had grown to 7,500 men. It was under the command of Lt Col Oliver Watkins, who had been in the Administration. Instead of returning to his own regiment at the outbreak of the war, he was instructed to form the Carrier Corps – with one officer to help him. Initially he built them up to meet the needs of Force B when it had arrived from India in 1914, and by 26 August there were 5,000 carriers, organized into five corps, each of 1,000 men, two administrative officers, a Medical Officer and a senior African. Each corps was sub-divided into ten groups of 100 men. The Kenyans were supplemented by 1,000 men from Uganda, who arrived on 27 August. There were considerable problems in raising these numbers. District Commissioners requisitioned them from headmen; they were registered, issued with identity discs and pay books, and their records had to be maintained – in a predominantly illiterate society. Travelling by train and ship were alarming experiences for young men who had left their home communities for the first time, and to whom the sea was incomprehensible. Not being used to latrines, poor sanitation caused serious problems, and by October 2,000 men were ill with spinal meningitis. A depot was set up at Kisumu, for handling the cargos of the lake steamers. 2,000 carriers had embarked for Tanga with Force B; they did not get far inland, and when the expedition withdrew many of them were left to drift in lighters with no food, water or shade. Militarization of the Carriers was extended and they became known as the Military Labour Bureau, but the name Kariokor was perpetuated by Africans and is still used for the suburbs of towns where their camps had been. There was an outcry from Uganda when the 1,000 men were returned there, in poor physical shape due to bad food. It was some time before a scale of rations similar to the askari was authorized, while there were cases of rations being adulterated to bulk them out. By the time of the advance through the Taveta Gap, local sources of labour were severely taxed and men were drafted in from Nyasaland, the Seychelles and Nigeria. The system of periodic rest and relaxation for the Carriers was abandoned, with a consequent decrease in both efficiency and health. Watkins went ashore at Dar es Salaam in the first lighter to enter the harbour, while German snipers were still active, with his carriers, to get the port back into operation. For this he was awarded the DSO.

In early 1917, when Hoskins assumed command, there were some 7,500 Carriers. These were increased to 135,000 and then to 150,000, four times the numbers of fighting troops. Each man carried fifty pounds, but he ate two pounds of food daily, so that, even without a "pay load", he had an outward radius of thirteen days only. Men were drafted in from Portuguese East Africa, the Belgian Congo and from the occupied areas of German East Africa. 9,000 were offered from the Gold Coast.

With the enemy at a strength of 1,100 Germans and 7,300 askari, most of the South Africans and the Indians having left, excluding the hospitalized, the Empire forces had fewer effectives than the enemy. Smuts had authorized an increase in KAR numbers to 8,000; Hoskins sought more. In January, 1917, recruiting began to raise the force to 24,000, organized into seven regiments, a total of twenty battalions. Training was limited, as time did not allow for extensive programmes and instructors had to be taken from operational battalions. Officers and NCOs were drafted in from Europe, unused to bush warfare. Language was a barrier; courses in Swahili were organized for both Europeans and Africans.

With the end of the rains in May, Hoskins sought to close in on von Lettow's men, now crowded into a small area in the south-west of the territory, but he was posted to the Middle East and replaced by van Deventer. At about the same time von Lettow was promoted to major general. Van Deventer had a port at Lindi and planned to strike in the Kilwa area before the next rains began. At the same time, Northey, based on Nyasaland, was to deal with the rest of the enemy, including any who succeeded in breaking out of Kilwa. 1 Division was redesignated Kilwa Force and made slow, painful progress in difficult country where ambushes became a way of life. 1/2 KAR gave flank support to the Gold Coast Regiment in one attack. The manoeuvre failed, but when the *Schutztruppen* counter-attacked, the newly recruited askari of 1/2 KAR stood their ground and charged in their turn, forcing the Germans to abandon their defences and machine guns.

Capt Wintgens, a column commander, chose independent action and was pursued for a while by 1/1 KAR, but they were recalled to garrison Njombe. The chase eventually involved Indians, KAR, Nigerians, South Africans and

Belgians. Mkalama was beseiged by the same column, now commanded by Naumann as Wintgens had been wounded. The Nigerian/Belgian column came to the rescue, but some KAR askari in the fort had served until recently in the *Schutztruppen* and, when they mistook the advancing Nigerians and the Belgians for their former comrades in arms, they took to the bush rather than face being hanged. Naumann continued for some months longer, with 2,000 men hunting him, then surrendered on 2 October, when he was surrounded. He still had fourteen Germans, 165 askari and 250 porters, had covered 1,600 miles and had diverted a totally disproportionate force from the main front. The KAR units after him were 1/6 KAR, 3/4 KAR, the KAR Mounted Infantry, and 4/4 KAR, all composed mainly of new recruits, although 1/6 KAR included some ex-*Schutztruppen*.

Northey concentrated on trapping Kraut and Wahle. The former went towards Portuguese East Africa, so Northey moved his Headquarters to Zomba, 500 miles to the south, in April, 1917, and sent 1/4 KAR across the Livingstone mountains and then by lake steamer to Fort Johnson, at the southern tip of Lake Nyasa. They disembarked and hunted unsuccessfully for Kraut on the east side of the lake. He evaded them and linked up with von Lettow near Lindi. An even larger force hunted Wahle, but he eluded the combined efforts of 1/4 and 2/4 KAR. The last big battle of the campaign was now imminent. O'Grady advanced his force from Lindi in flat-bottomed boats towed by motor boats. The 25 Fusiliers disembarked first, to spend five unhealthy days on a mud bank surrounded by Germans, during which time their carrier force had very little to eat. The Kilwa Force, mainly Nigerians, marched towards Lindi; most of them suffered from malaria and dysentery. On the way they were shelled heavily by some of the surviving *Königsberg* guns. As the two groups converged on 15 October, the Battle of Mahiwa began. The enemy were concentrated into a few square miles and trying to reach the Rovuma River. When the two columns were still twelve miles apart, von Lettow struck the Nigerians, who formed square. Both sides were in shallow trenches and the battlefield began to resemble France or Flanders, except for the high temperature and humidity. Casualties were heavy and rations were cut; thirst was a problem as the one waterhole was under German observed shellfire. The only chance of rescue lay with O'Grady, but by 18 October he was still a mile away. Finally the Kilwa Force broke out through a gap in the German trenches. O'Grady had failed to reach them in time because he was held up by Wahle and his men. Von Lettow closed on O'Grady and the surviving Nigerians who were with him, but they withdrew towards the coast. In four days of battle the Empire casualties were 2,700 from an infantry strength of 4,900. The German losses were 519 from a force of 1,500.

After resting on 6 November Hannyngton's Kilwa group began to harass von Lettow's rearguard; they made a general advance on the following day. On 15 November Wahle's force was attacked at Chiwata by O'Grady and Hannyngton, but they pulled out quickly, leaving behind about 650 askari, Europeans and porters, all unfit. Von Lettow also decided to march with only his fittest troops and porters. At Nabindinga, close to the River Rvumba, he sorted them out. The camp was surrounded by British troops and it was expected that, as he was bottled up in the last remaining tract of German territory, von Lettow's surrender was imminent. The men who were to be left behind burned their rifles and prepared to surrender. The remainder moved to the river quietly at night; 300 Europeans, 1,700 askari, with 3,000 women, children and porters. They took several hours to go, in a long thin column, leaving behind over 1,000 Europeans and askari, plus uncounted numbers of women, children and carriers.

The *Schutztruppen* began to enter Portuguese territory on 25 November; it took the straggling column two days. They were fired on by a Portuguese fort and took it easily, killing Major Pinto and 900 of his men. They found uniforms, food, even European items, 1,000,000 rounds of small arms ammunition and enough rifles for half the force. There were also thirty horses and six British machine guns. Portuguese askari were impressed to carry the loot and 150 Portuguese were left in the wreckage. The enemy then wandered for several months, without a clear strategy and not strongly pressed by the Empire troops. In November, 1917, an attempt was made to reinforce and supply von Lettow from Germany, using a specially designed Zeppelin. Every element of the aircraft, in addition to its cargo and crew, would be of value on arrival. The cargo was fifty tons of weapons, ammunition and stores. After delays due to bad weather she crossed the Mediterranean on the first leg of a 4,000 mile journey. The radio was put out of action by a storm. When it was repaired and they were over the Red Sea, a message of recall was received. She turned round and had an even worse journey back, with gales so strong that half of the cargo was jettisoned and she came down in the Balkans after a flight of four days and one hour, and 4,180 miles. There was a theory that the recall message had been faked by British Intelligence.

After Christmas British strategy changed. The unhealthy area around the lower Rovuma was evacuated and two thrusts against von Lettow were proposed, one from the coast, to push westwards, and one eastwards from Nyasaland. Three battalions of KAR were strung out along the River Rovuma to prevent any attempt to double back into the former German colony. The 25 Fusiliers, Nigerians and and Indians were withdrawn, leaving the campaign to the Gold Coast Regiment, the West Indian

Drummers and buglers of 6 KAR, with a detachment of recruits in the rear, c. 1906, when 6 KAR was a mixed Indian/Somali unit. The men are all Somalis, including the officer.

Early days in 5 KAR. First, the medical inspection.

3. Nearing the end of recruit training; note the bare feet and leather rifle slings.

4. Lieutenant-Colone[l] Patrick Mundy, DS[O], MC, Commanding Officer of 4 KAR, [at] Bombo on 14 Aug[ust] 1939, watching the battalion beginning [its] move to Mombasa [via] Kampala. He subsequently commanded the Somalia Gendarme[rie]. The gun is a 1914-[18] War souvenir.

5. Brigadier 'Fluffy' Fowlkes (centre), Commander 22(EA) Brigade, giving orders.

Regiment and the KAR, plus the Cape Corps, artillery units and the Royal Flying Corps. The Portuguese army did not take much part in the campaign; the *Schutztruppen* saw their forts as supply bases rather than threats. Von Lettow split his force into three columns again, Wahle went to oppose Northey in the east, while Koehl confronted a force landed at Porto Amelia. Von Lettow was between them, ready to reinforce in either direction and investigating the benefits of moving further south. A few patrols clashed in January and February; von Lettow expected an attack from the coast.

The first attempt to land a force at Porto Amelia, in December, was abandoned with some loss of kit, but a second was made successfully a few days later. Porto Amelia was a hot and unattractive town with a short pier and a general air of decay. By 7 January "Pamforce", commanded by Brig-Gen W.S.F. Edwards, was ashore, including their porters. The road ended six miles inland, after which they advanced as fast as pangas could hack a way through the bush. Dissatisfied with progress during February and March, van Deventer added two battalions of KAR under Lt Col G.F. Giffard, known as Kartucol. Pamforce was now about 8,000 combatants strong and posed a real threat; Northey was moving steadily towards them from the west.

At dawn on 12 April, about 100 miles inland, near the village of Medo, Kartucol came under heavy machine-gun fire when wading through a swamp. Their ammunition ran short and men who were sent for more were killed. They took up positions roughly in three sides of a square, digging small weapon slits in the mud. To their right the Gold Coasters were stopped by a minefield that included some buried *Königsberg* shells. There were several well controlled counter-attacks, and the hero of the battle was Lcpl Sowera DCM of 2/2 KAR, whose bravery gained him a bar to his medal. He climbed a tree to have a better field of fire for his Lewis gun, attracting the combined fire of most of the German machine guns. Later he took command of a section that had lost its NCO and led the way, capering in front of them. By hard fighting Kartucol and the Gold Coasters came together on the far side of the ambush, which had been based on some slightly rising ground. The enemy moved away to the south-west as night fell. Casualties were very heavy, but the relatively inexperienced askari of Kartucol had done well in their first battle. Pamforce sorted themselves out on drier ground before resuming the advance. When they did they had a sharp action on the east side of Mbalama Hill; Capt P.T. Brodie captured a machine-gun post, enabling B Company 1/2 KAR to move forward and occupy the hill. Brodie received the DSO, Sgt Morris the DCM and the two askari with them were awarded MMs.

Von Lettow went to delay Northey, first getting behind him and capturing a supply depot. There was a stiff fight with Northey's main force before von Lettow withdrew, leaving a rearguard to slow up the pursuers. Meanwhile, Schnee blundered into an ambush with part of the column from Porto Amelia, and lost many askari, 70,000 rounds of ammunition, 30,000 rupees of von Lettow's home-made money and much of von Lettow's own kit. The German columns united again and on 22 May avoided being trapped between Northey's men and Pamforce. Kartucol had met resistance at the entrance to the gorge at Korewa, when 2/2 KAR were in the lead. A second detachment was located further up the gorge, and at the end of the pass 3/1 KAR came on the enemy reserve troops, who were eating. Despite sustained pressure, the enemy broke out through a gap between B Company 1/2 KAR and 3/1 KAR. The Gold Coasters and the KARMI arrived too late to assist. Apart from eleven Germans and forty-nine of their askari killed or taken prisoner, almost all of their transport, 100,000 rounds of small arms ammunition, the last of the ammunition for the Portuguese guns, food, baggage and Schnee's personal kit were captured.

Von Lettow changed tactics again, retiring in echelon rather in a single column, with the aim of trapping some or all of Pamforce between two of his groups by attacking both flanks concurrently. This ploy did not work, but there were occasional collisions resulting in minor casualties. The British columns in the field now were Pamforce (1/2, 2/2 and 3/32 KAR under Giffard and known as Kartucol, and Rosecol, made up the Gold Coast Regiment and KARMI), Kartrecol (3 KAR), Shortcol, (KAR and the Rhodesian Native Regiment. This was commanded by Col Shorthose and known as 'Soxcol') and Grifcol (KAR from Nyasaland). To these were added Fitzcol (KAR) and Mobforce, from Mozambique.

Von Lettow's threat to the town of Quelimane was delayed when two companies of 2/3 KAR under Major E.A. Gore-Browne reinforced the Portuguese garrison. But on 3 July the enemy broke into the perimeter and 2/3 KAR withdrew across the River Nhamacurra, ninety yards wide and with a strong current. Many were drowned while others, including Gore-Browne, were shot while crossing. The total losses were: killed one officer, one BOR and sixteen AORs; wounded twenty-eight askari, three BORs and 174 askari. Von Lettow escaped with all the weapons and supplies he could carry. Fitzcol set out from Quelimane to reinforce a company of 2/3 KAR garrisoning Namirrue and by 21 July they were within twenty-five miles of the objective when firing was heard. 3/3 and 4/4 KAR were making camp and digging in on 22 July at dusk when they were attacked by von Lettow in great strength. 3/3 KAR ceased to exist as a battalion, and the CO, Lt Col H.C. Dickinson, was among those taken prisoner. He spent the rest of the war marching with the *Schutztruppen*. Fitzgerald pulled his column together;

what remained of 3/3 KAR (about half a company), the survivors of the 2/3 KAR company from Namirrue (badly shattered by gunfire and out of water), and 200 of 4/4 KAR. They fell back towards Quelimane without being pressed. The men of 3/3 KAR were engaged on lines of communications duty for the rest of the war; remnants of 2/3 KAR were moved to Quelimane and 1/3 KAR to Lindi.

At the end of July Kartucol found von Lettow after strenuous patrolling, and Fitzcol joined Kartucol thirty miles north-east of Namirrue. They had a few days' rest and benefited from the fresh food in the area. In the west Northey handed over to Brig-Gen G.M.P. Hawthorne. The Gold Coast Regiment was withdrawn, having had 1,790 men sick and wounded in two years of campaigning. Von Lettow planned to move along the east side of Lake Nyasa to Tabora. He thought that van Deventer would withdraw his troops from Portuguese East Africa by sea to Dar es Salaam, and move them by rail to Tabora. Van Deventer feared a break towards the north and effectively did what von Lettow expected. 250 miles south of the border, after a clash with one of Hawthorne's columns, von Lettow left all his sick and wounded in the care of a British Army doctor. Several small actions with three KAR battalions cost the Germans ninety-five casualties, 48,000 rounds of ammunition, medical stores and armoury spares, but the *Schutztruppen* escaped by splitting into several smaller columns. Epidemics of influenza and bronchial catarrh caused many to leave the march towards the Rovuma River and the border; the remainder were there by 28 September.

When their health had been restored, aided by raids on supply depots, they bumped into some shooting at the small town of Songea, and van Deventer hurried reinforcements up the railway towards Tabora. On 17 October von Lettow purged his column of his sick and wounded again, including the retired Maj Gen Wahle. The column then turned towards Rhodesia, attacking and capturing some newly constructed British forts. From three-week old newspapers they learned of the successes of Allied forces in Europe. German patrols were sent out towards Lake Tanganyika and in the direction of Fife, in Rhodesia. Fife was defended by the Northern Rhodesian Police, who beat off the main enemy body after two days of hard fighting. Despite this reverse, the column was still in fairly good shape and had 400 head of cattle with them. A mission station and hospital were raided and large quantities of quinine were captured; they then turned south-west, towards Kasama, 100 miles away. 1/4 KAR was close behind them, led by Major E.B.B. Hawkins, whose only map was an atlas of the world, with a scale of 200 miles to the inch.

A settler warned Hawkins of a German rearguard at a bridge over the

River Chambezi; he changed direction and crossed twelve miles below them on 9 November. On the same day von Lettow took Kasama, where the garrison consisted mainly of men released from the local jail. They replenished with food and ammunition and considered moving into Rhodesia when 1/4 KAR caught up with several companies of *Schutztruppen*, who dispersed into the bush.

By this time news of the Armistice had reached van Deventer, who sent two messages to von Lettow calling on him to surrender and to release his prisoners. Von Lettow sent two telegrams to Berlin by British communications asking for confirmation, but there were no replies. The prisoners were released and Dickinson said goodbye to von Lettow on behalf of them, spending an hour chatting about the campaign with him over cups of coffee. Some of the *Schutztruppen* askari were unwilling to surrender, as they had not been defeated and wished to retain their rifles. For a while the situation looked ugly, but trouble was averted when von Lettow gave each askari and porter a certificate detailing the amount each was owed, as much as four years' money in many cases. He tried to borrow the money from the British, but was unsuccessful. The men were paid, at von Lettow's insistence, by a team of German paymasters, after he had returned to Berlin.

Von Lettow was impressed by Hawkins' youth; he was in his early thirties and had started the war as a lieutenant. He also came to Hawkins' rescue in the matter of rations, handing over half of his herd of cattle, which were gratefully received by the hungry KAR. It was probably because of the shortage of food in the British camp that von Lettow declined Hawkins' invitation to dinner, although he appreciated the gesture.

The residual *Schutztruppen* consisted of 4,500 men, women, children and porters. The combatant element was 155 Germans and 1,156 askari. They surrendered a few of the Model 71 rifles and seven German machine guns, 208,000 rounds of ammunition, forty artillery shells, a Portuguese gun, thirty British machine guns and 1,071 rifles of British, Belgian and Portuguese origin. The surrender ceremony at Abercorn on 25 November was taken by Brig-Gen W.F.S. Edwards, in the pouring rain. Guards of Honour were provided by 1/4 KAR and the Northern Rhodesian Police. Von Lettow saluted the Union flag and read out the terms of surrender, which Edwards accepted. Von Lettow was introduced to the officers present and then introduced his own officers, including Governor Schnee. The Germans went down to Dar es Salaam and the askari were interned for a while at Tabora. The return to Dar es Salaam was a triumph, with receptions by the German community en route. An epidemic of Spanish influenza killed ten per cent of the surviving Germans and large numbers of the askari of the *Schutztruppen*. The Germans finally sailed for Germany on 17 January,

1919. Von Lettow, on a black horse, led the Europeans of Germany's only undefeated army through the streets of Berlin early in March, to a reception given by the Mayor.

Excluding Allied and Naval personnel, about 114,000 troops had been engaged in the conflict; the peak of 55,000 was reached during Smuts' tenure, and included three KAR battalions. The official British casualties for the campaign were 62,220, excluding those hospitalized for disease. Deaths from disease were 48,328, mainly due to malaria. These figures omit the carriers. Between 400,000 and 500,000 men had served with the carriers and, when Watkins was closing his books, 40,000 of them could not be accounted for.

The KAR had grown to be 35,424 strong, in twenty-two battalions, the KARMI and a Signals Company. Eleven per cent of the regiment were Europeans. The KAR casualties had been 8,225; British officers with the KAR had 22.6% casualties, mostly from disease. The KAR had come through the war with honour and the fighting skills of the askari, particularly in the bush, were well recognized.

Von Lettow paid a return visit to Tanganyika in 1953, when he was fêted by the survivors among his askari. He died in 1964.

Chapter 4

BETWEEN THE WARS – 1919–1940

"During the First World War and the decade that followed, tribal unrest was rife in many parts of the East African territories."

"East Africa was not taken by surprise on the occasion of the Second World War."

Lt-Col H. Moyse-Bartlett, 1956

This period covers demobilization, financial stringency, varying commitments, the Ethiopian War of 1935–36 and progress to general mobilization in 1939. Throughout this time Internal Security (IS) duties were frequent except in Nyasaland, so 1 and 2 KAR took part in IS operations more often than other KAR units. The changes in the fortunes of the KAR from 1920 until the first seven months of war are shown in the following graph:-

KAR and EA Forces Strengths, 1919–1940

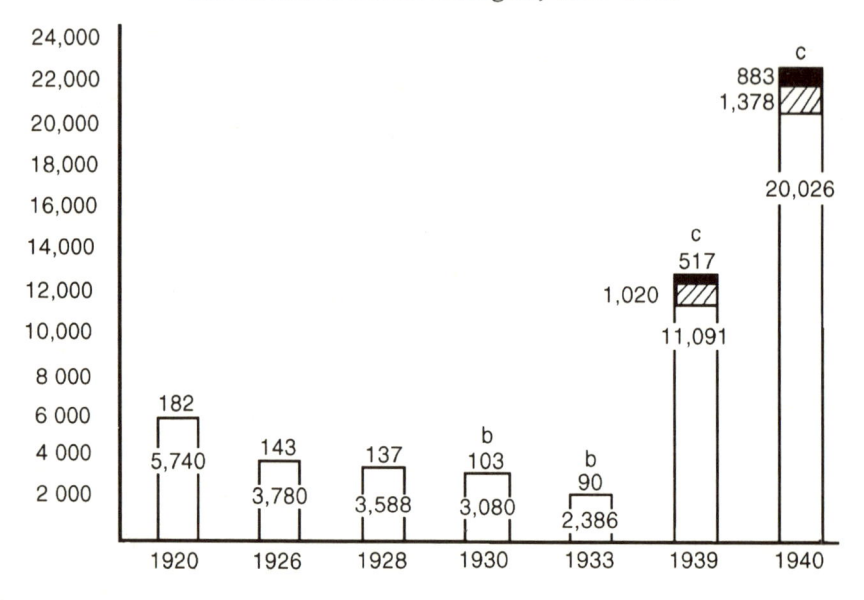

Year	Value	Additional
1920	5,740	182
1926	3,780	143
1928	3,588	137
1930	3,080	103 b
1933	2,386	90 b
1939	11,091	1,020 / 517 c
1940	20,026	1,378 / 883 c

Legend:-
Officers
BORs
AORs

Notes:-
a. excludes the Somaliland Camel Corps throughout
b. Includes S & T and bands
c. Includes non-combatants

After the 1914–18 war East Africa was in turmoil, complicated by the influx of white settlers from South Africa and Britain. The War Office wanted to stop paying for the Colonial Forces and the Colonial Governors wished to resume control of "their" troops – but only within their straitened budgets. This led to conflicts of interests and perceptions, as the Governors wanted the KAR primarily for IS and border control, dispersed to trouble spots, while the War Office wanted the KAR to be able to contribute to the defence of the Commonwealth and Empire. The Governors also wanted to reduce the numbers of men per battalion, but this would have reduced the units' flexibility and made them unsuitable for an Imperial rôle. The War Office considered that dispersion mitigated against training, discipline and sound organization. They also believed that, even for IS operations, a strike force should be held centrally, ready for rapid deployment.

At first the new commitment of Tanganyika was expected to need six battalions, but this was soon reduced to three: the indigenous 1/6 KAR and two Nyasa battalions. The passivity of the territory allowed a further reduction in 1923, when 2/1 KAR was disbanded; many of its soldiers went to 2 KAR. Zanzibar was also a reducing commitment; in July, 1923, all duties were taken over by the Police and the 2 KAR detachment was withdrawn. In July, 1920, Kenya became a Crown Colony, the Sultanate of Zanzibar became a Protectorate, and at about the same time the Administrator of Tanganyika was re-titled Governor.

The Jubaland was a constantly changing commitment. In 1925, having been a heavy and somewhat specialized IS responsibility for decades, it was transferred to Italy. The effect was to lose the IS task, but to add a new international border commitment. In 1940 it was hostile territory until occupied by the East African Force in February, 1941. It then came under the British Military Administration, with KAR and other EA units deployed in the area – an arrangement that lasted until 1950, when Italy assumed a UN trusteeship. Independence followed in 1960.

In the early 1920s the Mullah campaign was in its final phases, while the Northern Frontier District (NFD) was particularly turbulent, partly because of the unrest in Jubaland. There was unfinished business in Turkana, as no great military pressure had been exerted there during the war. New technology began to produce benefits, especially the introduction of radio (then called wireless), although it was not operational in Turkana and the NFD until 1927, the addition of better and more reliable motor transport, and, particularly after the end of the Mullah campaign, air support became possible.

In British Somaliland, even after the Mullah's death, the situation was not stable. This was partly due to an attempt to introduce an unpopular tax system, which resulted in the murder of a civil affairs officer at Burao. A consequence of his death was that B Company of the Camel Corps became a Yao Company, the askari being from 1 and 2 KAR in turn. When Sultan Osman Mahud reactivated one of the Mullah's old forts, a combined action with the Italians against him took the Camel Corps to the eastern part of the Protectorate in June, 1925. They blew up the fort, but operations continued until the Sultan surrendered at the end of 1927. There were riots in Hargeisa in September of the same year, and operations against the Esa people, near French Somaliland and around Zeila, which kept the Corps busy.

The first post-war plan was for the KAR to have ten battalions, but this was overtaken by events. The fortunes of the individual battalions are sketched out below:-

1 KAR

An outbreak of Spanish influenza in Nyasaland delayed demobilization, after which the battalions were demobilized in the sequence 3/1, 4/1 and 2/1; men who were retained joined 1 KAR, which became a six-company battalion, commanded by Lt Col G.L. Baxter DSO. By 31 May, 1919, Headquarters and four companies were in south-west Tanganyika and two in Nyasaland. The Nyasa companies were split between Zomba, Mangoche and Mlangeni.

2 KAR

By 31 May, 1919, 2 KAR (four companies) were in Central Tanganyika, mainly at Tabora, but with detachments at Dodoma, Mwanza and Kondoa Irangi. 2/1 KAR shared responsibility for garrisoning Western Tanganyika until they were disbanded in September, 1923. When the railway was extended to Mwanza early in 1928, No 4 company was disbanded and the garrison closed.

3 KAR

Initially the three battalions were concentrated at Nairobi, where they were reduced to two. 2/3 KAR continued in a Mounted Infantry role in the NFD until May, 1919, when it was disbanded, with transfers to 5 KAR. The bulk of 3 KAR was at Nairobi, with detachments in Northern Turkana, NFD, Zanzibar and the Masai Reserve. No 3 (Somali) Company attempted to mutiny at Moyale, and they were replaced by men from a variety of tribes by August 1920. The 3 KAR detachment left Moyale in April, 1922; the battalion was then still based on Nairobi, with two companies in Turkana and one at Gobwein. Despite this better concentration, the Inspector-General reported the battalion unfit for active service in 1923 because of over-dispersion.

4 KAR

Three companies of 1/4 KAR were concentrated in Uganda; mainly at Bombo, with detachments at Karamoja and Entebbe. 2/4 KAR was combined with 7 KAR and designated 6 KAR. After the Sudanese Government assumed control of Didinga the battalion was reduced to three companies, each of four platoons, but with only seven men per section. As Bombo was relatively isolated, it was proposed to move the battalion to Entebbe, but this did not happen and it was not until 1936 that 6 KAR's move to Jinja was authorized. This was an improvement, as previously the battalion had marched from Bombo to Kampala for ceremonial duties, leaving Bombo at midnight and arriving eight hours later.

5 KAR

5 KAR was in Jubaland with four companies; Headquarters were at Gobwein, but moved to Kismayu later. By 31 May, 1919, there were two companies in North Jubaland, one and a half in South Jubaland and detachments on the River Tana and in Turkana. In October, 1922, they took over control of the NFD, with Headquarters at Meru. On his first visit the Inspector-General considered them unfit for active service as they were spread over seven different locations. They were disbanded at the end of 1925, after the Jubaland commitment disappeared.

6 KAR

Initially they were responsible for the coastal areas of Tanganyika, with Headquarters and two companies at Dar es Salaam, one company at Lindi and the other split between Tanga and Arusha. They had been reformed in 1919, taking one company from 7 KAR, two companies from Uganda wartime battalions (see above), and one company from 2/6 KAR. When 2/1 KAR was disbanded in September, 1923, 6 KAR took over the whole of the eastern part of the territory, assuming responsibility for garrisoning Mahenge and Songea; Lindi and Tanga were vacated.

Somaliland Camel Corps

At the end of the Mullah campaign the Corps consisted of three camel-mounted companies and one pony-mounted. One of the camel companies was Indian, the remainder of the unit was Somali. The Indian company was withdrawn and a Yao company replaced the second Somali camel company in 1922, 100 men strong. A proposal for mechanization was not approved, as rounding up stock was hardly possible using vehicles. When mechanization was introduced eventually, the Yao Company was the first to be converted, as teaching Yaos to ride camels had proved neither practical nor cost-effective.

Inspector-General

During the war the central affairs of the KAR had been looked after by a Commandant and his staff, known as KARSTAFF. The post of Inspector-General was revived in October, 1919, and held first by Col G.M.P. Hawthorne, while Col. G.F. Phillips was Commandant. KARSTAFF disappeared in July, 1920, and Phillips continued as OC Troops Kenya, commanding two KAR battalions. This arrangement lasted until 1922, when Phillips left without replacement. Col. J. Harrington became Inspector-General in September, 1923, and took a robust view of the need to prepare the KAR for Imperial commitments. Harrington was succeeded by Colonel H.A. Walker (September, 1923, to September, 1927), who took much the same line as his predecessor, believing in a centrally controlled force and troops deployed according to military necessity. Due to Walker's insistence, the KAR Reserve of Officers was eventually formed in each territory in 1928-29.

The first Colours were awarded in 1923, initially only the four most senior battalions were to receive them. The subject had been raised first in 1907, but had been delayed due to confusion over the title "Rifles", which in other parts of the British and Indian Armies involved special traditions. After it was agreed that the KAR should carry Colours, a common design was accepted for all six battalions. The designs of the King's Colour are Union Flags, gold-fringed, with a Crown and the words King's African Rifles and the battalion numeral in a circle in the centre. The Regimental Colours are on royal blue grounds, with the centre similar to that of the King's Colours, except that a lion is in the centre and the battalion numeral on the fly.

All battalions were entitled to the same battle honours, even though they had not been in all of the battles. The honours were Ashanti 1900, Somaliland 1901-04, Kilimanjaro, Narungombe, Nyangao, and East Africa 1914-18. The Governors presented the Colours on behalf of the Sovereign. The King became Colonel in Chief on 25 September, 1925, a connection continued by King Edward VIII, King George VI and Queen Elizabeth II.

Pardoxically, the economies forced on the KAR by the depression of

1929-31 led to a sound organization from which they moved relatively smoothly on to a war footing. Some centralized control was essential if numbers were to be cut to what could be afforded. This was achieved by having two brigades, both capable of deployment wherever the need arose in British East Africa. As the Tanganyikans lived in a mandated territory they were not supposed to serve abroad; this was overcome by introducing the principle that the territories of East Africa were a single entity for defence purposes and, provided it was in the defence of their home territory, Tanganyikans could serve abroad. The brigade commanders were colonels; signals sections were added, commanded by Royal Signals officers, with one BOR and fifty-eight African signallers (from the KAR) with each brigade. The Supplies and Transport element was increased substantially, to six officers (from one), eight BWOs and BORs and 133 AORs. The vehicle strength went from thirty-seven to fifty. They were deployed mainly in support of the Northern Brigade, in the NFD. The OC was Capt (after the increase, Major) T.M. Brick RASC.

Each brigade was to have three battalions, two "forward", on border control and IS, with the third in reserve. The composition was:-

Northern Brigade; (mainly of Nilotic peoples) – 3, 4 and 5 KAR (the last was reformed on 1 January, 1930, from the transfer of officers and men from 3 KAR). Flexibility was ensured by requiring askari from Kenya and Uganda to serve in any battalion in the Northern Brigade. Their deployment was expected to be one battalion on the frontier west of Lake Rudolph, with one company at Bombo for IS. The second battalion would be to the east of the Lake, with Headquarters at Meru and a company at Wajir. The third battalion was to be in Nairobi.

Southern Brigade; (mainly of Bantu peoples) – 1, 2, and 6 KAR, with Headquarters and one battalion at Dar es Salaam, one at Zomba and the reserve battalion at Tabora. This ensured that battalions could deploy by rail in an emergency.

While these arrangements looked good, the units were small. Each was commanded by a major and had two companies each of four platoons, plus a Vickers machine-gun company of two platoons. The strength of a battalion was sixteen officers, one warrant officer and 442 askari. All buglers, clerks, dressers (i.e. first aiders/nursing orderlies) and gun porters were within this total, while the signallers were located at brigade headquarters. In consequence the residues were too small for serious training.

Improvements to transport and radio allowed troops to be more concentrated and many of the minor out-stations were closed. By September, 1931, the Regiment, in all its deployment areas, totalled 113 officers, 3,390 ORs and 875 reservists). This included Somaliland (16 plus 416, with 131 reservists). The Governors sought to dispense with the reserve battalions; instead, further savings were made within battalions, by reducing the Vickers companies to platoons, with four guns per battalion, commanded by the 2ics of the battalions. (The companies were re-established later.) The "native officers" who had served in 4 KAR as relics of Emin Pasha's organization were dispensed with. Battalions were required to contribute to the local economy by road-making, locust control and famine relief work.

In 1933–34 the RAF advocated a policy of control from the air; aircraft would work in close support of the police and the KAR could be reduced to a single brigade; 5 and 6 KAR would be disbanded and 2 KAR would merge with the Northern Rhodesia Regiment. The Governors did not accept that three battalions would be adequate for five territories, and thought that aircraft would not be much use in recapturing stolen stock. Before the discussion could proceed far the Italian/Ethiopian war began. Its effect on the KAR was a severe influx of refugees from Ethiopia into the NFD. Troops were called on to help the police in the NFD, and 1 KAR was warned for service in Somaliland. The Camel Corps was mobilized and a flight of aircraft deployed from Aden. All units received reinforcements. Christopher Consett, serving with his battalion in Belfast, volunteered for the Camel Corps. Shortly afterwards he embarked from Marseilles on a P&O ship. There were about eight officers travelling, including Maj Gen A. Wavell, on his way to Palestine to be GOC.

Consett disembarked in Aden and crossed to Berbera with his personal servant, Jama Warsama, on the SS *Tuna*, which was owned by the Cowasjee Dinshaw family. The *Tuna* was Somaliland's link with the world. Consett stocked up in Berbera from the Cowasjee Dinshaw shop, travelled by trade truck to Hargeisa to meet his company commander and left after one night for his platoon on the Ethiopian border at Borama. As they neared the town "I met a sight I shall never forget. It was three camels of the Camel Corps, with their magnificent askari, one of them carrying aloft a large Union Jack. They were patrolling the border – literally showing the flag – and it was a truly magnificent sight." At Borama the hand-over was brief, as his predecessor left at 4 a.m. next day, on a road-building detail, leaving Consett "with thirty camels and thirty Somalis in a quite uncovered camp near the landing strip; which played a large part in our lives, as three Vickers Vincents were on detachment from Aden."

In Kenya aircraft were also being introduced; in 1936 a Flight of RAF Valencias was in Kenya to move troops to trouble spots. Familiarization flights for the askari were from the RAF aerodrome outside Nairobi, on the edge of the game reserve, below the 3 KAR lines. "Crew" Stoneley went the airfield "to see the askari safely emplaned in one of these monsters. The Valencia was a twin-engined bi-plane with a sausage-shaped fuselage, intended to carry a platoon of infantry with their weapons. None of the askari had ever been near such a 'ndege', and they were astonished at its sheer size. The Valencia flew them around for about half an hour. I met the askari as they filed out of the aeroplane, and asked one what he thought about it. I suppose I had expected him to express some wonderment after flying at great speed high over the earth." But he was concerned at the cold.

Maj Gen G.J. Giffard, who became Inspector-General KAR in 1936, was appointed Inspector-General, African Colonial Forces (ie; covering both East and West Africa) in 1938. He saw the KAR's main task as countering an enemy thrust down the coast to Mombasa and possibly diversionary action in the NFD. In Somaliland the Camel Corps was not expected to fight more than a delaying action, pending reinforcement or evacuation. However, there was a prospect of combined action with the French in Djibouti. Giffard's assets were the Kenya (Territorial) Regiment (see Chapter 13; they were about 75% the strength of a British battalion), six small KAR battalions, a Coast Defence Unit at Mombasa, (a newly formed gunner/sapper organization), the KARRO and the KAR (African) Reserve.

Giffard pushed through his recommendations so quickly that they were considered by the Committee of Imperial Defence in London before the Governors had commented on them. The main proposal was for the first line battalions (two in the Northern Brigade and one in the South) to be brought up to war establishment in African personnel, ready to take the field. The lower priority battalions were to serve as cadres, with each company able to expand into a fully trained battalion from a combination of reservists and recruits within six months. There were shortages of money for weapons and equipment, and of Europeans. The War Office undertook to provide the money for the weapons (but the war started before they did), and the deficit in Europeans would be rectified from the KARRO and Southern Rhodesia. The Vickers machine guns were to be replaced by Bren guns, while mortars and anti-tank rifles were to be added. (Italian Blackshirt battalions each had some light tanks.)

In 1938 most of these proposals were implemented, with the support of the Governors. Signals and S & T were expanded, first line KAR battalions became lieutenant colonels' commands, brigade headquarters received all-military staffs and reinforcements were planned from West Africa. In June, 1938, Commander Northern Brigade identified four possible axes of advance into Kenya and expected to hold the line River Tana-Garissa-Garba-Tulla-Archer's Post, with 4 KAR on the right and 5 KAR on the left;

3 KAR would be building up its strength in the Nairobi area, while 1 KAR would have a company at Mombasa and be in reserve.

Communications were a high priority. Crew Stoneley was designated OC East Africa Signals Corps and developed the new organization to provide signals support within the two new brigades, plus rear links to the Division Headquarters expected to arrive from Britain, the supply of "area" signals covering Kenya, Uganda and Tanganyika, and a signals training unit for the askari. The East Africa Signals Corps took in all existing signals personnel from the KAR and also recruited. Pre-war all signals askari were Wakamba, but the other rapidly expanding military units wanted Wakamba too, so a "rationing" policy was introduced by Headquarters East Africa Command and a mix of tribes was recruited, including Kikuyu.

Two Kenya farmers with interest in and aptitude for signals technology joined the KARRO as potential signals officers. Robathan went to the Signals Training Centre and Depot in Nairobi, while Curtis became Brigade Signals Officer, 21 (EA) Brigade. Other officers came from the KAR reinforcement pool, some Rhodesians arrived from the Officer Cadet Training Unit (OCTU) in the Middle East, some potential officers were identified in British units, while "Africanization" helped to keep down the numbers of Europeans required. There was a EA Signal Corps Headquarters, two brigade signals sections, Northern Area Signals for Kenya and Uganda, and Southern Area Signals for Tanganyika and Nyasaland, plus the training centre and depot. When East Africa Command mobilized, Col Winkley arrived to become Chief Signals Officer, with Crew as his Staff Officer Grade 2. Dodge 1-ton truck chassis were modified locally to take short range radios.

Extensive training was necessary to operate the new short wave sets, using British Army procedures, with the aid of pamphlets from the Crown Agents. Drafts of signals personnel from Britain formed the nuclei of 11 (A) and 12 (A) Division Signals, with considerable reinforcement from East African sources. The Training Centre was commanded by Lt Col Peter Docker, with Major D.E. Robathan as 2ic. The latter was followed by Major John Swallow. Much of the equipment was improvised. Morse code – using both buzzer and lamp – and flag drill were taught. A special course for Regimental Signals Officers was run at M'bagathi Camp. Giffard authorized the purchase of American wireless components, which were built into locally designed and manufactured sets to give long-range communications. These radios were eventually replaced by No 11 sets from UK, and No 38 sets also arrived. There had been hopes of using captured Italian radios as the campaign progressed, but often they had been smashed, sometimes by our own forces. However, in Addis Ababa there were quantities of equipment and a Signals Park was formed to sort it out.

Other East African residents were drafted into the forces; Chris Bell, a school teacher, had no connection with the Kenya Defence Force (KDF) until he was visited at 10 a.m. on the morning after Italy's entry into the war, by "a KDF Sergeant who summoned me to report to Headquarters Mombasa at 10 a.m. the next morning. It was thought that the Italians might bomb Mombasa from Kismayu, not very far north. After three days in a dug-out, I was given two stripes and posted in charge of two Lewis guns on Biggs' tree, overlooking the water works. I had no military training since the cadet corps at school, I had never seen a Lewis gun, and we had so little ammunition that we could not actually fire the guns. There were no air raids and after about six weeks I was sent up to the transit camp at El Doret, en route for the OCTU at Nakuru . . . After OCTU I was posted to 1/6 KAR because I had passed all my Swahili examinations. The OCTU was largely staffed by ex-Indian Army officers who had served in the Great War (or, in one case I was told, the Boer War). Fortunately I knew something about Africa and the Africans."

The European ladies of East Africa also joined the Services, beating the system somewhat as the official *Kenya Gazette* notice establishing them from 1 September, 1939, was dated 16 September, 1941. With less than an official start, they were generally known by the 1914-18 title of First Aid Nursing Yeomanry (FANY); initially most of them were friends and neighbours of Lady Sidney Farrar (later MBE). She had served with the FANY in France during World War I and was determined that a comparable organization would be available in East Africa. By the outbreak of war she had recruited about seventy women and arranged for a lady of German extraction to train them. She was known as Sergeant Hessfleurger, "a rather fearsome woman who drilled and marched us for some months . . . and odd though the arrangement seems, she did her job on the raw material provided. We respected her and were sorry when she was interned with other Germans in the colony."

By September, 1939, they were housed in various commandeered houses in Nairobi, and ran a dispatch rider service between Nairobi and the KAR camps at Garissa and further north. They also staffed the fleet of ambulances held in readiness for casualties from Ethiopia. Mrs O'shea started as a telephone operator then requisitioned donkeys for animal transport, but reverted to telephones when the new GHQ opened. The demands for FANYs was so great that Lady Sidney went to Rhodesia and South Africa on recruiting drives. By the end of 1940 there were between 700 and 800 women in the Women's Territorial Service (EA). When Eloise O'shea became a lance corporal, twenty FANYs celebrated with the aid of one bottle of champagne and twenty egg cups. Their work changed as the war progressed; a deception plan included sending bogus bags of mail and signal traffic to Burma, so that the nature and extent of reinforcements were not disclosed. The FANYs took on additional duties as diverse as catering and intelligence work, both in East Africa and abroad, in Cairo, Somalia, Madagascar and Malaya.

A School of Instruction had been established at Nakuru, but in June, 1940, it was disbanded when Italy entered the war. A.D. "Mac" MacPherson had been a CSM Instructor with the Kenya Regiment before going to Nakuru in March; newly commissioned in June, he and another officer reported to the Coast Defence Rifle Company (CDRC) in Mombasa. The CDRC had been formed before the war to defend the coastal guns and searchlights, sited on the island of Mombasa and manned by a coastal artillery/sapper unit. The majority of the askari were seconded from 3 KAR, there was no headquarters, no British NCOs and they had Lewis guns at first, although Bren guns arrived later. Initially they defended Mombasa Island, but were replaced by the locally enlisted Arab Rifles in 1941 and guarded Italian prisoners of war from Ethiopia instead. In 1942 they returned to Mombasa and became part of 16 KAR, which was then forming under Lt Col Roger Hurst. MacPherson transferred to the Coastal Irregulars when they formed.

Command and Mobilization

Maj Gen Giffard was replaced as Inspector-General by Maj Gen D.P. Dickinson in August, 1939, and on 31 August the latter became GOC East Africa Command, with Headquarters at Kenton College. Movement of troops within fifteen miles of the Italian colonial borders was prohibited, to avoid provocation. The Kenya Administration abandoned Moyale and Mandera prematurely, but reoccupied them four days later. The "stand-by" signal went to all units on 22 August, complete mobilization was ordered four days later and the "precautionary stage" followed on 1 September, with the "War with Germany" signal on 3 September. Battalions carried out their transition-to-war measures and deployed according to their roles. On 3 February, 1940, East Africa Command passed under command of GHQ Middle East. The training of Ethiopian "Patriots" began, under East African direction.

1 KAR

In 1938 1 KAR was at Tabora; one company moved to Arusha during the Munich crisis, ready to support the police internment of the many Germans who lived there. Shortly after the Munich agreement the remainder of the battalion moved to Moshi, where their cantonment was being built; during the winter of 1938–39 they made bricks for it. By April, 1939, 1 KAR was concentrated in Moshi, except for one company at Arusha. During the third week there was a major alarm when a signal from Headquarters Southern Brigade relayed a War Office warning of a German aerial invasion of Tanganyika from Italian Somaliland; this coup was to take place on Hitler's birthday – 20 April. The Arusha company blocked the airfield runway with vehicles and took up defensive positions, but stood down without incident four days later. In August, 1939, the battalion was training east of Moshi, but when the German/Russian agreement was signed they returned to Moshi and mobilized shortly afterwards. On the outbreak of war, internment operations having been completed, they trained at Namanga for a short while before moving to Isiolo, (with one company at Wajir) under command of 1 (EA) Brigade.

2 KAR

Their first warning order arrived on 19 July: to re-occupy Iringa, to take over Mbeya from 6 KAR and to form an extra company of reservists. With the police they began to arrest Germans as soon as war was declared and by 23 September the task was complete. Deployment to their war station at Magabathi (with one company at Zomba), meant that they passed to 1 (EA) Brigade, (5 KAR going to 2 (EA) Brigade).

3 KAR

In December, 1939, 3 KAR was re-designated 1/3 KAR and became a machine-gun battalion by absorbing the machine-gun platoons of the other battalions and posting out the equivalent numbers of riflemen to the depleted units. The other battalions received mortars in this reorganization. Three companies of 3 KAR had machine guns while the fourth was a divisional headquarters defence company. In consequence, during the 1939–45 portion of the KAR story they appear as detachments only, which does not do justice to their achievements. They were Force Troops for the invasion of Ethiopia and were allocated formations and units as the tactical situations demanded. Later they became 3 (EA) Reconnaissance Regiment – afterwards titled 3 (EA) Armoured Car Regiment. In this rôle, too, they were deployed by sub-units and not as a tactical entity.

4 KAR

The battalion was at Bombo with a detachment at Lokitaung, whose job was, (in Peter Molloy's words) "as a base for keeping the Merille, Toposa and Danyiro from Abyssinia taking the cattle and women of our local tribe, the Turkana. It also enabled us to keep an eye on the Italians." In 1938 Lt

Col Pat Mundy took command. Peter said, "He produced an entirely new atmosphere in the battalion. He was determined to make 4 KAR the finest-trained battalion yet. He was old-fashioned, unmarried and, being forty-six, a generation older than the rest of us. He had a stiff left arm from his previous service." Before the declaration of war with Germany, reservists were recalled and the battalion concentrated at Bombo. They packed up their peacetime gear, as they were due to move to Jinja shortly in any event, and did not return to Bombo after the war. The battalion moved by rail to Mombasa (a two-day journey), dropping off a company at Mackinnon Road. In Mombasa they guarded Nyali Bridge and other vulnerable points around the town, under command of 1 (EA) Brigade.

5 KAR

This was the only battalion in the NFD at the outbreak of war. They re-occupied Moyale and Mandera, despite Italian representations, and moved to their war locations within the Northern Brigade plan, going first to Isiolo, with companies at Wajir and Archer's Post and the machine guns at Merti. On the declaration of war they moved to the Lorain Swamp-Merti sector. When Northern brigade became 1 (EA) Brigade, they passed from its command to 2 (EA) Brigade, as the latter was responsible for the defence of the western flank.

6 KAR

After interning aliens with 1 and 2 KAR, they moved from Dar es Salaam to Moshi before travelling to their war location at Nanyuki, under command of 2 (EA) Brigade. 2/6 KAR began to form at Dar es Salaam on 24 October.

7 KAR

The battalion began to reform at Bombo, then provided a company detachment at Lokitaung, taking over from the police. Two more companies were raised at the outbreak of war, for duty in Turkana. There was then a somewhat confused period in which many of the officers were transferred to 2/4 KAR. By August, 1940, these problems had been overcome, allowing 3/4 and 4/4 KAR to be raised and stationed at Bombo with 7 KAR.

(EA) Artillery

The formation of 1 (EA) Light Battery and of the development of the remainder of the EA Artillery are given in Appendix D.

Kenya Regiment

An abbreviated version of the history of the Regiment and its role, particularly in the provision of officers and BNCOs to the KAR in World War II, is in Chapter 13.

Other Arms and Services.

Signals and S & T expansions have been covered earlier. East African Engineers formed a Reconnaissance Squadron, a Field Company and a Field Survey Company. Medical, Ordnance, and Pay Services began to develop, as did the East African Military Police, while two Pioneer Battalions were formed. The East African Education Corps came into being at Nairobi on 7 February, 1942, mainly to teach Ki-Swahili to newly arrived officers and BNCOs, but a central school for teaching Ki-Swahili to Africans then developed, the Ki-Swahili language newspaper *Askari* was published, and broadcasts for African soldiers were made over local radio stations. With the creation of REME, EAEME was formed, taking personnel from the Sappers, S & T and Ordnance Corps. East African Forces were in process of becoming a balanced organization of all Arms and Services in addition to the KAR. The KAR expanded to a total of forty-four battalions by the end of the war.

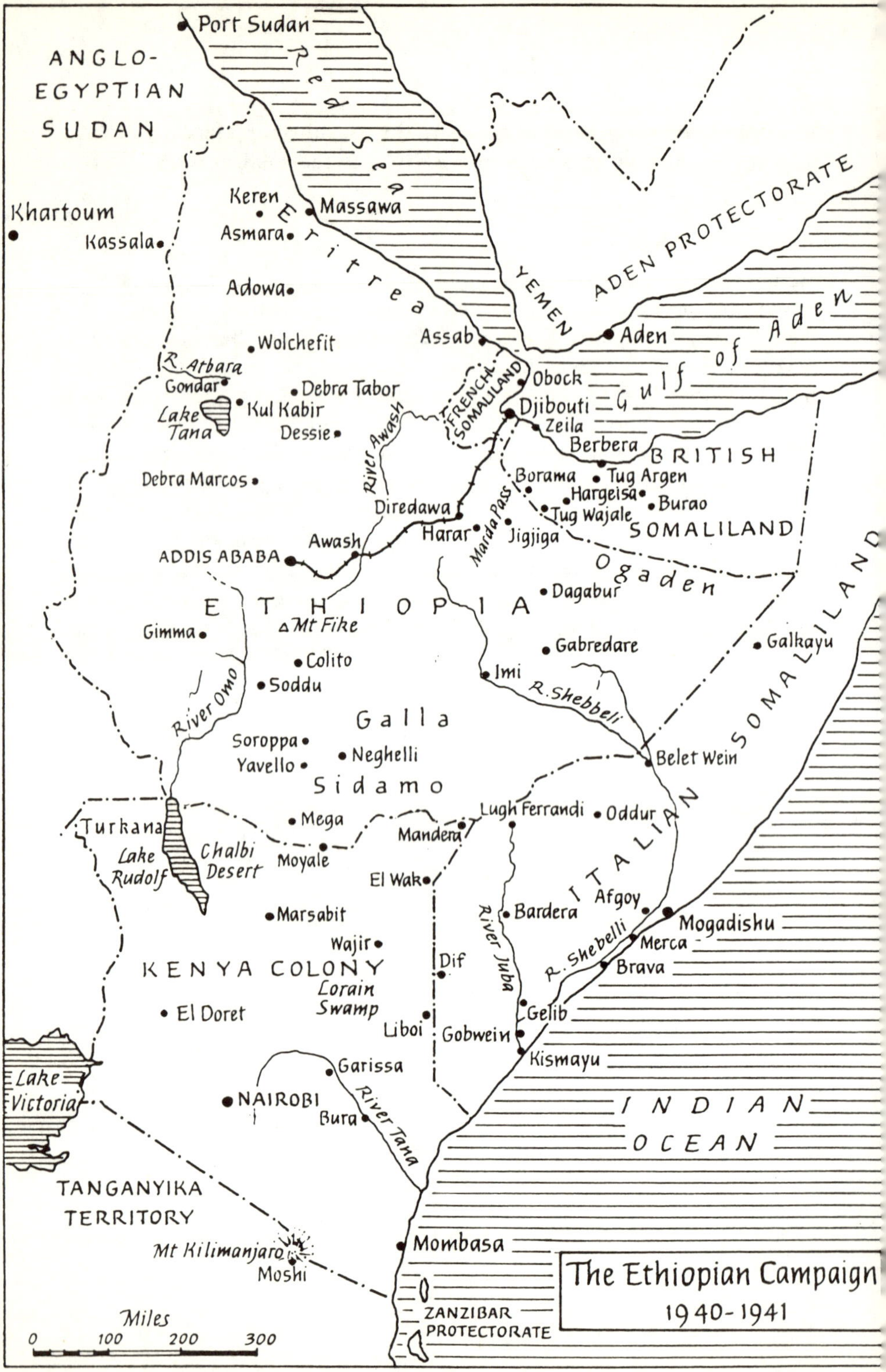

Port Sudan
ANGLO-EGYPTIAN SUDAN
Red Sea
Khartoum
Kassala
Keren
Asmara
Massawa
Eritrea
Adowa
Wolchefit
R. Atbara
Gondar
Lake Tana
Kul Kabir
Debra Tabor
Dessie
Debra Marcos
YEMEN
ADEN PROTECTORATE
Aden
Gulf of Aden
Assab
Obock
FRENCH SOMALILAND
Djibouti
Zeila
Berbera
BRITISH SOMALILAND
Borama
Tug Argen
Hargeisa
Burao
Tug Wajale
River Awash
Diredawa
Harar
Marda Pass
Jigjiga
Awash
ADDIS ABABA
Ogaden
Dagabur
ETHIOPIA
Mt Fike
Gimma
Colito
Soddu
River Omo
Gabredare
Galkayu
Imi
R. Shebbeli
Galla
Soroppa
Yavello
Neghelli
Sidamo
Belet Wein
ITALIAN SOMALILAND
Lugh Ferrandi
Oddur
Mega
Mandera
Turkana
Lake Rudolf
Chalbi Desert
Moyale
El Wak
Marsabit
Bardera
Afgoy
Mogadishu
Merca
Brava
R. Shebelli
River Juba
Wajir
KENYA COLONY
Lorain Swamp
Dif
El Doret
Liboi
Gobwein
Gelib
Kismayu
Lake Victoria
Garissa
NAIROBI
Bura
River Tana
INDIAN OCEAN
TANGANYIKA TERRITORY
Mt Kilimanjaro
Moshi
Mombasa
ZANZIBAR PROTECTORATE
The Ethiopian Campaign 1940-1941
Miles
0 100 200 300

MAP 4

Chapter 5

ITALIAN EAST AFRICAN EMPIRE – PART I
(Reference Maps 4 and 5)

"You, base city of Rome; Menelik, saviour of the world will not leave even one of your seed to bear your name."
Anonymous Ethiopian Court poet, 1895

Italy's Protectorate over Ethiopia was recognized by Britain in 1891, but Emperor Menelik denounced the Italian claims and Italian forces entered Ethiopia from Eritrea in 1895. After initial successes, mainly due to the slowness of Ethiopian reaction, the major Battle of Adowa was fought on 1 March, 1896. The Italians were taken by surprise by the Ethiopian Army's modern rifles and artillery pieces, which had been smuggled in with French connivance – at the price of concessions over Djibouti and the construction of the railway from the coast to Menelik's new capital of Addis Ababa.

When the Empress suddenly waved her large black umbrella and shouted out, "Courage, victory is ours. Strike," and led her court ladies towards the enemy, the Emperor decisively committed his 25,000 strong Shoan reserve to battle. Nearly 4,000 Italian and allied prisoners were added to about the same number already in Ethiopian hands. The Ethiopians might have driven the Italians into the sea, but they had lost about 7,000 dead and 10,000 wounded, many seriously. So they returned to Addis Ababa instead, with the Italian prisoners struggling after them over 500 miles of rough country in the rain, starving and in rags. Menelik made permanent peace with the French, British and Italians and took 10,000,000 lira for the return of 1,705 Italian prisoners. The remainder had died or else were African askari, many of whom had been mutilated. The humiliation of Adowa was deeply resented by the Italian army, who nursed hopes of revenge for forty years. Mussolini's ambitions and the army's resentment combined in 1935. A dispute at the important water wells at Wal Wal gave Italy the excuse to declare war on Ethiopia. She sent into Ethiopia a well-prepared army which was thoroughly acclimatized, had suitable clothing, diet and excellent medical facilities. It was a walk-over in military terms, and soon Haile Selassie moved to exile in England, where he stayed until 1942.

Marshal Badoglio rode into Addis Ababa in triumph and Italian colonists arrived with ambitious plans for road construction, building and farming. However, Italy's hold on the more remote areas was insecure, with partisan activity strong in the Shoa and Amhara provinces. In 1938 Prince Amedo, Duke of Aosta, became Viceroy, as both civil governor and commander in chief of the armed forces. Mussolini had told Hitler that it would be necessary to strengthen Ethiopia before undertaking large-scale operations, but little had been done and the Duke's forces were no longer the triumphant army of a few years earlier. On 10 June, 1940, when Italy declared war, the Duke commanded 290,000 troops, of whom 90,000 were from Italy. They had twenty-four medium and thirty-nine light tanks of doubtful quality. The air force's most modern aircraft were thirty-four obsolete Fiat CR 42 fighters, while the fleet in the Red Sea consisted of seven destroyers, two torpedo boats and eight submarines, four of which were out of action. There were shortages of artillery ammunition, petrol and diesel fuel, as well as various items of food. The fleet, although in poor condition, had considerable effect. When Italy declared war President Roosevelt banned American shipping from the Red Sea, which prevented supplies of material being shipped directly from USA to the Middle East. The Italian warships were also a constant threat to British shipping, now using the Cape route in view of the effective closure of the Mediterranean.

The Duke took the initiative, despite his disadvantages. In July he captured three towns in Sudan and Moyale in Kenya, before moving into British Somaliland. B Company 1 KAR was at Moyale with a platoon of 3 KAR machine gunners and a detachment of sappers, a total of 180 men. The village had been fortified secretly, houses on the perimeter had been reinforced with concrete, the whole area of 600 by 200 yards had been surrounded with triple Dannert barbed wire, trenches had been dug and pill boxes had been built; there was an underground command post and a field dressing station. The Lewis guns were antiquated, but they had some Boyes antitank rifles, four-inch mortars and grenades. Their water supply was outside the perimeter, so that tankers could be filled only when the Italians were not looking.

The GOC planned to use the NFD as a buffer, to impose delay and logistic difficulties on the advancing enemy. The time thus gained was to be used to receive reinforcements from Nigeria, the Gold Coast and South Africa. Moyale and Mandera were abandoned soon after the outbreak of hostilities with Germany, leading to a spate of cattle looting, armed robbery and inter-tribal feuding on both sides of the frontier, and the Italian authorities requested Kenya to resume the administration of the NFD as soon as possible. After they did so there was a period of close co-operation between the two administrations; the Italians assisted in the recovery of both government and private property that had got into the wrong hands.

On 10 June a British police superintendent and a friend, who had not heard of the outbreak of war with Italy, were taken prisoner when on an evening stroll. Two days later Moyale was bombed for the first time, but no serious damage was done. Towards the end of May three Hawker Hart planes reached Wajir, where there was a considerable stock of aviation fuel that had been moved by road from Nairobi. On 11 June Ted Crosskill, who was acting as Brigade Intelligence Officer to Brigadier "Fluffy" Fowkes, Commander 22 Brigade, visited the flight to brief them for an aerial reconnaissance. Two Caproni bombers arrived while he was doing so, damaged two of the Harts and set fire to the fuel dump, which burned spectacularly for two days.

A small-scale attack was planned on El Wak, a small fort just over the border into Italian Somaliland, sixty-five miles north-east of Wajir, both to show the Italians offensive action and to test the KAR's ability to fight. A Hawker Hart was due over the fort after the ground attack had gone in, but it arrived early. Fearing bombing, the Italian garrison moved into the bush. The KAR found the place deserted and started to search for maps, documents and souvenirs in a relaxed way. The Italians realized what had happened and counter-attacked, causing the recent victors to abandon their prize. The Hawker Hart was damaged and forced down. The KAR won the race to locate it, but the Italians pressed them hard. The pilot and the observer tried to repair it, then to tow it away, but the wheels seized up and it was burned.

At the fort of Moyale the main problems were snipers and shelling. The garrison countered with night raids to locate and harass the enemy. Enemy shelling was by small pack howitzers, but many shells failed to explode. A raid by Savoia bombers on 30 June was followed by shelling during the night, and a strong ground attack came in at dawn. Fighting was heavy until 8 a.m., but on the northern side of the fort it continued for a few hours more. Despite the heavy fire the defenders had four casualties and three trucks were destroyed. The Italians withdrew at about midday and the water tanks were refilled. Reinforcements then arrived: a second company of 1 KAR, a troop of 22 Indian Mountain Battery RA and the Brigade Commander, with an escort provided by the East African Recce Regiment. The battery had 3.7 inch howitzers and used Crosskill's data on enemy gun locations to conduct a counter-battery shoot. Over the next two nights the Italians kept up the pressure and it was decided to evacuate the fort. The order did not reach the defenders until the next day, and the commander, David Henderson, decided to pull out after dark, when the Italians were eating. Henderson brought up the rear, or thought he did, but three wounded askari who were judged unfit to move decided not to rely on Italian medical treatment and hobbled after him.

On 1 July Commander 22 Brigade proposed a two-battalion attack, but before it could be mounted an Italian thrust caused Brigade Headquarters to move back thirty miles to Debel. The brigade consisted of three battalions, the mountain battery, sappers, a Recce detachment and a field ambulance, and needed a position with enough water for a protracted stand. They found this at Buna, thirty miles further south, where they dug in and set up a light aircraft strip. On the way back they had been harassed by Italian patrols at night, led by a major nick-named "Twinkletoes" because of the small footprints he left behind. The brigade position was bombed, but with little damage as the bombers were met by the combined effects of thousands of rounds of small arms and the versatile howitzers of 22 Battery, with their trails dug into the ground to give them elevation. Buna was unhealthy and dysentery became a problem. In late August the brigade moved back to Wajir and the River Uaso Nyiro. The Italians followed, their morale boosted by their capture of British Somaliland.

The plan for the defence of the Somalilands was based on Djibouti and its strong French garrison. Wavell intended to put the senior French general in overall command and for the British to fall back towards Djibouti, but the plan was abandoned when the French capitulated in Europe. The Military Governor of French Somaliland, General Le Gentilhomme, was replaced by General Germaine, who supported the Vichy Government. This deprived the defence of most of its troops and left the British right flank wide open. The British fleet extended its blockade of Italian East Africa to include Djibouti and other minor ports.

British Somaliland was garrisoned by the Somaliland Camel Corps, with a motorized Yao company and the remainder Somalis – one camel-mounted company, a pony company and a reserve company. They had fourteen British officers, 400 askari and 150 reservists, and in October, 1939, received seventeen officers and twenty warrant officers and NCOs from Rhodesia. The unit was commanded by Lt Col Arthur Chater RM and was funded and controlled by the local (i.e. Protectorate) government. In 1939 Chater had asked for money to construct defences on the approaches to Berbera and had been given £900, which was used to build some water tanks and a few pill-boxes. A proposal to increase the unit by fifty men was not approved until May, 1940.

Wavell assumed command of the Middle East in August, 1939, but did not gain operational control of the Colonial Forces until 13 January, 1940, while administrative responsibility was not transferred until 1 June. His request to mechanize two companies of the Camel Corps was granted on 19

May. He also reinforced the garrison from Aden and East Africa, to inflict maximum casualties before withdrawal became necessary. The first reinforcements were a Punjabi battalion from Aden, 1 Northern Rhodesia Regiment, 2 KAR and the East African Light Battery with four 3.7 inch howitzers. The troops from Africa travelled by sea round Cape Guarda Fui. The gunners had been formed at the outbreak of war and had two days to refit before leaving Mombasa on 3 July. Chater believed he stood a good chance of holding his positions with two more infantry battalions and was allocated another Punjabi battalion and 1 Black Watch from Aden, which gave him nearly 6,000 men. Against him was the Italian Eastern Army of some 25,000 men, commanded by Lt Gen Guglielmo Nasi. He had five brigades; twenty-six battalions and twenty-one batteries, with tanks and armoured cars. The Italians probably wished to eliminate a British threat to their flank, to stop the raids by the Camel Corps and the Illalos, to strengthen their control of the Red Sea and they needed a victory for home consumption. They therefore decided to take British Somaliland.

There were three possible enemy approaches to Berbera; from Chater's left to right the first was via Sheikh and down the Sheikh Pass, a narrow road made during the Mullah campaign. The second was to use the main Berbera-Hargeisa road, which runs almost north-south. The third was

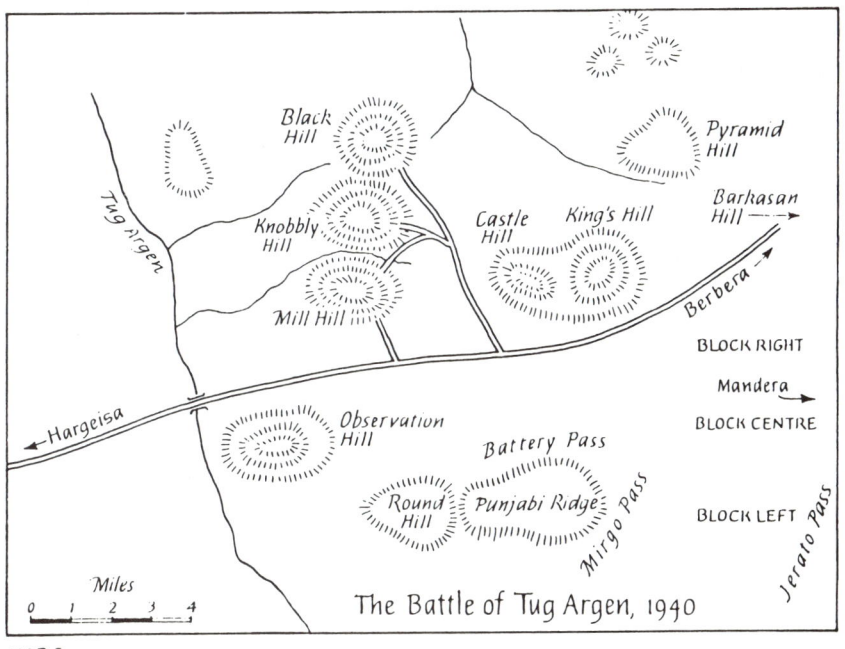

The Battle of Tug Argen, 1940

MAP 5

through Zeila and then along the coast to reach Berbera from the west, which was the new opportunity created by the French defection; it had two passes to assist defence, but the coast route from Zeila was poor. The Sheikh Pass route was no threat; the problem lay in the centre.

Chater selected a position astride the Hargeisa-Berbera road at Tug Argen, a dried-up water course south of Berbera. The tug is about 150 yards wide with a soft sandy bottom and steep banks in parts, with good fields of fire to the south through sparse bush. There are four hills on the Berbera side and two in depth behind, which were the backbone of the defence. (See Map 5). The features were called Observation Hill, to the left of the road, Mill Hill to the right, Knobbly Hill a mile to the west and Black Hill a further one and a half miles beyond, covering the right flank. The two hills in rear were Castle and King. There were other minor hills around, and a ridge to the left of Observation Hill which was occupied by D Coy 3/15 Punjab became known as Punjabi Ridge. The main routes into the position from the enemy side were the passes of Battery and Mirgo, to the east of the road. 1/2 Punjab covered the Sheikh Pass and the approaches via Zeila; 1 NRR (less one company), 2 KAR and 3/15 Punjab and the Machine Gun Company of the Camel Corps were in the main position, with the guns on Knobbly and Black Hills. In addition there was a detachment of three seamen and a 3-pdr gun from HMAS *Hobart*. 1 Black Watch were in reserve near Castle and King, while Force HQ was about five miles down the road towards Berbera.

The screen was provided mainly by the Camel Corps and a delaying action was planned at Hargeisa. The enemy crossed the border in two main columns, one directed initially on Zeila and the other on Hargeisa. They encountered the screen forward of Hargeisa on 2 August, when the Boyes anti-tank rifles of the Camel Corps destroyed one armoured car and damaged two more. However, this was a minor action before they came against the delaying position at Hargeisa. The screen was commanded by Major Christopher Consett; it consisted of B Company 1 NRR, D (Reserve) Company and a Pony Troop of the Camel Corps. They had patrolled offensively, attacked an Italian border post and burned huts full of ammunition, but Chater would not allow them to attack the assembling enemy over the border. They were attacked by one Blackshirt Division, one regular colonial division and thousands of Italian Somali irregulars, plus a company of medium tanks, and could only impose delay. Hargeisa's hastily dug anti-tank ditch was incomplete and Italian tanks found the gap. Consett arrived on his pony to see them going through the gap and hit the rearmost with a shot from a Boyes anti-tank rifle. The survivors then marched cross-country, around the advancing column of Italians, with their wounded and a few pack animals, to the Tug Argen position. A Rhodesian NCO was awarded the MM for leading his platoon through the enemy lines by night, their boots slung round their necks and their feet bound with puttees. Sale and Denaro of the Camel Corps were awarded MCs, but Consett was criticized by Chater for not attacking the enemy from the rear, and was not decorated. (He gained a DSO and an MC later.) The RAF struck at enemy targets, but the Italian air force was also active and the force of at least six colonial brigades, three Blackshirt battalions, three groups of irregular "Banda", twenty-five tanks and some twenty guns moved northwards towards the Tug Argen Gap. Refugees poured through the Mirgo Pass, patrols of D Coy 2 KAR had a brush with four Italian armoured cars east of the position on the evening of 10 August, and enemy transport was seen moving forward from Hargeisa. The main attack was launched on 11 August, the brunt being taken by 1 NRR.

The East African gunners were in action for the first time; they sent an Italian pack battery into hiding with their first shots. Thereafter they were busy for five days and nights, often firing at short range over open sights. The guns were in pits so they could fire all round the compass. During an attack on Knobbly Hill by 2,000 enemy, they broke up the force of the attack and, spotting an Italian general on a white charger trying to reform his men some two miles away, disposed of him and about fifty enemy with a single shell. S/Sgt Thom from Nivasha crouched for hours behind a three-foot-high parapet, dismantling, repairing and reassembling a jammed gun. An Italian attack led by eight tanks was dealt with by the gunners in the same afternoon. Assaults on Mill Hill were unsuccessful, although the guns were firing at 700 yards range at one stage, causing the enemy to abandon armoured cars and guns.

A serious threat developed quickly at the Mirgo Pass, where the hills between A and D Coys of 2 KAR had not been occupied as they were thought too difficult to penetrate. D Coy 3/15 Punjab came under heavy pressure and, when their ammunition ran low, fell back to the right rear of the KAR. They were resupplied during the night due to the initiative of OC A Coy 2 KAR, Capt T.H. Birkbeck, but a dangerous wedge had been driven into the left flank of the position. The Brigade Commander, (Chater was promoted on 6 June) ordered a counter-attack for the following day, to be carried out by A and C Coys 2 KAR, D Coy 3/15 Punjab and D Coy 1/2 Punjab, in a composite battalion commanded by CO 2 KAR, Lt Col Payne-Gallwey.

On 12 August each of the four hills was attacked by infantry in small parties, who made good use of ground and were supported by artillery. Mill Hill was the weakest position, as its defences were incomplete, and it was lost in the afternoon. The section officer, 2Lt A.G. Mollison, got his guns and men away in the direction of Knobbly Hill, but had to take refuge in a "tug" before they reached the wagon lines near Brigade HQ, although without the guns. Subsequently he was awarded the MC. In eighteen hours the battery fired 1000 rounds, and they had never been in action before. C Company 2 KAR, on Mill Hill, did not receive the order to join the composite battalion for the counter-attack on Punjabi Ridge until the early hours of 12 August.

The counter-attack was to eliminate the enemy penetration to the right rear of A Coy 2 KAR and to regain control of the Mirgo Pass. Partly due to the late arrival of C Coy 2 KAR from Mill Hill, the attack went in piece-meal. D Coy 1/2 Punjab attacked the ridge, supported by the mortars and small arms of A Coy 2 KAR. Two platoons reached the pass by the time C Coy 2 KAR arrived, at 1030 hrs. The attack was not renewed and C Coy took up a position next to A Coy, near the top of the pass, but an enemy brigade drove the composite battalion back to Block Hill Right, Block Hill Centre and Block Hill Left, with two platoons on the main road opposite Cats Hill. The whole position was in danger of being outflanked; the enemy were filtering across the road in small parties towards Castle Hill and enemy aircraft attacked the road convoys. Lt Col Payne-Gallwey was replaced in command of the composite battalion by Major G.A. Rusk MC.

Elsewhere on 13 August the enemy was less aggressive. An attack on Knobbly Hill at midday was beaten off with difficulty because only one gun could be brought to bear on the enemy and Italian machine-gunning was very heavy in consequence. Later in the afternoon, when some of the enemy worked round behind Knobbly, the second gun came into its own and shot downhill at the attackers at less than 900 yards range until they withdrew. By this time Knobbly and Castle were short of ammunition and water. A convoy was put together during the night, escorted by the Black Watch, who shot their way through some Italian patrols and sped into the defensive positions. Castle Hill and Observation Hill were shelled throughout 14 August until 4 p.m., when the latter was attacked by infantry, which was repulsed.

The key to the position was Observation Hill. It came under heavy fire throughout 15 August, then a singularly violent two hour bombardment in the afternoon was followed by an infantry assault. The position was overwhelmed by sheer weight of numbers. The Camel Corps machine guns were commanded by Captain E.C.T. Wilson, East Surrey Regiment. He kept them firing throughout four days of intensive fighting, although wounded by the same shell that killed his platoon sergeant, Omar Kajog. The water tanks were very vulnerable; had they been punctured the guns would have not been kept cool enough to fire at the high rate demanded. Wilson was wounded, suffered from malaria and had to continually repair the guns. He was captured when the position was overrun, but was thought to have been left dead when the hill was evacuated. He was awarded a posthumous VC, but emerged from captivity eight months later to accept it. He subsequently served in the Desert, then in Burma as 2ic 11 KAR. McCreath the gunner had a somewhat similar experience. One of his signallers got away from Observation Hill, but McCreath was presumed dead and was awarded a posthumous MC, which he received when he was freed.

On the evening of 11 August Maj Gen A.R. Godwin-Austen arrived from Middle East to take command, but as the situation was complex and Chater was handling it well, he left the conduct of the battle in his hands. However, after a few days he realized that the only way to save the force was to withdraw to Berbera, for evacuation by sea. Cats Hill changed hands twice on 14 August. C Coy 2 KAR captured Key Hill, forcing the enemy to abandon Cats, but C Coy was then heavily shelled and counter-attacked, so they withdrew and Italian guns and machine guns took over. On Chater's left the Italians kept up a cautious advance; a platoon of D Coy 2 KAR led by 2 Lt R.R.C. Peel held off a Banda force of about sixty men.

General Le Gentilhomme escaped from Djibouti to Zeila. Borama had been evacuated and the Camel Corps demolished the Dolo Pass, unfortunately with the District Officer on the wrong side. The flank was wide open. On 17 August enemy movement on the coast about forty miles from Berbera was bombarded by HMS *Ceres*, but this was only a delaying action. Anti-aircraft defence rested on the pompoms on the warships, until two AA guns arrived during the final stages. The decision to evacuate was taken on 15 August. 1 Black Watch and 2 KAR set up a delaying position around Barkasan Hill, about fifteen miles from Berbera, before the general withdrawal began. There was some shooting during the day, then units slipped away at dusk to embus near Pyramid Hill and move to Nasiye before embarkation.

On Barkasan the two battalions were separated by high ground and 2 KAR had little water. An epic bayonet charge by 1 Black Watch drove the enemy back 500 yards and slowed their advance for some hours. Outflanking moves then began, first against the Black Watch and, at around 3.45 p.m., around 2 KAR. The order to retire was sent at 2.10, but they did not receive it until 5.30. They had inflicted such heavy losses that the enemy did not press his attack on the next day; embarkation proceeded slowly but without interference. The Royal Navy had prepared an all-tide jetty and policed the town. The European and other civilian evacuees left first, followed by the troops. The final sub-unit, a 2 KAR platoon under 2Lt R.T. Roman, was picked up by HMAS *Hobart* late on 18 August. She marked her departure by shelling the government buildings in Berbera. Consett had been evacuated by the SS *Tuna* and returned in a destroyer on the following day to look for survivors along the coast, but found none.

2 KAR left behind them the greater part of their equipment, even some machine guns. In Aden during the next few days the battalion was reorganized, absorbing the Yao company of the Camel Corps. Before evacuation most of the Somalis in the Camel Corps and the Illalos were paid off. For some this had happened earlier – at Sheikh almost a week before, Capt O.G. Brooke had ordered C Coy to disband, taking their rifles with them. Brooke and his officers, with the anti-tank weapons, moved to Tug Argan with the Punjabis.

Casualties were surprisingly light, despite all the shooting; about 250 on the British side (of whom about half were 1 NRR) and 1,000 Italians. 2 KAR had one officer killed (2 Lt J.F. Purse of A Coy) and two wounded, two BNCOs wounded, two askari killed, ten missing and seventeen wounded.

Chapter 6

ITALIAN EAST AFRICAN EMPIRE – PART II
(Reference Map 4, 6, 7)

"Italian military power in East Africa was broken by a gigantic pincer movement."
The Abyssinian Campaign, HMSO, 1942

There were four converging thrusts; two were military and the third was mainly political, to return the Emperor of Ethiopia to his country and throne. The fourth was launched from Aden, to re-establish British Administration in Somaliland and open the port of Berbera. In addition the Patriot movement operated inside Ethiopia, to support the Emperor's advance and other operations. Wavell balanced the needs of the East African campaign against demands from the other fronts of Middle East Command; he switched 4 Indian Division from Sidi Barrani to fight the Battle of Keren, then rushed them back north again. Similarly 5 South African Brigade, followed by other SA formations, were moved hastily from South Ethiopia to the Middle East in March, 1941. Churchill wanted Wavell to leave the defence of Kenya "to the settlers" and to send troops from East Africa for employment elsewhere. Smuts stressed the need to keep adequate forces in East Africa, while Wavell was aware of the risk of Italian offensive action into Kenya and further south, and the threat they posed to Mombasa. The South African Division had been provided originally for use south of the equator only, and East and West African troops were not equipped or trained for the highly mechanized operations in the Middle East. A major strategic objective was to clear Italian naval vessels from Massawa and to open the Red Sea for Allied shipping.

In Rome Marshal Badoglio thought the Italian military assets in East Africa could be better employed. In Ethiopia there were about 300,000 Italian troops, including local forces. They were made up of 255,950 members of the Italian Army, of whom 182,000 were locally raised men in units and formations and in the "banda" irregulars. The remaining army component was two-thirds regular soldiers and one-third Blackshirts. Many of the Italians served with the technical Arms, particularly artillery and armour. The one combat division, the Savoia, was reputed to be battle-hardened, but life in an army of occupation had taken some of the edge off them. The rest of the "army" were armed police and customs officers of various categories. There were 325 aircraft of all types. Badoglio wanted the Italian Viceroy to attack into Sudan in support of the offensive against Mersa Matruh and Alexandria that Marshal Graziani was planning. The Duke was expected to secure either Khartoum or Port Sudan, but he claimed he needed – before he could start towards either of them – 100 more aircraft, 10,000 tons of fuel and 10,000 tyres. He was not enthusiastic about the policy either, believing that the security of the Empire was his first charge and that he could best achieve this by remaining passive and conserving his resources. Eventually, in an attempt to force his hand, some of his needs were shipped from Japan on the cargo ship *Yamayuri Maru*, but by the time she reached Kismayu the port was in British hands.

On 2 December, 1940, in Cairo, on the eve of his own offensive against Graziani in the Western Desert, Wavell discussed the strategy to be adopted against Italian East Africa with the newly appointed GOC East Africa, Lt Gen Alan Cunningham and GOC Sudan, Lt Gen William Platt. There was no intention to fight a major campaign. Wavell ordered Platt to prepare to recapture Kassala (which the Italians had occupied earlier), perhaps with reinforcements from Egypt if events permitted, to maintain pressure in the Gallabat area and to further rebellion in Ethiopia. Cunningham was told to advance to the frontier on the line of Kolbio-Dif, to operate in the Moyale area with small mobile columns, then in May or June (after the rains) to advance to Kismayu. These moves were to precede any advance into southwest Ethiopia and attacks from Sudan. Cunningham told Wavell that he could not take Kismayu earlier because of shortages of transport and inadequate water supplies. With the flanks secure at Kismayu and Kassala, Wavell intended to boost aid to the Patriots and to deploy troops away from East Africa.

Wavell had identified only two feasible routes into Ethiopia. The better one was via Djibouti to Addis Ababa, but with Djibouti in the hands of the Vichy French it was not an option. The alternative was from Kassala to Massawa, but there was only a single road through difficult country, to which the invaders would have been tied, which made the prospect unattractive. When Eden (Secretary of State for War) visited in November, they agreed to develop the Patriots' activities, and Lt Col O.C. Wingate was appointed Staff Officer Patriots. In late November he flew into Ethiopia and contacted Brig Sandford, the Commander of Mission 101, who was already engaged in Operation Planex. Brig D.A. Sandford DSO and Bar had been British Consul in Addis Ababa before the 1914–18 war, an artillery officer, with Sudan Political Service, then a farmer in Ethiopia, when he became a

. The leading scout car, flying the union flag of the Brigade Major 22 Brigade, Major Michael Biggs, entering Addis Ababa.

. **The battles for Kul Kaber and Gondar** — the road from Dessie to Debra Marcos.

8. West African gunners shelling Kul Kaber with their First World War 60 pounder gun.

9. Before the Kul Kaber battle. Birru and the two South African Sappers, Pienaar *(left)* a[nd] Brenner *(right)*, with the two Askari carrying anti-tank rifles.

friend and confidant of the Emperor. He left Ethiopia when the Italians invaded but returned to operate under the code name "Fiki Mariam" ("Love of Mary"). Early in 1940 Platt sent the District Commissioner at Gadaref letters prepared by Sandford, written in Ahmaric on linen and sealed in the name of the British Government. When Italy entered the war the letters went to eleven Patriot chiefs, who were invited to send mules to the Sudanese frontier to collect weapons, ammunition, money and food. Most of them availed themselves of the offer, but not all were 100 per cent allies of the Emperor. The Emperor had flown to Alexandria on 25 June, 1940, and was in Khartoum by 3 July.

Sandford entered Ethiopia in August with a captain, a medical officer, a radio, food for a month, money, letters from the Emperor and a representative of the Emperor, all carried by a convoy of mules. Another Mission 101 officer was less fortunate; his convoy was caught by the Italians and not heard of again. Sandford broke radio silence in mid-September to report a link-up with a prominent Patriot leader, who sent mules to the frontier with Sudan, at the River Atbara. Twelve of his men swam across and saw the Emperor in Gadaref, and returned with photographs and copies of his proclamation. In October and November Sandford persuaded rival chiefs to co-operate against enemy communications. General Nasi, the Vice Governor General, went to Gondar with troops to eliminate Mission 101, who were short of supplies and penniless. They had borrowed money from the Ethiopians, but their credibility was well established, particularly because their radio gave frequent news of the Emperor and the rest of the outside world. Wingate flew in to brief on a new forward policy and the use of regular troops to undertake sustained operations.

The change in policy materialized quickly, with the assembly of a mass of camels from all over the Sudan, large quantities of silver dollars from the mint in Bombay, 2 Ethiopian Battalion, which had been formed in Kenya from men who escaped to that country in 1936, an Ethiopian Operations Centre, (others were to follow) and 4 Patrol Company of the Sudanese Frontier Battalion. They penetrated ninety miles across the border and prepared an air strip at Bayala. The Emperor crossed the frontier on 20 January on horseback and reached Bayala on 6 February, 1941, where a cave had been prepared for him. The Emperor's route could be followed by the stench of dead camels, as so many had died of exhaustion on the way. In his cave, with the aid of a printing press, he set about establishing his authority, issuing decrees and receiving delegations from various parts of the country.

The rest of the Sudan Frontier Battalion joined the group, now known as Gideon Force, and with support from the RAF and the Patriots, cleared Gojjam Province of Italians. After this they turned south, a single column of 700 camels, 200 horses and mules that occupied four miles of single track. The Emperor followed with his bodyguard. At Burye on 27 February Wingate attacked an outer fort and took the whole complex by 1 March. An Italian counter-attack on 4 March was checked by the 2 Ethiopian Battalion. They killed 120 of the enemy, who called off the attack and fell back to Debra Marcos. Brig Frank Messervy's Gazelle Force, based in Sudan, harassed the Italian communications with Kassala effectively during the winter. Platt did not prevent the enemy escaping, but his subsequent progress was such that Wavell authorized him, at the end of January, to take Asmara with the aid of some Free French troops and others from Port Sudan. Events in the Middle East were going well and did not yet require any troops from East Africa.

When Wavell was in Kenya at the end of January, Cunningham told him that Italian morale had been badly shaken by British successes in the Middle East and that he could take Kismayu in February, before the rains, instead of in May. Wavell agreed and instructed Cunningham to get across the Mogadishu-Addis Ababa road to disrupt supply to the enemy in Ethiopia. On 12 February Wavell was ordered to send all available troops from the Middle East to Greece, but he decided to continue to eliminate the Italian Empire, although he warned Platt and Cunningham that some units would soon be needed in Egypt. On 24 February Cunningham was doing so well that he was ordered to advance to Harar to cut the railway line from Djibouti to Addis Ababa and, with the aid of the G(R) Force under the direction of AOC Aden, Air Vice Marshal G.R.M. Reid, to open Berbera port and establish a shorter line of communication into Ethiopia. Following the reverse in Greece, Wavell gave Platt one more chance to take Keren before withdrawing 4 and 5 Indian Divisions. He did so on 27 March, after which the Italians made little effort to defend Eritrea.

Civilian morale in Kenya improved when the first brigade arrived from South Africa, as the advance party of 1 SA Division. Until January, 1941, Cunningham had only 11 and 12 African Divisions, each of one West African and one East African brigade. They were deployed on a two-division front, with 11 Division on the right holding a line Malindi-Bura-course of the River Tana-Garissa, while 12 Division was at Wajir, extending westwards to Marsabit and Lokintaung, a total frontage of 650 miles. Troops were in defensive locations well protected by mines, wire and tank traps, with mobile reserves behind them. Energetic patrolling had gained ascendancy over the large area of desert between the opposing forces. Somali Irregular Companies, each 120 strong, were used to counter the Italian "banda", either operating on their own and or in conjunction with conventional troops. As the campaign progressed, more Irregular

Companies were raised from Ethiopian refugees and deserters, and from Turkana tribesmen.

When the full SA Division arrived, they took over the western sector and the other two divisions were side-stepped. There was no Force Reserve, although units out of the line for rest and training could have been used as such. Cunningham had very little artillery except in the SA Division. He put the problem to Smuts, who did not want to break up the Brigade Groups but agreed to SA Brigades being under command of the African Divisions when necessary, an arrangement which worked successfully.

Except around Marsabit itself, all locations were in desert country. The 400 miles from Marsabit to the sea was flat bush of varying density, and waterless. Tanks, armoured cars and in most cases soft-skinned vehicles could get through the bush without too much difficulty, except when rain made the black cotton soil impassable. Around Marsabit and to its west were the Chalbi Desert and the lava fields. The lava belts could be crossed by vehicles after preparation, but the Chalbi Desert could be crossed in dry weather without difficulty. Elsewhere bush stretched for many miles, often thin, but sometimes so thick that armoured vehicles could not force a path through.

Cunningham estimated he needed six brigades to reach Kismayu, one of which should be armoured. Before the attack began troops were moved closer to the enemy's defences, water was found and supply dumps established. Most units were 230 to 390 miles from the railhead, across inhospitable territory and over poor roads. The invaluable 36 Water Supply Company SAEC provided water convoys, explored for water and sank bore holes in the area between the Tana and Juba Rivers, on the route of the proposed advance.

The first move was against El Wak, where there was a battalion of Italian troops with sixteen guns. Both brigades of 12 (African) Division (1 SA and 23 West African) attacked successfully between 16 and 18 December, 1940, although many of the enemy got away into the bush. All the guns, quantities of stores and many prisoners were taken, with heavy enemy casualties but negligible losses in Godwin-Austen's Division. Because of low Italian morale and the quantities of water that had been found, it then appeared possible to take Kismayu before the rains with a force of only four brigades. The Italian Air Force sent out sorties daily, to attack the South Africans in particular, but three Hurricanes that had been defending Nairobi and Mombasa were moved forward. By 1 February they had established air superiority and the Empire force was free from air attack during daylight. 11 February was the date for the attack, to coincide with the full moon, as the initial advance was to be by night. The objectives were to capture Kismayu and to secure a bridgehead over the River Juba at Giumbo, but commanders were ordered to be ready to exploit as far as the line Mogadishu-Isia Baidoa-Lugh Ferrandi.

While this was going on near the sea, on the northern front 1 SA Division, under Maj Gen G.E. Brink CB DSO, faced three Italian Divisions (21, 22, 24), two of which were east of Lake Rudolf with some guns. There was also a banda force of 1,600 in the area. 1 SA Division consisted of 2 and 5 SA Brigades east of Lake Rudolf, and 25 (EA) Brigade at Lokintaung. Their tasks were to penetrate the Galla-Sidamo country, stir up the chiefs to rebellion and turn the Moyale-Mega escarpment. The two SA brigades east of Lake Rudolf faced 120 miles of waterless bush with only two routes forward. The poorer quality road gave access to Ethiopia around the Moyale-Mega escarpment. 2 SA Brigade took the fort at Giorai and 5 SA Brigade captured El Gumu and Hobok, but the local population showed little interest in revolt so Brink decided to open the Marsabit-Moyale-Mega road, but his supply route was disrupted by early rains. He made a two-pronged attack; 5 Brigade came in from the north to take Mega and 1,000 prisoners, but 2 Brigade was less successful in attacking from the east. Moyale was evacuated, but Cunningham concluded that the northern front was not the best way to reach Addis Ababa.

25 (EA) Brigade consisted of two newly formed battalions (2/3 and 2/4 KAR) plus supporting Arms and Services. They started west of the lake, tasked to take Kalam, and met no serious opposition until 9 February, when they were north of the lake in the country of the Merille people, traditional enemies of the Turkana. This enmity had been extended to include the Empire forces. 2/4 KAR could not reach the water holes, which were protected by large numbers of Merille spearmen. The one road open behind them could not take all their traffic and they were short of water. Eventually air action dispersed the Merille and some water trucks got through to 2/4 KAR with an escort of armoured cars, but Kalam was not taken until 24 March. On Cunningham's orders the Division went over to the defensive. Most of the South Africans were then withdrawn to Kenya and 25 (EA) Brigade joined 12(A) Division, whose front was extended northwards again. 1 SA Division Headquarters and 5 SA Brigade were put at the disposal of Headquarters Middle East Command, but 2 SA Brigade was retained for operations in British Somaliland and Ethiopia.

The El Wak raid made the enemy withdraw to the line of the Juba River, leaving behind only some banda and a strongly protected position at Afmadu. In the southern sector, between Gelib and the sea, were 102 Division, with four brigades, three banda groups and Kismayu Command. 101 Division was north of Gelib with two brigades and three banda groups.

Against them Cunningham used six fully motorized brigade groups. The Order of Battle (with emphasis on EA units) was:-

11 (African) Division (Maj Gen H.E. de R. Wetherall CB DSO OBE MC)
   22 (EA) Infantry Brigade (Brig C.C. Fowkes, CBE DSO MC)
      1/1 KAR, 5 KAR, 1/6 KAR plus 22 Mountain Battery RA (an Indian unit), a Field Company, 1 Tanganyikan Field Ambulance and a Signals Detachment.
   23 (Nigerian) Brigade
      1, 2 and 3 Battalions Nigerian Regiment, with a Light Battery, a Field Company and a Field Ambulance.
   Divisional Troops
      1 EA Armoured Car Regiment (less A Squadron), 1 (SA) Light Tank Company, one Medium Battery, four Field Batteries, an Anti-Tank Battery, Anti-Aircraft Artillery, two Field Companies, C Company 1/3 KAR (Machine Gun), a Kenyan Field Ambulance, a Field Hygiene Section and an Ordnance Field Park. All artillery and engineer units were South African.

12 (African) Division (Maj Gen A.R. Godwin-Austen CB OBE MC)
   21 (EA) Brigade (Brig A. McD. Ritchie DSO)
      1/4 KAR, 1/2 KAR, 1 NRR, 53 Gold Coast Field Company and a Zanzibari Field Ambulance
   24 (Gold Coast) Brigade
      1, 2 and 3 Battalions Gold Coast Regiment, with a Light Battery, a Field Company, and a Field Ambulance
   25 (EA) Brigade (Brig W. Owen)
      2/3 KAR, 2/4 KAR, 27 Mountain Battery RA, a detachment of Armoured Cars, 3(SA) Field Company SAEC, 6 (Uganda) Field Ambulance, a Signals Detachment and a Headquarter Company (who covered the rest of the front).

Divisional Troops
      A Squadron East African Armoured Cars, three SA Field Batteries, 53 (EA) Light Battery, four Anti-Aircraft sections, a SA Field Company, A Company 1/3 KAR (Machine Gun), a Hygiene Section and an Ordnance Field Park.

Force Troops
   1(SA) Infantry Brigade (Brig D.H. Pienaar)
      1 Royal Natal Carabineers, 1 Transvaal Scottish, 1 Duke of

Edinburgh's Regiment, 3 (SA) Armoured Car Company, Anti-Tank and Anti-Aircraft batteries, Medium Artillery, a Field Ambulance and A Company 1 Northern Rhodesia Regiment.

These units were deployed along the line of the River Tana to Garissa, then to Wajir, linking with the South Africans at Marsabit. Bura, Garissa and Wajir were the starting points for the various columns. The plan was for 12 Division to advance and take Afmadu, then to split into two columns. The SA Brigade was to capture Gobwein and form a bridgehead at Giumbo. The other column was to threaten Gelib, with the aim of tying down the enemy's reserves. 12 Division had most of the artillery and armoured fighting vehicles, in view of the importance of Gobwein. While this was developing, 11 Division was to reach Kismayu, 23 Nigerian Brigade led, moving from Bura via Lac Banda, but did not start until 15 February, after Gobwein had been attacked.

The Royal Navy's Task Force T bombarded Brava, movement on the coastal road, and prepared to shell Kismayu. A re-supply convoy was to enter Kismayu as soon as it was taken. If there was a delay, stores were to be beach-landed down the coast. SAAF raids on Afmadu, Dis and Gobwein destroyed ten enemy aircraft, and on the afternoon before the attack Afmadu and Gelib were both bombed heavily. A feint attack on the opposite flank, using little more than two platoons and some armoured cars, convinced the Italian Commander at El Wak that he had stopped the advance of a Division, and he reported accordingly.

Cunningham's forces carried sufficient food and water to last until 21 February, so he had to reach Kismayu by then. If he failed and if the beach-landing plan went wrong, the advance would have to be called off and the Force withdrawn to Kenya until after the rains. The advance to the border started on 15 January, the forward troops of 11 Division reached Badada by 11 February and those of 12 Division were at Beles Guani. 22 (EA) Brigade then pushed along a dusty track so quickly that the enemy evacuated Kismayu without a fight. Many of 22 (EA) Brigade, were moving to what would be their first time in action. At the beginning of January 1/1 KAR were at Bura, 5 KAR were on the Nairobi/Garissa Road and 1/6 KAR were at Mwingi. 5 KAR had been patrolling forward, and moved on 7 January to cross the River Tana and occupy a new camp on the Garissa/Liboi road. 1/1 and 1/6 KAR followed into the concentration area. The next bound was B Company 5 KAR's reconnaissance of the wells at Hagadera, which were occupied by A Company 1/1 KAR, with the rest of the battalion following. The brigade operated in three groups: armoured cars led the reconnaissance group, with two infantry companies and a sapper detachment. The main body and brigade headquarters were second, about an hour behind, then the administrative group and its infantry escort. Although the brigade was strung out on a single, narrow track, the whole column usually closed up for the night.

5 KAR occupied Wardeglo unopposed on 23 January, then moved to Liboi with the reconnaissance group by 8 a.m., 28 January. Some bombs or grenades were thrown at the leading armoured cars, but C Company drove the banda off and secured the main water hole. B and D Companies went next to the water supply at Hawina, where David Shirreff noted, "They again killed a few banda and captured some excellent loot, including some elephant tusks." By the afternoon the whole battalion was in Italian territory. Excitement was high, as 1/1 KAR were due to pass through 5 KAR and attack Beles Guani, where hard fighting was expected from some of 93 Colonial Infantry and 8 Banda Group. The leading company was to go to ground on making contact and give covering fire while two companies did a pincer movement. The askari in the leading company thought otherwise, charged with bayonet and panga and drove the enemy from the camp; all their MGs and several dead were left behind. 1/1 KAR lost one officer and three askari were wounded. There was some firing during the night, but no attack. 5 KAR had been ordered to move at 2 a.m. on 5 February, and sleep was out of the question; it was rendered even less so when "Kemble produced his bagpipes and marched up and down the perimeter playing until the time came to get into the lorries".

The move by truck from Liboi to Beles Guani in the dark was possible only because of the excellent night vision of the drivers. No lights were allowed, there was no moon and the road was a mere camel track. It was a further thirty-five miles to Afmadu. C Company 1/1 KAR were patrolling on foot about a mile from Afmadu when they came under artillery fire and retired. D Company patrolled during the following day. Afmadu was surrounded by perimeter wire and anti-tank ditches, backed by well-sited machine guns. The garrison consisted of 94 Colonial Infantry and a banda group, and another position was believed to be three miles to the south-east. The air bombardment of Afmadu, with support from the Mountain Battery, was stepped up on 10 February, while the mortars of 5 KAR and two platoons of 1/3 KAR (machine guns) created a diversion against the west side, and 1/1 and 1/6 KAR got ready to attack from the north.

On 11 February the bombardment began at 4.45 a.m. thickened up by the mortars of 5 KAR. When it stopped at 5.30 1/6 KAR got through the wire into the north of the objective. 5 KAR entered through the western gate shortly afterwards and the town was secured. The garrison had left in the night; 1/1 and 1/6 KAR set off in pursuit, but with little success. 5 KAR were also involved, after 1/6 KAR were ambushed and suffered casualties. Shirreff said "We never caught up with the enemy, but had the worst march of my experience, through dense bush in appalling heat." After Afmadu there were some changes in command; in particular Major R.F.A. Hurt took over 5 KAR and Major J.F. Macnab became Commanding Officer of 1/1 KAR. "Bulgy" Leach (OC 22 Mountain Battery RA) criticized the junior infantry commanders who had relied on air photographs for the selection of their objectives and had not confirmed them by personal reconnaissance. They had not co-ordinated with the gunners and registration had begun with incomplete information. He also believed that personal reconnaissance would have shown that Afmadu had been evacuated, and 2,000 rounds of precious gun ammunition would have been saved. This waste of ammunition led to the CRA being replaced.

The Gold Coast and South African Brigades moved through Afmadu and the Gold Coast Brigade attacked Bulo Erillo with great gallantry, losing most of the Europeans of 2 GC Regiment. The bridge over the Juba at Gobwein was burned before 1 SA Brigade could reach it, due to heavy shelling. The Juba is 580 feet wide at this point, and tidal. When it appeared that Kismayu had been evacuated, 12 Division sent 22 Brigade from Afmadu to secure the port; orders to do so reached Commander 22 (EA) Brigade on the morning of 14 February. The brigade was reinforced with South African armoured cars and artillery. Leaving 1/6 KAR at Afmadu, they set off to Kismayu with the brigadier sometimes ahead of the armoured cars in his enthusiasm. Ten miles from Kismayu they came to the wide belt of barbed wire that surrounded the town, and some land mines. These were cleared and while 1/1 KAR secured the high ground overlooking the port, 5 KAR entered it. C Company was left behind to tidy up, and a party in a dhow, led by the Brigade Major, 22 Brigade, (Biggs) visited the two island forts at the harbour entrance. The askari did not relish the trip, but when they reached the island of Miango ya Papa, they found four 4.7 inch coastal guns and a large number of artillery instruments. In the harbour they searched two ships; both were void of everything except rats and cockroaches. Kismayu was a dusty, untidy town, anything of any worth had been sabotaged or looted. To Shirreff's discomfort the water was "like drinking sea water". Three days after the main offensive began, six days ahead of the time table, Mussolini had lost the most valuable portion of the territory that had been ceded to Italy as a reward for her services during World War I. When Cunningham visited 22 Brigade in Kismayu, they were distressed that credit for taking the port had, according to the radio, been given to the South Africans. He denied this, but a news broadcast while he was there proved the strength of the brigade's claim.

The next major task was to cross the River Juba. With enemy artillery much in evidence at Giumbo and Gelib very strongly held, other crossing places were needed. The South Africans found one at Yonte, fourteen miles north of Gobwein, and the Gold Coast Brigade another in the thick forests of Mabungo, thirty miles north of Gelib. The Juba was the last natural barrier before the road network that led to Ethiopia. The South Africans crossed in collapsible boats on the night of 17/18 February and killed all of the Italian force after three counter-attacks. The Gold Coast men had an easier crossing on the night of 19 February. Gelib was now threatened from three sides, and 22 (EA) Brigade's role was to advance by a narrow track and get across the road eighteen miles to the east of Gelib, to cut off the enemy's retreat. With armoured cars and light tanks attached, the brigade was designated FOWCOL for this operation. They moved north and crossed the Juba at the Gold Coast bridgehead. Three days of hard work followed, with navigation by the aid of compass, messages dropped from aircraft and even an astronomical fix. In Shirreff's words, "Most of the time the South African armoured cars and light tanks could not force their way through, so our askari worked frantically in relays to clear a track". By the afternoon of 22 February (the day the attack on Gelib was due) they reached a broad track that ran south and moved faster. One group of enemy was encountered, then a field hospital, before FOWCOL reached the road eighteen miles east of Gelib in time to capture a battery of artillery and some Italian officers escaping towards Mogadishu. The town had fallen at 10 that morning, 102 Division was disintegrating and remnants of 101 Division were retreating up-river towards Bardera.

Some re-grouping was now necessary. B Company 5 KAR was still at Afmadu and C Company was at Kismayu. The remainder of the battalion joined 24 (GC) Brigade at Bulo Erillo, with C Company 1/3 KAR under command. A Company 1/3 KAR had supported 2 Gold Coast Regiment in their attack on Alessandra on 22 February. 22 (EA) Brigade now came under 11 (A) Division and received sharpish orders that they should get cracking at dawn. 1/1 KAR (Macnab) pursued the Italians to Modun, where the Nigerian Brigade passed through. HMS *Shropshire* bombarded the crossroads near Modun before Macnab entered Brava, and 22 Brigade was tasked to watch the coastal approaches to Mogadishu. A platoon of C Company 1/3 KAR was with the leading elements of the Nigerian Brigade when they met and dealt with resistance at Afgoy, and Mogadishu was entered on the morning of 26 February.

A push north towards Bardera (by 27 February), Isia Baidoa (28th), Lugh Ferrandi (3 March) and Dolo (5 March) followed, using light forces from 12 (A) Division. Many prisoners were taken, including the commander and staff of 20 Colonial Brigade; their African troops had deserted. Italian troops who had been bypassed in the urgency to get forward now started to surrender, mainly because of thirst. Chris Bell was with 1/6 KAR, camped west of Mogadishu on the Webi Shebelli where the river was a wide, sandy bed lined with bushes and trees. He was siting an outpost when two Italians came out of the bush waving white garments. When he prepared to march them into camp, more than 150 men in various stages of dishevelment appeared from their hiding place. Most of them had already thrown away their weapons.

Mogadishu harbour was not seriously damaged, but, until it was cleared of magnetic mines, the small port of Merca was used. 200 British and allied seamen who had been imprisoned there got the port working. But Merca was only a stop-gap and Mogadishu was soon handling 500 tons of material per day. There were excellent warehouses in the docks area and an Advanced Base was established. As no MT ships were available, replacement vehicles still made the difficult journey 800 miles from Kenya, over roads that had broken up into dust pans. The main logistic problem was to keep pace with the advancing troops until Berbera could be used. Apart from the vast quantities of other war material, there was petrol. At first they were told that there was none, but the offer of a reward revealed 350,000 gallons of motor spirit and 80,000 gallons of aviation fuel, which powered the next phase of the advance. Up to this point 31,000 of the enemy had been accounted for by death, imprisonment or by dispersion.

Cunningham was authorized to advance to Harar. Remnants of the enemy's Juba force were withdrawing on Jigjiga, there were three fresh Italian brigades between Jigjiga and Harar and one brigade in British Somaliland. The advance was resumed on 1 March by a column of the Nigerian Brigade, but the strength of the column depended on the ability to keep it supplied. When Lt Col J.A.S. Hopkins reached Dagabur on 10 March he was 590 miles from Mogadishu with some armoured cars and two companies of the Nigerian Regiment; the rest of the column was 100 miles behind. He fought a small battle for the town.

Fighter attacks on the Diredawa group of three airfields between 13 and 15 March destroyed twenty aircraft, including six in the air, for the loss of two Hurricanes. This success allowed the columns to continue their advance by day, even in the narrow passes through the mountains. By 19 March administrative arrangements were in place for 11 (A) Division to start its advance again, but initially only with the Nigerian Brigade; 1 SA and 22 (EA) Brigades could not move forward of Dagabur until 21 and 26 March respectively. Meanwhile, the G(R) Force moved from Aden to Berbera, under the command of Colonel A.H. Pocock MC, on 16 March. The force was two Indian battalions plus attached troops, including some Adanese Somalis. The port had not been demolished and was brought into working order quickly.

British Somaliland had been garrisoned by 70 Colonial Brigade, which had been cut off before they could withdraw through Jigjiga. They attempted to move via Borama and Diredawa, but apart from the Brigade Commander, General Bertello, who was seen in Diredawa on a mule a few days before it was taken, there was little sign of the brigade. On 20 March, when the Nigerians had captured Tug Wajale on the border of British Somaliland, two armoured cars and the Chief Engineer of the East African Force travelled through Hargeisa to contact the Berbera force, which had been there just four days.

Jigjiga marked the end of the plain and with it the rapid movement of motorized columns, led by armoured cars and geared to finding and getting round the flanks of any enemy. It was time for troops to fight on their feet, but the advance had been so rapid that the mule-based transport column and the mule-pack 3.7in howitzer battery that had been prepared for use in the mountains had not arrived. The main defensive position beyond Jigjiga was the Marda Pass, flanked by high hills with observation over the plain and the Jigjiga airfield, 9,000 yards away. The position was expected to be defended strongly, and GOC 11 (EA) Division called forward the SA Brigade for a two brigade attack on 23 March. But on 20 March the enemy appeared to be withdrawing, so he attacked next day using only the Nigerian Brigade. To minimize the risk of casualties from artillery fire, the Nigerians advanced rapidly by vehicle across the open plain and debussed to attack on foot. Aided by patrol reports from the last two days, they secured a height overlooking the Pass from the north by 8 p.m. and forced the enemy from the pass that night. It could have been held for a long time, being four miles wide, heavily wired, with gun positions dug into the hillsides and surrounded by tank traps and mine fields. A British Medical Officer thought he could have held it with his stretcher bearers, but the position lacked depth and the Nigerians turned its flank.

There were two other possible defensive positions before Harar, the Babile Pass and the Bisidimo River. The pass was strongly defended, but the Royal Natal Carbineers achieved surprise and the position was abandoned on 24 March. The Nigerians resumed the advance next day, to be delayed for a while at the Bisidimo by enemy artillery, but the South Africans' guns enabled them to move on by noon on 25 March. The GOC did not accept that Harar was an open town and sent armoured cars forward to occupy it before the Italians troops could escape. Instead they laid down their arms. Large quantities of munitions were captured, including some 105 mm guns, a type that had not been encountered before. The advance to Harar brought the total enemy losses for the campaign so far to 50,000, including dead, deserters and prisoners. Smallwood's Nigerians had covered 1,054 miles in thirty days, the last three and a half in difficult country and involving three strong defensive positions. They were now in the cold, wet Ethiopian Highlands.

There were only two brigades between the East African Force and Addis Ababa; the one possible defensive position was on the line of the Awash River, and there was no sign of it being reinforced. Cunningham was under pressure to release the South Africans and as many transport and other units as possible to the Middle East. Capture of the Djibouti-Addis Ababa railway would economize in road transport. On 27 March 1 SA Brigade moved towards Diredawa and the Nigerian Brigade advanced by a more southerly route through the mountains, both brigades tasked with getting to the Awash River. The pass down to Diredawa had been badly damaged and repairs were expected to take eight days; the South African Engineers, 54 (EA) Field Company and 1 Nigerian Regiment did the work in thirty-six hours. The Transvaal Scottish entered Diredawa on foot on 29 March ahead of the main body. There were some demolitions and seven Italians had been murdered by deserting Colonial Infantry. There were extensive demolitions between Diredawa and the Awash, but they were rarely covered by fire and caused little delay. The GOC kept the weight of his advance on the northern route and took the Italians by surprise, as they were expecting an attack from the south. They withdrew in two columns, one moving behind the Awash and the other southwards, through Sire towards Cofole.

The safety of the Italian civilian population was now a matter of international (as well as local) concern, as there were about 20,000 Italians in Addis Ababa and 100,000 Ethiopians. There was a lull in operations while high-level signals were exchanged, culminating in an invitation to the Italians to surrender all their forces and the ships in Massawa harbour, in return for care for the non-combatants. When the Italians did not reply after twenty-four hours, the advance was resumed.

Pienaar's brigade reached Meiso by 1 April, where they ran out of petrol. 22 (EA) Brigade had sufficient petrol for 1,000 miles by all vehicles, so they passed through the South Africans and reached the Awash with all three battalions by midday on 2 April. The river was about thirty yards wide and wadeable in several places, in a gorge with steep cliff walls. Both the road and rail bridges had been blown. There was a defending enemy force of 4,000 Italians with a variety of guns, 2,000 Eritreans, some tanks, a machine-gun company of the Savoia Division and an assortment of Blackshirts, police, Carabinieri, engineers and airmen, while a Shoan banda group was on its way by rail until the SAAF bombed their train. The River Awash crossing was a great success for 5 KAR, particularly for D Company under Capt TCC (Chippy) Lewin. At first light on 3 April the Commanding Officer (Hurt) made his reconnaissance with the aid of two armoured cars. The enemy positions were well forward, overlooking the river, generally on the line of the road and the railway. The railway bridge was about 1,000 yards east of the road bridge, where the ravine was particularly steep-sided. At the road bridge and to the west of the valley was slightly less sharply defined, with the steeper bank on the enemy's side, close to the river. Consequently their defences, machine and anti-tank guns, were deployed well forward and were easily located. The Mountain Battery shelled the enemy with little risk of retaliation. The most suitable crossing places were near the bridge and a ford about 1,000 yards west (i.e. upstream) of the road bridge. Patrols went out at 7 a.m.; some machine-gun fire was encountered, which was dealt with swiftly by the Mountain Battery.

D Company approached the river in the area of the road bridge with two platoons forward; Lt R.A. Landridge's was close to the bridge and Lt Valentine's platoon went about 500 yards east of the road bridge to locate the enemy's flank. Covering fire was provided by the third platoon, under Lt G.H. Howard. Landridge's platoon waded across, while Valentine's men, east of the road bridge, came under heavy machine-gun fire. Lewin ordered

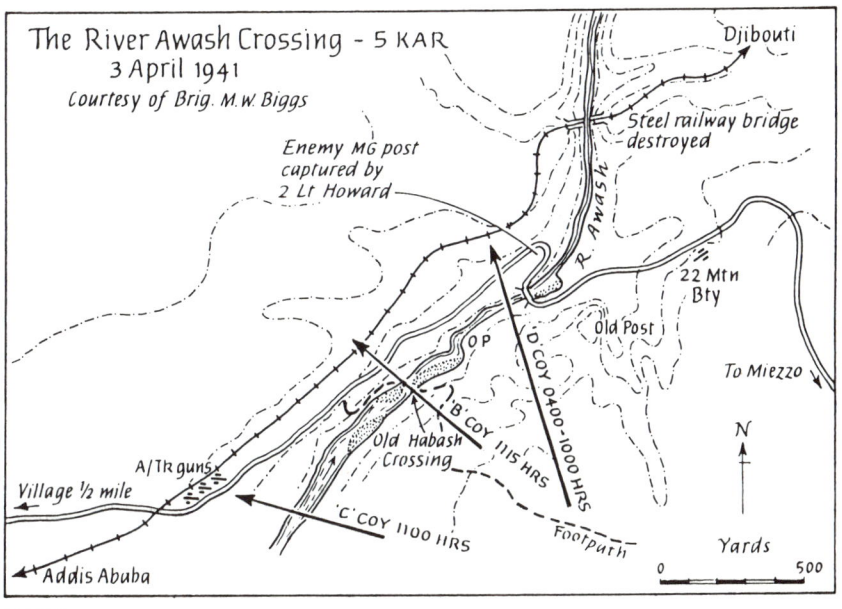

MAP 6

Howard's platoon over the river after Landridge's. On the way they were fired on by a machine-gun post that had been silent until then. Howard got to the post ahead of his men, leaned over the sangar and shot the crew with his pistol; the other occupants of the post immediately surrendered. Both platoons gained the crest and cleared out post after post of the enemy. Lt Ridley's platoon returned from patrol and joined the first two. Valentine's platoon extricated itself then followed the rest of D Company over the river.

At the ford C Company equally successfully crossed the river, turned east to roll up the enemy's right flank and moved to cross the road. B Company followed, moved between the other two companies and consolidated on the objective quickly. The operation owed much to Lewin's initiative. Landridge and Howard received immediate MCs and Lcpl Farah of Landridge's platoon was awarded the MM, as was Pte Boiyo of Valentine's platoon, who did good work with his light machine gun. The War Journal of 5 KAR notes that many senior officers saw the battle. In their historians' (i.e. Draffan and Lewin) words, "By this time a number of VIPs in their Red Hats had joined D Company's observation post on the east bank of the gorge and in no time the lip of the gorge resembled a poppy field." B Company and a platoon of 1/3 KAR followed up an artillery bombardment on Awash village, occupied it by 5.30 and took prisoners. The total captured were seventy officers and about 500 men, plus anti-tank guns and one tank. Deception had been complete and the bulk of the enemy had remained downstream where the crossing had been expected. The advance cut off the retreat of another group of the enemy, who surrendered later. An East Africa Force Badge was awarded to CSM Kirotho of Headquarters Company, who moved some transport out of artillery range when it was being shelled.

The South and East African Engineers rapidly built a road bridge of box girders and at 2 a.m. on 4 April 22 (EA) Brigade set off on its 150-mile dash to the capital. Fowkes had the resources to get there and the Military Governor of Addis Ababa urged him on, saying that the Italian Army had left the capital and the Italian civilians feared for their safety. There was no risk of air opposition as all thirty aircraft on the Addis Ababa airfield were destroyed by air attack on 5 April. An enemy column escaped from Sire, but some of them were disposed of a few days later.

Fowkes' determination to be first into Addis Ababa conflicted with Cunningham's obligation to Smuts, who needed a victory by South African troops to boost public support in the Union. Fowkes was told to halt and let the South Africans pass through, but he claimed that the message arrived corrupt and pressed on. Wetherall finally stopped him with a message dropped by a very low-flying Hartbeest, practically on to the bonnet of his car, just ten miles from the capital. A few armoured cars and infantry were sent in by 22 Brigade at the request of the Military Governor on the evening of 5 April to prevent looting. [Not all versions of events are consistent on this point.] Next day, at 1030 Wetherall, accompanied by his three brigadiers, Pienaar, Fowkes and Smallwood, entered Addis Ababa and received the surrender of the Military Governor. They were led by a single armoured car flying a Union flag; the escort was provided by C Squadron East African Armoured Cars, the South African Armoured Cars, 13 Platoon 1/3 KAR, 5 KAR (less B and C Companies), one Company 1/6 KAR and one Company of Natal Carbineers. 5 KAR moved on to the airfield on the far edge of the town, where 1,200 airmen surrendered. On the following day (7 April) the South Africans formally marched into the city, but the sharp-eyed father of a 1/6 KAR officer commented a few days later, when seeing the photograph in his UK newspaper, "As the African soldiers were lining the route, it seems reasonable to assume that they had got there first". The Duke of Aosta had left four days before.

The Union flag which had been on the armoured car was hoisted over the Palace for a while, until replaced by an Ethiopian flag in the afternoon. It had belonged to the father of the Brigade Major 22 (EA) Brigade, (Biggs) and had been flown in Bermuda when Biggs senior was Acting Governor. The Brigade Major's wife had sent it to him in the pocket of his greatcoat, when forwarding some kit from Nairobi, with a note saying, "Hang this over somewhere for me." Apart from its appearance on the armoured car and the surrender ceremony, it flew next at Gondar at the end of the campaign, and later in Burma.

With the aid of some Greek mechanics the railway was brought into action after three days, with a limited service between Diredawa and the Awash Bridge site. When the Advanced Headquarters arrived in Harar following the capture of Addis Ababa a high-power radio transmitter/receiver was found, which worked daily direct to the Vatican in Rome. As the operators and the equipment belonged to the Vatican, the Chief Signals Officer allowed them to continue with their daily schedules, while introducing covert monitoring of their transmissions to ensure security. The Headquarters Wireless Diagram then included a terminal working to a distant station in an enemy capital.

In the advance from Harar to Addis Ababa a further 15,000 Italian and colonial troops had been rendered inoperable for the usual three causes of death, desertion and being taken prisoner, while considerable quantities of ammunition, supplies and petrol had been captured. Casualties on the British/African side were killed 135, wounded 310, four were prisoners and fifty-two missing.

While 11 (A) Division was getting ready for the next, protracted phase of the campaign, 12 (A) Division were clearing the Juba and the Webi Shebelli valleys of enemy. By 3 March they were at Lugh Ferrandi and had pushed patrols out to Dolo and Oddur. A patrol sent out from Dolo on 6 March found Mandera unoccupied and the nearest enemy at Neghelli, while one from Isia Baidoa to Belet Wein reported the road to be impassable in wet weather. 1/4 KAR (21 (EA) Brigade) were repairing the Wajir–Moyale road when they learned that the enemy had evacuated Yavello, where there was an important airfield, and that the town was occupied by Patriots. Capt E.W. Temple-Borman went to investigate, with D Company 1/4 KAR, two platoons of armoured cars, a mortar detachment and a section of 1/3 KAR machine guns. The road to Yavello was known to be heavily mined. The story is taken up by Lt Col Peter Molloy OBE MC, then Adjutant 1/4 KAR, (although missing from the action as he was at the Staff College at Haifa) and Lt Col R.C. Glanville, OBE MC:-

"Yavello was occupied on 21 March by 1/4 KAR and a company of 1/3 KAR under command of Pat Mundy (Lt Col P.R.M. Mundy DSO MC). Soroppa was then carefully reconnoitred. Prisoners said that Soroppa was occupied by 61 Colonial Battalion and four guns of 35 Pack Battery deployed on a ridge known as Little Soroppa, while a forward position on Magpie Ridge was occupied only during the hours of daylight by one infantry company and one gun. The crest of Little Soroppa was approached from the Yavello road across a minefield covered by artillery and machine-gun fire. By 29 March it appeared that the Italians were prepared to evacuate, so the attack was set for 31 March.

"The troops available to Pat Mundy were 1/4 KAR, B Company 1/3 (MG) KAR, a platoon of South African armoured cars, field and anti-tank artillery and a detachment of 40 (AC) Squadron SAAF. The plan was for D Company 1/4 KAR, with a mortar platoon and machine-gun section under command, to capture Magpie Ridge at dawn. B and C Companies 1/4 KAR, commanded by Capt R.C. Glanville, were then to attack the enemy's left flank on Little Sorropa, supported by artillery fire and aerial bombing. Concurrently three platoons of the 2nd Irregulars were to get round the enemy's right and cut the escape route to Alghe.

"At 5.45 a.m. the first artillery salvo fell on Magpie Ridge. After a short bombardment D Company 1/4 KAR advanced and took the ridge by 6.15. Glanville then began his outflanking movement against Little Soroppa. Dive-bombing and machine-gunning added to the artillery attack. Shortly before 7 a.m. B Company was checked at the eastern tip of Little Soroppa by intense fire from heavy and light machine guns. Glanville led C Company round the flank and attacked the enemy's left rear.

"61 Colonial Battalion had a good reputation and C Company met stubborn resistance, as the whole ridge was studded with concealed weapon pits dug into the bases of ant hills. In the face of heavy fire C Company advanced up the ridge with bayonets fixed. Hand grenades were used with good effect and, shortly after 9 a.m. scattered parties of the enemy began running across the crest of Little Soroppa and vanishing into the valley beyond.

"Resistance did not cease until Glanville's forces reached the enemy battery. The success signal went up at 1015 a.m. and Pat moved his Headquarters to the vicinity of Little Soroppa and sent I NRR forward to exploit the victory. Our losses were very slight. About fifty of the enemy were killed, eighteen Italians and over 200 colonial troops were taken prisoner, and five guns and many machine guns were captured. The ground was too rough for armoured cars, but the Irregulars had reached the Alghe road about eight miles north of Soroppa, where they captured another nine Italians and 140 Colonials. Among the prisoners was Colonel Rolandi, the commander of 18 Colonial Brigade."

Pat Mundy was awarded a bar to his DSO, Bob Glanville received an immediate MC, Sgt J.E. West the DCM. One DCM, four MMs and five EA Force Badges were awarded to African troops. Molloy and Glanville described Pat Mundy as a "fine leader of men".

On 21 March a battalion of the Gold Coast Regiment, a light battery and some armoured cars occupied Neghelli, but were withdrawn due to a misunderstanding; they were replaced by a fresh group from Dolo on 30 March, when a patrol of 1/2 KAR (21 Brigade) occupied the town and then handed it over to 3 Gold Coast Regiment. The 1/2 KAR patrol then withdrew to Yavello. There were no enemy about, but there was unrest and conflict between the Somali and Boran peoples locally and punitive patrols were sent out. On 6 April Headquarters 12 Division moved to Neghelli and took over from 1 SA Division and the other troops who were to go to the Middle East. 12 (A) Division then consisted of 21 and 25 (EA) Brigades plus the SA units not being sent to the Middle East, while 24 Gold Coast Brigade (less 3 Gold Coast Regiment, at Neghelli) was Force reserve.

Cunningham now had to deal a knock-out blow to the remaining enemy and to release as many units and as much transport as he could to Egypt. It was necessary to get the Emperor back on his throne and to establish an Ethiopian administration, while law and order had to be restored in all of the recently occupied territories. The surviving enemy were in three enclaves at Dessie, Amba Alagi and Gondar, and their main force was in the Galla-Sidamo province. This was about 40,000 men with some 200 guns. The Duke of Aosta was at Dessie, while the remnants of the Italian civil administration were at Gimma. The South African Division Headquarters and 5 SA Brigade had gone to Egypt and 2 SA Brigade awaited shipment from Berbera, so the East Africa Force was reduced to:-

11 (A) Division, with 1 SA Brigade, 22 (EA) Brigade – less 1 KAR deployed along the lines of communication, and 23 Nigerian Brigade at Adama and Addis Ababa.
12(A) Division, with 21 (EA) Brigade attacking northwards, 24 Gold Coast Brigade with one battalion at Neghelli and the remainder restoring order in southern Somalia, while 25 (EA) Brigade were advancing towards Maji.

To move the units to the Middle East via Port Sudan or Massawa it was necessary to open the Addis Ababa road north to Asmara. The task was allotted to 11 (A) Division, using 1 SA Brigade, who were to fight their way northwards and to embark for Egypt from either of the Red Sea ports. Although Wavell wanted Dessie taken, Cunningham lacked the resources and asked for help from Sudan, which could not be available before 3 May.

For the rest of the Force the first priority was to open the route to Kenya by clearing the enemy from the area of the Great Lakes south of Addis Ababa. 11 (A) Division were tasked to take Sciasciamanna and 12 (A) Division were to advance on Dallae and Hula. The Gold Coast Brigade returned to 12 Division and was replaced by garrison battalions from Somalia. Italian civilians continued to call for protection from the Ethiopians; the Duke of Aosta was still Viceroy, but when he heard that a BBC broadcast had said that he had asked for terms of surrender, he sent a message to Cunningham saying that he (Cunningham) was responsible for the safety of the white population; this included the consequences of any actions of the Ethiopian Patriots. The Emperor reached Addis Ababa on 5 May, which gave further momentum to the Patriot movement. With the aid of the Operation Centres, each of one British officer, some NCOs, up to seventy selected Ethiopians and equipped with radios, explosives, money and personal weapons, the Patriots attacked the enemy's lines of communication and isolated garrisons, but personal gain and vengeance sometimes led them to tackle softer targets too. This included Italian troops who were ready to surrender.

As Djibouti could not be used to evacuate prisoners of war or civilians, they were taken down to Berbera, despite its limitations as a port. 30,000 prisoners were moved quickly to the coast through four staging camps, and a further camp was set up in Aden to hold 2,500 men in transit to Mombasa. Although great progress was made in getting the railway working, the Awash rail bridge could not be rebuilt and a road ferry shuttle service operated across the river.

When operations resumed on 6 April, 11 (EA) Division had 1 SA Brigade in Addis Ababa, 22 (EA) Brigade (two battalions) south of the Awash River and 23 Nigerian Brigade at Diredawa. 12 (A) Division had 21 (EA) Brigade around Soroppa, advancing north slowly because of the heavy rains, 3 Gold Coast Regiment was patrolling north from Neghelli towards Wadara, while the rest of 24 Gold Coast Brigade was in Somalia. 25 (EA) Brigade were to take Maji, then to hand it over to the Equatorial Corps in Sudan. Against the two African Divisions were 21, 22, 23, 24, 25, and 101 Divisions. Most units were well below strength, but they had around 200 guns, plus some anti-aircraft weapons, an unknown number of armoured cars and between twenty and thirty tanks.

With two weak divisions widely dispersed, 1 SA Brigade moving off towards Asmara and Egypt, and two battalions tied down in Addis Ababa on internal security and local defence tasks, Cunningham decided to use 2 SA Brigade, who were still at Berbera and unable to sail before 3 June. He put 1 Natal Mounted Rifles and 1 Field Force Battalion under command 11 (A) Division from late April until 27 May. In the Sciasciamanna area enemy anti-aircraft guns were in action often, while a mechanized column under General Bertello was ready to attack the lines of communication at Noggio. This formation was bombed many times in their harbour area. 22 (EA) Brigade worked down from the north to Bocoggi and took some prisoners on the way. They continued the advance by a better road, and by 24 April were moving south of Ponti Machi.

Cunningham wanted to unite 11 and 12 Divisions, which were converging. 12 Division was fighting its way slowly northwards in heavy rain, with the Gold Coast Brigade on the Neghelli road and 21 (EA) Brigade on the Lavello road. In their path were two strongly fortified positions where the Ethiopians had delayed the Italians for almost a year in 1935/36. The Gold Coast Brigade attacked the Wadara position on 3 May and had a hard-fought week before they were successful. 21 (EA) Brigade took the formidable Budagamo position on 5/6 May and moved on. The road conditions were terrible as the rains moved north with the troops, to reach Addis Ababa in August.

Reinforced, 11 (A) Division continued southwards, to capture

Sciasciamanna and to join up with 12 Division. Wetherall planned to advance with one battalion west of the Lakes to cut the Sciasciamanna–Soddu road, while two battalions moved directly on Sciasciamanna, crossing the Audada and Dadabd Rivers. As the enemy air force was out of action, a Close Support Group of light bombers, fighters and co-operation aircraft was formed and placed under command of 11 Division. The co-operation aircraft acquired the targets, mainly Italian units attempting to escape across country, and the combat aircraft were tasked immediately. Tanks and armoured cars were the priorities. The first real action in the Battle of the Lakes was fought by 5 KAR at Mount Fike, when they attacked with artillery support through thick bush, grass and swamp. Shirreff describes this as "the perfect battle", involving C and D Companies of 5 KAR, with two three-inch mortars and with the support of a troop of 18 Indian Mountain Battery. There was a lull when the enemy was thought to be developing an attack on 1/6 KAR south of Lake Lagana, but this did not materialize and 5 KAR resumed their operation. The two assault companies advanced in transport until they came under artillery fire, debussed and advanced on foot, waded across the River Gidu and built a ford of brushwood for the guns. D Company gave covering fire from the front, while C Company moved to some high ground to the left, where they overlooked the Italians from the west. They charged with the bayonet through scrub and captured 200 prisoners, three 65 mm guns, anti-aircraft guns, machine guns and rifles. There had been many desertions from the enemy, both before and during the action. The Commanding Officer, Lt Col R.A.F. Hurt (he received news of his promotion shortly after the battle) received the DSO for this action.

On 11 May 5 KAR advanced west of the Lakes, captured Bubissa and took some prisoners and guns, but were counter-attacked by six medium and three light tanks, plus a banda group. They fell back behind the River Gidu with the armoured cars covering the withdrawal and acting as decoys. The three armoured cars bogged down so badly that they had to be abandoned, but they were recovered later. 5 KAR's losses were 2Lt W. Warton captured, two askari killed and eight wounded. 2Lt D. Evans was awarded the MC for his part in this action, and three askari received MMs. (Evans was killed subsequently in Madagascar.) 1 Natal Mounted Rifles attacked the enemy positions overlooking Sciasciamanna on 13 May, taking 800 prisoners, two batteries of artillery and nine tanks. This provided the key to Sciasciamanna, which was entered on 14 May; Dalle was taken on 17 May and 22 Brigade (now called FOWCOL again) turned west towards Soddu, while the two South African battalions formed a defensive flank in the Dalle area.

In the north Amba Alagi had fallen and the Duke of Aosta was a prisoner, so supreme command devolved upon General Gazzera, who was at Gimma, which was the seat of government. There were good political and military reasons for taking Gimma and ending the campaign quickly, particularly as the occupation of Soddu would split the enemy's forces, reducing the likelihood of Gimma being strongly held. The immediate objective, therefore, was Soddu, to cut off 21, 22 and 101 Divisions, or what remained of them. The first plan was for an attack by both Divisions, but 12 (A) Division was still held up by the rain. However, 1 Gold Coast Regiment caught up with the rear brigade of 24 Division and captured the brigade commander and most of his brigade. Because the roads were impassable to vehicles, two battalions of 21 (EA) Brigade were halted and 1/2 KAR were put on an improvised pack basis. They continued the advance on foot to drive the remainder of 24 Division towards the South Africans at Dalle.

The enemy was preparing defensive positions east of the Soddu road, so 11 Division made an immediate attack; a brigade of 12 Division was to take over Soddu from them as soon as possible. As 1/1 KAR were still north of Mogadishu on line of communication duty, they were replaced in 22 (EA) Brigade by 2 Nigeria Regiment, while 1 Natal Mounted Rifles and 1 Field Force were kept as divisional troops. 1/6 KAR began the move towards Soddu after an action at Little Dabada, while the Natal Mounted Rifles captured Sciasciamanna. On 17 May they were on the road to Soddu, four miles past Sciasciamanna, with an advance party of A and C Companies, armoured cars and artillery. After eighteen miles A Company started to prepare a base for the battalion, while C Company (Capt R.M. Cresswell) carried on to a point seven miles to the east of Colito, where they met two enemy patrols. They debussed and attacked on foot with the support of seven armoured cars, then came under fire from what appeared to be the enemy's main position, at 400 yards range. A patrol advanced 100 yards in the scrub when a white flag was seen. This might have been an artillery marker or a signal flag, but it was taken for a flag of truce. Cresswell went forward with an armoured car and was mortally wounded. C Company then withdrew to their base, where the whole battalion was now concentrated.

It was not all fighting; Shirreff described the road to Soddu as "between mountains with steep precipices on one side, past little villages perched on hilltops from which the women ululated as we passed. Male Habash [Ethiopians] trotted alongside the lorries brandishing their rifles, others tried to sell chickens, tomatoes and mirra. We travelled slowly, stopping and starting until dusk and then camped by the side of the road, near a vegetable shamba [farm] which provided our dinner table with spinach, leeks, tomatoes and potatoes, a welcome change. As we made camp a contingent of the Patriot army passed through us. They were an amazing sight; the warriors and chiefs rode on mules and ponies, saddled with high wooden saddles and bridled with cruel double bits. Their waists were enclosed in several layers of cartridge belts and some had long hair sticking straight up from the head over a foot long. Borgi slaves and Galla footmen ran beside the mules carrying rifles and Breda machine guns. These were part of the nondescript force known as Henfry's Scouts, who, at this stage of the campaign, were far more trouble than they were worth."

The enemy had prepared defences on the line of the River Billate, where the road to Soddu crossed it, so on 18 May patrols from all four companies of 1/6 KAR went out to assess the enemy's positions in preparation for an attack next day. They found a defensive position in front of the river, but its flanks were hard to locate in the thick bush. Artillery registered during the late afternoon and 1 Nigerian Regiment mounted a flank attack at dawn on 19 May to find that the enemy had evacuated the position in the night, except for a few stragglers. 1/6 KAR took up the pursuit, while 5 KAR rejoined the main body of the brigade, having struggled back across the flooded River Gidu. On the way they discovered that the Italians had evacuated Bubissa.

1/6 KAR reached and occupied the town of Colito by 8.30 a.m. on 19 May and got across the track to Bubissa. Ahead of them the river was forty feet wide, its banks covered with thick vegetation and the bridge blown, but

The Battle of Colito, 19 May 1941

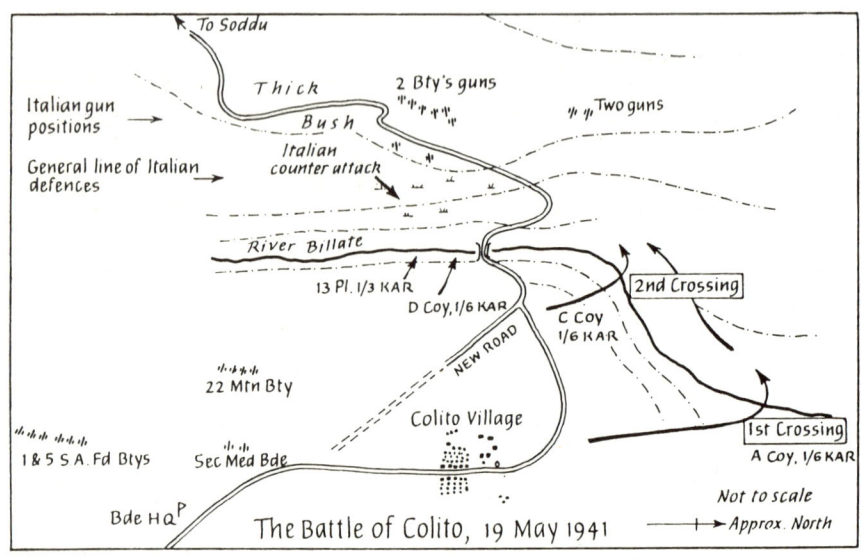

MAP 7

it was fordable in places. Enemy positions could be seen on the far side, as they had not been concealed as well as usual. In support of 1/6 KAR were two regiments of South African field guns, 22 Mountain Battery and a section of medium artillery, plus their own mortars. When the leading company came under fire the battalion 2ic, Major S.D. Field, sent Lt Thorne to find an outflanking route to the north, while the artillery engaged the enemy. C and then A Companies crossed the river by Thorne's route and attacked southwards towards the bridge site, with A Company on C's left. They reached the bridge and pressed on a further 1,200 yards through the enemy's position, clearing a succession of locations and taking many prisoners, while the rest of the battalion gave covering fire across the river. By 4 p.m. the enemy's transport park had been taken, some three-quarters of a mile beyond the bridge. D Company crossed the river near the bridge and 13 Platoon 1/3 KAR followed, man-handling their machine guns over the river with the aid of a fallen tree.

Before consolidation was complete the enemy counter-attacked with armoured cars, medium and light tanks. The Boyes anti-tank rifles seemed to be ineffective. Then Sergeant Nigel Leakey performed the act of gallantry that turned the battle, gained him the VC and cost him his life. Leaky had joined the battalion from the Kenya Regiment and was a dashing, somewhat unconventional NCO in the Mortar Platoon. With his bombs expended, he had joined in the attack as an infantryman, armed with a revolver and some grenades. He climbed on the top of one of the medium tanks and, with his revolver and then (according to some reports, with a grenade) he killed the crew through the hatch including, it was discovered later the Italian commander of the tank unit. This disrupted the attack. Leakey was last seen on top of another tank, attempting to repeat his success as a tank killer, but it carried him off into the bush and he was not seen again. He was just over twenty-one years old. The citation for his VC includes the words:-

"Sergeant Leakey, single-handed, halted a most dangerous counter-attack which threatened to destroy all our infantry who had crossed the river."

1/6 KAR took 489 Italian and thirty-one African prisoners of war, ten field guns, thirteen heavy and twenty five light machine guns, three tanks, diesel lorries and about 300 rifles. Between fifty and 100 enemy dead were buried and large numbers of their wounded were captured later. 1/6 KAR's casualties were three European and eighteen African dead. The success at Colito marked the end of the Battle of the Lakes; 1/6 KAR subsequently celebrated the anniversary of Colito annually and named their barracks after the battle. MCs were awarded to Field, Thorne, Onslow and Swynnerton.

The Battle of Colito opened the way to Soddu and its important crossroads, which were taken on 22 May, after demolitions on the route were repaired. Nigerian troops were first into the town; 5 KAR followed, their trucks sliding on the muddy roads, hampered by a shortage of tyre chains. Soddu was a fairly large Ethiopian town with an Italian fort and a number of European houses. 5 KAR was to take over the town and the thousands of prisoners so that the Nigerians could move on. C Company was counting the 2,000 Italians they were to acquire from a Nigerian company when there were shots. The Italians took refuge under the charge of two platoons while the remainder went to investigate. Another platoon had found a Patriot group looting a food store. The KAR's arrival led to a brisk battle. Shirreff recalled:- "We brought up all available Brens and opened fire on them. Some of the more courageous Italians also manned the wall and fired at the Habash (they still had their rifles). Thus there was the odd spectacle of British and Italians firing shoulder to shoulder at the marauding Habash. We killed several, the rest ran away and comparative peace reigned again." The fort was in a filthy condition and normal standards of hygienic conduct were enforced at the point of the bayonet.

The enemy then retreated to the deep gorge of the Omo River. While it was important to get to the enemy before they improved the defences at the Omo, some reorganization and rethinking were necessary. 12 (A) Division was still bogged down and could not contribute much from the south. The two South African battalions returned to Berbera to sail for Egypt, 1/1 KAR was moved up from near Mogadishu, the Nigerian Brigade was brought over to the front and the Nigerian battalion in Addis Ababa re-joined its brigade. However, in view of the shortage of time, 1/1 KAR remained in the Nigerian Brigade, who were to attack Abalti, south-east of the Omo, while 2 Nigerians remained with 22 Brigade/FOWCOL.

The Omo is one of the three great rivers in Ethiopia. It runs in an extension of the Rift Valley with mountains rising on either side to 2,000 feet above the valley floor. This causes a steamy environment, with prolific vegetation and mosquito-ridden jungle, in contrast to the cold of the mountains. The river was not yet in flood; Wetherall had to push on quickly, before it became deeper and wider. To quote Shirreff again, "Together the escarpment and the river formed a natural obstacle so formidable as to make any commander feel a bit doubtful, but I don't think our Brig had any doubts." There was a shortage of bridging equipment, as seventy bridges had been built or rebuilt during the advance. An approach to the Omo on two routes required two bridges; but the overall transport situation was barely sufficient to keep two brigades in action beyond Addis Ababa. Both brigades were to get over the river as quickly as possible, then the first across was to turn right or left, to attack the enemy opposing the other brigade. The Nigerians were at Abalti in the north; 22 Brigade was south of them and had a footbridge in their sector, if it could be reached in time. The road down into the valley had been demolished at many points, extensively mined and was under observed artillery fire. It was made passable to vehicles by 54 (EA) Field Company and 2 Nigerian Regiment. Even so, the advance guard failed to reach the footbridge before it was destroyed.

With the river over 100 yards wide and flowing at six knots, it was decided to put 5 KAR over in the few assault boats available, with the aid of sappers of 54 (EA) Field Company and some Nigerian watermen, on the night of 2 June. A precarious bridgehead was established with three platoons, but some of the assault boats were swept downstream and the bridgehead could not be reinforced or relieved for three days. Shirreff wrote, "Daybreak came on us drenched, miserable, cold and hungry and swollen with mosquito bites. Soon after first light we heard that the attempt was to be abandoned until the river subsided somewhat, and we marched the five miles back to our camp. Marching uphill warmed us up, and by the time we reached camp and smelled breakfast, we all felt much better. The Brig [Fowkes] was standing on the side of the road as we marched up the hill and shouted 'Bad luck, try again'. His presence as usual was extremely encouraging."

The bridgehead was attacked by enemy patrols and shelled constantly, while frantic efforts were made to find better crossing places. By daylight on 5 June two more companies of 5 KAR were across, with two of the Nigerians. A platoon of 1/3 KAR worked their way forward and machine-gunned enemy 105 mm gun positions. Although they were beyond the range of effective artillery support and very tired, 5 KAR managed a wide turning movement to the north and got across the road to the footbridge. Blackshirt troops counter-attacked many times, but were beaten off. The Nigerians established a second bridgehead and the sappers repaired the footbridge for the rest of 5 KAR, then other units of the brigade, to cross. Riding in some captured lorries, 5 KAR surprised a party of Italians who had destroyed part of the cliff face. They had blown one demolition prematurely and destroyed an Italian convoy by mistake.

Despite the appalling state of the roads, just 100 yards of pontoon bridging arrived after driving night and day. The bridge was in position by 10 June, when the brigade commander crossed with a troop of armoured cars and a section of light tanks, to link up with the Nigerian Brigade further north. The Nigerians had managed to get a rope over the river and attempted a crossing, but were not successful until the night of 4/5 June. They advanced 2,000 yards, then swung to their right to cut off the enemy's defences on the river. 1/1 KAR followed, but went straight forward for 9,000 yards to the base of the escarpment. They cut two sets of wires leading to demolition charges and moved on to take Abalti. The enemy was taken completely by surprise; a Forward Artillery Officer was found asleep in his observation post and Italian staff officers who had come forward from Gimma to ascertain the position drove straight into the middle of the KAR. In the two crossings of the Omo 3,900 prisoners and twenty guns were taken.

The enemy east and south of Gimma withdrew northwards. In view of the large number of civilians in Gimma its occupation would be an embarrassment, so the next thrust was made in the direction of Lechementi, to cut the opposition in two again. The civilian problem in Gimma then asserted itself. General Bisson, who had assumed command there, was in constant touch with Fowkes, who had been ordered not to accept responsibility for Gimma's population. Gimma had been invested by Patriots and free-booters (about 12,000 potential looters) before 11 (A) Division arrived. Fowkes reported that their putative leader was not in effective control, but representatives of the Emperor who arrived from Addis Ababa failed to exercise any authority. As operations were developing to the north of the town and a route through it was necessary, 22 Brigade was ordered to enter it, which they did without incident on 21 June. Among the 12,000 Italian and 3,000 African prisoners taken were four generals and eight brigade commanders.

There was gold in Gimma, which led to Bulgy Leach being threatened with excommunication from the Roman Catholic Church by the Bishop of Gimma. The Italian military authorities had handed half (other reports say a quarter) of a million pounds worth of gold to the Bishop for safe-keeping. Fowkes detailed Leach (the brigade's senior Roman Catholic) on the grounds that the gold would not have been given to the Church if the town's occupation had not been imminent. An attempt to negotiate with the Bishop in French ended when the Bishop said, "If you so much as set a foot on church property for such a purpose, I will excommunicate you." So Bruce Wilson, having confirmed that he was a Protestant and did not fear excommunication from the Church of Rome, was sent to find the gold. He was back within the hour, with it neatly wrapped in hessian and carried in five-gallon drums.

Captain John Pitt saw the advance to Gimma as "the race between Brigadiers", and noted that when a brigade was delayed by an abandoned Italian lorry, and their Brigade Commander arrived at the obstruction, he urged its clearance on the band of irregulars who were engaged in looting it by saying, "Go up north and bugger up Brigadier xxxxxx if you want to; don't you dare block my way again."

Parts of the enemy's 22, 23 and 26 Divisions were still in the field, in relatively small groups. The rains had started and, even on the new main supply route, traffic had been reduced to one-way working for many miles. On 27 June 1/1 KAR attacked and took Dembi, capturing General Nam and 700 prisoners. West of Gimma General Bertello gave himself up to 22 Brigade, to end his flight from Somaliland. Conventional troops could not achieve much more, particularly in the heavy rain and with poor roads, so Cunningham asked the Emperor to step up the activities of the Patriots. However, General Gazzera broadcast a message on 3 July that he was sending a car-load of officers to negotiate the surrender of all troops in the Galla-Sidamo. The negotiations were completed speedily. A group of 600 Italians and some banda remained on the north borders of Djibouti, where the local Danakil people had turned against them, but they surrendered in two parties on 8 and 11 July. A column commanded by Col Marventano had been pressed by Wingate's patriots and surrendered on 22 May, to be handed over to 11 (A) Division at Ficche.

That effectively concluded the campaign in the south, which had begun on 11 February. At no time were more than three brigade groups plus two battalions engaged against the 40,000 troops in the Galla-Sidamo. After the fall of Sciasciamanna only two brigade groups were used. 22 (EA) Brigade claimed as their share, in the last 400 miles of the advance, twelve generals, 25,000 prisoners, eighty-five guns and vast quantities of war material, plus the hoard of gold bullion from Gimma.

With the end of the main campaign some courses and leave were possible. To attend a course in Kenya Pitt travelled via Addis Ababa, crossing the Omo by a "flying ferry", a captive vessel that was hauled backwards and forwards, taking two vehicles at a time. In Addis Ababa he stayed at the Albergio Imperiale, now an Officers' Details Camp, arriving in time for dinner, bath and a comfortable bed. At breakfast he had a choice of a six, nine or twelve egg omelette (Ethiopian eggs were very small). He went shopping and bought a pair of diamond ear-rings, watches for his wife, sister and cook, a large Perelli rain cape and some Italian champagne. As he said, "Quite a good haul".

Early in November operations began against Gondar, in the north-west of Ethiopia, which Mussolini had selected as the last Italian redoubt, under the command of General Nasi. There had been several changes in the intervening months. Cunningham had gone north to command 8 Army and responsibility for the residual operations in Ethiopia rested with Headquarters East Africa Command direct. Until Platt arrived to take over, Wetherall was Acting GOCinC East Africa Command. The rains had ended. Fowkes had been promoted to command 12 (A) Division, with his Advanced Divisional Headquarters at Amba Georgis, east of Gondar.

Gondar is on a plateau some 7,000 feet high, with mountains up to 10,000 feet on all but the south side. The 34,000 enemy troops had plenty of time to develop their defences, and had a good supply of fresh food locally. There were two possible approaches for a force big enough to crack this very hard nut. One was from the south-west, from Dessie via Debra Tabor, while the other was from the north-east, from Asmara. Both were blocked by strong enemy positions; the Asmara route was remarkable for the ninety-nine hairpin bends that lay between the valley floor and the crest at Wolchefit, where a garrison of 5,000 men with thirty guns had complete observation over the valley. But the position was isolated from the main defensive location and it had been harassed by Major Ringrose and his Patriots, so that it was now cut off. Air attacks were pressed strongly while forces were assembled for an assault. Then the garrison surrendered to 25 (EA) Brigade on 1 September. The East African Engineers repaired the demolitions and the road was open again by 8 October.

Until the surrender of Wolchefit Fowkes had preferred the Dessie route and had assembled Southforce, made up of 1/6 KAR, the EA Pioneers and a battery of medium artillery, to advance northwards. The Wolchefit surrender and the effects of the long, hard rains led him to switch his main effort to the route from Asmara. He had 25 and 26 (EA) Brigades (both consisting of new and untried battalions), EA Armoured Cars, artillery and engineer units, the durable and invaluable 22 Mountain Battery and some South African Engineer Corps units. There were the Argyll and Sutherland Highlanders, gunners and sappers from the Gold Coast, a battalion of the Sudan Defence Force advancing from the west, a battalion of Ethiopians and some Belgians. The RAF and SAAF maintained air superiority and the Patriots were active. 25 (EA) Brigade was commanded by Brig W.A.L. James, and consisted of 2/3, 2/4 and 3/4 KAR. They had been in the area of Lake Rudolf, but had been relieved by a battalion of 21 (EA) Brigade, had concentrated at Nanyuki and then sailed to Massawa. Brig W.A. Dimoline commanded 26 (EA) Brigade, which consisted of 2/2, 4/4 and 3/6 KAR. 26 Brigade had taken over in British Somaliland when 2 SA Brigade left for Egypt. They then moved to Harar, responsible for security on the lines of communication from Berbera to the River Awash. 1/3 KAR and their machine guns were in demand; for the Gondar operation A Company was attached to 25 Brigade and D Company to 26 Brigade.

25 and 26 Brigades were north of Gondar, while Southforce was built up to consist of 1/6 KAR and a battalion of EA Pioneers, plus a battery of sixty pounders from the Gold Coast, a Squadron of EA Armoured Cars and a

Field Company of South African sappers. Southforce was commanded by Lt Col R.G.T. Collins, who had succeeded Lt Col Colin Blackden as CO 1/6 KAR on 26 October. For the Kul Kabir operation 1/6 KAR was led by Major N.C. Robertson-Glasgow and the EA Pioneers by Lt Col Michael Blundell. They met a small but resolute garrison at Kul Kabir, where extensive demolitions had badly damaged the road. The Italians had around 1,900 men from three battalions and other organizations, including Caribinieri and military police. Nasi had ordered them to hold out for two more months, as he expected the Germans would then rescue them. The garrison had developed its natural defences; at one place the Pioneers had to tunnel through an enormous boulder, thought to weigh 1,500 tons, that was blocking a road.

The first attack against Kul Kabir was at dawn on 13 November, but Italian artillery and machine-gun fire pinned down the attackers until they withdrew under cover of darkness. Some of the British officers with the Patriots criticized the plan as having been made without adequate reconnaissance and that a lack of radio communication between the various elements of the force had prevented them from acting together. The right flank of 1/6 KAR had withdrawn without orders, but the ground they were on was difficult and everyone was tired, having started their long approach march at 1.30 a.m. The Italians put in a spirited counter-attack which was successful. Southforce was weak in artillery, unable to call for fire support when it was needed, and too far from the main force for them to help. Collins was critical of the performance of the Patriots.

For the next attempt the two forces operated in conjunction. A poor track was found, which led from the Asmara road down to the plain between Kul Kabir and Gondar. By 19 November it had been made passable, although tractors were needed to get vehicles up in some places. It was screened from Italian view except at one place, and was beyond the range of their guns. The track had been used by the Italians when they took Gondar in 1936, but they had assumed that it could not be made passable for large numbers of vehicles. It served Fowkes' purpose and enabled the two columns to co-operate. 25 Brigade moved down it ready for the second attack on Kul Kabir on 25 November.

There was a brisk fighting nearby, at Chilga, when Sudancol, (the SDF Composite Regiment, a troop of Sudanese Artillery, with Pioneers and Patriots), attempted to take a position commanded by Colonel Miranda, who had three battalions. The position was well wired and the SDF took heavy casualties before they withdrew. Guy Campbell, who was with Sudancol, considered the operation "a bit of a shambles", but it had drawn off some reinforcements from Gondar. The position did not surrender until

28 November, the day after Gondar fell; a message from Nasi was dropped to them by a British aircraft to order them to do so.

After preliminary heavy aerial bombing and a pounding by the Gold Coasters' big guns, 25 Brigade attacked Kul Kabir from the north-west, while Southforce and the Patriots struck from the other side. 2/3 KAR reached their objective, but were shelled and counter-attacked off it. They were rallied by Major "Bombo" Trimmer, who led them back up the hill and, with two companies of 2/4 KAR, reached the ridge, where they withstood three more counter-attacks. For his decisive action Trimmer received an immediate DSO. The Patriots under Birru were expected to attack a feature nicknamed "Pimple", which overlooked 1/6 KAR's objective on a ridge. Capt Peter Molloy (4 KAR) was sent to join Birru on 20 November, accompanied by two SA sappers and two KAR askari armed with Boyes anti-tank rifles. Birru did not like the plan and Molloy spent some time during the night attempting, unsuccessfully, to warn his brigadier by radio that Birru might not co-operate. On the next morning at dawn Birru's attitude was still "We will see." After a half-hour Molloy set off with his two sappers, hoping to shame the Patriots into following him, which some of them did until deterred by shellfire. On the way to Pimple, Molloy met Capt Ted Onslow and a platoon of 1/6 KAR, who were about to tackle Pimple because 1/6 KAR was held up by fire from there. They agreed a combined attack, with Onslow coming in from the north-east with the aid of Sapper Pienaar, while Molloy and Sapper Brenner attacked frontally. Pienaar and then Onslow were wounded from an adjacent position, Onslow being rescued by one of his askari under fire. Molloy decided to attack Pimple with the sole aid of Brenner, intending to push a grenade through a weapon slit into the corner pillbox. They were seen and Brenner was wounded. He and Molloy were pinned down in the hot sun for several hours, until the Patriots suddenly, at 2 p.m. stormed up the hill and took Pimple just as 1/6 KAR secured the ridge. The two askari had given covering fire with their anti-tank rifles so enthusiastically that, by the time Molloy rejoined them, they had exhausted their ammunition. In the intense fighting all three of the Italian battalion commanders were killed. 25 Brigade had now secured all of their objectives and, in conjunction with the remainder of the Division, including the invaluable Gold Coast guns, were ready to tackle the southern face and weaker defences of Gondar.

Fowkes planned to attack towards Azozo with 25 Brigade and use 26 Brigade to secure Deflecha Ridge concurrently; 3/6 KAR were to contain the enemy in the Ambazzo area meanwhile. This involved 26 Brigade being put on to a pack basis at short notice, using local donkeys and mules, to enable them to go down into the valley of the River Megach and up the opposite side to reach their objective. The attacks were launched on 27 November, with Fowkes controlling events from a Battle Headquarters in slit trenches at the edge of the escarpment. 25 Brigade and the Patriots burst through the Azozo defences and swept on to Gondar. The Patriots' blood was up and they rushed into the town itself. A squadron of East African Armoured Cars followed them closely and Major Yeatman, the Squadron Leader, accepted General Nasi's unconditional surrender. 25 Brigade then rounded up thousands of prisoners and restored order. 26 Brigade had encountered minefields under artillery and machine-gun fire, which caused heavy casualties before they attained their objectives. After the surrender, Italian engineers assisted in clearing the minefields.

The final blow in the battle for Gondar was when Nasi's last surviving aircraft, a CR32, attacked the vehicle in which the newly joined Commander Royal Artillery (Lt Col J. Ormsby) and Biggs (then GSO2 Int) were travelling. Ormsby's femoral artery was severed and he died soon afterwards, and Biggs was wounded. Pitt's platoon of 1/6 KAR was resting at one stage in the battle when, through his looted binoculars, he saw a group of Patriots moving along a ridge. An Italian "broke cover and dashed off; the Patriots gave chase, caught him and formed a form of rugger scrum; then someone stood up with something held aloft. Later, when some of us went along the ridge we found a mutilated body. Mercifully it seemed that he had been killed before the Patriot collected his 'trophy'."

Biggs' Union flag flew at Gondar until, in his words, it was replaced "by a bigger and better one". The Crown Prince, representing his father the Emperor, had been at Fowkes' Headquarters for some days before the battle. He addressed a large crowd from the castle balcony with the GOC beside him. Later a victory parade was held outside the city, when all the units and vehicles were drawn up for inspection and to march past Maj Gen Wetherall, Acting GOCinC East Africa Command.

The Gondar operation caused the heaviest casualties of the campaign. The askari were against a firmly entrenched enemy, in a series of positions of great natural strength, under one of Italy's best generals. They were at a disadvantage in artillery and attacked repeatedly across open country, often through extensive minefields. Excluding Patriots, the casualties were eight officers and 108 soldiers killed, and fifteen officers and 370 soldiers wounded.

After the Gondar battle Peter Molloy escorted the Italian commanders to internment near Massawa. They started on 29 November 1941; Generals Nasi, Poli, Martini and Piccinelli were squashed into a staff car which Molloy drove, followed by two lorries loaded with senior staff, ADCs, baggage and a few askari guards. They missed the staging camp en route to Massawa, so they drove twenty miles on to Adowa. It was a modern colonial city with 10,000 Italian inhabitants; as an "open city" it had no garrison and only one very young English officer of the Occupied Enemy Territory Administration, with a pretty Italian mistress. Nasi spoke to the head of the Italian community and soon a delighted reception committee arranged accommodation; all Molloy had to do was to fix the time for them to meet in the morning and to wonder about the penalty for losing four Italian Generals. They set off again next morning, accompanied by a hooting mob of Italian cars in front and behind for the first few miles. They reached the Governor of Massawa's summer residence in the hills without incident, but the Generals took an instant dislike to their new guards, who were South African Security Police, and were horrified to lose Molloy. Before leaving Molloy shook hands all round and parted with genuine regret from "his Generals", whom he had come to like and admire. Nasi called the party to attention and saluted; Molloy drove out of their lives.

The Italian fleet at Massawa dispersed in March, 1941. Four submarines made the 16,000 mile journey to Bordeaux round the Cape, a sloop and an auxiliary cruiser reached Japan, but the remaining five destroyers launched an attack on Port Sudan. They were seen by the RAF at dawn on 3 April; two were sunk and the others were scuttled. The port of Massawa was relatively undamaged and the area was soon developed into a Middle East base.

The new Headquarters East Africa Command opened at Nairobi on 15 September, 1941, with Wetherall as Acting GOCinC until Platt arrived on 5 December. He reported direct to the War Office and the Command extended from Eritrea in the north to the Zambesi in the south. It was organized into four Areas: Eritrea (with its Military Administration), 12 (A) Division under Fowkes was responsible for Ethiopia and British Somaliland, 11 (A) Division became Central Area, covering ex-Italian Somaliland (Somalia), and Southern Area, under Maj Gen G.R. Smallwood DSO MC, consisted of Nyasaland and Northern Rhodesia. Smallwood was also military adviser to the Southern Rhodesian Government, with his Headquarters at Salisbury (now Harari). A few weeks later Eritrea left East Africa Command and came under GHQ Middle East.

In November, 1941, the British Government decided to evacuate all 34,000 Italian civilians from Ethiopia. Women, children and elderly men were repatriated to Italy under the supervision of the International Red Cross from Berbera, which involved setting up transit camps en route and screening to ensure that escaped prisoners of war did not slip away with the evacuees. 2/2 KAR were much involved in this. Evacuation began in

General Nasi's headquarters — the 13th century Portuguese castle at Gondar. This photograph was taken the day after its capture on 28 November, 1941.

The view of the town from the castle.

16. Lt.-Colonel Michael Biggs, GSO1 & 11 (EA) Division, being presented with the OBE by General Sir Claude Auchinleck. On the right is Brigadier John Macnab.

17. Members of 55 (T) Field Battery, 302 (EA) Field Regiment, with their 25 pounder g at Ranchi, 1945.

EAAC stand at the Army Exhibition in Nairobi, August, 1944. A Humber armoured car mounting a .50 Besa heavy machine gun and a .303 Besa machine gun.

Major Richard E. Thorne commanding the Somalia Gendarmerie contingent on the VE Day Parade in Mogadishu, 1945.

24. Control and Protection of the Civilian Population: a fortified village in the Kikuyu Reserve.

25. 7 KAR on patrol; a water patrol in the Aberdares.

December; in the following month 10,000 men were moved to Kenya and other territories. By May, 1942, 9,000 women, children and "infirm males" were repatriated through Berbera, and by November, 1942, another 8,700 in these categories had left Eritrea. But several hundred Italian men were still at large and posed security problems.

The Emperor was back in Addis Ababa, but had begun to suspect that there was a British plot to colonize his country. On 4 February, 1941, Eden made a statement in the House of Commons to the effect that military measures necessary for the control in Ethiopia (including operations against the Vichy French in Djibouti) would be agreed by negotiation with the Emperor. These negotiations were protracted, not least because the Emperor believed that there was oil in the Ogaden that Britain wanted. Eventually an agreement was signed on 31 January, 1942, which set the boundaries for KAR and East African forces for the next nine years in some areas. Direct British control was limited to a twenty-five-mile strip along the Djibouti border, the railway corridor from Djibouti to Addis Ababa, a number of cantonments (Addis Ababa, Harar and Diredawa were the most important), and the area that is now the Fifth (Somali) Region of Ethiopia.

Djibouti was the one serious task remaining; there were six Senegalese battalions who were expected to fight if ordered. The concrete defences had been built originally to keep out the Italians and could not be destroyed by the comparatively light aircraft available. The aim was to secure the Djibouti docks intact so that the railway line and the docks could be used to re-start Ethiopian trade. The capture of Diredawa had cut Djibouti off from most of its supplies, the Royal Navy blockaded the port and the French were expected to surrender in six weeks. Leaflets were dropped calling on them to give in, with the inducement of an early return to prosperity if the port reopened. Negotiations proceeded for some time, including an offer by Wavell to call off the blockade and to rush in a month's supplies if they all became Free French. The blockade was strengthened by a Free French sloop to disrupt the profitable blockade running from the Yemen, and Brig Dimoline's 26 (EA) Brigade moved from Aden to Assab. The brigade included 3/15 Punjab Battalion and 2/2 KAR (from Berbera). Supporting Arms and Services came from the defunct East African Force. It was now thought that the Senegalese would be less likely to fight, but several factors (including operations elsewhere) deterred any direct assault on the defences. Protracted negotiations continued, including a British offer to evacuate all French women and children to Madagascar and the French Governor's threat to destroy the port. 26 Brigade was then called away for the Gondar operations.

Preparations for the Gondar battle had included the formation of 28 (EA)

Brigade in Kenya. After various changes of plan it consisted of 2/1 KAR, 7 KAR and 10 KAR. The last had been at Yatta, was upgraded to a first line battalion and re-designated 4/6 KAR. 2/6 KAR remained in the Sudan. 28(EA) Brigade was tasked to relieve 26 Brigade for Gondar, and arrived at Jigjiga (less 7 KAR) under the command of Brig I.R.C. Bruce MBE in October. 7 KAR and A Company 1/3 KAR went by sea to Assab to relieve the Punjabis, and the remaining companies of 1/3 KAR were distributed along the Djibouti frontier and the railway line. The Danakil people assisted in enforcing the blockade on the landward side, but wanted protection from their traditional enemies, the Wajirati. A patrol from B Company 1/3 KAR, commanded by CSM Thompson and consisting of two armoured cars, two trucks with machine guns mounted and two trucks of riflemen, was checking a report about a group of Wajirati when they were ambushed. The Wajirati immobilized the trucks by shooting the drivers and the tyres; one machine gun jammed, the other did not get into action and both armoured cars blew gaskets. The patrol withdrew after two hours with the loss of nine askari killed and four wounded, two of them fatally. That was the end of patrols. The Company moved to Sardo and was used mainly on garrison duties until relieved by the East African Pioneers, when they returned to Kenya.

Blockade-running had grown to such proportions that the French were refusing to accept some supplies provided by the British for the women and children of Djibouti, and some Ethiopian chiefs profited from the smuggling. Two Somali Guard Companies had been raised to assist in guarding prisoners of war, but with most of the prisoners gone they were used to enforce the blockade. They were increased to four and then to six companies, enabling all the KAR to be withdrawn. When Japan entered the war the naval blockade ended and there was no point in retaining the landward blockade alone. The morale of the French in Djibouti was seriously depressed by the surrender of Madagascar on 5 November and the Allied landings in North Africa. The Governor flew off, ostensibly on leave, and did not return. On 28 November Col Raynal and his battalion of Senegalese, together with most of the garrison artillery, crossed the frontier to Zeila with their arms and equipment. Because it was feared that the Vichy French might blow two vital railway bridges between the port and the frontier, they were positioned ready to strike down the railway to seize the bridges, which they took intact on 26 December.

A fresh round of negotiations began with the Acting Governor, with the American consul from Aden intruding and a Foreign Office official (Mr Henry Hopkinson) visiting. The last caused some amusement to Tony Scawin and his company of Somaliland Scouts at Ashia, as he arrived in a London suit, bowler hat and umbrella. An agreement was signed on 28

December and on 31 December Generals Le Gentilhomme (now High Commissioner for French Possessions in the Indian Ocean) and Platt were received by a Guard of Honour in Djibouti. Tony Scawin's company set out on the long march to Borama, but eventually met some trade trucks that had been sent out to carry them across the desert.

The problems with communications in Ethiopia and Somaliland led to the formation of one of the most multi-national units ever to have served in the British Army. Called Somaliland Signals, it was based on the Corps Signals unit which had served Cunningham's Headquarters, supplemented by local recruitment and a Signals Company which had been formed in Somaliland. An independent Somali Signals Squadron in Mogadishu provided the communications for the Administration and the Somalia Gendarmerie. By mid-1944 Somaliland Signals consisted of roughly equal parts (120–150 each) of British, Africans, Somalis and Ethiopians. There were four different ration scales and four OR messes in Hargeisa. The Somalis did not like the AOR uniform (a come-down from Camel Corps styles), the Ethiopians despised the Africans and the Somalis took a low view of everyone. Lt Col Henry Jenkins was in command. Others in the unit included a Mauritian of French descent, who was the senior cypher officer, Canadians, Kenyans, South Africans and Rhodesians. The generators were in the care of an Italian ex-POW, the Africans were from three or four different territories and the tailor was a French-speaking Somali. They operated long distance W/T links to Nairobi, Mogadishu, Addis Ababa, Aden and Djibouti, plus some posts in the Ogaden. Most of their equipment was obsolete, unsuitable or captured. But it worked; when General Anderson (now GOC EA Command) visited he saw it was a "Good, live show".

Brig A.R. Chater, who had fought the Tug Argan battle eight months before, returned to Somaliland as Military Governor soon after the landing of the G(R) Force in March, 1941. The Camel Corps reformed quickly. Capt Oliver Brooke had half of his company on parade within twelve hours of his return to Burao. The remainder were there on the next morning, apart from one man who had died. Brooke's personal servant then disappeared, to return with some of Brooke's kit he had buried; his sword was recovered later. The Somali Guard units were formed quickly by two British officers, Lts R. Bassett and D. Sadler, assisted by RSM Awaleh Farah of the Camel Corps, who became the RSM of the Guards and then of the Scouts. Initially the unit wore captured Italian uniforms, black shirts and shorts of coarse green canvas. These were very unpopular, saved only because the shirts had collars. The unit expanded to six companies, designated numbers 31 to 36, the numbering believed to have derived from the numbering sequence of Scouts units in the rest of the British Army. The Military Units Ordinance of 1 May, 1942, required the askari to be attested, and they received the same pay rates as the KAR askari, except that it was in rupees. They were designated Somaliland Scouts on 1 July, 1943, and adopted the cap badge of crossed spears with an S superimposed; the crown was added in 1950. Initially the CO was a major, but with six majors as company commanders, the unit was upgraded to a lieutenant colonel's command. For a time battalion headquarters were at Harar. The companies usually operated in pairs, not only in the Protectorate but also in the Reserved Areas, Ogaden and the Haud of Ethiopia (as long as those areas remained under British administration) and in Somalia. 35 and 36 Companies were in north-east Somalia for six months to protect the RAF airfields from which Wellesleys flew anti-submarine sorties. Shifta in the Dagabur area necessitated 35 Company patrolling that area for three months, before they moved to Segag, near the source of the Webi Shebelli, where they had some brushes with the Arussi Galla people, with support from armoured cars of the Somalia Gendarmerie.

With the war against Japan demanding large numbers of troops, it was proposed to raise a Somali brigade, but Chater advised against it. Instead 71 (1 Somaliland) Battalion KAR was raised on 1 September, 1942, and 72 KAR in January 1943. The former served in Burma, as described in Chapter 8, while 72 KAR was intended to be a training and drafting unit, and moved to Kenya. In September, 1944, sixty-three men deserted, although they had been detailed for a draft. Some of them returned later, but the unit was disarmed for a while, then returned to Somaliland and disbanded in February, 1945. The Camel Corps was due to be converted into an armoured car unit, to move to Kenya for training and then possibly on to Rhodesia. On the night of 5/6 June, 1944, 150 askari broke into the armoury in Burao, taking rifles and ammunition. A few shots were fired but no one was hurt. The barracks were looted by men of the town, but most of the clothing and blankets were recovered by a police cordon. Next day the Corps paraded short of the 150 men, over 200 rifles and some ammunition. Some men returned later and were tried by Court Martial. At the EA Armoured Car Depot at Gilgil thirty Camel Corps askari who were on a course in June, displayed "dumb insolence" and were returned to Somaliland. The mutiny was not a complete surprise; the Somalis were apprehensive of going to Kenya, feared for their religious customs and for their life-style, which derived from their long association with the Indian Army. The change in culture to that of a mechanized regiment did not suit many and the uniform was unpopular, being thought degrading. A Court of Inquiry was held into the causes of the mutiny and the Corps was disbanded in September, 1944. Many of the men transferred to the Somaliland Scouts.

The Scouts were engaged in dealing with clan clashes in the northern Ogaden, Reserved Areas and the Haud, while the southern Ogaden and Somalia were patrolled by the Somalia Gendarmerie and the KAR. The Gendarmerie had been formed from a mixture of Tanganyikan police, Nyasa askari and Somalis. It included armoured cars, some pony-mounted units and, for a while, a camel company. The prospect of a return to Italian rule in Somalia and to Ethiopian control in parts of the Ogaden caused unrest, while the British proposal for a Greater Somalia (Somaliland, Somalia, Djibouti, the Ogaden and the NFD) was debated in the United Nations and in Somali coffee shops. Eventually opposition from Ethiopia, France, USA, Italy and Kenya killed the idea and Italy returned to Somalia under a UN mandate in 1950, charged with preparing the country for independence in ten years. The immediate effects were disbandment of the British Military Administration, the Area Headquarters in Mogadishu and the Somalia Gendarmerie. It also broke the supply route from Kenya to Somaliland, which passed under control of GHQ Middle East, with local operational command exercised by AOC Aden. This meant withdrawal of the residual East African units in Somaliland (a supply depot, hospital and workshops) to Kenya and closure of the Sub-Area Headquarters in Hargeisa.

Maj Gen Dimoline, on his last visit to Hargeisa as GOC, said in conversation with the Scouts' CO, Lt Col Oliver Brooke, "I'll concede that the Somalis probably killed more Japanese than any other battalion [in Burma], but one could not rely on them". Scouts officers believed themselves to be in the Camel Corps tradition and were sometimes accused of having cavalry affectations. An officer of 407 (EA) Command Workshops is widely (but probably apocryphally) reputed to have said, "The trouble with you Somali Scouts is you are all too lah-di-dah; all you think of is playing snob's hockey on horseback."

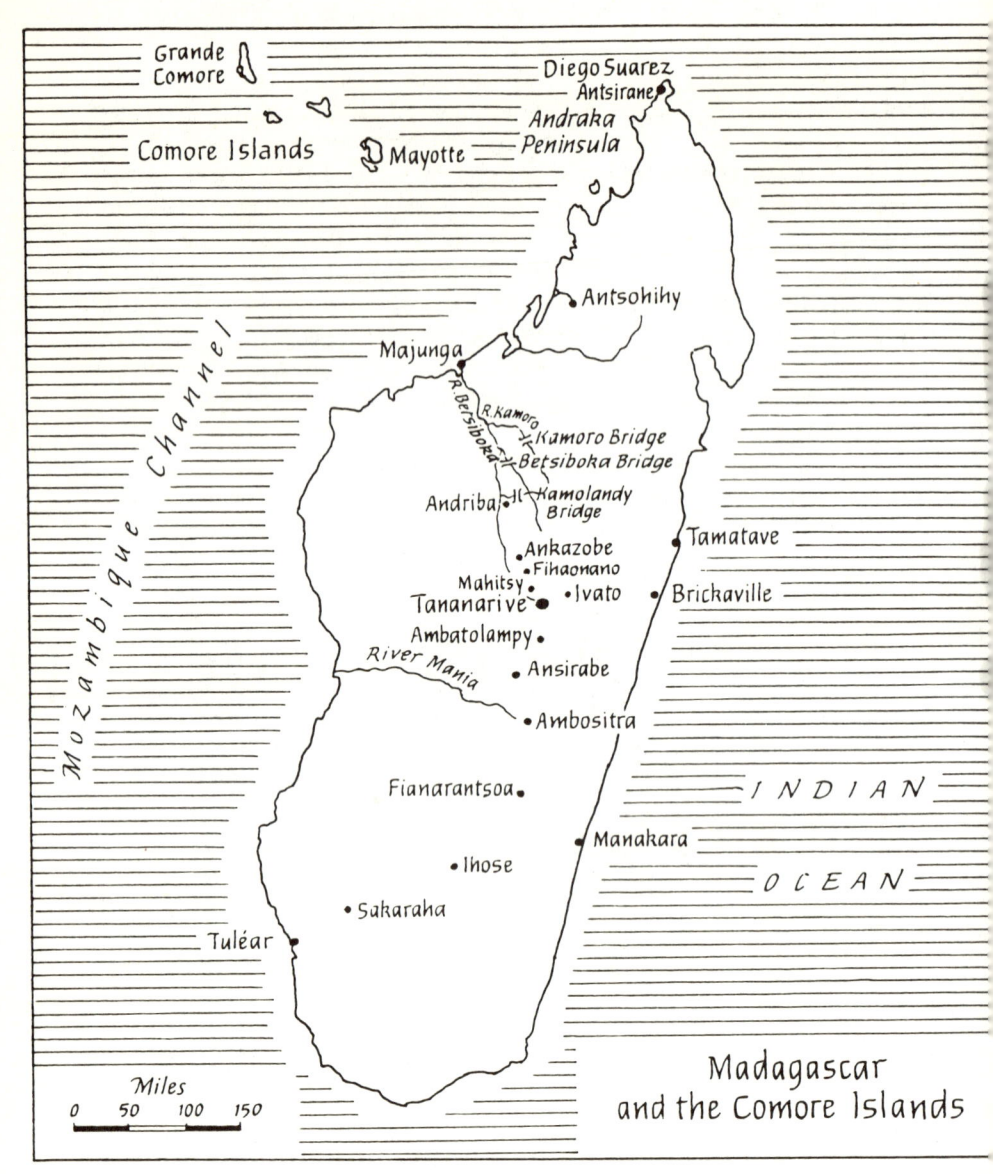

MAP 8

Madagascar and the Comore Islands

Chapter 7

MADAGASCAR
and Mauritius

"The key to the safety of the Indian Ocean."

FM Jan Smuts

The island of Madagascar is some three hundred miles east of south-east Africa, opposite what was, in 1942, Portuguese East Africa. Between them is the 300-mile-wide Mozambique Channel, a major shipping route. The island is about 1,000 miles from north to south; it was a French colony and sided with Vichy France. General de Gaulle urged Churchill that Free French Forces, with British sea and air support, should take over the island, but there were not enough French troops of adequate quality available for the purpose. Events in the Bay of Bengal and Ceylon then gave added importance to Madagascar, and it was decided to mount an all-British operation to protect the shipping routes round the Cape and on to the Middle East and India. There was a serious risk that Japan would base a submarine fleet on the island. Hitler had been briefed on the possibility on 12 March, 1942, but thought that Vichy would not allow it.

The aim of Operation Bonus was to deny Diego Suarez and other principal centres to the Japanese, but not to occupy the whole island. There were shortages of naval ships, troops and landing craft. When President Roosevelt attached some US heavy naval vessels to the British Home Fleet an equivalent number of RN ships were released to Ironclad, as Bonus was re-named. The fleet assembled for Ironclad included HMS *Ramillies* (battleship), HMS *Illustrious* (carrier), two cruisers, eleven destroyers, minesweepers, corvettes and fifteen assault ships, commanded by Admiral Sir Neville Syfret. Troops were found by delaying the arrival in India of 13 and 15 Brigades of 5 Division, 29 Independent Brigade and a Commando. The two Brigades of 5 Division were to be released immediately the objectives had been achieved, but 29 Brigade could be retained for up to two months. The British formations were to be replaced by African ones as soon as possible. Maj Gen R.G. Sturges commanded the land force.

The solution to the shortage of landing craft had a longer-term effect on the fortunes of East African troops. In Burma, General Wavell wanted to take the port of Akyab by amphibious assault. He was promised the landing craft and the requisite air cover, but the former were diverted to Madagascar and the latter arrived late. An attack by land resulted in the defeat of the six British brigades involved, and it was two years later, when an East African brigade was in the area, that Akyab was taken.

The UK components sailed from UK on 23 March, 1942, and the fleet assembled off Durban by 22 April. Added impetus to Ironclad came from a Japanese attack on RN ships at Ceylon in early April, when two heavy cruisers and a carrier were lost. The last (i.e. fastest) convoy left Durban on 28 April, and by 4 May the entire force was within striking distance of its objectives. Ironclad was the largest amphibious operation for British forces since the Dardanelles campaign, and was directed at Diego Suarez, at the north of the island. The first assault went in at 4.30 a.m. on 5 May, when coastal gun emplacements were seized with little difficulty, followed by Fleet Air Arm attacks on airfields and shipping. HMS *Hermione* carried out a feint attack on the east coast; by the afternoon 29 Brigade had landed on the west coast and the Commando had crossed the Andraka Peninsula (the northern arm of Diego Suarez Bay) despite French opposition. A destroyer landed fifty marines on the dockside at Antsirane, two miles across the water from Diego Suarez. She left under a hail of fire while the Marines captured a naval depot and freed about fifty British prisoners. Antsirane was surrounded before daybreak on 7 May, the harbour forts were bombarded and fighting ceased by 11 a.m. There were less than 400 Army casualties.

Smuts continued to press for the occupation of the entire island; his case was reinforced when a large Japanese submarine that carried both a mini-submarine and a reconnaissance aircraft got within striking distance of the fleet. The plane flew over them and, a short while later, the midget submarine hit both *Ramillies* and a tanker with torpedos, putting the battleship out of action for two months. The two-man crew scuttled the midget and attempted to escape by land, but were shot by a British patrol. Smuts offered Churchill a South African Brigade to help clear the island.

The French Governor General of Madagascar was unco-operative, so other operations were mounted against him and his troops, under the command of Lt Gen Sir W. Platt, GOCinC, East Africa Command. On 10 September 29 Brigade captured Majunga, on the west coast. 22 (EA) Brigade then landed, passed through 29 Brigade and moved on to Tananarive, the capital. 29 Brigade captured Tamatave on the east coast, the South Africans cleared the coastal roads, and the capital was captured on 23 September. A final action on 19 October led to the Governor General surrendering on 5 November.

22 (EA) Brigade was commanded by Brig A.W. Dimoline; after the siege

of Djibouti and the Gondar battle they left Ethiopia at the end of 1941 by road, and by mid-March, 1942, were at Yatta Camp for leave and training. Early in June, 1942 Dimoline left for Diego Suarez and the brigade moved to Mombasa to embark on the *Winchester Castle*. There was a hitch when they sailed, as the Commander Far East Fleet (Vice Admiral Somerville) did not like the way the brigade "manned ship" on leaving harbour, and they were recalled so that the compliment could be paid properly.

The *Winchester Castle* had landing craft lashed alongside, and en route to Diego Suarez troops practised moving in and out of them. On 7 June they landed by assault craft and replaced units of 29 Brigade as follows:-

1/1 KAR (Lt Col J.F. Macnab), with 959 all ranks, landed on White Beach and relieved the Royal Scots Fusiliers on the Ankorika Peninsula.

5 KAR (Lt Col P.A. Morcombe), with 971 all ranks, went ashore on Ocean Beach to replace 2 Northamptonshire Regiment (2 NORTHANTS) at Cap Mine.

1/6 KAR (Lt Col R.G.T. Collins), with 896 all ranks, moved in over Ocean Beach to take over from 6 Seaforth Highlanders.

The British units were still in slit trenches, living mainly on bully beef, and were astonished at the appearance of tables and table linen in the KAR units, followed by the service of a three-course luncheon. It took a little time for fresh rations to be organized, but there was a welcome addition to the menu when a British CSM in 1/6 KAR found and brought to his company commander a wooden box which proved to contain a very fine ham. With the wisdom of Solomon the company commander shared the ham equally between the British officers' and sergeants' messes. Shortly afterwards they received the first brigade orders to be issued since the landing. These congratulated all units of the brigade on their achievements to date, and the "lost and found" section included a request for news of a ham "the personal property of the Brigade Commander". A less fortunate experience with food arose because the Fleet Air Arm, in attacking Diego Suarez harbour, had dropped a bomb down the funnel of the largest French destroyer. The vessel was loaded with bully beef (there was a factory further south, which 1/6 KAR liberated later). The bomb ruptured the tins and the resultant smell was memorable.

The brigade was equipped with No 1 rifles, Bren guns and two-inch mortars. Some of their vehicles had been requisitioned in Kenya before they went to Ethiopia. They had been painted in Army colours initially, but this was wearing off and the names of Kenyan traders were becoming apparent. They took over the three-inch mortars and the Bren carriers of the British battalions. Their previous mortars had been made in the workshops of the Kenya and Uganda Railways from wagon axles and had a range of 1,000 yards with a following wind, but the bombs wobbled as they left the barrels. The British battalions helped to train the askari to use the carriers; one ran into a minefield, killing a corporal of 2 NORTHANTS and injuring several askari.

Their first operation after arrival was to take Mayotte Island, about 250 miles west of Diego Suarez, garrisoned by about 100 armed police. Operation Throat's objective was to take the island's installations and facilities because of their importance for the control of shipping in the Mozambique Channel. Thirty British Commandos from Force 101 and C Company 5 KAR were embarked on two destroyers, HMSs *Dauntless* and *Active*. The attackers were ashore by 4.45 a.m. surprised the police in their beds and the aim was achieved without loss of life. David Shirreff was commanding a platoon in C Company and was enthused by the prospect of impending action. They had seen no action for a year; for six months they had been on garrison duties in Ethiopia and, since being in Madagascar, they had dug trenches, done brigade fatigues, unloaded lighters and made roads. They had just benefited from a few days of training, including practising "jumping out of assault boats and staging attacks on the hills inland". The effect was "a tremendous difference and the troops were well keyed up and keen for a scrap".

At 1 a.m. the Commandos and the other C Company platoons had gone in, while David was "left chewing a pipe on deck anxiously waiting for the first shot or the wireless signal to leave. The guns were trained on Dzaudzi and the crews were longing to start firing. Minutes went by and nothing happened, until at last the message came that the Dzaudzi landing had been successful and I was to land at Mamudzu." They set off in the boats at 2.30 a.m. in the pitch dark. Fortunately the British platoon sergeant spotted a light which could only have come from a house in the town, so they turned inshore. They landed and started breaking into the European houses, capturing the Chef de District in the first. A road block was established, and the askari who manned it were soon proudly escorting three voluble Frenchmen who had tried to escape by car; the noisiest was the Chief of Police, high on the "wanted" list. David had told his askari that he and the British sergeant were the only Europeans not to be detained; all others were to be arrested. The next haul at the road block were two priests and a RN sub-lieutenant who had gone ashore without orders. At the barracks David found Corporal Barreh telling a fat Comorian sergeant to fall in his men at the double. A bugler blew the fall in and about sixty slovenly-looking police were rounded up; most of the remainder were caught by the other platoon. The landing at Dzaudzi had gone equally well; the Commandos had scaled the cliff, captured the radio station and caught the Governor in bed – a great stroke of luck as he had planned to escape to Grande Comore later that day. Dimoline, who had watched from HMS *Dauntless*, said he was well pleased with the KAR's first combined operation.

Towards the end of July, 1942, occupation of the rest of the island was authorized. Smuts sent a South African brigade to assist, which included a Commando of South African-built Marmon Harrington armoured cars with heavy machine guns mounted in the turrets. Their armour did not always keep out .303 rifle bullets, but they were invaluable assets when allotted to 22 Brigade. The French were confused when they heard Afrikaans on their radio intercepts and mistook it for German.

The French opposition amounted to about 7,000 troops, a mixed bag of French regular soldiers, Senegalese, locally recruited Malgash and French settlers. The Governor General was M Annet and the force commander was Gen Guillmet. He had several French regular officers including at least two colonels and one lieutenant colonel. There were a few aircraft, including Potez light bombers and Moraine fighters, but not enough to be a serious threat. The French intended to make a fighting withdrawal towards the south of the island, holding out for as long as they could.

22 Brigade's task, in conjunction with 29 Brigade, was to clear the island as quickly as possible. 22 Brigade was relieved of its coastal defence role by 27 (Northern Rhodesian) Brigade early in August and moved into camp near Sakaramy, about eighteen miles from Diego Suarez, for three weeks of intensive training. Meanwhile, 29 Brigade had moved to Mombasa and was preparing to rendezvous with 22 Brigade at sea. The operation to clear the island was called Stream Line Jane, and was in three phases. Stream was an assault landing by 29 Brigade to secure the port of entry at Majunga, 350 miles down the coast, south-west of Diego Suarez. Line was the advance by 22 Brigade from the beach head to the capital – Tananarive, and Jane was the landing by 29 Brigade at Tamatave, plus a diversion by a battalion of 7 (South African) Brigade and smaller temporary landings elsewhere.

Tananarive is about 360 miles from the port of Majunga, along a winding road with bush on either side, which crossed rivers and ridges of hills. It was important to defeat the French before the rains started in September and to deny them time to improve their defences. For its role in Jane, Dimoline organized his brigade into three Fighting Groups (FGs), each with a battalion, a gunner battery, a troop or more of SA armoured cars and a company of EA troop-carrying vehicles. Engineer detachments were added as necessary. The initial basic compositions of the FGs were as follows:-

1 FG – 1/1 KAR, plus a field battery of 9 Field Regiment RA

2 FG – 5 KAR plus 56 (U) Field Battery

3 FG – 1/6 KAR plus a field battery of 9 Field Regiment RA.

The first task was to seize two river crossings on the Tananarive Road, over the River Kamoro at mile 99 and the River Betsiboka at mile 131. It was allotted to 1 FG, who led with the SA armoured cars, followed by B Company 1/1 KAR, 145 Light Anti Aircraft Battery RA and a RE detachment.

29 Brigade went ashore north and south of Majunga before dawn on 10 September. By 7 a.m. the town had surrendered, for a British loss of five killed and nine wounded. At 4.15 a.m. the Forward Body of 1 FG began to go ashore at Red Beach, but the armoured cars stuck in the soft sand, compounding the delays that had already occurred in unloading. The advance eventually began with Lt King's platoon in the lead, then the OC, Major Dawson and the mortars, while the rest of the FG joined the rear of the column as they cleared the beaches. At 4 p.m. King reached and seized the bridge over the River Kamoro from a few *gardes indigènes*; Dawson followed. Meanwhile the rest of the FG were still getting ashore. By 9.30 Dawson and the advance guard were six miles short of the River Betsiboka bridge when they halted because of the darkness and because the use of the armoured cars' headlights would have forfeited surprise.

At 6.30 next morning the armoured cars reached the river to find that the bridge had been demolished. The centre span had collapsed into three feet of water when the main cables were cut; that apart, there was little damage. The French unsuccessfully attempted to bomb the bridge. By 10 a.m. two platoons of B Company and the mortars were over the river on foot and had cleared a bridgehead, and six askari had been wounded. The French lost ten killed, four wounded and thirty-seven captured. The bridge was repaired and the armoured cars were over by dusk. Twenty-four hours later the whole of the Forward Body had crossed, ready to resume the advance. This briskly-fought action set the tactical pattern for much of the rest of the campaign.

C Company 1/1 KAR was ashore by the afternoon of 12 September, with one troop of artillery, followed by the remainder of the FG on the next day. The Forward Body resumed the advance with three troops of armoured cars and Lt Hignett's platoon in the lead. Air reconnaissance had shown that the French were destroying bridges and building road blocks all the way to Tananarive. Dimoline closed up to the Forward Body and continually urged everyone to press on. C Company, commanded by Capt Robertson, passed through and took over the lead on 14 September, with the rest of the FG close behind, except for D Company, who guarded the bridge sites until relieved by 1/6 KAR. By 9 a.m. on 15 September Lt Col Macnab caught up with the Forward Body at the Kamolandy bridge, where the planking had been removed by the withdrawing French. A temporary deviation was made and by 1 p.m. they were across the river. Two hours later they reached Andribae, but were then delayed by a major demolition two miles south of the town. They were leaving the coastal plain and into hilly country.

The road blocks were cleared during the following morning and by 10.30 they reached the River Mamokamita at Anjiajia. The river was about 150 yards wide and the bridge spans had been cut at both ends. Although the river was fordable, the French held the crossings in some depth. In a flanking movement by two platoons Lt Fraser was killed and Sgt Odilo took over the platoon, captured a machine-gun post manned by a French crew and mopped up the left flank. For these feats he received the MM. Shortly afterwards 2Lt Palmer was wounded, but by 1 p.m. the action was over. Some of the opposition had been provided by Senegalese soldiers, who fought well here and throughout the campaign. On at least one occasion, they, using long French bayonets, fought against panga-wielding askari and lost. The total KAR casualties were Lt Fraser and four askari killed, 2Lt Palmer and seven askari wounded. A Company now moved into the lead.

During the night of 16/17 September the ford was made passable for vehicles. A and B Companies resumed the advance in the morning and took the airstrip at Marotsipoy by 4 p.m. The sappers set to work at once and twenty-four hours later it was able to operate as a forward support base. The next two days were spent in meeting and clearing road blocks. The objective was Ankazobe, but there was little fighting, although sixty-four stone-built road blocks obstructed the route. At 5 p.m. on 18 September the Forward Body was still five miles short of its objective. Six more road blocks were overcome early on the following day before they reached a demolished bridge a little way outside the town. Enemy positions on the far bank were shelled, mortared and machine-gunned; then A and B Companies attacked left-flanking. But the enemy had already withdrawn all but one platoon, which soon followed. A bridgehead was established quickly and a ford was made. This took some time, and it was the following morning before two armoured cars were across. A second ford was made, and by 7.30 D Company 1/1 KAR got its vehicles over and resumed the advance. The Forward Body pressed on to reach Fihaonana; the bridge decking had been removed, but it was replaced quickly by local timber and D Company moved into the village to find it empty. 300 miles had now been covered with little opposition, but Tananarive was sixty miles further on and a major battle was expected for it. Brigade Headquarters were at Ankazobe, together with 3 FG, which was in brigade reserve, having got all of their transport ashore.

A sharp battle for Mahitsy developed on the 21st. The Forward Body was delayed by a bridge demolition until 11.30 a.m. when D Company, some armoured cars and a troop of 28 Field Battery crossed, followed by the battalion's Operational Headquarters and A Company. An hour later they reached the outskirts of Mahitsy, where the leading armoured cars were fired on by a 75 mm gun and several machine guns. Mahitsy is at the base of a line of wooded hills, in a marshy valley with paddy fields. The French defences were on the hills, with excellent visibility. Capt J. Mulholland's D Company deployed off the road and attempted to advance with artillery support. They were soon pinned down by enemy fire, although Lt Willey's platoon captured a machine-gun post after gaining fifty yards, having had three askari wounded.

Neither air reconnaissance nor the Commanding Officer's own patrol could locate the enemy, who had ceased firing, so Macnab set up an observation post on high ground. At about 4 p.m. there was an outbreak of heavy firing, apparently from the hills and ridges on either side of the road. Only two hours of light remained, but he decided to attack, using A Company to support D Company on the right of the road and B Company, under Major Dawson, on the left. In the fading light Capt J.E.S. Clarkson rounded the enemy's left flank and the French retired for about 300 yards along the ridge, under cover of smoke from grass fires. Clarkson co-ordinated with D Company on his left and they resumed the advance, but the French had withdrawn. Meanwhile, B Company made a wide left-flanking movement to clear a small village. They captured a machine-gun post and, with the aid of artillery fire, silenced a 75 mm gun. B Company moved forward to take up defensive positions for the night. The KAR's losses were one askari killed and five wounded, but the enemy's casualties were unknown because of the grass fires burning along the front.

Dimoline was for pushing on at all costs. On the morning of 22 September A Company, on the ridge, captured two prisoners and two 80 mm guns before siting an observation post at the end of the ridge overlooking the causeway into Mahitsy. The causeway had been blown in three places and was covered by fire from enemy positions. The battalion's plan was to make a wide right-flanking attack by using B and C Companies, while A Company 1/6 KAR came forward to clear the road blocks. The attack was delayed by heavy shelling by two 65 mm guns that caused eleven KAR casualties before they were silenced. The attack began at 11.15 a.m; while it went in, Lt Willey's platoon of D Company, supported by artillery and fire from the armoured cars, attacked and overcame the machine-gun posts covering the causeway. One platoon of A Company crossed the demolitions and met a platoon of C Company coming back through the town from the south. A

Company 1/1 KAR and A Company 1/6 KAR then occupied the high ground beyond the town.

The enemy strength had been three infantry companies, supported by machine guns, mortars, a 75 mm gun, two 65 mm guns and two 80 mm guns. All the artillery pieces were captured, so that half of the enemy's artillery was now in British hands. The enemy also suffered heavy casualties and forty prisoners were taken. The French attributed the loss of Mahitsy to the bush fires, and thereafter took precautions against them. The KAR's success at Mahitsy and subsequently caused large numbers of the Malgash soldiers to desert.

During the night of 22/23 September D Company 1/6 KAR cleared a large roadblock south of the town, and at dawn two troops of armoured cars, A Company 1/1 KAR and one troop of artillery moved off, followed by the rest of the Forward Body. Eleven miles short of the capital they met some light enemy forces and cleared them with mortars and the armoured cars' guns. The enemy then fought a delaying action to allow their forces to withdraw south of the capital. Their position on a ridge covered the airfield at Ivato. A and B Companies moved forward and Sgt Walasi gained an MM when his platoon captured two field guns. The ridge was taken for the loss of one askari killed and three wounded.

The mayor of Tananarive met the Brigade Commander to surrender the town and airfield. Dimoline then formally entered the town, accompanied by Macnab and all of FGs 1 and 3 and cheered by an enthusiastic crowd. Between 24 and 26 September they occupied barracks in the town and guarded the airfield. 1/6 KAR took over from B and C Companies, Macnab became Commander Tananarive Area and 1 FG was broken up. In the thirteen days since they had landed, the casualties in 1/1 KAR were one officer and seven askari killed and one officer and thirty-one askari wounded. The enemy's remaining forces were fourteen infantry companies in the field, plus another five on garrison duty, none of whom had been engaged. 3 FG was at Majunga in French barracks and two companies of 5 KAR were still engaged in unloading at the beaches, hampered by a shortage of landing craft.

While 3 FG was preparing to continue the advance there was some tidying up to be done. TWEEDCOL, a column commanded by Major H.D. Tweedy (D Company 5 KAR, with armoured cars, mortars and a sapper reconnaissance party), patrolled north of Majunga to link up with a South African force from Diego Suarez. 19 KAR arrived and relieved 5 KAR, who had many of their vehicles ashore, but still not enough to maintain them when deployed for operations.

Meanwhile, 29 Brigade had occupied Tamatave and expected to link up with 22 Brigade shortly. 3 FG began its advance on 26 September; B Company 1/6 KAR relieved C Company 1/1 KAR on the Tamatave road, while B Company 1/1 KAR was replaced by Battalion Headquarters 1/6 KAR and two companies, together with three troops of armoured cars and a gunner battery on the Antsirabe road. The enemy were deployed in three lines at Behenjy. After artillery had shelled the first line, D Company 1/6 KAR advanced along the road with platoons on both sides, to find the first position abandoned. The second line was cleared later in the morning, when one askari was wounded; three Hotchkiss guns and ten prisoners were captured. Concentrations of fire from mortars, guns and the armoured cars made the enemy vacate the third position with slight loss.

Ambatolampy was occupied in heavy rain, where sixteen British men and women internees were freed. Also on 28 September, B Company rejoined the battalion, to be followed by C Company from Tananarive shortly afterwards. South of Tananarive the countryside was well wooded, with plenty of local material for road blocks. Malgash labour was used to clear them, but progress was slow. Two enemy companies were reported to be on a ridge near Sambaina on 30 September. A Moraine fighter attacked some of the forward troops, after which patrols moved on to the high ground, followed by Capt Ted Onslow's A Company left of the road. B Company was in reserve. At 5 p.m. when A Company deployed on a two-platoon front, they were mortared; 2Lt J.M. West was killed and five askari were wounded. After some small-scale attacks the action was called off until the morning, when Sambaina was found empty. Three Hotchkiss guns and three mortars, plus quantities of ammunition, were taken. Road blocks were still troublesome, with occasional rifle fire to harass the men engaged on clearing them.

Antsirabe was a pleasant mountain resort, a sort of hill station for the French. The bridge three miles north of the town was blocked by a steam roller, which was removed and Dimoline entered the town at 6 p.m. with his Advanced Headquarters and 3 FG. The main supply route was now 400 miles long and vulnerable at the river crossing, particularly at Betsiboka where the damaged bridge was breaking up, but the French made few attempts to disrupt it. On 4 October Commandant Machefaux and an infantry company that was fifty per cent Senegalese, moved through the bush to the right of the KAR and parallel with them. D Company laid an ambush near the lake, supported by armoured cars and mortars. It was a limited success; the enemy escaped, but they lost one French NCO, a light machine gun, thirteen rifles, a radio, grenades and ammunition, plus some secret papers. A second attempt to capture the wily Commandant also failed.

On 7 October the advance was resumed, directed at Ambositra, while 2

FG concentrated at Antsirabe. As only light opposition had been met since leaving Tananarive, strong defences were expected. On 9 October the enemy had a minor success after B Company 5 KAR had passed through B Company 1/6 KAR and taken the lead. A small concealed position, in hilly country and on a winding road, had remained undetected until the bulk of the Forward Body's transport had passed through, when a light machine gun opened up on the back of a 5 KAR signals truck, killing two askari and wounding eight others, two of whom died later. Road blocks were now more frequent. 2 FG, in the lead, concentrated north of Kiajna in the face of sniping and machine-gun fire. Ilaka was occupied by 2 FG at 9 a.m. on 10 October. One enemy company was identified in the hills south of the town, so C Company patrolled towards them along a high ridge, while A and D Companies concentrated on clearing road blocks. Lt Barkas' platoon located the left flank of the enemy position and attacked downhill to capture one French officer, one French NCO and six Malgash. D Company then struck at the enemy's main position, supported by mortars and the armoured cars. Thirty prisoners were taken; 5 KAR had no casualties.

The River Mania posed no obstacle as the enemy had abandoned the position after an air attack, so the KAR waded across without delay. But, fifteen miles beyond the river, a major position was thought to be covering Ambositra. On 12 October C Company 5 KAR, commanded by Major D.H.A. Kemble, set out on a wide outflanking move to the west, to take Ambositra from the rear on the following day. The objective excited a great deal of interest in 5 KAR as it was the centre of the wine industry. Kemble and his men had a strenuous march and an uncomfortable night, but these paid off next morning when, as their regimental history relates, "they descended the precipitous hillside at dawn on the 13th and took the town completely by surprise before ever the battle to the north had started." They captured five French officers and thirty-eight others. However, Kemble had no means of reporting his success, and Morcombe had to begin his attack without knowing if the backstop was in place. The countryside was well wooded, with several bridges on the winding road, and many ridges well suited to defence. A Company was leading on the 12th, with a section of armoured cars, when they met a concealed French 75 mm gun. The first armoured car was allowed to pass, but the second was engaged at 70 yards' range and received a direct hit, killing four askari and wounding ten others. Lt W.H. Williamson of A Company was seriously wounded. Sgt Seymour, also of A Company, collected some men, charged the gun and captured the crew. He received an immediate MM for restoring the position so promptly.

On the next day (13th) 5 KAR patrols located enemy on both sides of the road, at Amnbophitia to the west, and at Antanjona, as had been expected.

When 2Lt R. Corbet-Ward and a platoon of B Company made an initial reconnaissance in heavy mist, they were forced to retire with one askari killed and one wounded. While A Company moved forward on the road, removing road blocks and repairing bridges, the CO decided to clear the area to his right before attacking the main position. The attack was ordered, using D Company and Corbet-Ward's platoon from B Company, together with two mortars under the command of Lt Evans. As the attack was about to begin, A Company came under fire and eight men were wounded. The company went to ground until D Company's operation started. At 11 a.m. the attack went in, with fire support provided by a troop of 56 (U) Field Battery. They moved against well-sited trenches covered by interlocking arcs of machine-gun fire. The French fought hard; in the final assault 2Lt Corbet-Ward and three askari were killed. The position and eighty-two prisoners were in 5 KAR hands shortly after noon.

For the attack on the main position, D Company of 1/6 KAR reinforced 5 KAR. A reconnaissance aircraft reported that Kemble's company was in position and A Company moved forward, cleared a hill and was then held up in some paddy fields. Two enemy companies were thought to be ahead. D Company went forward to join in the attack, arriving by 1.30 p.m. Artillery registered during the afternoon and at 5.15 the first major shoot of the campaign began, firing over 1,000 rounds in half an hour and causing large-scale (mainly Malgash) desertions. The hill was finally cleared when Major Tweedy led a 5 KAR Company and D Company of 1/6 KAR in an attack. The 5 KAR History records that "enemy bugles were heard sounding what seemed remarkably like 'Cookhouse' and the enemy could be seen evacuating the positions not already overrun." Although some enemy withdrew to the east and none fell into Kemble's trap to the west, over 200 prisoners were taken. KAR casualties for the action were one officer and four askari killed, one officer, one BOR and ten AORs wounded.

A Company 5 KAR and D Company 1/6 KAR cleared the battlefield on 14 October, while B Company moved forward to Ambositra and C Company helped to clear the road. Heavy rain hampered movement and slowed repairs to bridges, but A Company entered Ambositra on 15 October, followed by 3 FG the following day. Patrols detected some enemy movement on the high ground south of the town. The road runs through sheer rocky hills, with the ridge of Andriamanalina to the west and the high bulk of Ambabahambala to the east, culminating in a feature called "The Knuckle". Air reconnaissance reports showed that the passage between the hills was covered by enemy artillery, mortars and machine guns. The enemy position was very wide, with the flanks protected by isolated posts. It was also deep, but it was held by only two companies, one on each side of the road. The artillery strength was unknown and the enemy might reinforce the position. Dimoline called forward 3 FG, ready to attack on a wide front. Patrols had identified routes to the east and the west of the enemy. The Andriamanalina feature was the first objective, as it commanded the country further south. Accordingly, Dimoline decided to attack the front and the right of the enemy's position, while 1/6 KAR outflanked to his left to cut off his retreat. To support this wide outflanking movement, A Company 1/6 KAR became porters, carrying ammunition, mortar bombs and rations.

At 2 a.m. C and D Companies 1/6 KAR set off, led by Major Robson, battalion 2ic. After two hours they came upon an enemy artillery observation post, but thick mist obscured the enemy's position, necessitating a change of plan. C Company (Capt "Toto" Mans), with a detachment of mortars, was to move to the high ground to the left of the enemy's last known position, and then to march along the hills west of the track, followed by the rest of the battalion. At 7 a.m. they bumped a machine-gun and rifle position, which they captured for the loss of an askari killed and three wounded, one of whom died later. The enemy withdrew with C Company following, until they bivouacked for the night in a village where they obtained chickens and rice from the local people. D Company had followed, to the north of the road, moving in short bounds and delayed by occasional sniper and mortar fire. Radio contact was lost and the Battalion Intelligence Officer had to go forward to locate C Company. The remainder of the battalion moved up to join Robson in the pouring rain. While 1/6 KAR was busy, 5 KAR reconnoitred the enemy's right flank. Two of A Company's prisoners pointed out the enemy's positions and artillery fire was directed on them. The enemy strength was still estimated at two companies, one on either side of the road, supported by two 75 mm guns, mortars and machine guns. At 4 a.m. on 15 October the rest of 1/6 KAR began to close up to C Company; one AOR was wounded by sniper fire en route. The CO changed the line of advance from the exposed high ridge to lower ground to the west, to avoid a French ambush. Having got near Antanimenalava by 1.45 p.m., orders were issued for a night approach march. B Company went forward at 5.30, but it was well after midnight before the rest of the battalion arrived at the forming-up point, having moved in single file. Early in the morning of 18 October A Company and the carrier platoon set off to get round the enemy's right flank.

The plan was for B and C Companies of 5 KAR, on the opposite flank, to capture the northern end of the Andriamanalina Ridge, and then for A Company to take "The Knuckle". Next, all three companies would push inwards, rolling up the enemy positions and moving towards 1/6 KAR. C Company 5 KAR was to provide fire support, then move forward along the road as the advance progressed. At 4.30 a.m. on 19 October all three batteries of the brigade's artillery opened fire for what proved to be the greatest concentration of the campaign. After fifteen minutes 5 KAR attacked on both flanks. They had been hidden by mist and position after position was taken, often with little difficulty, frequently from a flank or from the rear. By 5 a.m. B Company had secured the high feature on the ridge and then swept down with D Company behind them. A Company took "The Knuckle" almost without opposition and by 8.15 the battle was over. Commandant Brunot surrendered, followed shortly afterwards by Colonel Metras.

Thereafter B Company made the running, cutting the central road. C Company moved to set up a roadblock further south, while the rest of the battalion followed B Company. The leading company reached Metras' Headquarters at Ivato, where the radio and seven men were captured and some French doctors gave hot tea to the victors. Refreshed, B Company then advanced again, taking over 100 prisoners, three machine guns and two 75 mm guns that had been sabotaged by their crews. By 10 a.m. they had linked up with C Company 1/6 KAR. C Company 5 KAR moved down the road covering sappers clearing road blocks and came under fire from four machine guns. Two platoons attacked, expelling the enemy in thirty minutes. It only remained for 5 KAR to clear the battlefield while 3 FG took over the lead. For no casualties, the KAR had captured some 700 prisoners, including fifteen French officers and 166 French soldiers, two 75 mm guns and quantities of ammunition. The French had eight companies left and no guns. B Company 1/6 KAR resumed the advance and soon captured a 35 mm gun and 100 rounds of ammunition. They came under fire before dusk, when a sporadic action was fought which petered out in the mist and the darkness. The main effort continued to be clearing roadblocks, usually of stone and felled trees, harassed by isolated snipers and the occasional machine gun. The next village was passed through without opposition, and 3 FG moved on towards Fianarantsoa, thirty-six miles ahead, through hilly country with plenty of good defensive positions. The French had selected the line Mandalahy–Alkamisy for their next stand. The Brigadier's plan was for 3 FG to continue the advance while 2 FG made a wide out-flanking movement via Vohiparara. This was carried out by TWEEDCOL, consisting of B and C Companies 5 KAR and two troops of armoured cars. The enemy's position was in depth along a series of high, bare ridges with wooded valleys in between, occupied by two companies to the east of the road and one to the west. The grass had been burned off, there was no camouflage and they had been attacked from the air for several days. The main attack was mounted by A and C Companies of 1/6 KAR, plus a mortar detachment, and led by Major Robson, the 2ic. They made an approach march through six miles of swamp and bracken during the afternoon and formed up in some paddy fields ready to attack at dawn.

On the other flank, TWEEDCOL bumped a small enemy force that withdrew when B Company outflanked it. C Company then encountered the main enemy position and made an immediate attack that ended with a bayonet charge. Four askari were wounded; the enemy lost fifteen killed, seven wounded and nine taken prisoner. At 2 a.m. TWEEDCOL reached the western end of the enemy's position, where they captured three French and nineteen Malgash in their beds. By dawn they had secured Colonel Tricoire, who surrendered the entire position. Total enemy losses were thirty-one Europeans, sixty-five locals, Hotchkiss guns, light machine guns and mortars. An unknown but considerable number of Malgash had deserted. The way was now open to the former capital of Fianarantsoa, where Lt Col St Lawrence surrendered the town. The 5 KAR historians present a somewhat less formal scene. They describe the entry of the town as "a bit irregular, as it was led by the 2ic and the Intelligence Officer in a most disreputable old truck, loaded with squawking ducks and geese". 5 KAR spent two days at Fianarantsoa before resuming the advance. Many of the enemy had been bypassed during the rapid advance and it took several days to round up almost 800 prisoners and to evacuate them.

Annet, the Governor General, and the senior military commander were at Ihosy, behind a trail of road blocks. Air reconnaissance had discovered a naturally strong position at Vatova. While 1/6 KAR took over garrison duties at Fianarantsoa, with A Company at the port of Manakara, 2 FG resumed the advance, led by A Company 5 KAR and attached troops. They came up to some defensive works being constructed near Antanandava, where the country opened out into something like moorland. For the first time the carriers could go into action, under Lt Watson. The enemy was forced to withdraw after a smart skirmish, not least because shooting by the carriers had set fire to the grass. They abandoned some very useful motor cars which were promptly annexed for company commanders' use, and one Hotchkiss gun. Lt D. Evans of the mortar platoon was shot in the forehead; the sniper had used a telescopic sight. It was the more tragic as he, who had been a particularly effective mortar officer, was the last casualty of the campaign. A Company continued to clear the enemy from the woods in heavy rain, eventually finding the French artillery staff hiding in a monastery. D Company led during 3 November, encountering road blocks; C Company took over from them next day, patrolling towards Vatova, where a defensive position was located. The enemy was thoroughly dug in on the hills flanking the pass that was the approach to Ambalavao, their positions connected by underground passages. The ground was open on all sides and the enemy had extensive fields of fire over all the likely approaches. The plan was for C Company under Major Kemble to attack from the right flank, while the remainder of the battalion moved rather gingerly down the main road.

The artillery bombardment began as C Company reached their start line, but then bugles were heard, sounding the "cease fire". When the guns closed down, C Company advanced at the double down the hills to the French Headquarters, where Capt Meyer explained that he had been informed by telephone that Gen Guillmet had ordered the cease fire. The "bag" was fifty-four French and 220 other prisoners. The telephone line to Ambalavao was down, but an important message was said to be awaiting Dimoline there. On the following morning a small force of 5 KAR, with two staff officers and a Newsreel cameraman walked into Ambalavao to receive Guillmet's request for an armistice, pending the opening of negotiations. Annet sent his ADC by plane from Ihosy to negotiate. 2 FG entered Ambalavao unopposed and at one minute after midnight on 5 November the armistice was signed by Dimoline and the ADC. It was exactly six months since the landing; the 5 KAR History notes, "Under French law a campaign must be six months in duration to qualify for a campaign medal."

The French had intended to make a fighting withdrawal throughout the length of the island, but they seemed to lack the will to do so. The KAR, by contrast, had covered 600 miles in six weeks, against an enemy that was usually on ground of their own choice and at almost twice their strength. They captured nearly 3,500 prisoners, sixteen field guns, fifty heavy machine guns and many other weapons. Casualties were four officers and twenty-three askari killed, seven British and seventy-five Africans wounded.

7 South African Brigade returned to South Africa and 27 (NR) Brigade continued to garrison Diego Suarez, while 22 Brigade Headquarters were established at Antsirabe, with battalions at Manakara, Ihosy and Tulear. The battalions rotated through Tananarive, spending six to eight weeks there at a time, and otherwise did jungle training in anticipation of going to Burma. The "battle drill" pamphlet was translated into Swahili and proved very effective. Due to a shortage of British platoon commanders many of the platoons were now commanded by African sergeants. The training programme included sand table models, tactical exercises without troops and field exercises. The culmination was an exercise directed by the Brigade Commander, with 5 KAR, 56 Field Battery RA, and C Squadron 1/3 KAR Armoured Car Regiment. The "enemy" were 1/1 KAR.

In the early stages of the operation, when Diego Suarez harbour facilities were still damaged and most cargos were landed over the beaches, troops were used for beach clearance duties and road repairs. They had to be relieved of these tasks as soon as possible. By 7 May part of 5 Group Headquarters Pioneer Corps, led by Lt Col D.J. Dean VC TD, had set up a civilian labour office and had taken over the Malgash prisoners of war and 100 Arab dock labourers. Up to 2,000 Malgash POWs daily did dock and other labour jobs; later they were released from the French Army and employed as civilians, allowing a POW camp to close.

Dimoline had read about some Indian troops who had marched seventy miles in twenty-two hours, and gave Toto Mans three weeks to train his company of 1/6 KAR to beat it. At the end of the three weeks of tough preparations, fifty men, with Mans and the British CSM, set out one night, led by an askari with a hurricane lamp. The lamp man twisted his leg and fell out after the first mile, but the remainder went on to cover eighty miles in twenty-one hours, a record they held for many years. Guarding POWs was a heavy commitment. The 1/6 KAR solution was to build a POW cage in the centre of their camp to hold the Senegalese. After a while a *sous officier* asked to see the CO. The 2ic interviewed him; the substance of his request was that he and his colleagues had seen the relationship between the British officers and the African soldiers. They had decided that things were far better in the British Army than the French, and they all wanted to transfer. Unfortunately, this was not possible.

In June, 1943, the brigade moved to Diego Suarez, as the island was now controlled by the Free French. Gen Le Gentilhomme became Governor General; 5 KAR provided the Guard of Honour at his installation. In May, 1944, 22 Brigade returned to Kenya.

The 5 KAR historians' summary of the campaign was:-

"The campaign had been a good one, with no undue hardship and plenty of fresh poultry to be had for the asking, but it was not a pleasant undertaking, as one could not help feeling that one ought not to be fighting erstwhile allies, and that casualties on both sides were a needless waste of gallant lives."

Mauritius passed to Britain under the Treaty of Vienna in 1815. It had its own garrison unit, the Mauritian Regiment, officered in the main by French Mauritians. They were smartly turned out but had little field experience. It was decided, in 1943, that they should be toughened up in Madagascar before going to Burma. Because of threats from Japanese submarines the island could not be left unprotected, and 17 KAR replaced them in November, 1943, after an unpleasant voyage. The Mauritian Regiment reluctantly embarked and left for Madagascar. 17 KAR were no more welcome in Mauritius than 2 CAR were at the beginning of the century, and matters were not improved when they were deployed in "aid of the civil power" in circumstances that were close to strike-breaking. That apart, it was a pleasant posting.

The Mauritians had at least as uncomfortable a voyage to Madagascar as 17 KAR had. They disembarked at Diego Suarez at the hottest time of day and paraded in full kit for over an hour. Their CO then decided that they would march for three hours to their camp. This was a disaster, as the men were unfit and things were not improved by the inability of officers to communicate with their men. The camp was infested with snakes, scorpions, cockroaches and large centipedes. It was probably an accident that set the jungle on fire; the flames spread to the camp. The Mauritians refused to obey their officers; technically it was a mutiny, but like other such incidents, it could and should have been avoided.

1/1 and 5 KAR were called in to restore order, bolstered by British ranks from 3 and 1/6 KAR to provide additional control and to restrain any excesses. It took a day to isolate the ringleaders, who were guarded by 3 KAR. 1/1 KAR guarded the rest in the remains of their camp. An underlying cause of the mutiny was the presence of Nyasa troops in Mauritius while they were away from the island: shades of 1900.

Chapter 8

BURMA

"The uneasiest of all our imperial possessions."
Maj Gen James Lunt

The East African forces came to the Burma front late, having dealt with the aftermath of the Ethiopian campaign and Madagascar. As it had been calculated that East Africa could sustain one division in the field in Burma, 11 (EA) Division, consisting of 21, 25, and 26 (EA) Brigades, was provided, together with two reserve brigades (22 and 28). The two "independent" brigades had few supporting Arms and Services, and were intended for use as reinforcements, according to circumstances. Instead, changing strategy and a shortage of manpower led to them being committed to battle at different times and in different sectors of Burma. The East African Scouts were detached from 11 (EA) Division to 81 (WA) Division (15 Corps) in the Arakan from January, 1944, until June. 11 (EA) Division moved into the Kabaw Valley under the command of 33 Corps from August, 1944, and reached Shwegyin, on the east bank of the Chindwin, in December, 1944. 28 (EA) Brigade were tasked to simulate 11 (EA) Division in the next phase of the operation, from January until April, 1945, on the right flank of 4 Corps. 22 (EA) Brigade was the last in the field, initially in 25 (Ind) Division (15 Corps) in Arakan. They were then under 26 (Ind) Division and finally with 82 (WA) Division, all between November, 1944, and May, 1945.

Burma, now called Myanamar, is over 261,000 square miles (677,000 square kilometres) in extent, about the same size as Spain. Clockwise from the north, in 1939, Burma's neighbours were China, French Indo-China (now Laos), Siam (now Thailand), then the sea, finally India (but now including some of Bangladesh). The country is mountainous, with four south-flowing rivers as the main axes of communication. From east to west they are the Salween, which forms the boundary with Siam for part of its course, the Sittang, 250 miles long, over 700 yards wide at the mouth and very fast-flowing in the monsoon. Third is the Irrawaddy; its major tributary, the Chindwin, joins it fifty miles west of Mandalay. About 800 miles of the Irrawaddy are navigable. The Chindwin starts in India and is navigable by shallow-draft boats for much of its length. The capital city of

Burma, 1941–1945

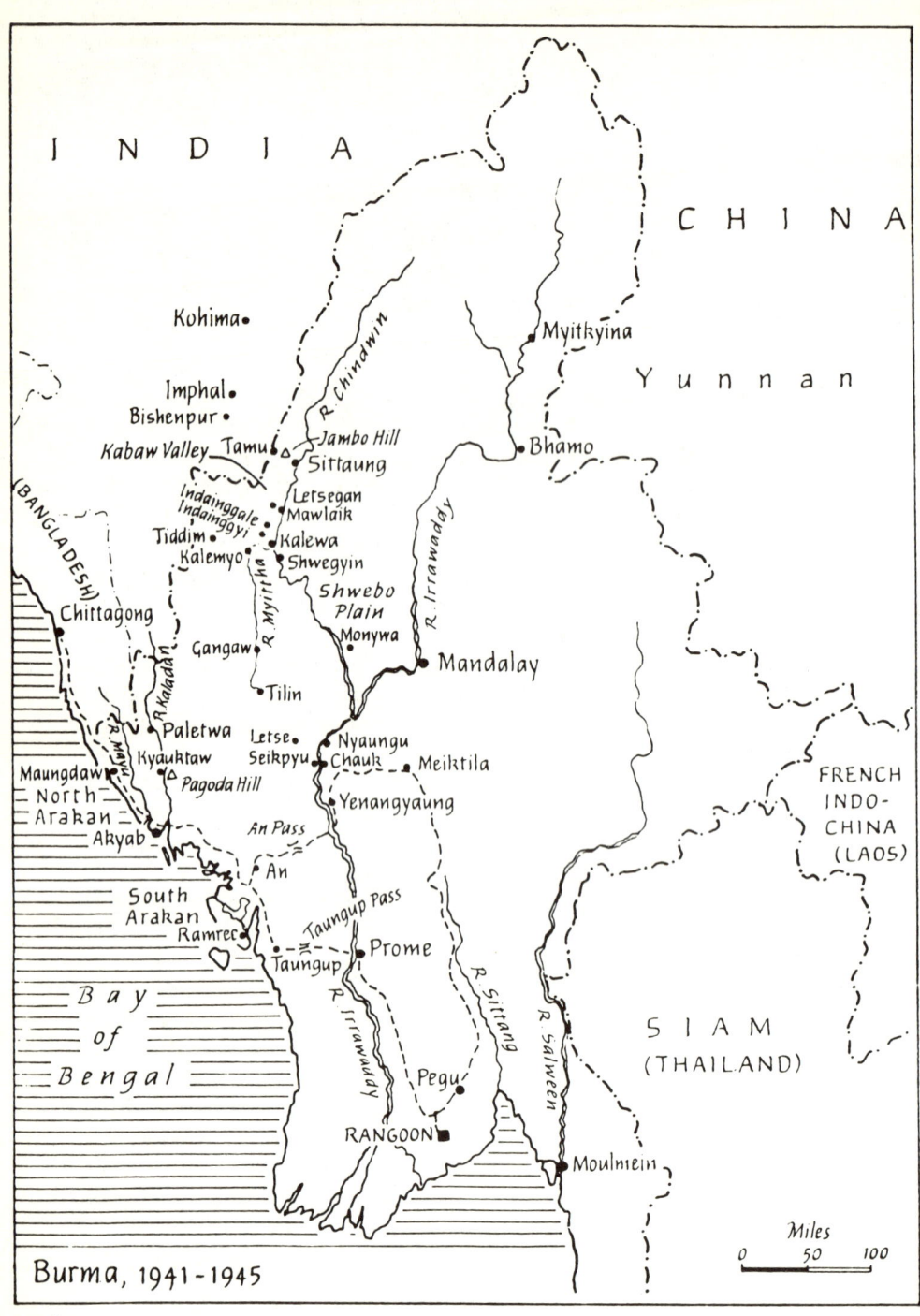

MAP 9

Rangoon (now Yangon) is between the estuaries of the Irrawaddy and the Sittang. There are three seasons; from October to February it is relatively cool and dry. This is followed by two hot, dry months, then the monsoon from May to October. The rainfall is mainly in the monsoon, and reaches 200 inches per year in places; yet the area of the oil fields, Yenangyaung, is almost desert. Half of the land surface is forest of various kinds, according to altitude. It was (and is) thinly populated.

Britain acquired Burma in three phases between 1824 and 1866. It was administered from India until 1935, after which the Governor reported direct to London. British interest was mainly in trade, for which peace was enforced, roads and railways built, river traffic developed, minerals (particularly oil and gems) and timber extracted. Despite the many innovations, there was a shortage of all-weather roads, some of the railway was single track and metre gauge and there were few airfields. Those that existed were mainly on the route from India to Singapore. In 1941 half the population (10 million) was Burmese; the rest were Karens, Shans, Kachins, Nagas and Chins, plus minorities of Indians, Japanese, Chinese, Malays and Siamese. The Burmese Rifles were four battalions strong at the outbreak of war; there were several battalions of Burma Military Police with a Gendarmerie-type rôle and two British regular battalions.

In 1941 Britain did not want a war with Japan, as she was already overstretched in her struggle against the Axis powers. Japan had been at war with China since July, 1937, and her forces were well trained, equipped and battle-hardened. War with Japan became inevitable when USA and Britain used oil sanctions against Japan to force her to withdraw from China and Indo-China, and the Japanese navy had to start using their oil reserves. Vichy France allowed Japan air bases in French Indo-China, and in November 1941 General Chiang Kai Shek warned Churchill that Japan would attack from Indo-China to cut the Burma Road, on which China depended for US aid. His request for air support led to the build-up of the American Volunteer Air Force in Burma and China.

When negotiations failed, with only fourteen months of oil stocks left, Japanese landed troops on the Kra Isthmus and attacked the US fleet at Pearl Harbor on 6 December, 1942. Next day they invaded Malaya and two battleships (HMS *Prince of Wales* and HMS *Repulse*) were sunk by Japanese bombers. Responsibility for the defence of Burma changed many times; finally it reverted to India on 25 February, 1942. When he returned to India as CinC, Wavell found that the troops he had counted on for the defence of Burma had gone to Malaya, and the two African brigades he expected from East Africa had not yet left there.

Burma had four strategic benefits to the Allies; it was a buffer zone for the defence of India, the logistic support for China ran across it (China was tying up twenty-eight Japanese divisions), it had oil, and its airfields were part of a chain to reach Singapore. A relatively small Japanese invasion force attacked from Siam and gained complete surprise. 17 Indian Division lost most of its equipment and almost ceased to be a fighting formation. The key facilities in Rangoon were destroyed and it was evacuated, disrupting supplies to China. Lt Gen William (Bill) Slim took over command of Burma Corps, (BURCORPS) on a hasty posting and promotion from Iraq, and extracted them by the longest retreat in the history of the British Army. This was 900 miles, mainly on foot, hampered by refugees. They fell back to the Yenangyaung oil fields, which were destroyed in April, and then towards India. With them went 38 (Chinese) Division, while units of the Fifth Chinese Army reached India by the Ledo route. Joe Stilwell, the US general commanding the Chinese, marched out to Imphal. Six Chinese divisions moved back to Yunnan Province, pursued by strong Japanese forces. BURCORPS destroyed most of its heavy equipment at Shwegyin on 10 May and made for the Kabaw valley, to struggle up 90 miles of misery, sickness and decay to Tamu; but from the experience Slim realized the valley's potential as an axis of advance. BURCORPS reached Imphal in the monsoon, on 20 May, and was dismantled. The Chinese went to Ramgarh, where United States forces re-equipped and trained them. On 16 April Wavell had ordered his Joint Planning Staff to start working on the re-occupation of Burma.

India became a base for the recapture of Burma, Malaya, Singapore and the Netherlands East Indies. American railway units improved the Assam railway system and roads were built. The lessons of the earlier campaign were applied at all levels, including the Quetta Staff College and in training formations, but the internal political and the Internal Security situations in India were distractions, particularly Gandhi's "Quit India" campaign. A Japanese fleet controlled the Bay of Bengal until they were redeployed to the east after the American Pacific Fleet destroyed the Japanese carrier force in the Battle of Midway. This opened up the prospect of taking the island of Akyab and its airfield. The operation was a failure; Slim was recalled from leave to take charge and stabilized the front. Commanders then changed rapidly. In May General Sir George Giffard took over from Irwin at Eastern Army and began to examine the options for taking the offensive. Before a second Arakan offensive could be launched, Slim went to command XIV Army at Calcutta on 16 October. Lt Gen Phillip Christison replaced Slim at 15 Corps.

Allied strategy agreed at the Quebec Conference in August, 1943, was for a series of amphibious operations under South East Asia Command (SEAC) and Admiral Lord Louis Mountbatten. No heavy fighting was expected on the mainland once a land route to China was open. Mountbatten moved his Headquarters to Kandi in Ceylon, with Stilwell as Deputy Supremo in addition to his other responsibilities. The three service Commanders in Chief were Somerville, Giffard and Peirse. Giffard became CinC 11 Army Group; Stilwell and Slim should have been under his command, but Stilwell refused and proposed instead that he should report to Slim for the early stages of the operations. This meant that Slim dealt with Mountbatten direct when Chinese or American issues were involved, but it ensured that there was a single land forces commander for the early phases of the forthcoming operations.

SEAC's tasks were to engage Japanese forces as closely as possible to create a diversion from the Pacific theatre, where offensive operations were in hand, and to improve contacts with China by developing the air route and a road through North Burma to connect with the earlier route into China. Most of their plans were abandoned when Stalin insisted on a "Europe first" policy, and the landing craft were withdrawn from SEAC. Chiang Kai Shek would not move his Yunnan Armies without the major amphibious assaults, which left only an overland advance by 15 Corps in the Arakan, Stilwell's advance on Myitkyina with Wingate's Long Range operations in support, and an advance on the Central front by 4 Corps to the Chindwin.

The Japanese had been substantially reinforced and had planned an offensive in two parts. Their main thrust, called U-GO (Plan C) was directed at Imphal, with a secondary operation into Arakan, known as HA-GO (Plan Z), to destroy 15 Corps and to draw British reserves away from the main battle. The Arakan offensive began on 4 February, 1944, but the attack in the Central sector was delayed until 6 March. In Arakan the infiltrators were trapped between 5 (Ind) and 7 (Ind) Divisions south of them and two Divisions (26 and 36) striking down from the north, under the command of 15 Corps (Christison). 81 (West African) Division protected 15 Corps' left flank in the Kaladan Valley, forty miles east of 7 Division, with difficult country between them. The reconnaissance unit for 81 (WA) Division was the East African Scouts, who were the first East African troops into action in Burma and the first to sustain casualties.

81 Division's own reconnaissance regiment had become a Corps Troops unit; the East African Scouts were less orthodox. They had been raised in April, 1942, for coastal protection in East Africa, as the Coast Irregulars and armed with captured Italian weapons. In March, 1943, they became the East African Scouts and their role changed to scouting, "to move ahead and on the flanks of our forces, to obtain information on enemy dispositions, to raid his lines of communication and to harass his flanks while protecting our

own." Emphasis was on bushcraft, and they were not subjected to rigid military discipline, as that might inhibit their natural aptitude. They were recruited from Nyasaland in addition to the original areas of South Tanganyika and Kenya. The officers were selected for their experience with Africans and knowledge of African languages. The CO was Major T.C.C. (Chippy) Lewin (later Lt Col Lewin OBE MC); the only regular officer was P.A.N. Lindley of the Buffs, a Sandhurst graduate who had arrived at Mombasa with 399 other "Imperial" subalterns in February, 1941. After service with 10 and 4/6 KAR, he joined the EA Scouts in the Arusa/Moshi area, where the rest of 11 (EA) Division was concentrated. Here they were issued with .303 rifles, Bren light machine guns and some Tommy guns, but no support weapons. There was one radio set for the CO and one truck for the Quartermaster. The officers included an unfrocked priest from South America, an Argentinian farmer's son, a diamond miner from Tanganyika, a Scot from Nyasaland, two settlers from Kenya and a Medical Officer.

They had travelled to Colombo by troopship with the rest of 11 (EA) Division and trained at Kandy. The routine included route marches, games and fitness training, soccer, hockey and rugger, more route marches and everlasting weapon training. The final exercise was a fifty-mile march over rough country in three days, carrying all their needs. When they reached Comilla, where Slim's Headquarters were, they learned that they were to be attached to 81 (WA) Division, which they considered "a bit flattering" and were all the more keen to show that "they were worth knowing".

In late November and early December, 1943, 81 (WA) Division (Woolner) moved into the Kaladan valley, totally on air supply. Their Nigerian Brigade was with Wingate, and the two remaining brigades were, in the Japanese view, "a comparatively lightly equipped enemy". The EA Scouts joined 81 Division on 29 January, 1944, near Paletwa. They had four rifle companies, but no Support or Headquarter Company, no porters and only two-thirds of their officers, due to sickness. They began operations with little delay; B Company was detached to cover the gap between 5 and 6 Brigades and the main body joined 6 Brigade to cover its eastern flank. They made many long, tough patrols carrying all they needed. Sometimes they lived on tea alone, supplemented by occasional meals from local people.

6 Brigade (less 1 Gambia) followed the east (left) bank of the Kaladan, and 1 Gambia moved down the west bank, 5 Brigade, with B Company of the EA Scouts, struck inland to follow the Pi Chaung, a sizeable waterway that flowed south, parallel to the Kaladan. The going was very difficult, across thick, jungle-clad hills. On 20 February, when trying to cross the Pi, B Company came under fire from the far side and lost Capt Sladen, the Company Commander, one AOR killed, and three askari wounded. Later,

when crossing the Pi, a boat capsized with the loss of one AOR and several weapons. B Company rejoined the rest of the EA Scouts to advance down the east bank of the Kaladan, with 1 Sierra Leone and 1 Nigerian Regiment following. On 16 February their patrols reached the Kyauktaw–Thayettabin road and moved on to occupy Pagoda Hill, opposite the town of Kyauktaw, on 18 February.

Pagoda Hill, on the east bank of the Kaladan, gave observation over Kyauktaw on the west bank, which 1 Gambia had taken. To increase pressure on the Japanese, who were starting to withdraw, the Corps Commander ordered GOC 81 Division to extend his front towards the River Mayu, forty miles westwards across difficult territory. This involved moving some 10,000 men back across the Kaladan, 400 yards wide at its narrowest, in a variety of craft including local dugout canoes and rafts made from folding bridge pontoons. The confirmatory order included an estimate that the enemy could concentrate a force of up to five battalions in the Kaladan valley, but not before mid-March, and gave the additional task of denying Kyauktaw to the enemy, and made the thrust westwards subject to it. The EA Scouts were left on Pagoda Hill, as it was thought troops could be switched back from the main body if Kyauktaw was threatened.

The EA Scouts had patrolled east and south of Pagoda Hill for some days and knew the area quite well. They had several contacts with the enemy, with casualties on both sides. A successful attack was made, with artillery support, on 23 February, four miles south of Thayettabin, and was their deepest penetration. When the majority of the Division left, C Company was on Pagoda Hill, D Company at Thayettabin, and Battalion Headquarters with A and B Companies at Binapara. Patrol clashes continued, and D Company successfully ambushed a body of Japanese at 1930 hrs on 1 March with four LMGs, but were mortared and then assaulted shortly afterwards. They withdrew to join the rest of the battalion on Pagoda Hill at 0430 hrs on 2 March. The attackers were about two-thirds of a battalion strong, with an infantry gun. Pagoda Hill was jungle-clad and jutted high out of the flat plain. The golden pagoda on the summit at its southern point was visible for miles; it was not an easy position to hold.

Hearing the fighting, GOC 81 Division sent 1 Gambia back to the Kaladan. Just before dusk Lewin reported that he was being hotly attacked from the east and shelled from the south, but thought he could hold out. But the shelling unsettled some of the Scouts, who did not stay in place. At first light one company and then the rest of 1 Gambia crossed the river, but the open paddy fields were covered by enemy fire and they sustained casualties in an attempt to advance up a chaung. They eventually reached the hill in the dark and CO 1 Gambia dispersed his troops widely around it, by means of his map. Artillery support was not available and mortar support was limited. It was too late for them to dig in and they were attacked during the night and early morning. CO 1 Gambia concentrated C Company of the Scouts at the base of the hill to the east and reinforced Lewin, on the top of the hill, with a platoon of 1 Gambia. In the night of 2/3 March Japanese infiltrated from the north, cut off D Company 1 Gambia and attacked up the north side of the hill, while C Company 1 Gambia was attacked from the east.

The war diary of the Scouts reads:-

3 March, 0630. Japs attacked in large force from Lammadaw up north slopes of Pagoda Hill. Assaults twice driven back completely with the use of grenades and LMG fire. Final assault of Japs at 1100 hrs successful due to the effect that ammunition was almost exhausted, and unit had to withdraw to the south to 1 Gambia position. During this action Lt Mathison was wounded. CQMS Hutchinson was wounded in the foot and multiple grenade wounds in the side. Lt Robinson also wounded, multiple grenade wounds. It was in this action that Capt Stevenson who organized the defence of the hill was awarded the MC and CQMS Hutchinson the MM.

On 2 March 1 Gambia, less some detachments, withdrew to the south of the hill, and a second battalion arrived from the south, having crossed the river lower down. The survivors of the Scouts withdrew over the Kaladan some four miles south of the hill by 1800 hrs. At first it was feared that about 150 of them were missing, but by 4 March many had been located with 1 Gambia and 1 Sierra Leone. The two officers who had been reported missing were found; Lt Robinson, although wounded, swam the river with his equipment, Tommy gun and binoculars. 81 (WA) Division then concentrated and withdrew north of Praing Chaung. Brig Jeffreys wrote, "The main thrust went straight to the top of Pagoda Hill, held by Lewin and his Scouts" and "the Scouts had a very hard time in a type of set-piece battle for which they had not been trained. Many of them, particularly their officers, fought gallantly." The GOC commented on the unit's successes in long-range patrolling and in hit-and-run tactics, but thought the shortage of British officers had caused them to become exhausted from constant patrolling. The unit was now down to about 400 men and was reorganized on a three-company basis. It received a draft of reinforcements, but postings out reduced them to twenty-two Europeans and 197 AORs in three companies, able to provide fourteen patrols, each of one European, five armed askari and three porters. They continued with long-range patrols and a detachment

Crossing the Sangana River in the forest.

A bivouac on the moorlands; Mount Kinangop in the background.

42. Royal East African Navy. HMEAS *Rosalind* entering Mombasa Harbour, October, 1958.

43. Guard of Honour for HM The Queen Mother at Mombassa Airport, February, 1959. The officers of the Guard are Lieutenants B. Mitchell and M. Sutcliffe.

operated in the 6 Brigade area for a few days towards the end of March. Two more drafts left, so that by 18 April there were just 100 all ranks. They guarded an airstrip for a while before leaving for Comilla, where they disbanded on 31 July. (Moyse-Bartlett says they moved to Ceylon and were disbanded there in November.) Pat Lindley thought the Scouts were an experiment that did not succeed, and he doubts the premise on which it was based. Perhaps the unit was over-specialized, and no one can guarantee that a specialized unit will not get drawn into a set-piece battle or other rôle for which it has not been trained and equipped. As Pat observed "training is everything".

The Japanese 15 Army attacked in Operation U-GO, which was intended to last no more than three weeks, aiming to reach Imphal, Tiddim and Bishenpur. 33 Division struck 17 (Ind) and then 29 (Ind) Division, having advanced up the Kabaw valley, but could not break into the Imphal Plain. The three other divisions positioned themselves to attack Imphal from several directions. Slim's counter-attack plan was in four phases; concentration of forces, attrition, counter-offensive and pursuit. Concentration included bringing from Arakan the formations that could be spared; he particularly wanted 5 (Ind) Division and 3 Special Service Brigade. On 14 March Slim alerted Mountbatten to the urgent need for transport aircraft to move them, which the Supremo diverted from the China airlift without authority. He had instructed Giffard to start moving troops from Arakan on 5 March, a lack of response to which led to Giffard's removal a few months later. Mountbatten was certain that his intervention had been critical, and wrote to his wife on 30 March, "If the battle of Imphal is won it will be almost entirely due to Dickie over-riding all his Generals".

On 10 July the Japanese began a general retreat; to the east Stilwell had reached Myitkyina and had secured Slim's left flank. Both Giffard and Slim wanted to follow up the Imphal victory and pursue the defeated Japanese. Mountbatten agreed and authorized the first two phases of a land offensive. His own orders were changed shortly afterwards, to the recapture of all Burma at the earliest date, while continuing to improve access to China. On 24 July, 1944, Giffard ordered Slim to prepare for a land operation in December. The first task was to clear the way to the Chindwin, using Stopford's 33 Corps, while the rest of XIV Army refitted and retrained. For this Stopford had 5 (Ind) Division and 11 (EA) Division, plus the irregular Lushai Brigade.

11 (EA) Division, usually known as the Rhino Division because of its divisional sign, had formed in East Africa in February and moved by brigades to Ceylon, both as part of the island's garrison and for jungle

warfare training. It had three infantry brigades – 21, 25 and 26; there were eleven infantry battalions, three each from Uganda and Nyasaland, two each from Kenya and Tanganyika and one from Northern Rhodesia. The infantry were:-

21 (EA) Brigade; 2 (N) KAR, 4 (U) KAR, 1 NRR

25 (EA) Brigade; 26 (TT) KAR, 34 (U) KAR, 11 (K) KAR

26 (EA) Brigade; 22 (N) KAR, 36 (TT) KAR, 44 (U) KAR

Divisional Protection Battalion; 13 (N) KAR

Divisional Reconnaissance Battalion; 5 KAR, who joined the Division at the end of August.

The Division had a full complement of supporting Arms and Services, all manned by Africans with British officers and some British warrant officers and NCOs. A major set-back had been the loss of almost all of 301 Field Regiment EA Artillery, when the troopship *Khedive Ismail* was sunk after they had been at sea for a week. She was in a convoy with four other troopships and some escorts. The regiment was 850 all ranks, but some of the junior officers were transferred to another ship and their cabins allocated to female passengers. On 12 February, near the Maldives, a very large Japanese submarine fired four torpedoes, two of which hit the *Khedive Ismail* and she sank in two minutes. The escorts depth-charged the submarine to the surface and used their Oerlikons to stop the crew reaching the deck gun, which was 5.5 inches calibre; the escorts had 4-inch guns. The submarine was sunk by torpedoes. The few survivors from the *Khedive Ismail* included one of the ten Kenyan Women's Auxiliary Service members and 113 of the 787 gunner askari, some after several hours in the water. Lt Guy Yeoman was reunited with nine members of his troop in Ceylon. The surviving gunners were posted to 303 Regiment and an Indian field regiment was attached to make good the Division's deficit in artillery.

The Division was commanded by Maj Gen C.C. Fowkes CBE DSO MC. Training continued until June/July, 1944, culminating in Exercise "Tayari". The Division moved from Ceylon by sea to Chittagong and on to Imphal, where they joined 33 Corps. The Corps' task was to advance to the Chindwin by two routes; 5 (Ind) Division was on the right (west) flank, to clear the Tiddim road and 11 (EA) Division was to advance down the Kabaw valley, nearer the Chindwin. The Kabaw had been a principal Japanese escape route. The Division was to clear the valley and reach the Chindwin by a diversionary thrust to Sittaung, then a push straight down the valley to link up with 5 (Ind) Division at Kalemyo. They had the advantage of surprise, as the Japanese had expected an advance down the Tiddim valley only. They received jeeps and four-wheel-drive 30 cwt trucks; one gunner regiment converted to 4.2 inch mortars and Indian stretcher bearers joined the Division.

The Division replaced 23 (Ind) Division at the beginning of August, when 25 (EA) Brigade (Brig N. Hendricks) relieved an Indian Brigade at Tamu, at the head of the valley, and was under command of 23 (Ind) Division for a short period. On 5 August Headquarters 25 (EA) Brigade and 34 (U) KAR (Lt Col C.D. Trimmer) entered Tamu. There was utter chaos; most buildings were rubble, and dead and dying Japanese were everywhere. Attempts to provide medical care and food for the Japanese survivors were not well received, as most of the enemy preferred death to surrender and wished to take as many of their opponents with them as possible, using hand grenades. The rotting Japanese corpses were dealt with by the very busy hygiene squads. Heavy rain delayed the movement of artillery, but 25 Brigade advanced towards Sittaung on a narrow track thirty miles long which the enemy disputed at every opportunity. Their orders were to reach and cross the Chindwin, then move south down the eastern bank to cover the Division's left flank. The advance was led by 11 (K) KAR (Lt Col T.H. Birkbeck), the youngest battalion in the Division. They had formed at Jinja in February, 1941, and had guarded POWs at Nyvasha.

MAJOR-GENERAL C.C. FOWKES CBE DSO MC COMMANDER OF 11 (EA) DIV.

143

Initially they were multi-national, but were now all-Kenyan. They had been inspected by Mountbatten earlier and the askari had been impressed by his similarity to King George's face on the coinage; with the King's brother to lead them, they could not fail. They encountered some Japanese on 6 August, when a patrol killed ten of the enemy and captured two more before they met a river 150 yards wide. This was crossed with the aid of two assault boats and an overhead wire left behind by the enemy; jeeps and trailers were floated over in tarpaulins. B Company located a bunker defended by about thirty or forty of the enemy, cleared it and the advance resumed, while stragglers were rounded up. On the following day artillery fire removed some opposition, then came Jambo Hill – a heavily wooded feature to the left of the track, held by a company of Japanese. D Company assaulted after a bombardment by 59 Field Battery, at 10.40 a.m. on 18 August, and the enemy abandoned the position leaving several dead. A and D Companies attempted to trap the survivors and killed two of them. C Company sent a patrol to a small hill east of Jambo Hill and broke up an imminent counter-attack, taking a machine gun before moving further east. Jambo Hill cost the lives of Major R. Fulton and one AOR, while Lt W.R. Norbury and fifteen askari were wounded, most of them by grenade fragments. The enemy lost thirteen killed. Lt Norbury received the Division's first MC and two askari were awarded MMs. Fulton's death shocked the askari. Like the other officers, he had been wearing black face paint, but his rôle as leader had made him conspicuous. One Wakamba asked why his officers had to go in front and be killed. He thought officers should confine themselves to indicating enemy locations and then get out of the way until the askari had dealt with them. That way, he explained, they would still have their officers.

The action was watched by the GOC, who asked a wounded officer "if it hurt". On being assured that it did, the general said that he knew, having been wounded four times during the 1914–18 war. The GOC's presence and his congratulations were great motivators for the askari. The wounded were carried to pick-up points by Indian stretcher bearers; the ambulances were driven by American Volunteer drivers. Despite the battalion's losses, Jambo Hill was an encouraging start to the campaign. Slim issued an Order of the Day on 31 August saying that 11 (EA) Division had lost no time in showing itself to be of the highest fighting quality, congratulated them on their achievements to date, but left them in no doubt that great things were expected of them.

Because of the monsoon 11 KAR were put fully on to air resupply. It was very strenuous to get artillery units forward, mainly because of the fast-flowing chaungs, and considerable time was spent cutting logs to corduroy the roads. The first attempt at a supply drop was unfortunate, as a sack of rice or flour in free fall killed a soldier of A Company. The incessant heavy rain of the monsoon not only drenched everyone continuously, it made observation for both aircraft pilots and gunners difficult and at times impossible, so that co-ordination with attacking troops was rare. Many infantry attacks had to be made without full support, although poor visibility occasionally gave opportunities for surprise. Bridges over chaungs, constructed with great effort, were washed away in moments. The preparation of food was always difficult, while good sleep was rare. The main health hazards were malaria and scrub-typhus. The latter was controlled by the detection of infested areas, when the mites were killed by spraying. Sores, foot rot and stomach complaints were also prevalent. In the first month of operations about 1,000 men were evacuated from the valley for medical reasons, of whom 750 were Africans.

Patrolling forward, 11 KAR still leading, enemy positions were located about 2,000 yards beyond the last of the Jambo Hill features. The targets were bombed, shelled and mortared for two days while the brigade was concentrated and an attack planned, but the enemy withdrew. 34 KAR took over the lead and 11 KAR became the brigade reserve, which involved road building and towing artillery. 34 KAR secured two river crossings; at the second they killed four of the enemy. As the KAR moved towards the Chindwin, fifteen miles away, Japanese resistance hardened and they were shelled for the first time, when 26 KAR took some casualties on 29 August. There was stiff fighting at the last natural obstacles before the river, two steep cliffs south of the track. A and D Companies 34 KAR made wide right-flanking moves on to the two cliffs from the south, with D Company on the first and A Company on the more easterly obstacle. The cliff tops were narrow ridges about ten feet wide, but the early morning mist concealed the attackers until it was too late for the enemy machine guns to do much damage. Thereafter, advancing on a two company front, 26 KAR reached the Chindwin at Sittaung to find the place smashed to pieces, littered with abandoned vehicles and equipment, dead everywhere, two sick Japanese and a mass of black flies. A Company 26 KAR remained in Sittaung while the rest of the brigade improved the roads and an Anglo-Burmese liaison officer helped to organize boats, porters and elephants. Assault boats and outboard motors came forward and on 8 September A and B Companies 26 KAR crossed the 500-yard-wide Chindwin. It was flowing at about five knots and there was a great deal of flotsam, including logs that could have stove in the fragile boats. Patrolling began on the east bank, with a few minor clashes with the enemy. One boat with a machine gun fitted was christened HMS *Rhino* and scored some successes, earning 26 KAR Mountbatten's congratulations for their "naval engagements".

The Corps Commander sent a message of appreciation: "Heartiest congratulations . . . to all ranks for getting across the Chindwin – the first troops to do so". He complimented them on "the enterprise, determination and endurance shown". On 20 September 26 KAR (now commanded by Lt Col J.P. Carne, previously 2ic 34 (U) KAR) handed over their bridgehead to an Indian formation and, with the rest of 25 Brigade, began to withdraw to Tamu for rest and training. This took ten days as they built roads on the way. On average ten trees were used for every yard of road, cut down and trimmed to length by pangas. Getting the first bridgehead over the Chindwin had cost the brigade forty-five casualties, against 412 lost by the enemy, of whom 253 had been killed.

The remainder of the Division had begun their advance down the main valley towards Kalemyo and Kalewa, with 36 (TT) KAR (Lt Col N.C. Robertson-Glasgow) leading and 13 (N) KAR (Lt Col H. French) on the left flank. Despite its justly hideous reputation, the Kabaw looked beautiful. Gerald Hanley wrote of the blue mountains and the darker jungle, with patches of paddy fields so bright green as to be almost sickly. But the dark green gloom under the arches of the teak trees seemed to isolate them from the rest of the world. Rain fell for fifty-five days non-stop, amazing askari from semi-desert lands. The valley was about twenty miles wide, but the tracks were narrow and hemmed in by teak trees, so most of the division were employed on road construction and maintenance, particularly corduroying.

To the East Africans' right, in the Tiddim valley, 5 (Ind) Division reached Milestone 100 on the road to Kalemyo and Kalewa by early September. Air supply was working well for both formations; there was no sign of the Japanese air force and the supply planes flew without escorts. The struggle was against small groups of Japanese troops, usually unco-ordinated; but the main efforts were against the elements and the mud. Some of the enemy were now surrendering, influenced by psychological warfare pamphlets, but others still had the determination and resource to fight on, and land mines were encountered from time to time. A truck ran over one near the river at Sunle, killing three askari. Mules also suffered from the mines, some of which remained from BURCORPS' retreat up the valley two years before.

The advance paused to allow units to close up, while 3 KAR patrolled forward and on both flanks. A Company took a dug-in position defended by two machine guns, killed one and captured one of the enemy, and recovered a British three-inch mortar. A brigade base was established at Sunle and a dropping zone established; the first air drop was on 25 August. 44 (U) KAR (Lt Col T.H.S. Galletly) went into the lead south of Sunle and crossed the river with some difficulty on 26 and 27 August, then met a series of minor outposts. They captured two members of the Japanese Indian Forces when clearing them, then pushed on, but the Sunle river had become impassable and the GOC slowed down operations for a while. Elephants and mules became the principal means of resupply for several days, while the entire brigade maintained the tracks. 22 KAR (Lt Col K.H. Collen) and 44 KAR then moved forward in bounds and a bridge was built over the Nam Pawla Chaung. Patrolling forward continued, with minor brushes. In one of these Lt N.D. Smith of 22 KAR was severely wounded and died soon afterwards. The western side of the valley seemed clear, but there were still enemy between the valley and the Chindwin.

5 (K) KAR (Lt Col P.A. Morcombe) became the reconnaissance battalion, and four sections were attached to 26 Brigade for patrol duty. One patrol lasted for five days and returned to report the enemy in strength at Mawku. The GOC decided to attack, but the roads had to be improved first for supporting Arms to get forward. The monsoon then intensified, destroying a ferry. Some troops were put on half rations for a while, but air supply enabled them to survive. By contrast, many of the Japanese were reduced to eating grass. When the weather improved somewhat on 24 September 22 KAR, with two companies of 44 KAR under command, located some of the enemy late in the day; after reconnaissance, they were ready to attack on 26 September. The first move was by C Company 22 KAR and led to the deaths of Lt G.A.C. McCormick and his sergeant, but Cpl Asifa took command of the platoon and overran the objective, which was mopped up by Lt D.J. Payne's platoon. Twelve Japanese were killed, most by grenade and bayonet, and eight escaped. The two-company position was well stocked and parts of it were newly dug. Two companies outflanked the position and set up road blocks to the south, killed ten Japanese and captured several more. These successes made the enemy withdraw, and by the end of September the first phase of the Division's move down the valley was over.

21 (EA) Brigade (Brig J.E. Macnab) entered the valley with 4 (U) KAR (Lt Col J.E.D. Watson) leading, and concentrated at Witock. After a few days of patrolling and road work, they began to clear the area Mawku-Mawlaik before moving towards the Chindwin. Under command were 17 Battery Mountain Artillery, a sapper reconnaissance party, a field ambulance company and mule transport. A Company 4 KAR leading moved off on 12 September to meet a chaung about thirty-five yards wide, which they crossed by means of a flying ferry hastily constructed by the sappers. There were some minor clashes on 21 and 24 September; the second involved about thirteen Japanese. CSM Bevan and one AOR were killed, Lt T.F. Eaton and three askari were wounded. Ahead was a high steep ridge about

600 yards long and some thirty yards wide called Leik Hill, where the enemy had dug in; it had been called "the main gateway to the Chindwin". Both sides patrolled aggressively and about fifteen Japanese unsuccessfully attacked B Company during the night of 28/29 September. The enemy then jittered them for the rest of the night; an officer and five Japanese soldiers were found dead outside the position at first light. The ridge was steep, with almost precipitous sides, covered by tangled jungle, and the top was a knife-edge. Patrols could not learn much as visibility was bad, but air strikes and mortar fire softened up the position. The Japanese cut the battalion's telephone cables and passed some bogus messages in English. On 4 October two platoons of D Company got into the enemy's position, but found only a few foxholes and other defences. The patrol was attacked as it withdrew, but drove off the enemy. On 10 October the main attack began with an air strike, followed by an advance by C Company. Half way up the hill rifle and machine-gun fire made them pause. Following mortar and artillery bombardments, a further attack at 11.48 a.m. came against a sheer cliff fifteen feet below the summit, and Watson called off the attack. Casualties were one soldier killed, one European and twenty-six askari wounded.

The next attempt was fixed for 22 October. In the interim the Brigade was concentrated and extensive patrolling gathered more information about the Leik position, including ways round it. Using one of these, a patrol by 2 KAR reached the Japanese supply route, killing one and wounding one of the enemy, to break the battalion's "duck". 4 KAR had decided against another frontal assault. Unfortunately they had to attack with no artillery support, except for B Company's operation against a secondary feature, because the intervening ridges prevented the 3.7 inch howitzers hitting their targets. The weather suddenly improved and the troops, who had been sodden for weeks, went into action in the dry. 4 KAR made a wide swing to the right and attacked from the south, up the lines of the two narrow ridges, with D and A Companies on the left ridge and B Company on the right, concealed by a smoke screen. Heavy fighting cost several casualties, including Major A.C.G. Aspinal (OC D Company) and Cpl Sebi Alijabu, who was the first to reach an enemy bunker. PSMs Yoweri and Ali Farajalla distinguished themselves by their gallantry. A Company charged to the sound of bugles and Acholi whistles and, undeterred by enemy fire, reached their objective, but D Company was held up by enemy fire from the enemy's main position. Lt P.G.W. Anderson of 2 KAR, an attached mortar FOO, aided by Sgt Sparkes and his mortar askari, knocked out a troublesome sniper to clear the way for two platoons to advance and destroy the bunker with an explosive charge. When D Company reported its success, C Company passed through them, but were held up by machine guns in an area that gave no scope for manoeuvre and where only one platoon at a time could be deployed. They halted for the night and tried "jitter" tactics on the enemy in the bunker. Next morning the enemy had gone, apart from a small rear party who were disposed of quickly. In the bloodiest fighting of its war experience, 4 KAR lost nineteen dead and 102 wounded. Japanese losses are not known, but many weapons were captured.

2 KAR then moved against the Longstop feature that had resisted B Company 4 KAR on the previous day, almost surrounded it and called down air strikes, shells and mortar fire. Patrolling was aggressive and PSM Selika Walani was awarded the DCM for his gallantry when attacking a particularly resistant enemy post. A and D Companies attacked the main position on 29 October, unsuccessfully it seemed, but the enemy pulled out during the night. Next morning twenty enemy corpses and one wounded man were found in the position. Concurrently, 1 NRR patrolled west of Mawku and threatened Japanese communications with Mawlaik. These moves assisted C Company 2 KAR, who had met another naturally strong enemy position on some steep cliffs. Two air strikes and an unsuccessful assault were followed by occupation of the position on the following morning. 2 KAR then took over the general area of the cliffs. By this time the battalion had lost seven askari killed, three Europeans and thirty-three askari wounded. D Company secured the mouth of the Mawku Chaung with only minor casualties and the Chindwin was crossed for the second time when Capt D.H. McCalman took a patrol along the east bank, met a few enemy stragglers before lying up at night, then recrossed the river on the night of 5/6 November. Shortly afterwards 1 Assam Regiment took over left flank protection. After a few brisk encounters, 4 KAR reached Mawlaik with Lt T.F. Eaton's platoon in the lead, to find it almost deserted and badly damaged by bombing. 4 KAR prepared an airstrip for casualty evacuation, while 2 KAR occupied the high ground south of the town and explored an island that had been a Japanese base. 5 KAR (Lt Col T.C.C. Lewin vice Lt Col Morcombe, evacuated sick) came under command of 21 Brigade on 5 October. Earlier they had fought a series of engagements, notably the Battle of Letsegan.

5 KAR had spent three weeks road building, collecting air drops and making bashas after leaving the base camp at Tamu on 18 September. They had concentrated at Chinyaung by 15 October and were allotted mule transport. B Company 22 KAR had located a strong position on a hill named Point 3069, a mile and a half east of the Letsegan Rest House. With D Company 44 KAR and 101 Mortar Battery of 304 Field Regiment under command, but less C and D Companies who were on detachment, 5 KAR marched seven miles to the objective on 17 October. They began intensive

patrolling next day in the thick forest, to locate the defences and to know the ground. On the 20th there was an air strike and next day D Company and the mortars rejoined the battalion. The track from Letsegan to Mawlaik went over a saddle between two hills, both of which were occupied by the enemy. Point 3069 was on the right, with a steep escarpment confronting 5 KAR. Lewin's plan was for B Company to attack the westerly hill while two companies under the 2ic (Draffan) took Point 3069 from the rear. They advanced on the morning of 22 October, screened by mist. This cleared in time for an air strike on the western feature, but B Company was slow to follow it up because of some flooded chaungs. A mortar bomb had wounded five of them, including the Company Commander (Townley), and the airstrike had made some good fields of fire for the Japanese. A platoon led by PSM Kipchoge of D Company broke into the position and Ssgt Bull's platoon charged the trenches. The enemy ran down the hill to the rear, into A Company's field of fire. The western feature was then abandoned. Letsegan was the toughest battle fought by 5 KAR in Burma. They lost fourteen African soldiers killed or who died of wounds, four officers and seventy-nine askari wounded. Lewin was awarded the MC and Ssgt Bull the MM.

5 KAR then joined 21 Brigade, as described earlier, to relieve 1 Assam Regiment on the left bank of the Chindwin. The 2ic, in command of DRAFORCE, took two companies over the river in tarpaulin rafts stiffened by bamboo and stuffed with grass. These were useless for mules, so the mortars were left behind. By the evening of 15 November A and B Companies were across and deployed, while sufficient Burmese porters had been recruited for the advance to begin. The porters, of all ages and both sexes, worked in return for food and one eighth of a parachute per person per day. 2 KAR were on the west bank with a Special Boat Section under command. This was a reconnaissance section, but they engaged a Japanese motor boat. In two canoes and using their LMGs, they killed eight and captured one of its occupants. 1 NRR went into the lead on 19 November, after 2 KAR had a series of engagements, and soon came up against a strongly held position north of Nanmawke Auk. 4 KAR closed up in support, but the enemy pulled out before they were attacked. 1 NRR remained on the west bank of the Chindwin but the rest of 21 Brigade crossed over to joint DRAFORCE on the eastern bank. Jeeps and trailers were rafted down the river from Sittaung, while some assault boats and outboard motors were flown in to them.

In the main Kabaw valley 26 Brigade moved down to Yazagyo, where enemy resistance stiffened, leading to several weeks of intensive patrol activity with 36, 44 and 22 KAR taking turns in the lead. 6 Platoon of B

150

Company 36 KAR had a typical encounter on 15 October when, having fought their way through an ambush and killed eight of the enemy, the platoon commander, CSM J. O'Hara, was shot by a Japanese soldier who had feigned death. B Company continued to advance down the track while A and C Companies dealt with enemy on Point 1107. Two platoons of D Company overran the main position, but they came under fire from defences in depth and withdrew. The OC (Major J.E. Frith), CSM Birtwistle, Sgt Brown (22 KAR mortars) and several askari were missing, three askari were dead and fourteen wounded. An attempt to find the missing men on the next day cost the lives of one officer and one AOR.

A brigade battle was planned; 44 KAR was to make a wide swing round the enemy's right, cross the track behind them and probe northwards, while 36 and 22 KAR were to maintain pressure on the enemy from the north. 44 KAR got on to a feature called Neck in the enemy's rear by 23 October, having crossed a chaung in some small boats and killed seven Japanese in a dugout. The brigade had been reinforced by a squadron of light tanks (C Squadron, 7 Light Cavalry) and a company of Indian infantry (D Company, 3/4 Bombay Grenadiers). The plan was to pass 22 KAR through 36 KAR, bomb the position from the air and shell it by 303 Field Regiment, then for 22 KAR to attack the succession of hill features. But the first flight of Hurribombers struck the troops forming up, killing seven askari, wounding twenty-nine and putting a tank and some vehicles out of action.

B and D Companies 22 KAR made little progress on the first day because of a series of well concealed strong points. However, the tanks (Stuarts, thirteen tons with a 37 mm gun) and the Bombay Grenadiers did better on the right of the road, destroying a bunker. The air photographs used to plan the attack did not show all the details of the ground, and some replanning was necessary. Next day patrols found that the enemy had abandoned two small but awkward hills during the night, but a third, called Pun, was still held and the Grenadiers were machine-gunned from it. A Company came forward to assist, with tank support, and attacked through thick undergrowth under showers of grenades. CSM K.F. Sucking was killed when commanding the left flank platoon, and Sgt Akim Muhango took over. The assault was held up by fire from a bunker and the reverse slope. Until these had been dealt with, further progress was unlikely, so the forward elements of 22 KAR withdrew and artillery fire was called down.

A second attack began at 3.30 p.m.; Lt Mills was killed in the early stages, while 8 Platoon was caught up in a fire fight with some snipers on the right flank. C Company attacked on the north side of the chaung, and Lt K.E. Nidd gained his objective with few casualties; he was awarded the MC. However, counter-attacks backed by grenades fired from positions hidden in the long grass compelled two platoons and the Company Commander (Blaydon) to withdraw. The action at Brown Hill was remarkable for the courage and determination of Cpl Wisiki Bauleni of 22 KAR, who was awarded the DCM. His citation is quoted in full:-

"On 27 October, 1944, No DN 9327 Cpl Wisiki Bauleni was the leading section commander of 13 Platoon, C Company, during C Company's attack on Brown Hill Burma. Within 100 yards of the start line Cpl Wisiki was wounded by a grenade for the first time. Undeterred, Cpl Wisiki continued to lead his section forward, being wounded twice more before finally reaching his objective. In spite of weakness and loss of blood from three wounds, Cpl Wisiki refused to be evacuated and continued to direct the fire of his section on to a Japanese counter-attack which was then launched. This attack was then beaten off, but in the course of it Cpl Wisiki was wounded for a fourth time and only when unconscious was he evacuated."

The battalion had lost one officer, one CSM and eleven askari killed and two officers and fifty-three soldiers wounded. 36 KAR were brought forward for the next attack, on the morning of 30 October with the aid of two air strikes and an artillery barrage. The enemy had withdrawn, leaving five dead. 22 KAR then passed through and, with 44 KAR, two troops of tanks and two batteries of 302 Regiment, resumed the advance against a series of delaying positions. In one of these actions on 1 November Lt A.J. Scott was killed, but his platoon disposed of thirteen of the enemy. C Company 44 KAR, on the left of the road, drove about fifty Japanese from half-dug positions and captured a gun, a machine gun and a British 3 inch mortar. On the other side of the road 22 KAR were blocking a Japanese escape route from the Tiddim valley. Fifteen Japanese got away, but they left most of their equipment.

5 (Ind) Division had reached Tiddim itself and the two Divisions became mutually supporting, while 11 Division was able to operate on a two-brigade front for the first time when 25 Brigade moved up on the right. A column was formed to strike down the Bon Chaung to cut the Kalemyo–Kalewa road. 36 KAR got into difficulty meanwhile, when they came to three strongly defended hills in thick jungle. They took the first one, but were without artillery support and exposed to heavy fire from machine guns and grenades, losing Capt B.W. Sellar, Lt G.I.W. Grier and eleven askari killed, while Major Onslow and thirteen askari were wounded. The action was broken off and, in view of its losses, the battalion was employed as the Divisional Headquarters Protection Battalion, being replaced by 13 KAR on 12 November.

Since entering the valley the Division had been free from Japanese air activity. Most air strikes had gone in without disruption except by the weather, and air resupply had been similarly unaffected. Casualty evacuation by air had become routine, even by gliders. This involved very careful preparation of the landing strip for the glider's arrival, as there was only one chance for the aircraft to land safely. While the casualties were loaded the American crew arranged for take off. This involved laying out a tow rope for 200 yards ahead of the glider, with a loop at the far end held up by two posts, ready for the "snatch". A Dakota then flew low over the glider and engaged the loop with the hook at its tail, to drag the glider into the air very smoothly. Light aircraft (Moths and L5s) were used, fitting in whenever they could. Behind the battlefield long-range bombers made interdiction raids on enemy supply routes through Siam. Being used to air supremacy, it was a shock when, on 8 November, twelve enemy aircraft struck the Honnaing area, causing casualties, mainly in 11 KAR. The battalion lost its Medical Officer (Capt L.S. Adler) and Sgt Mwanza was mortally wounded, while Capt H.R.C. Curtis and 2Lt H. Maclean were both wounded.

22 KAR had a couple of days of hard fighting, supported by 303 Field Regiment and a squadron of tanks, around Moshi. As the day went on Japanese resistance increased and some minor withdrawals were necessary to allow the artillery to register before nightfall. Japanese artillery shelled the battalion during the evening and the following day 25 Brigade started its move down the right flank towards Kalemyo. To keep abreast, 22 KAR had to take Indainggale, which involved reaching the line of the chaung just north of the town. C Company was in thick bush when they came across thirty Japanese with four machine guns. They attacked quickly with tank and artillery support, and two companies went round a flank to get behind the enemy's position. The enemy withdrew when they heard the tanks, and the battalion reached the chaung early next morning. 22 KAR continued east of the road with 13 KAR on the west, both battalions with patrols well out and plenty of artillery support. The aim was to convince the Japanese the main attack on Indainggyi would be from the north. An attacking column was formed, designated SKEECOL, under the Divisional Commander. It was led by Lt Col T.H.S. Galletly and consisted of 44 KAR (less B Coy), 26 KAR, C Company 5 KAR and two mule troops. They were to move down the Bon Chaung and round the rear of Indainggyi to cut off escape to the east. C Company 5 KAR and 44 KAR made rapid progress, bypassing minor opposition until coming on about fifty Japanese on a hill. After two days of reconnaissances and preparatory moves, a three-company attack found the position abandoned. C Company 5 KAR then reached the road, bumped into thirty of the enemy and killed seven. A battalion road

block was set up to seal off escape to the east, which killed twenty-eight Japanese in the next two days. An enemy attempt to neutralize it by gaining control of a neighbouring feature was defeated by a two-company attack by 44 KAR, supported by guns and mortars. A Company removed a Japanese position from a small hill at the second attempt and with some assistance, and cleared the east bank so that mule convoys could reach 44 KAR, who were short of rations. B Company had a stiff fight for a small hill, took it on 23 November, saw 25 Brigade advancing down the road towards them and hastened to link up.

While 26 Brigade advanced on Indainggyi, 25 Brigade had ten days of rest and reorganization before going to the Yazagyo area as Divisional reserve, but also tasked with local patrolling. On 9 November they were ordered to advance to and capture Kalewa, which involved crossing the Neyinzaya Chaung. There was open parkland and tall elephant grass along the line of the chaung, and the weather improved with the end of the monsoon. This meant better artillery and fighter-ground attack support, drier and more solid roads, better food supply, better health; but also increased Japanese resistance, including suicide groups to sabotage convoys, tanks and supply depots. Headquarters Japanese 33 Division had been at Indainggyi, and elements were still near. Some of the Japanese were recent arrivals in Burma, better fed and equipped than those met earlier in the campaign, and showed more fight. Instead of living on grass they now carried mess tins full of rice and vegetables. The askari enjoyed the rice, and enemy mess tins were valued prizes.

The askari had tried all sorts of rations, including a field service ration of maize meal, meat, ghee, vegetables, potatoes and minor items. A light-scale ration was issued to jungle patrols, portable and ready use. A variant was the lightweight jungle ration, sealed in a tin like a sardine can, that contained mainly high energy foods. There was also the eight-man composite ration pack, in a can that could be used to cook the food. The Africans and British disliked the soya link, a form of sausage that was monotonous, tasteless and almost ubiquitous. Hatred of the soya link was illustrated when Mike Calvert's brigade flew in as part of Wingate's force: "soya link" meant failure and "pork sausage" was used to report success.

11 KAR took the lead in the 25 Brigade operation, while 34 KAR kept the lines of communication open. A Company 34 KAR was surrounded at one stage, and fought its way out after seven hours. 11 KAR linked up with 5 (Ind) Division on 13 November, when a patrol met some 4/7 Rajputs. During that night a road block manned by A Company 11 KAR on the Tiddim road trapped about two companies of Japanese. The askari held their fire until the enemy were within five yards of the position, when they

killed four and wounded an unknown number. The next day, 14 November, the COs of 11 KAR and 4/7 Rajputs entered Kalemyo. The one Japanese soldier remaining in the ruins was killed by an askari's burst of Sten gun fire. While 11 KAR, with a battery of 3.7 howitzers under command, took over the defences of the town, the rest of 25 Brigade concentrated at Segyi.

The Japanese would not stand and fight long enough to be destroyed, but only sought to delay the advance. Indainggyi had been blasted, then occupied without opposition. 25 Brigade moved on Bon Chaung with 11 KAR in the lead, supported by a troop of tanks and a platoon of Bombay Grenadiers; the group was commanded by the 2ic, Major E.C.T. Wilson VC. His CO recently remarked that there was only one disadvantage to having a VC as 2ic; it made it impossible for him to duck. 34 KAR unsuccessfully attacked a group of old Japanese bunkers recently reoccupied by about seventy enemy, then an air strike hit B Company, killing four and wounding nineteen. Despite this, 11 KAR crossed the Bon Chaung and their patrols met some of SKEECOL soon afterwards. This made the Japanese retire to the Myittha River gorge, leaving most of their artillery and transport behind them. The Kabaw Valley was clear of the enemy and 11 Division had linked up with 5 (Ind) Division; the East Africans had achieved the main part of their task. SKEECOL was broken up and 26 KAR reverted to 25 Brigade.

The next step was to establish the Chindwin bridgehead. 21 Brigade was pushing down the east bank; if they reached the Shwegyin–Chaungzon road, the Japanese might fall back and not defend the Myittha River gorge and the approaches to Kalewa. However, this was not to be, and 25 Brigade started to clear the thirteen-mile-long gorge between the mouth of the Bon Chaung and the Chindwin. Several close ridges ran north–south, the road was on the north bank of the river where there was little room for a substantial force of infantry and there were few suitable gun positions. Most of the bridges had been destroyed and there were mines in abundance. The mines accounted for a bulldozer and two jeeps, as well as the tracks of three tanks. 11 KAR were halted by a road block in the early afternoon. Finding three positions strongly held, the leading company withdrew while the artillery bombarded and the remainder of the battalion laagered for the night. On the south bank 34 KAR made good progress despite heavy going, and found an RAF pilot who had been shot down three days earlier. An attack down the road on 26 November was unsuccessful and cost two tanks; it was called off to allow the artillery to take over. On the south bank, next day, 34 KAR moved forward to get ahead of the enemy on the north bank, while C Company 11 KAR approached the enemy across the steep ridges to the north. The Brigade Commander decided to attack on the following morning, taking advantage of the progress made and the intelligence collected by 11 KAR. 26 KAR came forward for the attack, with B and D Companies left-flanking and the other two on the road to exploit success. Initially D Company was in reserve, but later moved up on B Company's left because of the width of the front. B Company reached the road but D Company was held up by machine-gun fire and they got no further that day. But the enemy pulled out during the night and a B Company patrol led by PSM Hassan Yayoyi Ali, which had lain up near the enemy's position overnight, found it abandoned next morning and moved back along the road to meet 26 KAR. 26 KAR took over the lead and at dusk reached a chaung where the gorge widened, and were shelled. They were ordered to cross the chaung at once. A Company got a patrol across to the north with some difficulty, while D Company crossed lower down. The remainder of the battalion then closed up on the west bank.

Progress was difficult as the tanks were confined to the relatively level ground near the road, while the steep ridges left of the road restricted infantry manoeuvre and prevented artillery fire from reaching the reverse slopes. Lt W. Poppleton was mortally wounded while leading his platoon. Mortar fire was used when possible, but communications were not easy. At one stage a No 48 set was used, working to a tank whose crew telephoned the fire orders to the mortars. Again the Japanese moved out during the night and 26 KAR reached Kalewa, despite demolished bridges and anti-tank mines, by 1.30 p.m. on 2 December. Shortly afterwards 1 NRR entered the town from the north. It had been deserted for some months, was in ruins and stank of death. The sight of the Chindwin was a great boost; their next objective was to capture Shwegyin. Fowkes hoisted Biggs' Union flag over a pagoda-type building by the river, its third appearance over a captured town. An enemy gun caused trouble from across the river. It moved frequently, but withdrew after four days.

On the east side of the Chindwin, 21 Brigade was moving southwards against a series of well-sited Japanese positions among small hills. Hurribombers gave close support, but could not always locate their targets. A cross-country move away from the river was not practicable and the brigade continued down the river on a two-battalion front. To expand the bridgehead another brigade was needed east of the Chindwin. 25 Brigade put 34 KAR over on the night of 3/4 December, with the aid of the Deception Platoon and 26 KAR in the Kalewa area. The assault battalion crossed about three miles upstream of the town, using two beachheads, but six askari were drowned when their assault boat collapsed. C and D Companies pushed inland quickly to occupy a feature known as the Ridgeway, with battalion headquarters and B Company close behind, while

A Company covered the bridgehead. The opening moves went well, but D Company came under heavy machine-gun and mortar fire. C Company tried to move south, but was held up, after which A Company was committed. During the day the battalion lost six askari killed, while one officer, one British warrant officer and twenty-six askari were wounded. Patrolling and exchanges of fire marked the second day; A Company began to move forward early on 6 November, but encountered heavy mortar fire and withdrew under cover of smoke; fourteen askari were wounded. 26 Brigade then crossed the river and took 34 KAR under command. The more exposed positions on the Ridgeway were withdrawn, leaving A Company and some other elements in place. Some askari of B Company refused to accept their rations before relieving A Company next day, but eventually and reluctantly they took over the Ridgeway positions. Apart from thirty NCOs, A Company refused to move back to the Ridgeway on the morning of 8 November. 22 KAR crossed the Chindwin in daylight, in ferries operated by East African sappers. They moved up on 34 KAR's right and 34 KAR moved into reserve in the Kaing area.

22 KAR were followed across by 13 KAR, who took over the left of the bridgehead. The enemy withdrew during 8 and 9 December, and 22 KAR resumed the advance on 10 December. A patrol found a party of fifteen Japanese laying mines and evicted them with the aid of mortar fire. By the end of the day 22 KAR reached Kongyi, and 13 KAR passed through them, captured Shwegyin and linked up with 21 Brigade. 21 Brigade had dropped off one battalion on the north side of the bridgehead and was pushing on to cut the Shwegyin–Chaungzon road, bypassing minor pockets of the enemy and disposing of small parties of the enemy's rearguard. The defenders had the benefit of broken ground, and artillery on the west bank could not be used for fear of causing KAR casualties.

While the bridgehead was being expanded, equipment to build the longest floating bridge in the world had moved down the Kabaw valley road and through the Myittha gorge to Kalewa. It was a floating Bailey bridge 1,154 feet long and was assembled between 7 and 10 December, in twenty-eight working hours. The GOC crossed first, followed by a stream of vehicles, weapons and equipment. Slim visited 11 Division on 7 December, crossing the river by a raft to see the KAR's advance on Shwegyin; it was his first time in the area since the retreat in 1942. Other visitors included the Corps Commander and Supremo, who walked over the bridge with the GOC, and congratulated the division on its "highly successful advance". Six enemy planes attacked the bridge on 11 December. One was shot down and two others damaged; they dropped some bombs and used their cannon and machine guns, wounding two askari.

21 Brigade took over the northern sector of the bridgehead and 26 Brigade was south of them. Shwegyin was a mess, not only damaged buildings, but also the hulks of British tanks, guns and vehicles from the retreat of 1942. 2 Division moved through the positions of 21 and 26 Brigades to relieve the East Africans, who returned to India. 25 Brigade left by air, then 21 Brigade crossed back over the Chindwin and followed them. 26 Brigade remained operational, and carried out the last KAR action of this phase of the campaign using 13 KAR, who sent out "TICKYFORCE", commanded by Major E.C. Spurr, who searched for 200 Japanese who had been reported in the area of the Kanni–Ywadaw track. They found none and rejoined the battalion on 24 December, when it had already begun its move to Indainggale. With 5 KAR they flew out of Burma to the rest camp at Dimapur.

Nearly five months of fighting had caused the deaths of twenty-six British all ranks, ninety-five were wounded and seven were missing. The African losses were 233 killed, 976 wounded and thirty-five missing.

While 11 Division had been making its advance and river crossings, the next phases of the campaign were being planned. Stilwell had gone, Giffard left when the land forces chain of command was recast and Slim's responsibilities were reduced. He was dismayed at the loss of Giffard, whom he considered a great tower of strength and military common sense. Giffard was replaced by Gen Sir Oliver Leese, from 8th Army in Italy.

Slim urgently needed airfields, as his transport aircraft were operating close to their maximum effective range, but the only suitable ones were in Arakan, still in Japanese hands. There was sufficient lift to sustain forward four and two-third divisions, including 28 (EA) Brigade. The enemy was expected to hold the Shwebo plain, forward of Mandalay, between the Rivers Chindwin and Irrawaddy. 19 (Ind) Division (Rees) had crossed the Chindwin at Sittaung and by 2 December was forty-five miles beyond his crossing place. Four days later he linked up with 36 Division at Indaw, to create a single front from the Indian Ocean to China for the first time. But the Japanese had not held the line of hills essential to defend the Shwebo plain, and Slim realized he had misread the situation. Instead of moving more of XIV Army into the area between the two rivers, he decided to destroy the enemy in the Mandalay–Thazi–Chauk–Mingyan area.

The key objective was Meiktila, the maintenance area supporting both 15 and 33 Japanese Armies, with its airfields and its road and rail junctions. Slim decided to simulate a major build-up over the Chindwin by 33 Corps, to draw as many Japanese troops into the river loop as possible, then to move 4 Corps to the Irrawaddy via the Gangaw Valley further south. When 4 Corps had taken Meiktila, 33 Corps would strike from the north. A dummy

4 Corps Headquarters put out a volume of realistic messages, while strict radio silence was imposed on the genuine one. 11 (EA) Division's vehicles, call signs and formation signs were transferred to 28 (EA) Brigade, who simulated all of 11 Division. Valuable time was lost when some transport aircraft were diverted without warning. They were replaced eventually, but the Japanese had prepared for the offensive, and the monsoon was closer. The main task was to move 4 Corps 328 miles by a very rough earth road in two months, in secrecy.

4 Corps consisted of two Indian divisions (7th and 17th), 255 Tank Brigade (with Sherman tanks), the Lushai Brigade and 28 (EA) Brigade. The Lushai Brigade was in action in the Gangaw valley. It had been formed hastily at the time of the Kohima and the Imphal battles, to defend the Lushai Hills. It was commanded by Brig P.C. Marindin, and had disrupted enemy traffic in the Tiddim valley, with the aid of levies from the Chin Hills. It was lightly (even poorly) equipped; they were said to have a single map, which Slim used once despite its many vermouth stains. By 15 November the brigade was forty-five miles south of Kalemyo; they reached the Chindwin twenty miles south of Kalewa by the end of the month and started to raid across it.

28 (EA) Brigade was commanded by Brig W.A. Dimoline and had 7 (U) KAR, (Lt Col S.D. Field), 46 (TT) KAR, (Lt Col G.D.P. Adams) and 71 (Som) KAR (Lt Col D. Campbell-Miles). Other units were 63 Field Company EAE, 21 Inf Bde Company EAASC, 9 Inf Bde Workshops EAEME and 108 Casualty Clearing Section EAAMC. The brigade moved from Ceylon via Calcutta and had trained south of Imphal. It was to take over the Corps' right flank from the Lushai Brigade while simulating 11 (EA) Division. They moved south by transport at the end of December to the Minthami area and relieved the Lushai Brigade on 11 January. 7 KAR replaced the 1st Chin Hills Battalion, 71 KAR the 1st Bihar Regiment and 46 KAR the 1/9 Jat Battalion. Opposite them were some well-dug-in enemy positions, which were attacked by air on 10 January before the Lushai Brigade took them. 28 Brigade passed through the Lushai into the lead. B Company 71 Battalion set up a road block at a chaung and encountered the enemy, suffering the Brigade's first seven casualties. 7 KAR mopped up the southern part of the position and the Gangaw was clear of Japanese by 12 January.

The brigade followed up the withdrawing enemy quickly, with 7 KAR on the road and two companies of 71 KAR (with mule transport) in the hills to the left. 46 KAR took over from 7 and, a few miles short of Tilin, met some road blocks of felled trees, which caused delays until ten elephants came forward to remove them. There was some minor skirmishing before

Tilin, when one askari was killed. C Company 46 KAR entered the village on 22 January and located a Japanese position on a track to the left, where they killed fifteen and wounded twelve. 7 KAR took over the lead beyond Tharaka, with two companies of 71 KAR on the right flank. Road blocks and a machine-gun post were encountered, with only slight delay, and by 30 January 7 KAR were 105 miles from Gangaw.

7 (Ind) Division was to cross the Irrawaddy at Nuyaungu; 28 (EA) Brigade was to make a feint south of their crossing site, at Seikpyu. The Japanese had prepared positions on the west bank of the Irrawaddy, to cover the Yenangyaung oilfields. The country was open and troops had to dig for water, artillery support was limited to one field battery and the brigade had to cover a divisional front. Dimoline split his force to use both routes to Seikpyu. The right hand column (MILCOL) was 71 KAR and a troop of 347 Field Regiment RA. The remainder (DIMCOL) moved parallel with them. A patrol of 7 KAR in DIMCOL came on some Japanese, took them by surprise, killed two and captured some documents. From Burmese returning from forced labour on Japanese defences they learned what lay ahead. MILCOL was ambushed with the loss of two Somali askari and one Burmese guide before coming up to an enemy position on a hill near Kinsok. A platoon attack to the right made little progress, but B Company came in from the left with artillery and mortar support to take the objective by 6 p.m. The enemy counter-attacked before dark but were driven off. They opened fire twice during the night but did not renew the attack and in the morning seventeen dead Japanese were found outside the perimeter, while maps and weapons were captured. B Company's losses were one officer and one Somali soldier killed, four Somalis wounded.

46 KAR got ahead on the other route, with 7 KAR in support, a patrol from the latter killed two of the enemy, while a follow-up platoon killed one more and took a prisoner. During the night of 6 February MILCOL had several skirmishes and in the morning fourteen dead were found and several carts were captured, six of them loaded with food. 46 KAR had a minor engagement and killed seven enemy in a chaung. MILCOL rejoined the brigade on 8 February, three miles from the ridge before Seikpyu, where the Japanese were well dug in on a five-mile front. The plan was to take the southern sector first, where there were thirteen large, mutually supporting bunkers. A two-battalion attack was mounted, with 7 KAR on the right and 46 KAR on the left; both battalions patrolled forward and made contact on 8 February. Next day C and D Companies of 46 KAR took two forward positions, losing two Europeans and seven Africans killed. D Company 7 KAR had one officer and four askari killed, sixteen wounded and one missing, but did not reach their objective. Both battalions continued to

patrol forward to the main positions, suffering some casualties. C Company 71 KAR found field defences being built by about 400 Burmese under Japanese supervision; the Japanese left hastily and A and C Companies moved forward. B Company sent a patrol into Lanywa who wounded three of the enemy.

The feint crossing of the Irrawaddy began when sappers crossed the river south of Seikpyu during the night of 12/13 February to lay several explosive charges timed to go off at dawn. Artillery bombardment began at 5.30 a.m. while D Company 7 KAR supported with their mortars and machine guns. An hour later 46 KAR did much the same things at Sale, then the town of Chauk was bombed heavily and left in flames. Further north there was another feint. Deception was total; the Japanese rushed reinforcements towards the feints, the centre was left lightly protected and 7 (Ind) Division crossed in the afternoon with relative ease. 4 Corps followed up quickly and the race began to reach Rangoon before the monsoon. Japanese counter-attack was inevitable and they still thought 28 Brigade was the whole of 11 Division. Some enemy were on the river on 14 February and next day 7 KAR came under heavy attack in the Seikpyu area. A Company was surrounded and withdrew during the morning, with B Company giving covering fire, while two sections of C Company were over-run. They were then shelled by a 75 mm gun for the rest of the day. 7 KAR lost two officers and twenty-two askari killed; one officer, one British warrant officer and thirty-five askari were wounded. The Japanese isolated the two forward companies (B and D) when the rest of the battalion withdrew into the brigade box at Myegyandaw. The forward companies were shelled for two days by a 75 mm gun before they were relieved by B and D Companies 71 KAR on 18 February. Sniping and jittering continued for the next day. 46 KAR was withdrawn and used on flank protection, when they suffered casualties.

B and D Companies 71 KAR were surrounded by 19 February, with a road block between them and the brigade box. A 7 KAR patrol from the box also encountered enemy across the road. Dimoline concentrated the brigade at Letse, where there was adequate water and where he could fight on ground of his own chosing. As 71 KAR withdrew at dusk they were shelled and the CO (Campbell-Miles) was severely wounded; Major J.R. Carbonell assumed command. Most of the brigade, including the hospital, a landing strip and dropping zones were in the Letse box by 20 February, with 7 KAR as rearguard. 46 KAR were three miles to the south at Ywathit, to deny the water there to the enemy and to keep his artillery at arms length. 46 KAR were jittered for two successive nights, then in a dawn attack eighty Japanese penetrated between two C Company locations and overran the leading section. The counter-attack was successful, with the loss of one European and eight askari killed and fourteen wounded. There were at least forty enemy dead. 4/14 Punjab, an armoured squadron, a section of machine guns and a second artillery battery arrived as reinforcements and 7 KAR was evacuated. The administrative units were moved to a fresh box. Dimoline left on promotion, replacing Fowkes, and Brig T.H.S. Galletly took over 28 Brigade on 12 February.

Patrolling and air strikes continued. A patrol of 71 KAR found the enemy mortaring a Punjabi position and attacked, killing about twenty, but were machine-gunned while they were withdrawing with their wounded, screened by artillery smoke. On 26 February D Company 71 KAR advanced with tanks towards some enemy positions on a ridge at Springs. They cleared the forward slope, killing sixty-two of the enemy, but could not exploit their success as the tanks and artillery could not engage the enemy on the steep reverse slope. Thereafter offensive action was confined to ensuring the security of the brigade boxes at night. In the following week A Company and a platoon of B Company 71 KAR fought a group of about 200 Japanese, killing thirty-six of them for the loss of one officer and one askari. 46 KAR occupied some forward positions on 2 March, but withdrew under fire. The last action before the tanks reverted to Corps command was on 6 March, following three days of patrolling. C Company 71 KAR and B and D Companies 46 KAR moved on Springs through close country. Japanese infantry attacked the tanks, but 46 KAR reached the objective after an air strike and shelling, to find it unoccupied. Returning to assist the tanks, they drove the enemy off in the direction of Subokkon. With the support of mortars 46 KAR attacked there next day. Concurrently, 71 KAR located a strong position on Point 436, later called Somali Hill. They attacked it on 9 March with the aid of a heavy air strike, but many of the bombs missed the objective. The Somalis followed up quickly and took most of the position by midday, when a shortage of grenades and mortar bombs made them halt. There were then two Japanese counter-attacks, in the course of which four Japanese officers and 102 soldiers were killed, for the loss of one Somali killed and seventeen wounded, plus one British soldier wounded.

On 10 March D Company 46 KAR plus two platoons attacked Subokkon, killed twenty-five and captured a machine gun. The battalion attacked with three companies on 15 March, but met stronger opposition than had been expected. Facing encirclement they withdrew having counted fifty-seven enemy dead, for the loss of one European and eight askari killed and twenty-four wounded. A major attack on the brigade was now imminent, as the enemy had lost Meiktila on 4 March and was counter-attacking everywhere. Two companies of 46 KAR were on Somali Hill and 71 KAR was in the box when, on the evening of 19 March, the enemy shelled them intensively, followed by jittering through the night. D Company 71 KAR, the Defence Platoon and the Field Works Platoon came under heavy fire before an attack in their sector. Heavy shelling began again at 4 a.m. 20 March, concentrated on 71 KAR and Brigade Headquarters, followed after an hour by an assault on D Company's sector. Weight of numbers took the Japanese into the position and by dawn they were in Letse village and the high ground to the east, overlooking the box. 71 KAR were ordered to counter-attack at once and Carbonell threw all he had into the battle, including Battalion Headquarters, D Company, the Fieldworks Platoon and the stretcher bearers. The Somalis fought with great ferocity and forced the enemy to withdraw. As their smoke screen was not very effective, the Indian Mortar Battery did great execution on the fleeing Japanese. With Punjabi and KAR help the situation was fully restored by 10 a.m. A Japanese prisoner said that the attack had been mounted by 500; of these 253 were killed and many weapons were captured, including six officers' swords. Somali casualties were twenty killed and eighty wounded.

On the following day a patrol of 46 KAR reported thirty Japanese well dug in on a hill overlooking the box. An attack by C Company 71 KAR and D Company 46 KAR at 10.30 a.m. found the enemy there in three times that strength. C Company was heavily mortared and withdrew after killing seventeen of the enemy. D Company lost one European and one askari killed and pulled back. On 22 March 2nd Battalion, South Lancashire Regiment relieved 71 KAR. 46 KAR remained for a further two weeks, taking part in operations until the Brigade was withdrawn on 9 April and moved to Dohazari. The Japanese counter-offensive was petering out. The brigade had achieved its objectives and had accounted for over 1,200 of the enemy, suffering casualties of thirteen officers, five British other ranks and 151 African and Somali soldiers killed, fifteen officers, eight British other ranks and 420 Africans and Somalis wounded, with a further thirty missing. These were the heaviest casualties in any East African brigade.

22 (EA) Brigade followed 11 (EA) Division into Ceylon when the Division moved to Burma. The Brigade was commanded by Brig R.F. Johnstone. 5 KAR had joined 11 Division soon after arrival in Ceylon, so that there was only one KAR unit, 1 (N) KAR, commanded by Lt Col R.D. Blackie. The other battalions were 1 RAR and 3 NRR. In late November, 1944, they joined 15 Corps in Arakan, where a general offensive was due, in step with 4 Corps' operations. The objectives of the first phase were Akyab and Ramree islands, to prevent Japanese reinforcement of the central sector and to control the main axis into the Irrawaddy valley from Prome. South of Akyab is a single range of hills with steep ridges covered by dense

vegetation. There are two important passes over the range from the coastal strip to the Irrawaddy valley. The northern is the An, about sixty miles long. The other is the Taungup, 110 miles in length. The coastal strip is mainly mangrove swamps and a mass of minor waterways. Ramree Island controls access to both passes.

15 Corps consisted of 25 and 26 (Ind) Divisions, 81 and 82 (WA) Divisions and 22 (EA) Brigade. By February 81 Division had cleared the Kaladan valley and 82 Division had taken the Kalapanzin/Mayu valley, after which 25 Division had captured Akyab. 26 Division then took Ramree Island. The next task was to clear 200 miles of coastal strip as far as Taungup, which included the western exits of the An and Taungup passes. Amphibious operations by 25 Division and 82 Division were successful and, at the end of February, 82 Division moved on An and 53 (Ind) Brigade (25 Division) occupied a bridgehead at Ru-Ywa. 4 (Ind) Brigade (26 Division) landed at Letpan and cut the coast road between the two passes, then turned south to Taungup. This left about ninety miles of coast road north of them still occupied by the enemy. 22 (EA) Brigade was tasked to take over the Ru-Ywa bridgehead from 53 Brigade, bypass the Japanese garrisons at An and at the mouth of the An pass, and join 26 Division outside Taungup. The brigade had been patrolling further north and had then garrisoned Akyab, when 1 KAR was the first unit in, on 28 January.

All transport was left behind and they moved by landing craft to Ru-Ywa, to replace 53 (Ind) Brigade on 17 March. Next day they were ordered south to link up rapidly with 4 (Ind) Brigade outside Taungup. They had ten days for a move of ninety miles through Japanese-occupied territory, with many hills and two major chaungs to cross. The first chaung, the An, was covered by part of the enemy force defending the pass and its approaches. There were electrically controlled minefields in the mouth of the chaung and small parties of enemy were along the road. 82 Division could spare only sixteen decrepit 15-cwt trucks, barely adequate for the minimum of daily maintenance, and the brigade discarded some stores and reduced the ammunition they carried, to progress at the speed demanded. On 21 March 1 KAR passed through 3 NRR (Lt Col J.W.E. Mackenzie) and south to the An Chaung with 2 Gold Coast Light Battery and a company of 71 (Ind) Field Ambulance in support. They made steady progress, despite losing two vehicles and seven casualties from mines. On 25 March they were on commanding ground over a major crossing of the chaung, with patrols on both sides of the water as far as the sea. Two electrically controlled minefields were exploded to open the chaung to navigation. The guard on the minefield severely wounded an officer and two askari. One of the wounded soldiers rescued the wounded officer under machine-gun fire.

Three landing craft arrived in the afternoon of 25 March with supplies, and ferried the main body of 1 KAR across the chaung. One company had already swum over, floating their kit on improvised rafts. 1 RAR (Lt Col G.H.W. Goode) were due to take the lead after An Chaung, but more speed was demanded, so 1 KAR continued in the van. During the period 26 to 28 March, when the brigade was crossing, there were frequent clashes by patrols and some casualties on both sides, and a lot of Japanese jitter parties. The next objective was the Mai Chaung, but a shortage of fresh water led to the brigade being regrouped so it could advance by definite bounds. There were three battalion groups and a fourth consisting of 1 RAR guards and the Forward Maintenance Area, until stocks could be moved forward.

1 KAR were within eight miles of Letpan by 28 March, with 1 RAR Group two days behind them and 3 NRR Group one day after 1 RAR. The brigade was ordered to hold the southern ferry point on the Mai Chaung and the whole brigade was in position (less the Forward Maintenance Area Group) by 1 April. 1 KAR began to relieve 4 (Ind) Brigade. Three companies moved in transport, but the fourth company had to march thirty-one miles in thirty-six hours, a splendid achievement by heavily laden men who had led the brigade's advance for ten days through 127 miles of difficult country. A thirty-six-hour rest was essential, but the Brigade Headquarters opened at Dalaba on 2 April and the brigade was in its operational areas seventeen days after leaving Ru-Yaw.

82 (WA) Division took over the area and 22 (EA) Brigade from April. 22 Brigade's first task with 82 Division was against the northern flank of a Japanese force covering the Taungup pass. They moved down the Tanlwe Chaung, crossed the hills and reached Taungup Chaung, to cut the pass at mile ninety-nine. 1 KAR patrolled down the Tanlwe Chaung, 3 NRR covered the left flank of 4 (Ind) Brigade, and 1 RAR protected the Divisional Headquarters and the forward lines of communication. A 1 KAR patrol surprised some Japanese at their midday meal, captured a company flag, killed three of the enemy and wounded three more before withdrawing; but the Japanese, thoroughly confused, kept up firing, mainly at each other, for a further half hour.

3 NRR was relieved by a unit of 4 (WA) Brigade on 10 April and on the next day (less one company) began a deep flanking move against the Japanese lines of communication. They used an elephant track over difficult country, carrying four days' rations, four mortars, two 22 sets and charging engines. A troop of medium artillery supported them and 102 Light Regiment WAA was added later, while two companies of 1 KAR were nearby. After two air strikes by Hurribombers and Spitfires and a bombardment by the West African Light Regiment, 1 KAR attacked and cleared the

Yapale area. Retreating Japanese bumped a road block set up by 3 NRR and lost six men when trying to break through; 3 NRR had four men wounded. 3 NRR and then 1 RAR went into the lead, inflicting casualties on small groups of enemy. After the Japanese escaped in the dark, they entered Dalet on 17 April.

The brigade came against stiffening resistance as they closed up to a well-prepared and strongly defended position with all its likely approaches covered by registered artillery fire. Holding actions from the north and north-west were planned, with a deep encircling attack along a ridge nicknamed Chevalier. The brigade deployed with 3 NRR to the right and 1 RAR to the left, with patrols along the Chevalier ridge. A patrol led by an African located a machine-gun post while investigating the ridge; he got his men away by spraying the Japanese post by Bren gun fire from the hip. As there was now no surprise via the ridge route, a direct attack was made on the main position of Berger, 900 feet high, covered with thick bamboo and with Japanese dug in on the only feasible approach. 3 NRR reached two minor features to the south-east, then, following a heavy air strike, supported by all the guns and mortars the brigade could muster, 1 RAR attacked Berger and the adjacent Valerie positions on 26 April. 1 RAR's first major operation went very well; Berger was secured and the follow-up company passed through and on to Valerie, despite meeting some road blocks and not having air support. Total casualties, including those from shelling and mortaring during the night, were six killed and twenty-four wounded.

While this was going on an African corporal of 3 NRR got his section astride a likely Japanese withdrawal route. His ambush killed five Japanese, then withdrew without loss. Thick bamboo prevented accurate artillery support, but 3 NRR attacked on 28 April, supported only by their mortars, but the shape of the ground forced them into an area covered by enemy guns and they withdrew, having had three killed and ten wounded. Patrolling and air strikes continued across the brigade front; on one occasion a company commander and 2ic were killed within a few minutes of each other. Plans for a major attack on two positions called Abbott and Lockwood were made for the night of 30 April/1 May, but the Japanese abandoned them during the night after heavy firing. 1 KAR led the pursuit and by 3 May the whole brigade was on the Taungup Chaung between Blondell and Lauder, with 1 RAR leading. A patrol of 1 KAR entered Kyauktaga on 2 April to find only nine Japanese there, but by the following day the enemy had manned some previously prepared positions overlooking the town, and the brigade had a tough battle before they cleared the way to the pass entrance. 1 RAR had five killed and eight wounded when they approached some well-prepared positions with good fields of fire, well-supported by artillery and 90 mm mortars. As the brigade's guns had not been able to keep pace with the infantry in the close country, 1 RAR was supported only by their own mortars and air strikes.

The Japanese bombarded the whole brigade position on 5 and 6 May from the area of the Taungup Pass, to empty their ammunition dumps. On 7 May a strike by Thunderbolts and Spitfires failed to dislodge the enemy from Powell. Artillery support was being planned when the brigade was ordered to regroup on the Taungup Chaung at Mile 100. This suspension of operations was caused by a shortage of transport aircraft. Priority was given to 4 (WA) Brigade, whose supply route had been disrupted by heavy rain. By 8 May the brigade was on the Taungup Pass between milestones 100 and 106; 3 NRR pursued the enemy through the pass as far as Milestone 58, but without making contact. They captured a great deal of material, including an old British 25 pdr gun.

In the past week the brigade had killed some sixty of the enemy and wounded about the same number. The brigade's losses in the whole operation were three officers killed and five wounded, two British soldiers wounded, fifty-six askari killed and 141 wounded, with two missing. The brigade was disappointed at not having encircled the Japanese at Taungup Pass, but they were not equipped to make a wide-swinging manoeuvre fast enough to ensure surprise. Instead they had forced the enemy to withdraw and to lose much material. The one successful outflanking action was by 3 NRR on 11/12 April, when they had 200 coolies to carry their supplies, a benefit that was not repeated. In his report the brigade commander complemented the sappers of 59 (EA) Field Company (Major I.R.R. Hollyer) for constructing jeep tracks close on the heels of the infantry. 71 (Ind) Field Ambulance gained the gratitude and admiration of all ranks, while the evacuation of wounded by the L5 light aircraft continued until the monsoon prevented the planes from landing on the inadequate strips. Brig Johnstone's most generous words of praise were for the askari, most of whom had never been under fire before: "Their energy and endurance on the march and on patrol through some of the worst country in the Arakan, their constancy and discipline under the stress of persistent mortar and artillery fire, and their cheerfulness throughout the appalling weather conditions which developed during the latter stages are beyond praise. Their doubts and delusions have gone and they are confident in the knowledge which can be born only of experience." That assessment could apply equally to the other East African units in Burma.

The East African formations had every right to feel proud of their achievements in Burma. 25 Brigade had become operational first, at the height of the monsoon, to make its two-month-long advance to Sittaung and to get over the Chindwin. 26 Brigade had struck down the main axis of the Kabaw valley, moving parallel to 5 (Ind) Division to their right, achieving great tactical surprise during the initial stages of their advance, when conditions precluded adequate artillery support. By the time the Japanese had reacted and reactivated the abandoned defensive works around the Yazagyo-Indainggale area, heavier weapons could be moved forward and supplied with ammunition, and the division deployed on a two-brigade front. 21 Brigade had some of the toughest fighting on the division's left flank, pushing across trackless hills and forests with just a few mountain guns in support, dependent on mules for transport and air drops for resupply, and on light aircraft for casualty evacuation. Brig J.F. Macnab was proud of them; in an Order of the Day he said the men of 21 Brigade had played "a major part in forcing the Japanese to abandon the gateway to Mandalay", and noted that they had killed some 300 Japanese and taken eight prisoners.

22 Brigade was the last into action in Burma, but had a longer war record than the others. It covered more ground and was in continuous contact for longer. It was the last out of action and had also served in more different divisions than the other brigades. 28 Brigade was the "youngest" and its operations were against an enemy that had reacted to the thrusts further north by counter-attacking in strength. The brigade was on the exposed right flank of 4 Corps and suffered heavy battle casualties.

While the Burma campaign was to a very great extent an infantry war, the supporting Arms and Services were all part of the teams of the Division and the brigade groups. 22 and 28 Brigades were often dependent on temporary attachments for support. Armour was represented by the 1st (EA) Reconnaissance Regiment, (Kenya Armoured Car Regiment) East African Armoured Corps. Originally they had been in armoured cars, but got tanks eventually.

There were field and anti-tank artillery regiments, although the anti-tank unit was converted to heavy mortars. Capt John Watson-Baker, who was with 302 (T) EA Artillery, was impressed by the askari's ability to master the technical aspects of gunnery, but thought the 25 pdr guns too cumbersome for the conditions, and lacked the crest-clearance to shoot behind steep-sided ridges, even when the trails were dug in. Preparation of a gun position in the Kabaw Valley could take over two days, including felling trees to give clearance and building gun platforms with logs before the guns could be winched or manhandled into position. Local defence was of great importance, and jittering parties often troubled them. Shooting was forbidden by night and reliance was placed on the bayonet and the panga. Approaches to gun positions were booby-trapped or guarded by camouflaged panji pits.

When in position the guns were laid on a common bearing, the "Zero Line", but as the positions were usually enclosed, aiming posts had to be used instead of distant features. Optical instruments suffered in the high humidity, particularly the troop directors and dial sights, while the paper on artillery boards corrugated in the damp. 25 pdr ammunition was in short supply and some was unreliable due to poor storage and handling. Apart from the delay this caused, there was always the risk of the loss of a complete gun crew from a misfire. When they reached the far bank of the Chindwin and the country opened out, the 25 pdrs came into their own again. Capt P.P. Wise of 304 (EA) Anti-Tank Regiment was captured and held by the Japanese for three days, pegged down to the ground for part of the time. He escaped and returned to his unit with valuable information about the enemy.

The divisional sappers were 54, 58, and 64 (EA) Field Companies and 62 (EA) Field Park Company, commanded by the Commander Royal Engineers, Lt Col J.T.S. Tutton RE. Their rôles had been mainly mine clearance, bridging and road construction, with river crossings a speciality. One of the biggest was 21 Brigade's crossing of the upper Chindwin, aided by Lt D. Shackleton and his platoon of 58 Fd Coy. They were mule-borne and supplemented by 200 Burmese, and got the whole brigade across in thirty-six hours. This included 2,500 men, 600 mules and fifty tons of stores, mainly on tarpaulin rafts. Lt Dixon and his field platoon of 62 Field Park Company took over operation of the ferry, continuing to use the mixture of rafts and other craft until a Spitfire mistook them for Japanese and sank them. Most of the engineer stores were air-dropped, but the more fragile items, such as outboard engines, mine detectors and ranger boats, were air-landed.

Signals units made invaluable contributions to the East African formations' successes in Burma. The combination of steep hills, monsoon conditions, humidity, the loss of reception as the day got warmer, the weight and limited reliability of the radio sets, the problems with batteries and charging engines, the constant laying of telephone cable, and its replacement when it was taken for other purposes, were great challenges; even greater, the distances over which the formations operated and the speed of their advances. The East African Signallers did at least as well as any other units in Burma.

Apart from supplying the variety of ration scales and packs that East African units required, EAASC personnel played a great part in the operation of the air despatch organization. The composite troops in each brigade ensured that immediate needs of combat supplies were met, coping with the uncertainties of the transport links that served them. John Tremlett was with 21 (EA) Infantry Brigade Transport Company as far as Palel, then joined

25 Brigade at Tamu. He was with them until Kalewa, when he moved to 2 (EA) Field Ambulance, until returning to his original unit at Ranchi. A major problem was the punctures caused by the enormous metal "staples" used to hold logs together, but which became displaced with use. When not on a jeep basis they had six-wheel-drive Dodge thirty-cwt load-carriers.

Apart from the treatment of battle casualties, health care and preventative measures were major roles for the RAMC and EAAMC medical staffs. Capt V.R.S. Damms RAMC served with a Uganda battalion and, by the time they had got to Ceylon, saw his job as being to keep the battalion fit, instead of just curing them. Shortly after arrival in Ceylon he sanctioned the use of a water supply, only for the corpse of a cholera victim to be found in it. He had a cholera outbreak on his hands and had to vaccinate the whole battalion. Despite its indifferent reputation, the vaccine worked, and the battalion was free of cholera within six days. Dysentery and malaria were dealt with at source by fly and mosquito control, with due care paid to the siting of camps, latrines and kitchens. DDT became available during the campaign, and was regarded for a long time as a war-winning weapon because of its effective control of insects. Mepacrine was also held in high regard, but Damms believed that mosquito control had reduced the disease to a minor nuisance before the tablets became available. Scrub typhus was a problem in both Ceylon and Burma; the answer was to avoid the areas where the infecting ticks could be brushed off the bushes on which they lived. In operational areas this was supplemented by aerial spraying. Smallpox and cholera vaccinations were compulsory for everyone, at three-month intervals. Foot rot was countered by everyone going barefoot at times, but on other occasions footwear was compulsory to prevent hookworm from being caught from the earth around latrines.

The majority of wounds were caused by grenade fragments, but Japanese grenades were far less lethal than British ones. Wounded men were often operated on in the forward areas, particularly if casualty evacuation was delayed for any reason. During 21 Brigade's independent operations the Zanzibar Field Ambulance often cared for as many as 100 patients awaiting evacuation. Sgt Owoko Okumo, Cpl Pointino Zilibugyire and others of 10 (EA) Field Ambulance rescued a British Warrant Officer airman who came down in thick jungle. He had been wandering for seven days without food and was on the far side of a wide, deep and fast-flowing chaung. The two NCOs swam across the chaung with 200 yards of signal wire and brought the airman across, hand over hand, with help from men on the home bank. Owoko secured the concentration of the exhausted pilot at a critical moment by shouting at him not to be a bloody fool. Later on the same day Sgt Owoko rescued an askari who had got into difficulty when crossing the chaung. The

Belgian Casualty Clearing Station had Belgian officers and a staff of Congo Africans, including under-surgeons. They could establish a working hospital with great speed once they arrived on site.

Veterinary services were limited and 10 (EA) Field Ambulance was sometimes called in to assist. Patients included mules and elephants. One elephant became so used to the routine that it would stop outside the medical unit of its own accord and wait to be fed with biscuits while its injuries were dressed.

The East African Military Police's main function was traffic control, particularly at the chaung crossings and in the Myittha Gorge when the roads were packed with traffic of all kinds, each with its own concept of priority: jeeps, mules, tanks, guns, bridging equipment and amphibious vehicles, in choking dust clouds.

The padres were always close to the action, carrying their kit alongside the askari, administering baptism and communion services in the field, comforting the wounded and conducting funerals when necessary. They also registered the graves. They were particularly effective at medical units, where their presence was much valued by doctors and patients alike.

When Maj Gen Fowkes left the Division he issued a special Order of the Day to mark their achievements. In it he said that others would now take up the torch that the Division had carried, while they prepared for their next tasks. He thanked all ranks for "their bravery, devotion and loyalty" during the operations, ending, "It has been a great privilege for me to have led you". Fowkes was evacuated on medical grounds in January, careworn and sick. He was replaced by Maj Gen Robert Mansergh, who soon returned to 5 Division (he had been Commander, Royal Artillery), when the GOC died in an air crash. His successor was the previous commander of 28 (EA) Brigade, Maj Gen W.A. Dimoline CBE MC, who toured all units in the division and wrote in the Divisional newspaper *Rhino Review* "I thank you all for the very kind way in which you have received me," and ended his message, "To you all, therefore, I say – good luck, good health and good hunting."

After leaving the operational zone, the Division went first to Dimapur, where the routine of training was relieved by cinema shows, ENSA concert parties and the Division's own troupe, the Rhino Boys. A leave camp at Jorhat was enjoyed by many askari. In April the Division moved to Chas, a particularly repellent place of great heat and dust storms, where welfare services were inadequate. The semi-hill station at Ranchi, which they reached in May, was better. Had the war continued, the Division's next task would have involved crossing the Rivers Sittang and Salween, so they spent several months practising crossing the Ganges, before celebrating VJ Day with two days of non-stop parties.

Lt Gen Sir Kenneth Anderson visited from East Africa soon after taking over as GOC, bringing the good wishes and greetings of the people of East Africa. A party of Chiefs, including representatives of the Sultan of Zanzibar, also came to see how their soldiers had fared. They brought news from home, and were questioned by the askari for several hours. The Chiefs were entertained by the officers and the askari, visited missions and experimental farms and called on HE the Governor of Bihar.

Bishops visited to catch up with the backlogs of baptisms and confirmations. Several hundreds were confirmed in mass services for both Roman Catholic and Church of England askari. Members of the division attended services at Ranchi cathedral, and before they left presented a plaque to the Cathedral recording that the officers and men of the 11 East African Division had been welcomed and enjoyed the fellowship of worship in the Cathedral.

Training switched to vocational subjects. A three-inch-mortar course was converted to instruction in brick-making, and a cadre for African NCOs became a school. The sappers taught civilian skills; model houses were designed and built to illustrate the principles of construction and bricklaying. Unit gardens were developed, both to improve the diet and as instructional media, stimulated by inter-unit competitions. Major John Turnbull, 2ic 13 KAR, ran an agricultural course and a very successful farm. The literacy rate among the askari had improved during the campaign, encouraged by their interest in writing home and receiving letters in return. One gunner unit had a literacy rate of 15% when they arrived in Colombo; when they returned to East Africa 85% of the men could read and write.

An extensive Victory Searchlight Tattoo was held at Ranchi on four evenings, between 23 and 27 November, 1945, in aid of divisional welfare funds. It was organized by Lt Col Michael Biggs, Commander, Royal Engineers, and his Committee; 1,500 men of the division took part. It began with a selection of KAR marching songs in Ki-Swahili and Chinyanja, a Guard of Honour provided by 5 KAR and commanded by Major R.A. Landridge MC, with the band of 6 KAR, the Drums of 2 KAR and the massed bugles of all the battalions in the division. There was physical training to music by 44 KAR, then a display of motorcycling by Divisional Signals, followed by 2 KAR's "historical sketch" set in "a Corner of Darkest Africa" in 1903. 36 KAR gave a lantern drill display, ending by spelling out with their lamps in Ki-Swahili "Greetings from 36 KAR". Item 7 was music from the drums and bugles, followed by a pageant in three acts dealing with the impact of war on a typical askari. Dances by the Nandi and Akamba of

11 KAR and by the Sukuma of 46 KAR preceded the Grand Finale, which began with 6 KAR's Regimental March "Ngoma", then the Last Post, Abide With Me, God Save the King, the Regimental March again and then lights out. The salute was taken successively by the GOC, Maj Gen Briggs, Lt Gen Sir Arthur Smith and Lt Gen Godwin Austen. The last was Quartermaster General, India and had been GOC 12 (African) Division. The Tattoo choir was formed and trained by Rev Robert Down at the personal invitation of the GOC.

Sports days were very popular, while race meetings gave opportunities for fortunes to be made and lost, usually the latter. As Ranchi was an equine infection area, the animals were moved about thirty miles away. Riding was popular with many officers and the horses needed exercise. The mules had their admirers too, and Padre Down was touched, when visiting an askari from the mule transport unit who was in hospital when the unit was disbanded, to find the man distressed at not being able to say goodbye to his mules. Capt A.J. Birkett of 350 EA Composite Platoon was in charge of the "Riding School" set up by Brig Radford (Commander, Royal Artillery). He cared for thirty to forty ponies of various tempers, along with rheumatic chickens, one-legged ducks and goats in kid, which had been donated rather than being put in the pot as convalescent rations.

The cricket team toured around Calcutta to win two and draw one of their seven matches. At the Assam International Games the division came third; their wins included 200 yards, 440 yards and international relay races, and throwing the javelin. The International Soccer Team gave the division's teams two interesting and exciting games, but won both of them. A rugger team took part in a competition organized by the Calcutta Rugby Club. They defeated the Calcutta Anglo-Asians 3–0. The final was against the home team, and the Rhinos won the Calcutta Cup 1946.

Most men just wanted to get home; there were some uncharacteristic acts of indiscipline while they were waiting, but a priority system based on the British age and service system was introduced, and almost ten per cent of the askari were on their way by the end of 1945. Although arrival and resettlement planning had gone forward in East Africa, not everyone had quite the home-coming they had expected. 71 (Som) KAR, the victors of Letse, were landed by lighters at Berbera in the dark from a troopship anchored about a mile outside the port. There was no one around except one solitary and completely indifferent policeman, so the whole battalion slept on the beach in considerable discomfort for what remained of the night.

General Sir George Giffard gained one of the highest ranks and the most senior appointments in the Army of any KAR officer, being Commander in

Chief 11 Army Group for part of the Burma campaign. In 1912, when Lt Giffard, he was 2ic B Company 1 KAR in the Jubaland. Two years later his company was withdrawn to Nairobi on the outbreak of war. He took part in the German East Africa campaign and attempted to relieve a small garrison of Kashmiri troops who were trapped in a sisal factory, when he was commanding three companies of 3 KAR. By March, 1916, he had four companies of 1 KAR under command, then in October Lt Col Giffard took over 1/2 KAR; his reconnaissance with his brigade commander (O'Grady) at the end of the year laid the foundation for a series of successful actions in the first days of the New Year. On 17/18 October, at the battle of Nyangao "at great personal risk [he] was rallying his troops in the forward line" for a bayonet charge. Maj Gen van Deventer recorded that "no column had marched further or fought harder" than Giffard's. He was awarded the DSO.

In 1936 Giffard became Inspector-General KAR and two years later was appointed Inspector-General, African Colonial Forces. He put East Africa on to a war footing, increased troop numbers, arranged for first line KAR battalions to become units of Lt Col's command, and developed the command and control structure. In May 1943, he entered the Burma scene as Commander Eastern Army; Slim saw "A tall, good looking man in the late fifties who had obviously kept himself physically and mentally in first class shape . . . He abhorred the theatrical, and was one of the very few generals, indeed men in any position, I have known who really dislike publicity." Also, "He understood the fundamentals of war – that soldiers must be trained before they can fight, fed before they can march and relieved before they are worn out." He did not want commanders overburdened with administration and believed that "soundness of organization and administration is worth more than specious short cuts to victory." Slim was always grateful for Giffard's unstinting efforts in support of XIV Army.

Before the Arakan offensive, Giffard met Slim's request for more troops by allocating 81 (WA) Division, less one brigade, to 15 Corps. With the monsoon imminent, Giffard had agreed that 15 Corps should pull back its forward troops to a line that could be held economically, which was healthier and easier to maintain. In August, 1943, when SEAC was formed, Giffard became the land CinC under Mountbatten and Slim took over XIV Army. Giffard's Army Group Headquarters were in Delhi initially; he was not at his best in the extensive and high-level debates of the early days of Mountbatten's time as Supremo, but he "always kept to the fore the element of practical soldiering". Giffard's reorganization of the rear areas led to a variety of improvements, including mail deliveries and the build-up of welfare services. With Auchinleck, Giffard set up two training Divisions (14 and 34) where battle-experienced officers and NCOs of XIV Army passed on hard-learned lessons to reinforcements before they joined active formations with XIV Army. Both morale and tactical ability benefited.

Slim was impressed by Giffard's dignified behaviour during the difficult period of Stilwell's refusal to work under him. Giffard was an active CinC, visiting Headquarters and formations in the forward areas; he was in the Arakan shortly before the Japanese offensive, and narrowly escaped being shot down by Zeros. On one visit to Slim's Headquarters, Slim's reaction was "General Giffard had the invaluable knack of not interfering, yet making one feel that he was there, calm, helpful and understanding". Later, when the threat to Imphal developed, Giffard let Slim have Wingate's 23 Brigade, to cover the Ledo railway and Dimapur, in addition to the planned reinforcements, and was "as always, a tower of strength in emergency."

Giffard failed to move formations from the Arakan to Imphal quickly and so angered Mountbatten that his days were numbered. His fellow CinCs and the Supremo's Chief of Staff, Pownall, all criticized Giffard. Peirse wrote to Portal, "The General is slow"; Somerville thought him "stolid, critical and generally sound", but lacking in ". . . speed of thought and action". Mountbatten had considered getting rid of Giffard on medical grounds, but wrote that "he is such a straight and upright old gentleman that . . . he would not agree to such a subterfuge." Brooke had agreed that Mountbatten could dismiss Giffard if necessary. Mountbatten recorded, "The trouble is that we all like him. He is, however, non-aggressive, a non-co-operator, and unwilling to recognize me as the one responsible for the Burma campaign". The incidents in March brought to a head the difficulties between Mountbatten and Giffard, but it was not until the reorganization of November, 1944, that an integrated Anglo-American Headquarters, Allied Land Forces South-East Asia was formed, and he left. Slim said, "It was a sad blow. XIV Army owed much to his integrity, his judgement, his sound administration, his support in our darkest hours and to the universal confidence he inspired among us. We saw him go in grief. I and others built on the foundations that he laid."

General Sir George James Giffard GCB DSO was Colonel Commandant of the KAR from 1945 to 1954; he died on 17 November, 1964.

Chapter 9

VICTORY AND AFTERWARDS

No one of his rank was better qualified to command the East African Contingent on the 1946 Victory Parade in London than Lt Col Derek Watson DSO, a judgement reinforced by his subsequent KAR service. Watson was with the KAR for seventeen years and commanded three battalions (2 KAR as acting CO, 3 KAR and 4 KAR for two separate tours). His leadership of 4 KAR in Burma was much admired, particularly during the battle of Leik Hill (22 October, 1944), which was essentially "his" battle, when he gained his DSO. Later, not finding staff work to his liking, he persuaded Maj Gen "Fluffy" Fowkes to send him to a battalion. He was with 3 KAR for a year, when, not thirty-six years old, he was selected to command the Victory Parade contingent. His battalion was in Somaliland and he handed over to Lt Col Carne of the Gloucestershire Regiment (who was awarded the VC in Korea later). There were several disadvantages; he had not seen his family for about a year, his wife had been over-paid by the Paymaster and he was having to repay it, going to England would involve loss of his Overseas Allowance, yet (there being no married quarters), he would have to continue to pay the rent of his flat in Nairobi. When he pointed these out, he was reminded of the honour and the privilege involved.

On 12 April, 1946, those selected for the parade began to assemble at Langara Camp. They practised drilling in twelves, as that was how they were to march through London, received battle dress and inoculations and were documented. Before leaving Nairobi they paraded down Delamere Avenue. HE the Governor of Kenya and Lt Gen Sir Kenneth Anderson, the GOC, took the salute. The contingent consisted of detachments from the Kenya Regiment, the RNVR, the East Africa Reconnaissance Regiment, the KAR, the Northern Rhodesia Regiment, the Tanganyika RNVR, the Somaliland Scouts, the East African Artillery, the EA Engineers, the EA Signals, the Chaplain's Department, the EA Service Corps, the EA Military Police, the Pioneer Corps, the EA Military Nursing Service and the Women's Territorial Service. They totalled 350, including a composite Band and Drums, and took with them the Colours of 1, 2, 3, 4, 5 and 6 KAR and those of the Kenya Regiment.

The contingent left Nairobi by rail on 4 May, with the Kenya Police Band, families and friends to see them off. At Mombasa they embarked on the SS *Antenor*. John Swallow recalled that the NAAFI had issued them with seventy-one cases of "essential nourishment", despite troopships being officially "dry" at the time. They labelled it "band instruments, wanted on board" and put it in the baggage room. The band were playing their instruments on the quayside, but no one seemed to notice. During the voyage a steady stream of passengers found it necessary to check up on the instruments; all seemed to carry small bags.

Watson recalled:-

"On 28 May we disembarked at Prince's Landing Stage at Liverpool and entrained for London. On arrival there I was extremely surprised to see my parents at the station; I had not seen them since August, 1939. Some kind friend at the War Office had let them know of our arrival. The askari remarked how like my father I was. We travelled to Kensington Gardens where we were all in tents. The rations were awful! This was the first time that I realized how short of food people in Britain were. The askari had a cooked breakfast and a cooked lunch, and that was all. We had those awful soya link sausages for breakfast. I used to go to the De Vere Hotel and have kippers for breakfast, as I hadn't had one since 1939. Our lunch was sandwiches, and that was the last meal. For the first two days I kept the askari in camp to clean up after the voyage, and to acclimatize them to the ladies who climbed up the wire trying to lure them out." The press accused Watson of confining the askari to camp, which was soon disposed of. "A Guards officer was appointed to us. He was charming and most useful, as he arranged for a Guards Drill Sergeant to drill us up and down the park for a couple of hours each day by the Albert Memorial, with the desired effect. He gave me an excellent lunch at the Guards Club prior to 6 June, when we were inspected by HM The King, accompanied by the Queen and the two Princesses. Lt Gen Anderson and Maj Gen Dimoline were there; the latter dressed, like us, in battle dress and white webbing. The Minister for War came and inspected us, but the askari had hoped he would have been in uniform. There was also an extra parade for the East African Signals Detachment. The Princess Royal, as Colonel in Chief of the Royal Signals, wished to see all the Signal Detachments on the Victory Parade. This involved a march to St John's Wood Barracks without the aid of a band. It was the usual type of parade for Royalty, inspection, march past, etc. A drinks party was held for HRH to meet the officers, (including 'Dimmy', who was late Royal Signals). John Swallow was to tell HRH all about his chaps, having been briefed that he would be relieved after three minutes, but the next officer did not arrive and John struggled on for what seemed an interminable time, trying to cope with HRH, who was not known for her ability to keep conversation flowing.

"On 6 June I had the honour to present the officers to King George VI. In the photograph King George is shaking hands with me; Major Ted Onslow, my 2ic, is next to me. We were lined up on either side of one of the roads in the Park.

"The great day was 8 June. We assembled in Hyde Park. I have never felt so proud in all my life as I marched out of Marble Arch Gate at the head of the East African Contingent, with the Band and Drums in front dressed in tropical kit. I had that prickly feeling behind my eyes as I saw and heard the cheers of the crowds who were packed deep on both sides of the road and at every window. It was something one will never forget. Little did I think, when watching the 1914/18 Victory parade from the balcony of the Cavalry Club, that I would be marching in the next Victory Parade. The weather was kind to us, it was not too hot and it did not start raining until we had passed the saluting base. The thickness of the crowds on the pavements was unbelievable. The clapping and cheering was terrific. Sadly I cannot remember what we did after the parade. I know I ended up sitting on the roof of my father's Morris Isis outside Buckingham Palace, waiting for the King and Queen to come out onto the Balcony.

"I went to three official receptions. The first was at the Overseas League, to meet the Royal family. The luncheon at Hampton Palace was the highlight of the official functions and was extremely well organized. Capts Stan Wood and Ray Braithwaite remember it well because all the labels on the wine bottles were Royal and all the cigarettes had little gold crowns. The Band and Drums did a tour of Scotland which they enjoyed, and John Drysdale took his Somalis down to Cardiff, where they received a tremendous welcome from the Somali community. They had several days of entertainments and were given large sums of money.

"John Swallow took his Signals askari to the Signals Training Centre at Catterick, which they enjoyed, and were amused to see recruits receiving the same treatment that they had in Africa. At Darlington station the askari had plenty of time to load up, but were used to the Kenya and Uganda Railway, and had not even found the guard's van by the time the train pulled out. Most detachments enjoyed their visits, although some of them, gazing out of the windows and seeing no mud huts, were heard to ask, 'Where is the Reserve?' The general comment was that they had no idea that there were so many Europeans, and the number of butchers' shops impressed them enormously. At our final farewell party the Guests of Honour were Earl and Countess Mountbatten, and I introduced them to the guests. She was magnificent for the way she talked to everyone, but I remember the Earl saying, 'For God's sake hurry up, we will be late for our next appointment'.

"On 21 June, my thirty-sixth birthday, we entrained at Euston for Liverpool and re-embarked on the SS *Antenor*. It was a quieter return trip than on the way out; a smallpox patient was disembarked at Gibraltar, and we all had to be re-vaccinated. We passed an aircraft carrier in the Red Sea, which signalled, 'What KAR aboard? – signed Roddy Ward'. He had been my company 2ic at the beginning of the war, in 2 KAR, also my best man. He was going home on leave; it was the last time I heard from him, as he died soon afterwards. We disembarked at Mombasa on 13 July and dispersed at Nairobi. There was no official parade; our return was rather like a damp squib or a glass of flat champagne.

"Finally, I wouldn't have missed the Victory Parade for all the tea in China. It was the most marvellous 'Thank you' given by the people of Britain to the Services for what they thought we had done to win the war, but I think victory was entirely due to Churchill and the magnificent spirit of those in Britain who deprived themselves of everything so that the fighting forces should be given all of the help they needed."

Victory parades were held widely, including in Nairobi and, perhaps somewhat incongruously, in Mogadishu. Some East African soldiers had celebrated victory in London a year before. Alex Findler met them near Westminster Abbey by chance in August, 1945, when he had just been discharged from the Military Hospital at Millbank. He was walking across Parliament Square, when:-

"Am I seeing things? They had told me I had babbled away in Swahili when I was delirious, but this is ridiculous, and in any event I am fit now. But there they are, five tall, bush-hatted askari in heavy greatcoats despite the warmth, standing in the middle of Parliament Square. As I approach I catch the familiar cadences of that lingo which I have known for the last two years. My Swahili greeting is met by a chorus of 'Jambo Bawana's and a flurry of saluting and foot stamping that startled the pigeons. They explained, 'We have been prisoners of war in Germany, Bawana'. 'In Germany?' 'Yes, Bawana, we were in a Pioneer Company in the Desert and were captured at Tobruk. When we were released we were brought back to England and have been waiting for a long time for a ship to take us home. We have been given a day's pass from our camp, so that, before we go home, we can say that we have been to London and seen the Capital of the British Empire.'

"I feel somehow responsible, as these chaps have spent years in a POW camp in a strange country, and this visit to the heart of the Empire must be a big day in their lives. How can I say hello and then leave them? I propose some refreshment. Yes, they would like some chai; as we drink our tea at a mobile canteen I try to think of my next move. The corporal asks me where King George's church is. He had attended a mission school and, on return home, would like to tell his teachers he has seen the 'Kanisa ya Kingi Georgi'. My initial thought is Windsor, but what about Westminster Abbey? That's where he was crowned. 'Kingi Georgi's church? Why, it is just up the road; let's go'. The Corporal is delighted, so off we march, as the Corporal orders the others to fall in behind, and find myself humming 'Kwende Safari'. The askari and I entered an empty Abbey; there were no tourists and we stood bareheaded around the Tomb of the Unknown Warrior as I explained its significance to my solemn companions. As we proceeded, hushed and treading lightly through the nave, past the elaborate tombs and monuments, the silence was broken by the awed whispered exclamations of my companions. the centre of the nave was full of seats, with the front pews cordoned off. A verger offered assistance, and I told him about my slight subterfuge regarding 'Kingi Georgi's Church'. 'You are not far off the mark', he said, 'because the King and Queen were actually here last week'.

"I repeated this information to the askari, who were deeply impressed; then the Corporal asked which was the King's chair. He pointed to one of the special-looking chairs behind the barrier, and then he looked to see if the field was clear, lifted the silk rope and said with a thumbed gesture, 'As a special treat the Corporal can sit on the chair, but make it quick.' I repeated this invitation to the stunned Corporal, who was encouraged by a swift push in the back and a whispered 'Upsisana'. Ducking under the rope he tiptoed across to the chair, lowered himself onto it and sat wide-eyed on the very edge with that sort of ecstatic smile that nature has allotted only to the African.

"We had another cup of chai, with the Corporal shaking his head and repeating how he will tell them back home how he sat on the chair of Kingi Georgi. Doubtless, in the tradition of African story telling, the chair would soon become a throne. There was hand-shaking all round in the two-handed African manner, many asanta sanas and kwa heris, then the Corporal called the others to order and I was treated to an improvised but rather ragged 'grand salute', which under the circumstances was a very commendable effort. Walking off towards Whitehall, I glanced back to see five happy askari waving their bush hats. I waved back."

East African Pioneers played an important part in the Middle Base depots and ports during the war. After 1945 the Middle East labour force included 87,000 German POWs, who provided just about every skill needed to keep the base operational. By July, 1948, they had reduced to 20,000, against a requirement of 40,000. Various options were considered, including attempts to encourage the remaining Germans to stay as voluntary civilian employees. The uniformed East African Pioneer Companies had been run down earlier and the last six companies had been disbanded in February, 1947. The abrogation crisis led to the withdrawal of all Egyptian staff from the Canal Zone base.

Meanwhile, in East Africa the project to build an alternative base at Mackinnon Road had started, with demands for more labour. The Middle East requirement was covered by pioneers from Basutoland, Bechuanaland and Swaziland, and from Mauritius, Rodrigues and the Seychelles. Some Cyprus-based employees did not remain long, and the 40,000 Egyptian workers showed no sign of returning. The official history of the Pioneer Corps says:-

"An equally important source was the East African Pioneer Corps, especially formed to meet the abrogation emergency. Recruiting began at Machakos, Wakamba County, for the first unit to be formed, 2201 Company, which formed up at the Athi River Depot on 23 December, 1951. Three days later the company sailed from Mombasa on the SS *Mohamedi*, disembarking at Suez on 5 January, 1952. A week later the company was at work at the Ababiya docks and had put sufficient men through their range courses for them to provide armed guards for camp defence duties. The company was 416 strong, with four British officers and four British other ranks. NCOs were found from within the unit, which included a number of former members of the Kings African Rifles."

The RPC History says that some 10,000 EA Pioneers were recruited, organized into twenty-two companies. Of these 7,000 came from Kenya and 3,000 from Uganda. The first group moved to the Canal Zone in March, 1952, and were employed in logistic installations and units. They were on two-year engagements in the main, and, although some Egyptian workers had returned to British employment by this time, it was decided to recruit a further 10,000 to replace the men who were time-expired. There was a re-engagement bonus, so some of the NCOs in particular remained.

Concurrently recruiting for the Mackinnon Road project was in hand, with the assistance of Labour Commissioners. An EAPC Collecting Centre was set up at Tororo (Uganda) for initial recruit processing. Competition for labour increased due to the employment opportunities at the Owen Dam site. Unrest in and around Kampala made it an unsatisfactory recruiting area, so the recruiters moved into the Western Province and then into the East and West Nile Province. Due to a navigational error attributed to indifferent maps, they even recruited in the Belgian Congo.

To complete the Pioneers' story it is necessary to jump to February, 1954, when Headquarters MELF was asked to repatriate 1,500 EA Pioneers ahead of schedule, so that they could serve as guards for Mau Mau detainees. The response was not only a refusal, but the request for another six companies (each of 400) to be raised, two immediately. However, the labour situation eased sufficiently for some men to return in the next two months for guard duties. The introduction of civilian contractors to manage the Canal Zone installations reduced the need for East African Pioneers, and in September, 1954, the RPC and EA Pioneer Corps Depot at Kabrit became a release and repatriation centre. To quote the RPC history again:-

> "Despite opposition in some quarters to their employment as Guard rather than Labour Companies, the East African Pioneers quickly established a high reputation in this area; not a single case of theft or break-in occurred at any site they protected, including many valuable or attractive items". The last EA unit to serve in the Canal Zone was 2216 East African Pioneer Company, who left for home in February, 1956.

At Gilgil in 1945 David Ashley Hall had just transferred from the EA Artillery to the East African Military Police as a sergeant, and reported to the RSM. Apart from the RSM, there were four other British NCOs, thirty members of the Italian Caribinieri "under command" and fifty African NCOs; the Company Commander was in Nairobi. On the first day he was documented and issued with a Matchless 350cc motor cycle (the RSM had a Harley Davidson which might be looked at, but not touched). On Wednesday the RSM gave him a guided tour of their area of responsibility and a demonstration of how to time a speeding officer, who proved to be from the unit David had left at the beginning of the week and an "unauthorized driver" as well. Two more days of practical training followed, particularly in running the charge office, then on Saturday the RSM announced that he was taking the other British NCOs to the mobile Army Kinema Corporation, which had just arrived, and David would be in charge for the evening.

Left alone, David sat on the tall stool behind the high desk, with a pint pot of sweet tea hidden out of sight, and awaited custom. Just as it got dark a very "pink and white" KAR subaltern came into the charge office with four askari carrying something rolled in a lorry tarpaulin. They set it down on the floor and the subaltern explained ("proudly" David thought) that they had found a dead African. David said he was not responsible for dead civilian Africans; the subaltern countered that the corpse was that of an African soldier. Playing for time, David recorded every detail in the Occurrence Book, thanked the officer and bade him goodnight. But the subaltern would not leave without the tarpaulin, as he had signed for it. The askari speedily decanted the corpse on the charge room floor and took the tarpaulin, leaving David with his new friend and a mug of very cold tea.

Wondering how to escape the RSM's criticism for cluttering up the charge office, David reviewed the options for storing the body. He ruled out the cells (prisoners' objections) and the sergeants' mess verandah (hyenas); there was the hospital. In the duty truck he went to the Military Hospital, where a Sister was in sole charge, it being Saturday night and the AKC in town. David saw her as "battle weary, bitter, group happy, and unwilling, very unwilling to accept a dead and bloody body into her aseptic wards". But, being more scared of the RSM than of her, he flourished his very new warrant card and reminded the Sister that she was "enjoined" to provide him with any assistance he might require. It worked! She produced an African bearer with a hurricane lamp and sent them up a small hill to the mortuary, which was apart from the other hospital buildings. All was dark.

The mortuary was a small corrugated iron shed with a concrete floor and an iron table. It had a fly-proof door with a strong spring, which slammed shut, making the bearer drop the hurricane lamp, which went out. Blundering around in the darkness, they knocked over the iron table with the corpse on it. Table and contents hit the corrugated walls "with a clatter that must have been heard in Nairobi, eighty miles away". In the dark all David could see were the whites of the Africans' eyes as, fearful of adverse effects of the dead man's spirit, they attempted to escape by pulling down the walls of the mortuary. At this point the RSM's reassuring, stentorian voice roared from outside, "Ashley Hall, if the bugger's alive let him out; if he is dead, stop playing with him." Returning from the cinema to find himself locked out of his own charge office, he had set off in pursuit. Normality returned and David was accepted into the EAMP fold.

Induction of another kind awaited 2Lt Anthony McMurtrie when he arrived in Nairobi in October, 1948, fresh from the Eaton Hall OCS. His posting to 1 KAR in Nyasaland derived from a chance remark that he had an uncle there as a missionary; he was put in charge of a convoy to Zomba, carrying maize principally, to build up food stocks there. Anthony recalled:-

"The Brigade Major who had detailed me for this had not mentioned that the transport was hired from a rather dubious Arab contractor, and that the fourteen twenty-two ton lorries and two trailers were very near the end of their natural lives. The motley crew were not much more presentable. They were mostly Ethiopian and Somali drivers, with four Italians and a White Russian, who proved to be the most intrepid drivers and highly innovative mechanics. The Quartermaster, on hearing that I would not be returning to Nairobi, regretted that he could not issue me with a camp bed. Nothing daunted, I went down town and blew a whole week's pay on a safari bed. I did insist on a map and a hurricane lamp, despite being told, 'No need old boy. Just head south on the road to Zomba, you can't miss it'.

"Our fourteen lorries were laden with huge sacks of maize, on top of which were perched some sixty askari, their wives and children, household possessions, bicycles and gramophones. The men were returning to their units in Lusaka and Zomba after lengthy leaves in Kenya. The party also included four soldiers in handcuffs, for return intact to Lusaka to be 'dismissed with ignominy'. My 'team' consisted of just three – a very canny Scots CQMS, a rather less experienced RAEC sergeant and a stalwart African RSM who acted as interpreter. No one else spoke English. Our preparations complete, we set out finally on Wednesday 13 October at noon, after a frustrating wait for the end of the fast of Ramadan. It was not the best date to have chosen. Our route over the next four weeks passed through five territories – Kenya, Tanganyika, Northern Rhodesia, Mozambique and Nyasaland, across some of the most spectacular country one could hope to see in a lifetime. We averaged 100 miles per day for twenty-three days, with temperatures over 90 degrees F. On our best day we achieved 174 miles, on our worst just sixty. We went 1,600 miles due south-west to Lusaka on the first leg, and then 700 miles due east to Zomba on the second. The bitumen road out of the city soon gave way to a metalled surface, then to gravel and finally murram. Occasional stretches of 'strips', as wide as the wheel track, gave welcome breaks from the endless corrugations, clouds of red dust and the head-bumping potholes.

"Out in the bush we spotted the nomadic Masai tribe jogging along in single file, bundles of firewood on their heads, guarding their emaciated cattle. As the journey progressed many wild animals came into view – but there was no time for photographs. In Tanganyika the road ran through volcanic ash country, which was worse after prolonged dry weather than it was after rain, as it pulverized, leaving severe potholes. During one stretch of 100 miles in Tanganyika we passed through five tsetse fly control posts, which involved spraying all the vehicles. A heavy climb up a steep escarpment with fairly dangerous hairpin bends and finally into Lusaka for a welcome five-day break waiting for a supply of diesel oil. The final leg took us along the so-called Great East Road to Fort Jameson, over the escarpment with steep gradients, sharp curves and single-line traffic for 100 miles, taking up to half an hour to negotiate each oncoming vehicle. There were about forty bridges on this section, including the Beit bridge, some 850 feet in length.

"Selection of the night-time staging post was critical because, as well as keeping clear of any village, we had to park on a downhill slope to enable the lorries to start the next day; not too near scrub, in case we started a bush fire, but nevertheless with enough dead wood around for cooking. This was a combination that kept my mind active from 4 p.m. onwards. Rations were issued daily, otherwise they would all have been consumed before the halfway mark. Everyone lined up alongside the ration lorry with outstretched hands and enamel bowls to receive maize flour, corned beef, ghee, cooking oil, peanuts, sugar, tinned milk and tea. One evening the queue seemed longer than usual. A few enterprising locals had joined, intent on enjoying the munificence of Bawana Kingi Georgi. After that the RSM presided with a nominal roll and a sharpened pencil."

Anthony took a sick parade each morning at 5.30:-

"I dished out aspirin, laxatives and acraflavine; men, women and children all went away duly satisfied to face another day."

He slept on top of a lorry cab because lion were around at night. An Arab driver who was thought to have gone mad was handcuffed until he could be taken to the nearest mental hospital. Next day one of the wives gave birth to a bouncing boy during the morning break, and climbed back onto the lorry a little later.

Apart from the state of the roads, there was an endless list of mechanical dramas, crankshaft, clutch and compressor failures, as well as boiling radiators, wheel changes and engine breakdowns due to the intense heat. None of the lorries could tow the water trailer, which was dismantled and loaded on a lorry. They carried all their diesel fuel between Nairobi and Dodoma, where they loaded another 300 four-gallon drums, to take them to Lusaka.

"Before leaving Nairobi, I had been severely warned not – under any circumstances – to start a bush fire. My horror can be imagined on descending from my lorry one morning to see a nice ring of fire spreading out from where some men had been brewing up. All hands set to work with a will, the men beating the fire with branches. It was not until we were able to create a natural firebreak that we succeeded in putting it out after one and a half-hours. Significantly, I can find no reference to it in my journal, but the memory is fresh after some forty-five years.

"On Wednesday 13 November, after 2,344 miles and enough initiative tests to last a lifetime, we drew up outside the boma at Zomba. Clambering down I gave my best Eaton Hall salute to the Commanding Officer, who, hearing that I was National Service, remarked to the Adjutant, 'I thought that we had dispensed with those now!' – and so to a hearty breakfast in the mess."

Elsewhere military life was assuming a more settled peacetime style of existence. In 1950 the Duke of Gloucester visited Kenya; the programme included the presentation of new Colours in Nairobi. Geoffrey Whitworth was with 5 KAR in Jinja and his company was to provide the Guard of Honour for HRH when he left Nairobi station. They travelled to Nairobi by train, but it was not an easy trip. Geoffrey remembered:-

"We were involved in one of the surprisingly few Kenya and Uganda Harbour Board derailments. We came off the line taking a sharp bend between Kaptagat and El Doret at 3 a.m. It was very cold. There were no fatalities, very few injuries, and none of my men was involved. The whole of the centre section of the train lay on its side, with many carriage roofs off. The dining car was completely wrecked. We kept warm with bonfires and the train staff shared out the unbroken contents of the Dining Car cellar. The local settlers were hospitable with breakfasts and baths, and we made Nairobi late that night, by MT sent from Nakuru. We were in time for the celebrations. The Guard of Honour turned out in immaculate order, despite the harrowing experience. We were very well looked after and all ranks had a good time."

But peacetime soldiering was not to last for long; the first rumblings of Mau Mau were already being detected by the more sensitive ears.

Chapter 10

MALAYA

"Full powers – heady stuff."

W.S. Churchill

The Malay Emergency was the longest and possibly the least popular in British post-war history. It lasted twelve years, from 1948 until it petered out three years after Malayan independence in 1957. It overlapped the Korean War, the Cyprus emergency, Mau Mau and the Suez invasion; then came the Borneo operation. It compounded British military manpower problems and frustrated the general wish to reduce National Service. At its height it involved 45,000 troops, including twenty-two infantry battalions, British, Gurkha, Malay, East African, Central African (including Rhodesian), Fijian, Australian and New Zealand (although not all at once).

Its origins lay before and during the 1939–45 war. Chinese and Indian workers had been brought in to develop the tin and rubber industries, but they were not welcomed by the Malay population. When the Japanese invaded in December, 1941, these two major industries were disrupted and most of the expatriate labour force lost their jobs. To survive, Chinese communities "squatted" on farms on the fringes of the jungle. The Japanese had a pro-Malay, anti-Indian and anti-Chinese policy which added to the Chinese sense of grievance. In consequence the main resistance to the Japanese occupation came from the Chinese community, based on the Communist organization close to its centre. The story of the resistance movement had been published at about the beginning of the emergency by Lt Col Spencer Chapman OBE, in his book *The Jungle is Neutral*. In it he described the movement's activities, including the rôle played by it's eventual leader Chin Peng. Chin was made OBE and took part in the Victory Parade in London in recognition of his achievements. He and his men were now our key opponents in the Malayan Emergency.

The Chinese had been frustrated by the post-war political situation in Malaya, and felt that they had not benefited from the victory. There were four States under direct British colonial rule, the Straits Settlements of

Penang, Wellesley, Malacca and Singapore. The rest of Malaya was Sultanates, semi-independent States responsible for their own internal affairs, assisted by British Residents, who advised the Sultans and reported to the British High Commissioner. In general the Sultans were not progressive and not sympathetic to the Chinese. The British Government proposed a new constitution to make all of Malaya, both the Straits Settlements and the Sultanates, into a federation with equal rights for all, irrespective of ethnic origins. This was popular with the Chinese and Indians, but not with the Sultans and most Malays. When, in 1948, UK withdrew the plan because of Malay opposition, the Chinese were resentful and felt they had been betrayed. The situation was exploited by the Malayan Communist Party, which was almost entirely Chinese in membership and very active in the trade unions.

The Emergency was declared after three rubber estate managers were killed in mid-June, in the very Communist area of Perak, in the north-west of the peninsula. This may have been premature, as Communist preparations were not complete. However, they had already set up secret camps in the jungle, within reach of Chinese villages, and moved into them.

The British organization was headed by the Special Commissioner for South East Asia, Malcolm MacDonald, who co-ordinated British policy throughout the region and who chaired meetings of the Commanders in Chief of the Far East Fleet, Land Forces and Air Forces. The High Commissioner of Malaya, Sir Edward Gent, was killed in an air accident on his way to UK later in June and was replaced, but not until October, by Sir Henry Gurney, formerly Chief Secretary in Palestine. The adverse effects of this interregnum were compounded by a change of Police Commissioner, as Colonel Gray, former Inspector-General in Palestine, had just arrived, Maj Gen Boucher was new at GOC Malaya, and the men holding the critical jobs of Attorney General and Financial Secretary, were both "acting" in those capacities.

The army's strength in Malaya was eleven infantry battalions; six Gurkha, two Malay and three British. In addition there was one British field regiment, while a further brigade was in Singapore. The Gurkha battalions had large numbers of new recruits, while the British battalions suffered from the high rate of turn-over and the constant erosion of training standards caused by National Service.

MacDonald identified two priorities: to gather intelligence about the Malayan Communist Party and to keep the mines and plantations working. The responsibility for intelligence was split, and there was a serious disagreement about the troops. The Police Commissioner wanted them as static guards, in line with his concept of MacDonald's priority, while the GOC wanted to use them on offensive operations in the jungle, subject to the police providing the requisite intelligence.

The Communists intensified their preparations, particularly their organization, training and logistics. While they were doing so, reported incidents dropped to about 100 per month for the first half of 1949, about half the rate for the previous six months. Gurney misinterpreted this, and estimated that the emergency would be over by the end of 1949. But when Chin Peng was ready the incident rate rose quickly and by mid-1950 averaged 400 per month. Targets included police stations and road ambushes, sometimes by as many as 100 bandits, or Communist Terrorists (CTs) as they were officially called after January, 1952.

The infantry battalions were increased to seventeen, then two more brigades were added. However, GOCinC Far East Land Forces, now Gen Sir John Harding, and the new GOC Malaya, Maj Gen Urquhart, considered that the troops were not being used to the best advantage; much time being spent on unproductive jungle patrolling. The plan was for the army to separate the activists from their logistic support in the "squatter" settlements while a political solution was developed that would give the remainder of the Chinese community land ownership rights and political equality, so that they had a future in Malaya as fully fledged citizens. A force of Special Constables was raised to take over the army's static guard duties.

A Director of Operations was appointed in April, 1950, Sir Harold Briggs. He quickly developed the Briggs Plan, which began in the populated areas and then moved to the rural ones. Areas were cleared systematically, not moving on until full clearance had been accomplished. A food denial plan was extended and the routes to CT food sources were ambushed frequently. Briggs chaired a Federal War Council which was attended by the GOC, and AOC, the Police Commissioner and the Secretary of Defence. The Council was replicated at State level, and Sir William Jenkin, formerly of the Indian Police, became responsible for intelligence.

After six disappointing months, Harding was convinced that power must be concentrated at the top (preferably in the hands of a General) to achieve any worthwhile results, and briefed the CIGS, Gen Sir William Slim, accordingly. At about this time the High Commissioner was killed in an ambush. A review by the new Colonial Secretary, Oliver Lyttelton, endorsed Harding's recommendations and Gen Sir Gerald Templer, GOC Eastern Command, was selected. Churchill, back in office as Prime Minister, insisted on seeing Templer, who had to fly to Ottawa where Churchill was attending a conference. Churchill's only contribution to the interview was the remark at the head of this chapter, which was taken as agreement to the appointment.

In February, 1952, Templer became both High Commissioner and Director of Operations. The latter post was vacant as Briggs had retired two months before. At the same time Gray was replaced by Sir Arthur Young as Police Commissioner. MacDonald and local politicians were concerned that so much power was in the hands of one man, who feared that Templer would concentrate on the Emergency to the exclusion of political advancement. Their fears were unfounded, as Templer quickly grasped all aspects of the situation and, while directing security affairs with zeal, he encouraged the development of a fully multi-racial society. He was aided in this when the Alliance Party formed. This was a grouping of Malay, Indian and Chinese political organizations opposed to the Independence for Malaya Party. It was led by Tunku Abdul Rahman who, as a member of a royal family, was in a uniquely strong position. In 1955 the Alliance Party won a major victory in the federal elections.

Templer had two able deputies; Gen Lockhart on the military side and Sir Donald MacGillivray on the civil as Deputy High Commissioner. With the aid of his strengthened forces, the introduction of bigger helicopters on a significant scale and the greatly improved flow of intelligence, Templer fully implemented the Briggs plan. As part of this, 410 new villages were created, and new legislation gave the Chinese firm title to their land, an important step forward that considerably improved Chinese perceptions of their future in an independent Malaya.

The Communists reacted by adopting a more flexible attitude to those who did not support them, and revised their tactics, operating in groups of about platoon size and concentrating on ambushes. There were regular rotation programmes for retraining and reindoctrination, and units were encouraged to grow their own food. This had its disadvantages, because they cultivated their crops in well-weeded plots, planted in straight lines; in consequence they were easily detected from the air. There was a technique that the KAR were to use, called "shamba bashing", in which a plot was watched from the air until the crops were near to being harvested, when it and the harvesters were attacked to the detriment of the harvesters. British operational areas were changed from Malaya's administrative boundaries to conform with the seven zones of the Communist organization; Chin Peng's sector in the Cameron Highlands was the most important of these. Each area was dealt with in three phases; intelligence gathering, food denial and a deep patrol to locate and destroy the terrorists.

In East Africa the Ogaden Region of Ethiopia had been handed over to Ethiopia, Somalia (excluding the British Protectorate) had become a UN Trusteeship under Italian administration, while, although there were some rumblings of eventual difficulty, the Internal Security situation was generally calm. The KAR was therefore not heavily tasked, while the manpower situation in Malaya had become pressing.

Lt Col J.O. Crewe-Read, who had been serving at the Greek Army Staff College at Salonica, moved down to Kenya in January to take command of 3 KAR, replacing Lt Col N. Hendricks. The battalion had been serving previously in the Ogaden and Somalia. In March they were on a brigade training exercises in the Lake Baringo area when they were visited by the GOC, Maj Gen Sir Arthur Dowler, and the Brigadier Training and Infantry GHQ MELF, Brig "Algy" Heber-Percy. This unusual level of interest was something of a surprise and was the prelude to the CO being told in confidence that 1 (Nyasa) and 3 (Kenya) Battalions KAR would be moving to Malaya as reinforcements in October, for action against the CTs.

The delay was to allow the terms of service for the askari to be agreed by the War Office, and for adequate leave to be taken. It was not until early 1952 that all was ready for the units to embark. Terms of service were based on an operational tour in Malaya of eighteen months plus two months for travelling by sea. Pay went up to the levels of other Colonial troops serving in Malaya (e.g. the Fijians) and the Gurkhas. This was a substantial increase and, coupled with generous home leave to settle families in their home villages, proved very popular.

The European complement was augmented by increasing the number of subalterns to one per platoon and by the addition of a 2ic per company, a Regimental Medical Officer (usually National Service), a Royal Army Education Corps WO or BNCO, (supported by several EAAEC WOs and NCOs), an Army Physical Training Corps instructor (WO or BNCO), a REME Armourer Sergeant, and an RAPC WO/BNCO. In addition a small REME Light Aid Detachment would be added in remote locations. The remainder of the British soldiers were an RSM, a British CSM in each rifle company, an Orderly Room Quartermaster Sergeant (WO2), a Regimental Quartermaster Sergeant (WO2) and a Colour Sergeant, many of whom had wartime service. In the main the subalterns were National Servicemen of high calibre, most of them had already secured places at universities at the end of their service. They went on courses in Swahili immediately on arrival in East Africa.

Roy Stockwell transferred to 3 KAR from 5 KAR together with several askari, and Dai Curtis joined from 4 KAR. Signallers were attached from EA Signals and drivers from EAASC. Not all of the attached personnel remained with the battalion on arrival in Malaya; many of the EAAMC went to the British Military Hospital at Kinrara, while a WO2 and a S/Sgt of EAAEC worked with the Forces Broadcasting Service in Singapore, broadcasting to the askari in Swahili. The RAEC WO/BNCO was employed in the Intelligence office.

The battalion was organized as four rifle companies and Headquarters Company. On arrival in Malaya No 5 rifles (rubber butt-pad and a flash eliminator) were issued, the Australian Owen gun replaced the Sten (which was considered too unreliable to take into the jungle); Bren guns modified for jungle use and Winchester carbines were also introduced. Mortars were not popular because of trajectory problems in the jungle canopy and the prohibitive weight of man-packing the bombs on patrol. In consequence the three-inch Mortar Platoon became an additional rifle platoon. The EY rifle (a reinforced SMLE No 1 rifle that fired a 36 grenade from a discharger cup fitted to the muzzle, with the aid of a ballistite cartridge and a seven-second fuze) was intended to replace the mortar at rifle platoon level, but it was disliked, even mistrusted.

As soon as the askari returned from leave, training started on the lower slopes of Mount Kenya, to familiarize all ranks with jungle operations. Concurrently a small advance party consisting of the RQMS and an African WO went to Singapore to plan the reception of the battalion, including arranging married quarters for the European families and drawing up the AFG 1098 scale of equipment to replace the kit to be handed over to the relieving unit, 23 KAR, before leaving Kenya. This posed a very heavy workload on the battalion's Q staff.

Early in January, 1952, 3 KAR embarked at Mombasa aboard the *Devonshire* and sailed to Beira to pick up 1 KAR, who had moved down from Nyasaland. The ship was not full, and all European ranks and some senior Africans were in cabins. The sea was calm throughout the voyage and the two weeks to Colombo were spent on PT, boxing and shipboard entertainments. The battalion included some Africans with 1939-45 war service who had travelled by troopship before, so any misgivings that the younger soldiers may have had about boarding the ship and adjusting to the routine afloat were speedily dealt with by the older hands. To replace them in East Africa, 23 and 26 Battalions KAR were formed.

A welcome break at Colombo allowed for company marches ashore, but there was no shore leave. The ship then sailed for Singapore where they were met by the advance party and staff officers from GHQ FARELF. While the European families moved into their temporary accommodation in Singapore (they went to Penang later, while the battalions were on operations), the battalions went to the Far East Training Centre at Kota Tinggi, in Johore. There, with the help of the Gurkha demonstration battalion, they did jungle training and drew up their scale of vehicles and 1098 equipment. Transport included six scout cars and some three-ton armoured trucks, jeeps, Dodge trucks and troop-carrying vehicles.

They were disconcerted at the lack of information given on the maps, and great emphasis was given to compass training for everyone. Battalion communications were by means of a version of the 18 radio set that had been modified in Australia to extend its range. Using a sky-wave aerial, voice communication was possible with patrols and between companies and Battalion HQ, although only at night when the aerial could be erected. Patrols used 68 sets (with dry batteries) and usually worked to 62 sets (wet batteries); the shape of the ground caused patchy performance, but sometimes the ranges achieved were impressive.

After three weeks of jungle training, 3 KAR moved to their operational sector, tasked to find and destroy the CT camps and their occupants. The sector was astride the branch railway line to Kuala Lipis in Pahang State, under command of 1 Malay Brigade. They took over from 1 Malay Battalion and set up Battalion Headquarters at Triang, in the stationmaster's house; rifle companies were deployed at villages along the railway. There was one train in each direction per day, escorted by Malay police. The line was prone to attack by CTs, who wrecked it by damaging the rails, causing derailments. Their most effective method was to loosen the fish plates, preferably on a bend, which made the rails splay. The out-going battalion had reported that the sector was relatively quiet. Patrolling was begun at once, both to gain experience and to familiarize themselves with the terrain. On their first Sunday, the down train was stopped by a cut line and the escort engaged the CTs. A 3 KAR patrol heard the firing and moved towards it. The leading scout bumped a CT and was shot at close range and killed. This was a most salutary experience for the battalion; a new air of purposefulness entered all that they did, and was reflected in their final record of eighty-eight CTs killed or captured in their sixteen months in contact.

They dominated their area by deep patrolling; the usual patrol was one officer and six askari with a radio. Normally the patrol would carry three days of "compo" (composite) rations and relied on streams and pools for water. Compo rations, mainly bully beef at scale of half a tin per man per day, together with rice, tea and sugar, were very popular with the askari. In camp they had the same scale of food as in Africa, maize meal ("posho"), fresh meat with vegetables, tea and sugar. Supply of the posho caused considerable problems. It was imported from Australia and was frequently too coarsely or too finely ground for African taste, with consequent complaints. Gurkha ration packs were popular with both Europeans and the askari.

The CTs put out propaganda that the askari were cannibals. This was refuted very effectively when a patrol, having killed two CTs, a man and a woman, found and brought in a baby whom they fed on tinned milk from the compo rations. In the four months on the railway line 3 KAR accounted for several terrorists and handed over to a Malay battalion an area that was more secure than they had found it on arrival. They were then assigned to a sector based on Kuantan, on the east coast.

They travelled down the River Pahang in flat-bottomed boats that were poled along. There was one night-stop before arrival at Pekan, the State capital and home of the Sultan, close to the sea. Transport was waiting to take them to their new company locations. Kuantan had been overrun by CTs at one stage, but the Gurkha battalion (1/10 GR) which 3 KAR replaced had restored relative peace. There was a sign like a thermometer in the town centre on which the Gurkhas had recorded their CT kills. It was taken over and used by 3 KAR in the same way. John Jessop (3 KAR Education Sergeant) was part of the advance party, to take over the Operations Room. The askari in the advance party got on well with the Gurkhas in the NAAFI canteen. John commented, "God knows what language they spoke, but they got on like a house on fire. I suspect it was English; but no Gurkha, in those days, would have admitted to having any English at all."

The battalion was widely dispersed, with some companies up to fifty miles from Battalion HQ at Kuantan. One company was at a tin mine (their duties included escorting consignments of tin from the mine to Kuantan for shipment), one on the railway and the other two in Malay villages. The CO travelled between locations using a 4x4 saloon at first, but he soon changed to a scout car or an Auster plane. The operational task was to dominate their area of jungle and to deny the initiative to the CTs. One, often two, platoons per company would be engaged in patrolling, while the balance of the company rested in the company base. Each askari averaged one patrol, usually of three days, per fortnight.

Air support was available from Lincoln bombers of the RAF, but 3 KAR had little experience of it. There were a few relatively small RAF helicopters; at Kuantan there was a squadron of Royal Navy Sikorski helicopters, used mainly for casualty evacuation. There were no helicopter gun-ships. Air drops were used to replenish long-range patrols; the main problem was for the aircraft to locate the patrol. African map reading in the jungle proved to be very good; it was occasionally supplemented by assistance from the Auster AOP flights, who would call for smoke to be fired by a patrol to disclose its position; then the Auster would radio a map reference to the patrol. Use of radio was limited by range and by the time of day when effective transmission was possible. Smoke grenades were used to indicate dropping zones where supplies could be parachuted in, but direct communication with RAF and RAAF aircraft was not always possible, and messages sometimes had to be relayed through their base airfield. On other occasions, however, it was possible to get through, as Bob Cobbing recalls, "It was always useful, if only to get a fix on your position, and the exchanges were occasionally enlivened by brisk Australian disregard for radio procedure and terminology, as they pointed out that our DZ was located in an entirely inappropriate spot. For our part we would point out in the politest way possible that, as it was difficult for us to see much more than fifty yards in front of us, they were pretty lucky to have been able to contact us at all."

A very good arrangement existed for co-operation between the Civil Administration, the Police and the Army. Every morning the District Officer, the senior Police Officer and the CO would meet for 'morning prayers' when events of the past twenty-four hours would be reviewed, intelligence information shared and plans discussed. Information came from Special Branch and routine patrols. However, it was not always effective. One operation set up on the basis of air reconnaissance photographs involved the air-lifting of Battalion Headquarters and two companies to attack an important CT headquarters; two other battalions were in position as back-stops. A careful approach led to a site that had been abandoned some time before, and much wasted effort. But things often went much better. For example, an emergency call from Brigade Headquarters reported that there had been an outbreak of CT activity at Trengganu. A flight by helicopter to discuss the situation with the Sultan and the police, followed by a thorough reconnaissance, led to the despatch of Headquarters B Company and two platoons to the area, where success was achieved rapidly. The battalion also recovered two elegant pig-spears with ebony handles, part of the Trengganu State Royal regalia, from a CT camp; the Sultan recognized them when visiting D Company mess. They had disappeared in 1942, during the Japanese invasion. The Sultan showed his appreciation for the battalion's effective work in the State by awarding the Trengganu State Distinguished Conduct Medal to J.O. Crewe-Read, the Company Commander (Major Tim Ewell) and to two D Company askari.

Throughout the tour in Malaya the morale of the askari was excellent. British families on Penang received details of progress mainly from the local press, which gave good coverage of operations. African Warrant Officer Platoon Commanders became particularly effective. One of them, Jackson Malengi, was attending the Imperial Defence College in London thirteen years later and rose to become a General and Chief of Army Staff in Kenya. The battalion had a great success in the Malay States' Games in 1953, and in the Command athletics meeting. Trained by the APTC instructor, they swept the board in the middle and long distance running events, breaking every record at one mile and above. The Kipsigis and Nandi askari were particularly good, out-pacing their British rivals and attracting comments from British soldiers "of a robust military character, as they saw their best athletes being left far behind". Might this have been the beginnings of the now legendary performance by African athletes at international events?

3 KAR had two officer casualties. John Mather was following up a wounded CT who had gone to ground when the CT threw a grenade (or fired a shot gun, versions vary), wounding John in the arm, from which he soon recovered. John killed the CT with a burst from his Winchester M2 carbine. Peter Harding had an unfortunate experience when he laid an ambush in the dark. When the CTs arrived he fired a Very light and seized the nearest of them, shouting in Swahili to his men as he did so, "Don't shoot, don't shoot". However, a Bren gunner failed to grasp the situation and fired, killing two CTs, including the man Peter was holding. A bullet passed through the CT and wounded Peter slightly in the shoulder and hand. The damage was not serious and he soon returned to duty. It was unfortunate that the men were killed, as prisoners were valued for the intelligence that could be obtained. The WOPC, a Nandi, was awarded the DCM for his part in this action. The CT fought very hard not to be captured. When prisoners were taken they were not allowed to be interrogated by the Army, but were handed over to Special Branch.

1 KAR returned to Nyasaland to be replaced by 2 KAR. 3 KAR was due to be replaced by 5 KAR, but Mau Mau had started and plans were revised because of the increased priority being given to Kenya. This led to CO 3 KAR flying back to Kenya to discuss the battalion's next moves. In consequence he missed their farewell parade, at which the Sultan of Pahang presented the battalion with a Malay kris [a ceremonial knife with a wiggly blade]. The battalion was given a propeller blade from an Auster by the AOP Flight, which held pride of place in the officers' mess in Nanyuki, when they moved there in 1957.

The battalion's achievements in Malaya were acknowledged by the award of one OBE (J.O. Crewe-Read), one MBE, a DCM (WOPC Kiberin), and several MMs, including WOPCs Kimani and Kitur. The latter received a bar to it later, during the Mau Mau operations.

Bruce Leeming, then nineteen years old, saw Malaya and 2 KAR as a National Service subaltern. After being at Zomba briefly, a month and two sea voyages by HMTs *Dunera* and *Dilwara* found him with several other 2Lts and the rest of 2 KAR at the Jungle Warfare School at Kota Tinggi, before moving to their operational area. He describes their deployment:-

"C Company was posted to the township of Sungei Lembing, in the north-eastern state of Pahang. Battalion Headquarters (CO Lt Col Blackie, Adjutant Michael Morton) were on the coast at Kuantan, the combat companies at strategic points around this pivot. Lembing, twenty miles inland, had grown up in the environs of a rich, isolated deep-lode tin mine" and they were to protect it. The entire settlement, mine and town, was surrounded by a twelve-foot barbed wire fence, guarded twenty-four hours a day by Malay police in observation towers.

On a typical occasion he was tasked by his company commander Ron Kidd, to destroy a CT shamba that had been identified from an air photograph. He left with eighteen men at 2 a.m. passing through the compound gates, where a Malay policeman saluted and said "Selamat jalan, Tuan" [safe journey, sir]. Although it was early, everyone was already sweating profusely when they halted for a short while in a Chinese graveyard to shake out into patrol order. One of the askari took fright at the proximity of the dead, but he was calmed and they moved into the jungle. After an hour of struggling through the clammy, matted creepers, tripping over rotten logs and being torn by thorns, they halted to check their compass bearings. A steep contour lay ahead and Bruce decided that they would go to it and sleep for a couple of hours before first light. Bruce continues:-

"The moon then disappeared altogether and it began to rain heavily. The ground between us and the hilly ridge was marshy. Hungry mosquitoes rose to meet us. Men slapped at the insects and were cursed by the NCOs for the noise. We sank into boggy holes and heaved ourselves out with great effort. In the dark we sweated blindly. The rain became torrential, turning the hillside into a greasy mudslide. Grasping at tree roots, we fought for footholds as we forced our way up to the plateau. It was desperately difficult keeping weapons if not dry, at least free of mud. On the hilltop we formed a wide circle and posted two sentries at thirty yards from its circumference. Sleep proved impossible in the rain, but tired muscles relaxed for a while as we sat against tree trunks, poncho capes over our heads. Near dawn the rain stopped. I ordered 'stand to'. Half awake askari stood up, weapons at the ready. All faced outwards round our circle, silent. This was an old army drill against attack at first light which we'd learned at Kota Tinggi. After ten minutes the sun was up and the sweating began again. Prickly heat pustules and old infected leech bites itched unbearably. We stank. But, after a brew-up, everybody cheered up. Half an hour later we set off to find the vegetable patch".

They did not find it, that day or the next; food ran short and no air drop had been arranged. There was nothing for it but to return to camp. However, sustained pressures were eventually successful, other gardens were located and destroyed, usually by burning, ambushes and occasional CT surrenders. Bruce continued:-

"Of course, some pleasant interludes also occurred during our jungle missions; a cloud of azure butterflies hovering close to the surface of an emerald stretch of river, a clan of gibbons passing noisily through the high leafy canopy overhead, from a tree cleft a prodigal spill of wild orchids – palest lemon and rust red petals vivid against the surrounding green. Furtive, blowpipe-carrying aborigines flitted across our track now and again. Once at morning ablutions, protected by two sentries, we discovered fresh pug marks and realized that our water point was being shared with a night-visiting tiger. Also in the area were elephant, tapir, leopard, wild buffalo, tiny mouse deer, boar, even bears, as well as snakes and countless types of birds.

"Although previous battalions in Pahang had done their work well, notably 3 KAR under Lt Col Crewe-Read, whom we relieved, there were still some high-ranking CTs about. Regional Committee Chairman Yoke Har was a fearsome fat Cantonese woman, said to have personally executed eight CTs for indiscipline. She had been involved in the murders of several unco-operative rubber tappers, in bus burnings and various other acts of heartless terror. Many of our patrols were geared to capturing her, often on a mere fragment of doubtful information on her whereabouts. But Yoke Har's intelligence sources were at least as good as ours, and she never crossed our path. At least not until an all-African patrol under WOPC Kazemba stumbled on her and her bodyguards travelling to a jungle conference in the south. Two of her men were killed, she was badly wounded and brought back to camp. The whole company was elated at this long-awaited success, and supplies were immediately ordered for a celebratory 'ngoma'. Pending transfer to hospital at Kuantan she was locked in a shed under close guard. She had been given a morphine injection, but was obviously in great distress, judging from her constant moaning. I knew how hot it must be in that little windowless room." He filled a bottle with water, had the door unlocked and offered the drink to the blood-soaked woman lying on a rope-strung charpoy. She was, he estimated, as old as his mother. She tried to knock the water from his hand, then the askari guard explained that she feared being poisoned, so Bruce drank from the bottle in front of her. "At once her expression changed, not to one of gratitude but simply to a dull acceptance. In seconds she was gulping down the lukewarm water." Months later, fully recovered, she was hanged in Kuala Lumpur's Pudu Gaol.

When the Malayan Communist Party formally laid down its arms and signed a peace treaty with the governments in Kuala Lumpur and Bangkok, Bruce obtained details of the CTs who had survived. The total was 1,188, comprising 670 Thais, 402 Chinese, 77 Malays, 13 Aborigines, 2 Indians, 2 Japanese (who had been in the jungle for at least 45 years), and one Indonesian. 200 of these were women.

In Malaysia as a rubber broker, after demobilization, Bruce saw democracy holding its own and the economy flourishing. He found himself "often thinking of the unsung contributions made so long ago by the likes of Pikinini Wadiwala Zakaria (WOPC), Billie Kazxembe, Wyson Lubeche, 'Piano' (who had become disconcerted in the Chinese cemetery), and the rest back in their native land. Those decades have not always offered them the same widening horizons and job opportunities."

Kenya: Mau Mau and after

MAP 10

Chapter 11

KENYA AND MAU MAU

"It had a profound effect in persuading influential Conservative political figures in Britain to bow to the wind of change in Africa."

FM Lord Carver, 1980

The causes of Mau Mau lay in the differing objectives of the various communities in Kenya. It was difficult to provide scope for African political evolution or job opportunities for educated Africans. There was resentment at the influx of settlers and Asian traders, who were thought to have stolen African lands. The Kikuyu were reputed to be the most biddable of the tribes; they were the largest and lived in the central area, north of Nairobi and east of the Aberdare Mountains. Through their proximity to the capital and because of the missionaries' educational programmes, the Kikuyu were generally better educated and many of them were employed in Government service at junior grades, and as domestic servants. But they had their own culture, some aspects of which were not in accord with European thinking; the Church of Scotland was opposed to the practice of female circumcision, and in 1922 the Church decided to oppose the practice publicly. This focus for Kikuyu resentment developed into a major grievance.

Jomo Kenyatta (originally Kamau wa Ngengi) was an early member of the Kikuyu Central Association; he moved to Britain in 1922, and wrote articles and books advocating African independence, which circulated among the Kikuyu community. He returned to Kenya in 1946 and became the leader of an active faction. The Government was attempting to improve social services and to assist African farming, but it was probably too little and too late. Kenyatta's views became widely held among the Kikuyu, but did not spread much to other tribes. When the Kikuyu Central Association was banned its members took control of the larger (and more widely supported) Kenya African Union, which was still a legal organization. It had connections with the Kikuyu Karinga Association, the African Orthodox Church and the Kikuyu Independent Schools Association; the Githunguri Teachers' College was a training base. Mau Mau was the military arm of the movement and was busy recruiting and establishing control over many Kikuyu through oathing ceremonies. These were eventually proscribed, but not before much damage had been done.

In 1952 Sir Philip Mitchell retired as Governor, but it was several months before Sir Evelyn Baring took up his post, during which time the situation deteriorated sharply. In mid-July the Police Commissioner reported that a general revolt of the Kikuyu was imminent. In the Legislative Council the European members called on the Government to take strong action. Kenyatta addressed a 25,000-strong meeting at Nyeri in late July. It had been organized by the Kenya African Union, but almost all those present were Kikuyu, who cheered every time Mau Mau was mentioned. Despite the efforts of senor Kikuyu, the oathings, intimidation and boycotting of Government activities gained pace. On arrival on 29 September Baring saw that he must act quickly or the Government would lose what support still remained among the Kikuyu, the trouble would spread among the other tribes (with serious implications for the KAR and the Police) and the European population would be at risk. He recommended the declaration of a State of Emergency and the arrest of Kenyatta and his closest followers. When the Lancashire Fusiliers arrived they did a "flag march" through Nairobi, and the Police, with KAR support, arrested nearly 200 members of the Mau Mau.

Two KAR battalions were still in Malaya and two newly formed battalions covered the Internal Security responsibilities in East Africa; a third battalion was split between Mauritius and Tanganyika. There was the Kenya Regiment, a part-time battalion of Europeans. East Africa Command was reorganized because the newly formed Central African Federation was taking command of the Northern Rhodesian and Nyasaland units. Within two weeks of the mass arrests, Senior Chief Nderi and a prominent farmer, Eric Bowyer, and two of his servants were murdered. Baring was hampered by the lack of intelligence, and took defensive steps first. He expanded the Police Force and authorized the formation of the Kikuyu Guard, both for protection purposes and as a potential focus for loyal supporters. In general British battalions operated in the areas of European settlement, the KAR in the reservation, the Tribal Police as directed by the Provincial and District Commissioners and the Kenya Police (under the Police Commissioner) in the towns. Sir Percy Sillitoe, head of the Security Service, recommended a unified control of intelligence and operations, but this took some time to establish. Several KAR officers returning from Malaya were dismayed that the lessons of that operation were being applied so slowly in Kenya. The murders of a farmer named Ruck and his family in January, 1953, caused many Europeans to march on

Government House, but Michael Blundell and Humphrey Slade persuaded them to disperse.

Maj Gen Hinde was appointed to be Director of Operations, but after Gen Sir John Harding's visit in February, 1953, Gen Sir George Erskine became Commander in Chief, with responsibility for the Army, the RAF and for the Police in emergency operations. Harding also sent to Kenya 39 Infantry Brigade Headquarters and two more British infantry battalions.

By the end of February 177 Kikuyu, nine Europeans and three Asians had been killed by the Mau Mau, and a month later the Lari massacre occurred. The KAR company normally in the area was at a prison south of Nairobi, in support of the Police. It was also unfortunate that the local Kikuyu Guard unit was patrolling in the forest, but there were only 150 of them, with pangas and spears, against about 1,000 Mau Mau, so their presence would not have been decisive. The Mau Mau surrounded the village and attacked each hut occupied by loyal Kikuyu, usually by tying wire round the hut to stop the door being opened, and setting it on fire with the aid of petrol. Any who tried to escape were killed. A detachment of Tribal Police arrived after a few hours, by which time 200 huts had been burned, eighty-four Kikuyu dead and thirty-one badly wounded; two-thirds of them were women and children, while 1,000 cattle had been slashed. The effect was to swing Kikuyu opinion against Mau Mau, and the Kikuyu Guard was strengthened and better armed.

Among the Europeans, however, there was growing mistrust of the Kikuyu, and numbers of dismissed servants and farm workers were sent back to the reservations, where some of them joined Mau Mau. To control movement, identity cards were introduced, but it took three attempts before non-forgeable passport-type books were in use. The newspapers were full of news of minor successes against the Mau Mau, with small quantities of weapons and ammunition being recovered and rifle factories being discovered and destroyed. These "factories" were little more than small workshops, with a dozen or so rifles under construction. The lack of weapons security by the European community saw several of them in Court for carelessness with arms and ammunition. On 3 February eight Kikuyu and two Embu men were hanged at Nairobi prison, six for being in improper possession of firearms and two for murder.

Erskine arrived in June. He was briefed that there were about 8,000 Mau Mau, although the actual number was around 12,000, of whom only 1,500 had modern rifles. They were in three areas: those in the Central and Northern Aberdares were led by Dedan Kimathi: the central sector in the Southern Aberdares was commanded by Stanley Mathenge, and "General China" was in command on Mount Kenya. In addition there were 30,000 supporters in the reservations, out of a total Kikuyu community of a million and a quarter.

The Aberdares provided a strong natural refuge for the Mau Mau. The lower slopes are covered with trees up to about 8,000 feet above sea level, semi-tropical forest with thick, prolific undergrowth. Next is a belt of bamboo for a further 2,000 feet vertically; it grows between thirty and sixty feet high. Above that again are the moorlands, from which the peaks rise to 11,300 feet. The Mount Kenya forest is similar, except that the mountain is higher, at 17,000 feet, and has snow in the upper regions.

Erskine had about 7,000 soldiers; three British battalions of 39 Brigade, 70 (East African) Brigade with five KAR battalions, an armoured car squadron, a heavy anti-aircraft battery and the Kenya Regiment. In a few months he had received a further British Brigade (49) with two battalions and an engineer regiment, so that his total assets grew to some 10,000 soldiers, 21,000 Police, 25,000 Kikuyu Guard and a flight of Harvard aircraft capable of dropping 19 lb bombs. He identified four areas of operations: the native reserves, the forests of the Aberdares and Mount Kenya, the European-settled areas and Nairobi itself. Erskine dealt with the Kikuyu reservation first, concurrently building roads into the forest to allow for deeper and more effective patrolling. This denuded the settled areas of troops and, although the Kikuyu Home Guard was becoming increasingly effective, the settlers were unhappy. They wanted a greater say in Government and better protection for their homes and families.

After the tribal reservations, Erskine turned his attention to Nairobi, where a series of cordon and search operations combed through the African population. Of the total screened, 16,538 were detained and 2,416 were returned to the reserves. The operation (Anvil) continued for a further two weeks and was the turning point in the campaign as it significantly reduced support to Mau Mau from the city. Crime levels in Nairobi fell and more Kikuyu joined the Home Guard. A policy of "villagization" was introduced, which had social and agricultural benefits as well as improving security. By January, 1955, Erskine had sufficient troops to switch his attention to the forest areas, and the rains had ended. Until then the RAF had bombed the forest using Lancasters, but with little effect on the Mau Mau, although the larger game animals suffered.

A combined police and army intelligence organization was formed under John Prendergast, with army intelligence officers integrated into Police Special Branch at the centre, provincial and district levels. They "turned" captured Mau Mau, using them as informers and later as infiltrators. "Pseudo-gangs" were formed, in which Kikuyu-speaking Europeans, generally members of the Kenya Regiment, were disguised as Africans and, with some of the "turned" former Mau Mau, went into the forest to locate the genuine gangs and their suppliers. The risk of a pseudo-gang being mistaken for the genuine article was avoided by rigid control and co-ordination.

Operation Hammer was the code-name for the clearance of the Aberdares in January, 1955. The forest was divided into areas of responsibility which units dominated by mobile and static patrols. Any Mau Mau attempting to break out of the forest would come against the Home Guard and the Tribal Police and their defences of panjis. Troops in the forest were organized into Forest Operating Companies, each of three tracker/combat teams. Each team had an officer or British NCO and eight soldiers, a radio operator, three African trackers, a tracker dog and a patrol dog, plus – for British battalions – an interpreter. One Forest Operating Company came from each of the five British battalions, two from the four Kenya KAR battalions between them, and one each from the Uganda and Tanganyika battalions and the armoured car squadron, a total of five British and five African companies. In addition each battalion produced a "Trojan" team of five men led by a Kikuyu-speaking NCO of the Kenya Regiment; they responded to any hot tips from the Police Special Branch.

The operation began above the tree-line, where the countryside resembles moorland, working down towards the forest edge and the waiting Home Guard and Tribal Police. The plan was too ambitious or there were not enough troops, and it degenerated into a large-scale sweep that caught or killed only 161 Mau Mau. In the Mount Kenya area Operation Flute was conducted more on the lines originally agreed, and the results were better. At this time an attempt was made, through the pseudo-gangs, to induce Stanley Mathenge and his group in the Southern Aberdares to surrender. Dedan Kimathi heard of it and frustrated the attempt, but the two gangs mistrusted each other thereafter.

By the time Erskine left in April, 1955, the active Mau Mau in gangs had been reduced from about 12,000 to 5,000; over 5,500 had been killed or apprehended in the past twelve months. The Kikuyu people were under tight control, both in the reservations and elsewhere, including large numbers in detention camps. The worst of the rebellion was over. Gen Sir Gerald Lathbury, who replaced Erskine, decided to use the pseudo-gangs and specialist units to track down the remaining Mau Mau activists, who were in small, scattered groups of the most determined and best trained men. The British battalions were in the settled areas and the KAR in the reserves.

Operation Dante was on earlier lines, to clear the forests around the Kiambu District. It was not a great success, but other methods continued to produce good results, and by the end of the year the number of Mau

Mau activists in gangs was down to 2,000, and most of the more expert gang leaders had been eliminated. Food denial to the reduced numbers was very effective, and sentiment among the Kikuyu had moved against the rebels. Smaller gangs were more difficult to track, but Kikuyu sources provided a constant flow of information about them. Inside the forest pursuit continued, but outside life was becoming more normal. Dedan Kimathi was wounded and then killed, General China was caught and imprisoned, but Stanley Mathenge just disappeared. The army withdrew from operations after four years, although the Emergency continued until 1960.

The Mau Mau casualties during the war were 10,527 killed, 2,633 captured, 26,625 arrested and 2,714 surrendered, while 50,000 of their supporters had been put into detention. They had killed 1,826 African civilians and wounded 918 of them, and killed thirty-two and wounded twenty-six European civilians. The Asian population had twenty-six killed and thirty-six wounded. The security forces had lost sixty-three Europeans, three Asians and 534 Africans killed, 102 Europeans, twelve Asians and 465 Africans wounded.

The total force deployed was 10,000 British and African troops, 21,000 Police and 25,000 Home Guard. The cost, shared between the British and Kenyan Treasuries, was £55 million.

This sketch of events gives a backdrop to the personal reminiscences that follow. During the emergency East Africa Command changed from what might have been a military backwater to a humming, strenuous place, with a jungle warfare school and a substantial expansion of the logistic services of the East African Forces, just after they had been run down following the reduction in operational commitments in Somalia.

The wars and Internal Security operations between 1945 and 1960 were essentially the province of the National Serviceman. Within the KAR, for the Malay Emergency and to a far greater extent the Mau Mau campaign, this meant the National Service officer. Some extracts from their experiences and a few from their Regular colleagues follow. It was on the junior officers that so much of the conduct of operations depended.

David Peters gives the feelings of one who has just returned from an extensive patrol. Senior officers with big hands and small maps have been the bane of junior officers throughout the ages. In Kenya it was no exception. He wrote:

"Meanwhile the company commander had climbed the steep track to Fort Gloucester. When the patrol emerged wearily from the bamboo he was disappointed at the subaltern's report. More senior officers wanted much more information. The subaltern, not for the first or last time, was not impressed by the ability of more senior officers to denote tasks by the circling of a finger on a map. For bigger tasks a whole hand was necessary. A very big hand could glide impressively over mountain and plain, forest and bush, cross rivers and gorges, traverse the ridges and ravines of volcanoes, march over arid wastes and through stagnant papyrus swamps. The troops followed the hand, but not over the flat smoothness of the map."

David described the campaign and his reactions to it:-

"The soldiers, police and loyalists who opposed Mau Mau were plunged into a strange, different war against the far recesses of the human mind. It was a campaign of a multitude of small actions by patrols, ambushes and even individual fights. In fact most actions were composed of man-to-man exchanges as one caught sight of the other between trees or round the corner of a hut. Perhaps more than in any other campaign, the troops experienced much weary frustration, fruitless effort and difficult movement, usually on foot, in appalling conditions. As always there was apprehension and sometimes fear. This fear was not of battle and its consequences, but of the unknown depths of Mau Mau savagery. Yet there were no major battles, not even a battalion engagement. Companies, even platoons, rarely fought actions as tactical entities. Soldiers never took cover against incoming artillery or mortar fire, or grenades or machine-gun fire. Troops did mass for huge operations in the forests of the Aberdares and Mount Kenya and in the Rift Valley, but only for deployment. There were no territorial objectives to capture, no great outflanking movements, no vital ground to defend. They did not have to take a hill with the bayonet, as 3 KAR did in July, 1917 at Narungombe; nor did they have to force a river crossing against tanks, as 6 KAR did at Colito in May, 1941, when cheering askari rampaged through the enemy position from end to end."

2Lt Tim Tawney served with 6 (TT) Battalion KAR. In April, 1953, he was posted with his platoon to the Police Post at Mukuruweini; company headquarters were at Nyeri. They moved by train. The first casualty was at Karatina, when a soldier with a Sten gun, who had not applied the safety catch, tripped in the dark and accidentally shot Cpl Mtatiro, one of the best NCOs. He died soon afterwards, the company's first casualty. On arrival at the Police Post in Mukuruweini, in the South Nyeri Reserve, they began refresher training:-

"Days were spent on routine patrols of the reserve, brushing up on the training which had been carried out in the palm plantations behind the old barracks near the docks of Dar es Salaam. Nights were devoted to ambushes."

A few months later Tim went to Mweiga for a jungle warfare course, run by a major who had recently returned from Malaya:-

"The first couple of days were devoted to the use of the Sten and Patchett 9 mm machine carbines, and consisted of 'jungle walks', when figures of baddies would suddenly leap out of a bush or from behind a tree, to be cut down with a (live) burst of fire. This was followed using the rifle grenade, a vile device. Subsequently our group of about six subalterns were taken by our mentor on patrol in the Aberdares. Needless to say, the shortest and smallest officer carried the Bren gun. This was no great chore when on forest tracks, but on the second day we entered the area of fallen bamboo, which, for those with a crutch clearance of approximately 2'6" was exceedingly hazardous, since the average drop through the fallen bamboo to the forest floor was rarely less than three feet; particularly when burdened with a Bren in addition to one's jungle pack. No sleeping bags were carried, only food and ammunition. Condensed milk, tea leaves and bamboo leaves all stewed up together on a little solid-fuel Tommy cooker, in a mess tin, tasted like elixir after a freezing night lying under a poncho cape basha in one's clothes. The abiding memories which really stick in one's mind are the smell of the bamboo – an old urinal on a seaside promenade – the total silence because of the carpet of dead bamboo leaves several inches thick, the eerie green light with no glimpse of the sun, because of the height of the bamboo and, after the sun was up, the occasional rifle-shot sound as a bamboo split from expanding in the hot air."

A few months later Tim, his platoon of twenty-two men and a dozen men of the Kikuyu Guard armed with a shotgun, knives and spears, were at a small fortified trading post at Kagicha:-

"Almost every day was spent in patrolling the allotted area of the reserve, and several night ambushes were laid to intercept Mau Mau supply couriers moving into the forest from the towns and the reserve.

In addition the platoon played its part in felling trees and marking with white paint an interdiction strip a mile wide along the edge of the forest. In one incident they trapped a terrorist in broad daylight, who dived into a patch of thick bush about forty yards across. The patrol surrounded the bush, and I threw a 36 grenade into the refuge. After a KG had shouted to him to come out, and received no response, the patrol was told to back off some thirty yards to give them a better field of fire, and not to shoot me or WOPC Febrika Kaliwa, who were going in. On entering the bush they found the terrorist hiding under a thick mat of bush; his arm had been almost severed by the grenade, and when he suddenly moved, the WOPC shot him dead. In the same area on another occasion, three men were found asleep in a clearing, not far from the interdicted mile strip. On being challenged they took off like rabbits; two got away and one was killed by a volley of shots. Night ambushes in the rain were miserable; nothing could be seen or heard more than a couple of yards away, and the hypnotic effect of the rain could only be countered by holding a bayonet under one's chin. Then there was the indignity of coming over a crest close to a neighbouring battalion's patrol area, and, being all black faces bar one, being shot up by them. I recall listening to a newly arrived brigadier giving orders to the Company Commander, Capt Piers Harley, Kenya Regiment. 'You will take your company into the forest for a three-day patrol. You will use that road from the reserve.' 'But, Sir, that road's a river!'"

Between March and June, 1954, Tawney was based with his company at a coffee shamba on the Muthaiga to Limuru road. Battalion Headquarters were at Kiambu.

"This followed a dreary spell acting as guard commander on Government House and at Gen Sir George Erskine's house at Muthaiga for a couple of months, enlivened only by the Italian Consul's daughter, who did not realize that her nylon bathing costume lost its modestly opaque qualities when wet. Sporadic patrolling and night work took place in the coffee shambas on the periphery of the city. On one of the many occasions when the order of the day was the 'sweep', the platoon had a nasty little flurry when clearing out some huts and a number of figures hurtled out of them waving pangas. It was an artificial experience, since at dawn one might be starting a sweep and by 1900 hrs sitting down to a slap-up meal in the New Stanley, where the range of weapons on view was startling."

Christopher Nunn had served with 3 KAR in Malaya and had extensive patrol experience. Shortly after arriving in Kenya he was with his platoon in the forest south of Fort Hall. They were based on a Police Post and were attacked with great ferocity by a gang of Mau Mau just after dusk. It was unusual for the Mau Mau to attack a well-defended position; their daring was probably due to having taken hashish and because they had good-quality rifles. Nunn was badly wounded during the first phase of the attack, but organized the defence of the Post until dawn, when the attackers disappeared. He was taken by ambulance over twenty miles of badly surfaced road, but died at about 9 a.m.

Jim Gordon joined 5 KAR during January, 1952, when the battalion was earmarked for the Malayan Emergency, and an advance party "of Fred Day (2ic), Major Brown, Mike O'Connor, Robin Montgomery and Cliff Thompson all went out to Johore Bahru. I am not sure how many askari went with them, but I believe they were lodged in the Jungle Warfare School. However, the Kenya Government decided, in view of the pending Kenya problems, the battalion's presence was necessary at home." The advance party was away for six or eight weeks. Jim Gordon also recalls the tragedy of the Mau Mau inflicting forceful circumcision on a female Church of Scotland missionary at Tuma-Tuma.

2Lt R.J. Horton went to Kenya in about August, 1953, flying in a Hermes, via Malta, El Adam and Khartoum before landing at Eastleigh Airport. He and 2Lt John Crow were taken to the Queen's Hotel (he believes), and they looked around Nairobi:-

"A great many Europeans in town seemed to be carrying firearms rather too openly, in our view. Most of the girls' dainty-pearl-handled jobs were most unlikely to be fired and might indeed provoke attack. The slogan post-marked on all letters posted on Nairobi at that time was 'Guard your gun'. All this made John Crow and I realize that we did not have much with which we could offer resistance. So we solemnly went out and bought a sheath knife each. After a couple of days in the big city we were picked up and taken to 4 KAR Battalion Headquarters at Fort Hall. I joined B Company; John Crow went to C Company I think.

"Almost immediately I went on to a forward base camp at a place called (?) Marera. It was a long hut with a corrugated iron roof and a small tented compound by it, surrounded by some barbed wire and a ditch. This was a sort of halfway house between Battalion Headquarters and the so-called 'forts' which were being set up as the most forward bases higher in the Aberdares, in the forbidden zone. I was soon to get to know a couple of these forts – I think Forts Winchester and Essex – pretty well. I am fairly certain that I took the first three-tonners (old QLs – relics of the WWII Abyssinian campaign) up to Fort Winchester. Previously only Land Rovers had made it, and the game was to avoid being ambushed when any of the heavy trucks got bogged down in mud or a crude bridge over a small ravine failed under a vehicle's weight. This was really only a one-off trial as I recollect, to see if a three-tonner could get through.

"A subaltern's main job at that time was to mount and to lead platoon-strength patrols from the forward forts. The forts were occupied by slightly under-strength companies, so patrols were usually half of the available men, leaving the remainder to garrison the fort. Fort Winchester was a hillock cleared of bamboo, with a panji ditch round it. The tents were put up over shallow trenches in which one slept. In the centre was a bamboo radio mast which provided our link with the outside world. I suppose we reckoned on activity in terms of an ambush – or being ambushed – or contact with Mau Mau about once a fortnight, with reasonably continuous patrolling between times. The distances covered must have sometimes been quite long; at one stage I reached snow level. I think this was when Intelligence told us that Dedan Kimathi was going to cross the mountains by a pass close to the feature known as the Elephant, and it was our task to try to take him, but we were unlucky. For some operations attempts were made to supply forts from the air, when conditions made ground supply impossibly difficult. But this usually meant that the weather was also bad for air drops. We were often short of food and at one stage we tried boiling up bamboo shoots. Drinkable water came from sections of bamboo and occasionally we were able to find some game. We also looked for cattle driven into the forest by Mau Mau, but, as far as I recollect, without success. Because of the shortage of food I started to smoke.

"In three months or so of operations in the forest, circa September–November, 1953, there were some modest incidents involving shooting in anger. One was really a company attack on a reported Mau Mau camp, just off the track to Fort Winchester. Leaving about fifteen behind to guard the fort and a small number of sick, as was usual in the forest, we set off in a group of about forty. This strength was justified because the gang we were to attack was thought to be about 300 and to be armed with up to 100 rifles and an elephant gun. We went down a well-worn track guided by an informer tied to the wrist of Capt Geoffrey Winstanley. On the way I picked up an empty Bren gun magazine from the bed of a small stream – so there was life about. Suddenly the very thick cover opened and we were able to start fanning out, and the next thing I remember is being caught pretty well in the open on a forward slope, with a lot of rifle fire coming from thick bamboo not far ahead. There was something going off that sounded like medium artillery – probably the elephant gun. Neither seeing nor hearing Geoffrey, after some effort I managed to get my lot up into some sort of attack position on the left flank, but my attempt to surround or flank the gang was too late and unsuccessful. They had evaporated into the forest, although there were signs that several gang members had at least been wounded, judging from some blood found round the camp. Unfortunately blood had also been shed on our side.

"Geoffrey Winstanley had been wounded in the leg, and the informer to whom he was tied had been killed, all by one of the initial bursts of fire. Also, my Bren gunner, whom I could see not far ahead in a good position, had been killed. Everything went wrong for us and we had bad luck, but we inflicted casualties and destroyed the camp. I took a crude home-made rifle, with a broken stock, left behind by the gang. This went back to the battalion Intelligence Officer, Capt Ian Grahame."

Richard Horton described the clothing and equipment available for operations:-

"My impression was that 4 KAR – and possibly all KAR units – were not well supplied. When I first arrived the QM had little to give me except a jungle hat. There even seemed to be a shortage of web equipment. At some stage we were given jungle boots (calf length, green canvas jobs, with black rubber soles), but they left the feet permanently wet and could be pierced by sharp bamboo. In the forest, clothing was quickly torn or rotted. We mostly managed to make our uniforms last, but members of the Kenya Regiment often had to resort to civilian items. I carried a Patchett, a 9 mm light automatic submachine gun, like a Sten gun but of supposedly improved design. It was supposed not to rust and to be more accurate than a Sten. It had a curved (rather than straight) magazine with, I think, a capacity of twenty-five rounds. In action one strapped two magazines together, so that a change could be made quickly. The main problem was with the 9 mm ammunition. It seemed to be of 1942 vintage and some of it was certainly Italian. This was highly unreliable, with a tendency to blow up in the breech. I got fed up with the Patchett, and never heard of it after East Africa.

The main platoon armament was a couple of bren guns, .303 rifles and a two-inch mortar. Askari carried pangas, which they used in preference to the bayonet. Grenades were not always carried, being dangerous to the thrower in thick bamboo, but were available. Phosphorous grenades were useful to destroy hutted camps in the forest in a hurry, particularly in wet conditions.

"Medical equipment was sparse, a few field dressings and that was about it. 4 KAR transport, apart from feet in the active zone, was provided mainly by the ubiquitous Land Rover, in its stripped-down version (easy to roll out of if shot at). There were also the old QL 3-tonners, left over from endeavours further north in the '40s. The battalion boasted a magnificent 1936 Austin ambulance.

"The forest and the whole of the Aberdares, with a three-mile limit outside it, were forbidden zones, which meant that, if it moved, you could shoot it. This made life easier when on patrol. Map-reading had to be reasonably good, so that you did not bump into other units through straying into their areas. Most successes were achieved by finding and following Mau Mau tracks; the askari were superb at moving quietly through the forest."

4 KAR left Kenya for Uganda in late 1953, for Internal Security duties and to garrison Uganda during the visit of HM the Queen, which was due in mid-1954.

In Kenya, in 1954, better intelligence and closer working between the police and the KAR bore fruit. Alan Liddell was a 2Lt and a platoon commander in B Company 23 KAR; he recalled his experience of the operation to capture Kaleba, the Mau Mau commander in the Mount Kenya region;

"The Kenya Police Special Branch was at the forefront of intelligence gathering, and no individuals more so than Superintendents Ian Henderson and Bernard Ruck. Brought up in Kenya, totally fluent in the Kikuyu language, brave and wedded to their duty, they entered the forest separately on many occasions to contact Mau Mau leaders to persuade them to renounce violence and to lead their followers out of the forest. They were always unarmed on these occasions, relying on their wit, fluent Kikuyu, detailed knowledge of the personalities involved, and courage backed by a strong belief. They are the only two men in the Commonwealth to have been awarded the George Medal and Bar.

"In October, 1954, Ruck was thirty one and had just been awarded his first George Medal. "General China", the first overall Mau Mau Commander on Mount Kenya, had been captured, tried and sentenced to death. He had been succeeded on Mount Kenya by Kaleba. Dr Gray Leakey had been taken alive from his home in the Chieni Forest area of Mount Kenya and was dead, believed buried alive by his captors. Kaleba was thought to have been responsible for this atrocity." Alan was visiting the Battalion Headquarters at Karatina, from his company in the Nyeri District, on the evening of Friday 22 October, 1954. He was in the mess anteroom after 11 p.m. most of the other officers had gone to bed, when:-

"A man in plain clothes came in and introduced himself as Bernard Ruck of Special Branch. I was intrigued to meet him. There was an air of urgency about him; he had information hot from Mount Kenya forest, via a surrendered terrorist who was outside with a Special Branch Askari. Ruck wanted an armed patrol to accompany him to capture Kaleba, who was reported to be lying up with several followers in the reserve between Nyeri and Kartina. I agreed to assemble the patrol, woke the Adjutant, Capt Harry Eggers, and told him what was happening. I also awoke WOPC Dickson Otota from my company, and he got four or five reliable askari, a radio set and operator from Headquarters Company. Ruck and I briefed our men and we were off within half an hour in single file behind Ruck, his surrendered terrorist and askari. Ruck had showed me on a map the approximate position of Kaleba's cave, and we agreed to be there by dawn, starting by walking up the railway line from Karatina. It was pitch dark and the usual chilly night that came with an altitutde of 5,500 feet in the Kenya highlands. We walked through the silence of the night, wattle plantations dotting the black hillsides, Kikuyu shambas vaguely visible, for some three hours along the railway line, then off to the east. Urgent Kikuyu-whispered chatter between Ruck, the askari and the terrorist thrashed out our next course.

"We now took off into the Kikuyu reserve, through patches of bush wet with heavy dew, skirting round shambas to avoid noise, up and down ridges. Ridges radiated out from Mount Kenya and formed the grain of the land in Kikuyu country, often with a stream at the bottom, sometimes a fully fledged river. No one was about, apart from ourselves. After about a further two hours the surrendered terrorist stopped and pointed to a hill ahead. With extra caution we climbed it using all available cover, and on its summit we saw in the grey half-light that precedes dawn the mouth of a cave surrounded by bush. There was no sentry. The terrorist was pointing at the cave as if to say,

'They're there'. As we approached we could hear snoring inside. Three of us dashed into the cave, Ruck shining his torch, and the remaining askari fanned out behind us, weapons at the ready. In the cave four startled people, three men and a woman, stood up but offered no resistance. We brought them out into the rapidly strengthening dawn and Ruck said, 'We've got him'. All except the woman were armed. Having disarmed them, they sat down with our askari round them. The woman and the two men jibbered with nerves. Kaleba had more presence, however, and said nothing. I reported to battalion headquarters by radio, asking for transport and an escort to meet us. Just behind the cave there was a good murram road. It all seemed rather an anticlimax. To Ruck it was the successful outcome of his intelligence-gathering work, but he took it very calmly. To the Mau Mau leadership on Mount Kenya it was a major blow, and we had captured the man who had organized Dr Leakey's abduction and murder, and much other terrorist activity."

Alan became Intelligence Officer at battalion headquarters shortly afterwards, for the last five months of his service. He replaced Mike Facey of the Kenya Regiment who had spent a year with the battalion and whose local knowledge had been invaluable. The officers of 23 KAR wore (or cut a dash in) tightly fitting khaki whipcord trousers made by the brothers D.V. and R.D. Patel. One day their shop had a new sign:-

D.V. Patel Regimental Tailors
to 23 (Kenya) Bn, The King's African Rifles
by Appointment

The sign also bore the "talata" (Arabic figure 3, the cap badge) on its red background. Self-appointed but very smart, and the sign stayed up.

Karatina was an administrative centre with a District Officer in charge. Alan continued:-

"To the north of the bustling area of Karatina was 23 KAR's Battalion Headquarters: a barbed wire enclosure compound, a sentry box at the main gate by the battalion sign, a black surround with a gold 'talata' on a square red background, and in white beneath '2/3 Bn King's African Rifles.' Although known colloquially as 23 KAR it was, strictly speaking, the 2/3 KAR and used the 'talata' on the same red background as 3 KAR. Our red background was square, however, while 3 KAR's was diamond-shaped. The battalion had been raised in late

1951 to replace 3 KAR who went to the Malayan Emergency. Inside the large rectangular compound were lines of tents – the large square office tents on the east side, the Colonel's, the Adjutant's, the orderly room, the I0's, the MO's, the QM's and so on.

"Tented accommodation for the askari of Headquarter Company (Major Hugh Clemas) ran in lines from north to south. On the west side were the MT lines and workshps and the Quartermaster's store (Capt Arthur Cainey), and at the north end of the camp were officers' tents, ablutions, officers' mess in the north-west corner, the sergeants' mess and cookhouses. The parade ground was at the south end of the camp. Lt Col Joe Bartlett was aided and abetted by our 2ic, Major Andrew Hlawaty, (3rd Hussars, late of the East African Armoured Car Squadron, the Royal West African Frontier Force and originally from the Polish Cavalry). He had a fierce, monocled, eagle eye for detail and form. One entered the mess by its shady veranda, steps up to a cement floor, a low wall enclosing front and sides, easy chairs, a line of tall blue waving gums just off the veranda. The walls of the main building were horizontally laid logs and the roof was a thick thatch on timber beams. The ante-room had a fine stone fireplace set into its thick log walls, pictures, rugs, soft furniture, magazines and a considerable degree of comfort. It was long enough to contain a full-sized billiard table at one end. The far dining room had a fine polished table big enough to hold all the battalion's officers and some guests, and an identical fireplace to the ante-room's. On cool nights a log fire was a welcome warmth and sight. Battalion silver shone on the long table around a centre piece presented by HM The Queen, Colonel in Chief, on her coronation, mounted and in uniform. The whole atmosphere, bearing in mind the circumstances of a battalion on active service, was one of warmth, comfort and relaxation, and more than a little impressive. Beyond the dining room was a service parlour and the kitchens. The officers' mess ran on well oiled wheels and was always under Major Andrew Hlawaty's eye, with Capt Geoffrey O'Coffey actually making it all work. He was variously 2ic Headquarters Company and Assistant Adjutant.

"Colonel Joe Bartlett insisted on officers dining together at least once a month. Naturally, operations and other exigencies took priority, but the standing order was that if one was not away on operations when a formal dinner took place, one attended. In blue patrols, whatever the weather – in my case it was often in the rain – one set off in a Land Rover, with escort and orderly, and slithered and skidded often a considerable distance from company camp into Karatina for a proper dinner. Orderlies, in white kanzu, red cummerbund and red tarboosh with battalion badge, stood behind our chairs and lent great tone to the proceedings. On occasions the KAR band played outside, surprising things like selections from the Merry Widow, in an open-fronted marquee. All this may sound odd forty years later, but it was the style of the time. It was enjoyable, an opportunity to meet brother officers in civilized surroundings, and very good for morale. I believe it is a major reason why so many of us who served in 23 KAR at that time remain in regular touch to this day. Guests were invariably present, such as the District Officer, officers from neighbouring battalions, for example the Buffs on our eastern boundary, 4 KAR to our south, occasionally a visiting dignitary, sometimes a settler from the settled area to the north. Returning to the rougher and readier circumstances of one's company camp in the cold late night watches, which one always did, was agony.

"Battalion Headquarters awoke at 6 a.m. to the bugler's reveille. Orderlies shimmered about their officers' tents with cups of tea and hot shaving water. Headquarters Company had a morning muster parade, sounds floated over from the MT lines, sometimes the less than dulcet tones of our MTO, Capt Ronnie Manders; one dashed off to the office tent to look at signals, SITREPS from the companies and neighbouring battalions, reply to them and prepare for the day's operations. After breakfast in the mess the day started in earnest. At 10, I usually briefed the CO, marked up his and the Operations Room maps, travelled with him to map reference RVs with one or more of our companies, or visited a neighbouring battalion to help prepare for a joint operation. Meanwhile, back at Battalion Headquarters the day passed in a great bustle and movement. Company trucks came in for stores, a company commander might be in for a briefing, the RSMs (we had two, one British and one African, Mr H. Tuffs and RSM Mulandi BEM) would be running a parade involving part of Headquarters Company and the Corps of Drums. Signallers ran to and fro bearing more or less intelligible messages, Capt Jimmy Marshall, the Battalion Signals Officer, sweated blood over recalcitrant wireless sets, the Adjutant had disciplinary infringers marched in and out at maximum decibels. All in all it was the normal hive of military industry in an operational battalion headquarters, doubtlessly repeated in eleven other battalion headquarters in other parts of Kenya on the same day. The industry would have been common to all, but the atmosphere at Karatina was uniquely a compound of our people, our location, the crisp highland air, blue sky and cotton wool clouds riding high, and our idiosyncratic spirit."

The battalion said goodbye to two elderly, retired officers who had decided to return to Britain after service in the Indian cavalry and farming in the Mweiga settled area. Alan wrote:-

"They had befriended 23 KAR officers and we had exchanged much pleasant hospitality with them. They attended a final luncheon in the officers' mess at Karatina, but the pièce de résistance, was when the battalion Corps of Drums paraded at Karatina station when the two veterans passed through en route to Nairobi, Mombasa and England. The sun was rising as the train from Myeri chuffed in at 6.30 a.m. The Corps of Drums in full fig, looking splendid, rolled its drums and marched down the length of the station platform to 'Funga Safari'. All available 23 KAR officers were present, and the two old soldiers took it all in for the last time, standing by their carriage door, tears coursing down their cheeks." Alan left the battalion soon afterwards, but returned to Kenya later as a District Officer and resumed his contacts with the KAR.

Robert I. Jones was with D Company 5 KAR in early 1954 and worked with the Kenya Police Air Wing. The company was stationed close to the Tree Tops Hotel, where, in February, 1952, Princess Elizabeth became Queen. When an aircraft pilot reported that Tree Tops was on fire, the duty platoon and three-inch mortars attempted to trap the raiders. They mortared them as best they could, then prepared for a long-range patrol, with trackers, on the next day. But heavy rain had washed the gang's tracks away, so they were recalled. Robert had "a very small and cheap Kodak camera which took only eight photographs. I took eight shots of what remained of Tree Tops and surrounds, basically a twisted fig tree and charred poles. Back in camp one of the Police pilots was going to Nairobi and asked if anyone had any mail to post. Possibly strictly against regulations, I scribbled a letter to the Editor of the *Daily Mail* in London and enclosed the film. I gave it to the pilot to post, but at Eastleigh Airport, Nairobi, he met a friend who was about to take off for London. He gave him the letter, to be posted in London. Yes! The letter got to the *Daily Mail*, and Yes! they published one of the photographs, about quarter of a page, with the caption 'Just a twisted tree where the Queen once stayed. This photograph was taken exclusive to the *Daily Mail* etc.' The photograph was taken on the morning of 27 May and was in the *Daily Mail* on 1 June. The negatives came from the *Daily Mail* with some prints, a couple of them enlarged, a copy of the issue it was in and a cheque for £15. I am told this was a ridiculously low figure, but who cares when one is nineteen? We had a good party."

They got the gang some weeks later, in the Aberdares, but were criticized for being outside their brigade area.

3/6 KAR had earlier associations with "General China", when they were still designated 36 TT KAR in 1944/45. Ian Sinclair remembers: "He was mess corporal of Headquarters Company in Ceylon and Burma. His name was Waruhia Itotia . . . He was 2ic the National Youth Service for some years . . . an excellent mess corporal."

67 AT Company EAASC provided animal transport to all units in the high altitude forests and mountains. The Company was based at Nanyuki and commanded by Capt M.F.M. Horner. When the terrorists moved to the higher altitudes in 1955, after operations "Hammer" and "First Flute", (in which they had been active), animal transport came into its own. Initially, at high altitudes the animals were lethargic and lost some condition, but were better when loads were reduced from 160 lbs to about 100 lbs. They were shod with "caulkins" (studded shoes) to enable them to climb the steeper slopes. The unit began in June, 1953, when one RAVC and two RASC soldiers arrived in Kenya to take over and train thirteen mules hired from a Nanyuki landowner. When fifteen askari had joined, the unit became operational in August, 1953, in the Aberdares. More mules were authorized and, by December, 1955, they were 67 AT Company EAASC, with 143 animals. Their first major operation was in February and March, 1955, when they supported B Company 2/6 KAR, during Operation Hammer. They carried three-inch mortars and ammunition, rations, supplies, water tanks and their own forage and picket gear up to 10,000 feet near Mount Kinangop and on to Fort Gloucester.

When the company was supporting 1 Bn The Gloucestershire Regiment near Lake Naivasha, during operation "Bulrush", one of the ponies was carrying ammunition and trip flares. A flare exploded, setting off others, and the pony bolted. Private Masyuka Kivati chased and caught it; the ammunition still exploding, he unloaded and led it away to dress its wounds. He was awarded the RSPCA's highest honour, the Margaret Wheatley Cross. By 1957 the unit was down to being 67 Independent AT Troop EAASC, and after working in the Northern Frontier District, they supported scientists of the International Geophysical Year on Mount Kenya.

The War Dog Training School was also at Nanyuki. Patrol dogs accompanied patrols and would "point" when in range of a human not part of their temporary "pack". In the Prohibited Areas this would almost certainly mean Mau Mau. David Peters recalled:- "The handler had a sub-machine gun, the dog and its accoutrements, including two leads, one short for normal purposes, the other some yards in length for casting about. A tracker dog hot on the scent provided an entertaining sight as it towed its handler through the undergrowth at a brisk pace. There was one hand for the lead, one for the gun, and none to fend off branches, brambles, creepers and spiders' webs."

The Air Despatch function started modestly. In December, 1954, John Spurway took over the Air Despatch Detachment of 70 AD Company RASC, with 37 Supply Depot EAASC. Their activities were essential to the efficiency of patrols in the forest, enabling them to stay out longer and to be more effective. The army had no high performance light aircraft. John continued:-

"So the Kenya Police Reserve were co-opted and helped the Army splendidly, using their Cessna and Piper Pacers for many resupply missions. The technique was to free drop five-men ration packs, or their equivalent into small clearings prepared by the patrols. Skill and accurate flying were paramount for the pilots, discipline and cool heads were needed for the dispatchers. Packs were prepared by the Detachment at Kahawa, using local materials such as small sacks, sisal, cloth bags and anything to ensure that the contents would survive a free drop and be in good condition on arrival. My packers became so adept at their work that eventually we successfully free dropped radio batteries as well as the rum ration in small cans.

"For free dropping the despatcher sat in the reversed front passenger seat of the aircraft, the packs having been placed on the rear seat of the four-seater plane. On reaching the dropping zone the pilot alerted the dispatcher, who placed two or three packs on his left knee, at the same time using it to prop open the aircraft door. The pilot dived towards the DZ clearing, pulled out at the last minute and gave the despatcher the 'Green Light' to eject his packs, sometimes no more than thirty feet from the ground, according to tree height. This unorthodox resupply method worked very successfully, and many KAR and other patrols were maintained in this way."

The army withdrew from operations in November, 1956, four years after the emergency started, but the emergency did not end until 1960 when Jomo Kenyatta left prison and led his country to independence.

Chapter 12

IMPERIAL TWILIGHT

"The young of today know nothing of what we went through. We were bulls in the KAR in those days."
Chief Kathuru Nyaga MM, 1959
(Ex-Sergeant 11 KAR, Jambo Hill)

One of the unfortunate effects of the Mau Mau era was that it disrupted and then compressed the process of bringing independence to the British colonies of East Africa. The pace was set by the United Nations when they gave Italy its ten-year trusteeship of Somalia, which ended in 1960. This obliged the Colonial Office to keep pace as far as Somaliland was concerned. France, in Djibouti, and the Portuguese, in what is now Mozambique, were less inclined to withdraw quickly. When the latter did, it was in extremely difficult circumstances and when the repatriation of colonists was a major cause of the revolution in Portugal, while Mozambique suffered a protracted civil war.

It may seem a slight paradox to begin before the Mau Mau period; however, when the withdrawal from the Canal Zone base was being contemplated and the Cold War becoming serious, the Mackinnon Road project came into being as a base for the Strategic Reserve. Had it been developed, it might have led to a totally different history for Kenya, with more African employment, a greater inflow of funds and a considerable boost to the economy in terms of infrastructure, local manufacture and a large market for locally grown foodstuffs. Some saw it as the Kenyan and military equivalent of the Ground Nut Scheme in Tanganyika, and it was often spoken about with similar distaste.

Mackinnon Road was a small railway halt about sixty-five miles out of Mombasa on the line to Nairobi. In the late 1940s it consisted of a disused airfield, set in a vast area of arid scrub desert. The nearest fresh water was in the Tsavo River, some seventy-five miles in the direction of Nairobi. The river was heavily stained with dull red silt; it was the home of hippopotamus and the haunt of elephant. Sappers went into action first, building pumping stations, filter plants and laying pipelines. Initially the troops were housed in bandas, but soon a supply point was established, distributing rations brought up from Nairobi. This was followed by a petrol depot, a barrack store and an abattoir, depots with their own railway sidings, Nissen huts as messes and dining halls, playing fields, a cinema, a large NAAFI and married quarters. In less than two years a huge camp had been created, while EAASC units were formed at a training depot at Athi Road, in what had been a camp for Italian prisoners of war, and which was eventually to be the depot of the Kenya Regiment. By 1950 nine EAASC Companies had been formed and the depot was closed, to merge with the All Arms Depot at Nakuru.

The Ordnance Depot at Mackinnon Road was designed to hold 200,000 tons of warlike stores, mostly stock to be transferred from Egypt, but eventually it was planned to absorb all the other stores depots in East Africa Command. The project was under constant review. As early as 1948, when construction had started, it became clear that there would not be the precipitate withdrawal from Egypt that had been expected. A more economical move was therefore proposed, projected over a longer time-scale. There were doubts about the capacity of the railway to handle the stock build-up, as it was assessed as being 200 tons per twenty-four hour period. Despite the difficulty of establishing a firm policy, an Advanced Ordnance Depot was set up by 1949. When a baobab tree, which has a life span of four hundred years, was planted at the depot by DOS MELF, the wish was expressed that the depot might come to maturity before the tree. It did not. In a letter to the War Office in April, 1950, ADOS East Africa wrote that the frequency of changes of plan was bewildering: "Since I arrived here last June there has been plan after plan set out on paper, but nothing has happened on the ground." The project was doomed and was abandoned in September, 1951, without becoming fully operational. It was one of the great "might-have-beens" and in a way was the beginning of the end for the British military presence in East Africa. One benefit, as already noted, was the boost it gave to the expansion of EAASC.

4 KAR had left Kenya for Uganda at the end of 1953, well before the end of the Mau Mau emergency, for Internal Security duties. The Kabaka of Buganda had been sent to UK. This was regarded as banishment by many of his supporters; in particular the Waganda felt that their national pride had been offended and civil unrest was thought to be in the offing. To the north of the country numbers of Sudanese refugees were crossing the border into Uganda in considerable numbers, which had to be checked. Another factor was the impending visit of HM The Queen, due in mid-1954.

Early in 1954 2Lt Richard J. Horton was on his own at Kampala with an under-strength company of askari at Kalolo camp, waiting for a riot, or rather for a call from the local police:-

"To turn out 'in aid of the civil power' to quell a riot. I was billeted at the side of Kalolo Camp in a Public Works Department bungalow, which had the essential aid of a telephone installed in it, otherwise I am sure I would have been in a tent. The telephone was for contact with the police and with Battalion Headquarters at Jinja. The only other equipment was a cooker, one 'table six foot', a 'chair folding' and one 'bed camp officers', as I remember it. Rather nerve-racking in a lonely sort of way, and very different from activities in Kenya. While waiting for something to happen it was essential to keep the askari busy. I remember I had them paint their helmets a particularly hideous, non-regulation shade of green, which, when they wore the helmets gave the impression that they had come straight from hell. Other time was spent in practising 'operations in aid of the civil power', in accordance with the relevant manual – noble British square, bugler, magistrate, banners with the inscription 'Disperse or we fire' and so on. It was not an enviable or comfortable situation, and – even at the time seemed very Kiplingesque.

"Most Waganda in the area wandered around for some time wearing bark on their arms as a sign of mourning for their lost Kabaka. However, the truth of the matter is that they did not really like him much anyway – or most of them did not. There was also no political party involved that was prepared to take on the police. It may also have helped that my askari were not Waganda, but from the Acholi and therefore not sympathetic to any Waganda. Whatever the reasons, the Waganda stopped milling about with bark on their arms, and I was able to return with my 'circus' to Jinja, and a less lonely existence.

"By this time we had to start getting the battalion up to standard for a full trooping parade, in readiness for the presentation of new Colours by Her Majesty during her visit in July, 1954. We also had to cover aspects of security during other parts of the royal itinerary, which included the opening of the Jinja Dam. The askari were not long out of a jungle fighting situation in Kenya, so this was a very tall order, but preparations were made in good time. A superb show was put on; it was quite an outstanding event which will always remain for me the highlight of my service.

"I cannot remember whether it was just before or after the Queen's visit that part of the battalion was, for a time, patrolling the Uganda-Sudan border, showing the colours in the old manner. I was not directly involved, but I was MTO at the time and had the considerable embarrassment of having only two three tonners (the old QLs again) and the 1936 Austin Ambulance on the road to support the endeavour.

"At the end of my time in Uganda I recall the hand-over by our splendid CO, Donald Nott, to Lt Col Green, just before leaving Africa myself to go up to Cambridge in September, 1954, to start a new sort of experience. And yes, before you ask, I did find it hard to settle down to the academic life after my year with 4 KAR."

David Happold did most of his National Service in 3 KAR, joining them in 1956, when they were in a tented camp outside Nanyuki, on the dirt (and often very muddy) road leading to the Mawingo Club. He described the scene:-

"It was a superb situation on the lower slopes of Mount Kenya, with glorious views of the forests and snow-covered peaks to the east, and to the extensive cotton soil and acacia plains to the west. The subalterns' lines were two neat rows of ridge tents with a small path of duck boards between them. Some enterprising officers made theirs larger by erecting a wall about three feet high, of horizontal bamboo poles, to which the base of the tent was fixed. This resulted in a much bigger 'room', with the ridge about eight feet above the floor. The officers' mess was a wooden hut with a tin roof, French windows opening towards Mount Kenya, and a large stone fireplace where there was a cedar-wood fire on most nights. Adjoining was the dining room and just outside was a small kitchen made of corrugated iron, equipped with an ancient wood stove where the cook produced magnificent meals with the simplest of equipment. On the side of the mess were the field officers' tents (much bigger and better furnished than the subalterns') and so on the other side was the loo, a huge pit surmounted by a wooden hut with four cubicles. Nearby was a shower hut, with hot water supplied from a 44-gallon drum which was heated by a wood fire.

"It was a lovely place to live, although in the wet season there was mud everywhere and one was likely to become drenched when moving from one part of the camp to another. I particularly remember Roy Stockwell, my Company Commander, his impressive handle-bar moustache, his enjoyment of a cold Tusker in a silver tankard in front of the roaring fire, and his extensive knowledge of the birds of Kenya. Many of the subalterns were National or Short Service; they included Barry Parton (Mortar Officer, who subsequently became a vet), Mike Ford, Nigel Mackerith, Berwick Coates, Michael Price (who later trained as an agriculturist), John Willis (Assistant MTO), Paul Wigram and Mike Scott (a Scots Guards regular officer). Mike Scott had an old land rover and two shenzi hunting dogs; I used to go with him and two Samburu askari, who discarded their uniforms and took up spears, to the plains to hunt warthog. I also collected butterflies and plants, watched birds and observed the fascinating marine life on the reef, during a short holiday in Mombasa and Zanzibar. I became quite certain that I would return to Africa after my training.

"In fact I returned sooner than I had expected. During my second year at University, (1959) I organized a five-man undergraduate expedition to the (then) Belgian Congo. We managed to get cheap charter flights to Entebbe but we had to reach Lake Kivu. I had a brainwave that the KAR might be able to help, and I wrote to Major General Tapp, GOC East Africa Command. He was delighted to authorize 4 KAR to meet us at Entebbe, take us to Jinja, collect our heavy equipment which had travelled by sea and drive us to the Congo border. We spent three days with 4 KAR and travelled in a three-ton lorry with several askari across Uganda. On our return three months later, 4 KAR met us at the border and drove us back to Entebbe; we spent three days in the Queen Elizabeth National Park, much to the delight of the askari.

"Six years after leaving 3 KAR, when I had completed my undergraduate and post-graduate studies, I returned to Africa as a biologist. All my professional career has been spent in universities, mostly in Africa... In recent years my major research has been on the mammals of Malawi. Those who served in 1 and 2 KAR will know that Malawi is a wonderful country and that the Malawians are extremely pleasant and friendly people. My short time with 3 KAR was a great experience in itself, but more importantly for me, it was of great value for what followed."

Roger Perkins had been with David Happold during their early days of National Service in the Devonshire Regiment. He was serving with 4 KAR. At that time the Suez Affair "Operation Musketeer" was in progress, with considerable disruption to transit through the Middle East (apart from other matters). Roger was stationed at Jinja with C Company when they were detailed to assist in mapping Uganda's northern border. He writes:-

"We had moved to Lomej by convoy but the vehicles had all gone back to Jinja. Nearly three hundred miles now separated C Company from the torpor of that lakeside town. We had escaped, for the coming weeks at least, from the predictable cycle of parades and basic infantry training which dominated life in King George VI Barracks. Our journey to Uganda's northern border had brought us through country which became ever more arid, and, towards the end, over roads which were little more than game tracks. Four European officers, with eighty African soldiers, were comfortably camped and ready for adventure. The officers had settled into a cluster of mud huts normally occupied by a lonely tsetse fly control manager. The askari had built their two-man grass huts and cleared a stretch of bush for netball and weapon training. Perched high on the rim of the Kidepo escarpment, we saw nothing but virgin Africa in every direction; the blue hills of Sudan to the north, the low rolling hills of Acholi to the south-west, and the broken mountains and hills of the Karamoyo Range to the east. Apart from a handful of naked Karamajong hunters, who came to watch our activities with detached curiosity, we were alone.

"This was not a conventional 'flag-wagging' safari. There were no resident villages who otherwise we might have impressed. Instead we were under orders to explore the terrain and assist the Government cartographers in Kampala by filling in some of the many blank spaces in their maps. With a supply of aerial photographs and tentative charts we would walk the ground and note the features missed by earlier surveyors. The Company Commander, Major 'Jonah' Jones, decided that he and Capt John Brandram should remain at Lomej and work around the immediate area. Jim Alford, my fellow subaltern, patrolled thirty miles towards the point on the map where the borders of Uganda, Sudan and the NFD of Kenya coincided, to assess the feasibility of a road being driven through the hills from Lake Turkana. My own task involved a march directly northwards into the Kidepo Valley, where I was to halt and camp as soon as I thought I was walking off the map of Uganda and onto that of our neighbour. Compass bearings taken from a number of surrounding mountain peaks would enable me to fix the theoretical frontier within a mile or two. Having arrived, I was to send out section-strength patrols with maps and pencils, and instructions to take notes concerning the ground and the 'going'. Apart from the value of this information, the project would provide an unusual opportunity for my three Section Commanders, Corporals Albino and Paskwilo and Lance Corporal Santonio, to use their initiative and leadership skills.

"The approach march, initially downhill and then across a bone-dry, sandy plain, occupied the first morning. The Kidepo River, so promising on the map, proved to be no more than a broad, golden meander of fine sand. Several hours' work with spades revealed the bed-rock and a trickle of muddy water. That hole, ten feet deep and twenty across, was my platoon's lifeline for the following two weeks. It was also a magnet for leopard, lion, elephant and assorted antelope which, every night, came to share our treasure. Climbing down to drink, they pushed avalanches of sand into the pit, and every morning we needed to dig again and restore the flow. Grass huts were quickly fashioned along the nearby river bank and a daily patrolling routine commenced. On the third day we had our first human visitor. A frail elderly gentleman dressed in a long black coat and a straw hat, quietly entered our camp and asked for a meeting. After taking tea and a little whisky, he announced that he was the emissary of the Didinga chieftain whose people lived in the hills to the north, in the Sudan. Would I consent to speak to his master, to discuss certain events which were causing him concern? He then revealed the news that Egypt had been invaded. This intelligence did not surprise me as we had been hearing rumours for some weeks past of preparations by the French and British Governments to recover the Suez Canal, and by the Israelis to occupy Sinai. But all that was 1,700 miles to the north, so what relevance could it have to the Didinga?

"On the following morning, after what must have been a four hour's march, our guest arrived. Accompanied by a solitary bodyguard gripping a clutch of spears, he was dressed for the occasion; khaki shorts, which had seen much hard service, a pyjama jacket, and a solar topee of a kind that must have been fashionable among ladies of the Church Missionary Society at the turn of the century. A sentry had been posted to alert me to his approach, and upon his signal Sgt Laban brought a small guard of honour to attention. I had selected six of my tallest Acholi for this duty. It seemed important to create a good impression, and the Acholi were renowned amongst the surrounding tribes for their warrior traditions. Having greeted our guest and escorted him to the shade of one of our few trees, I nodded to Sergeant Laban. With a fine sense of theatre, he gave his orders crisply but quietly, and the six askari gave a short demonstration of arms drill. He then dismissed them and the serious business began. One of my askari was a Karamajong who understood the language of the Didinga. Speaking to him in Swahili, I enquired into the chieftain's health, that of his family, the condition of his crops and the likelihood of rain in the near future. I had learned earlier in my short KAR career that it was considered discourteous under such circumstances to go directly to the heart of the matter. When these pleasantries had been exhausted, I asked how I might be of service.

"A wiry little man, with a deeply wrinkled face and a natural dignity which matched his station, he proceeded to describe distant events with a clarity which was astounding in a man who had no access to newspapers or radio. Under the terms of the Anglo-Egyptian Condominium, as he explained, his people had for many years lived in peace. For impartial justice they could always turn to their District Commissioner. All that had ended three years earlier when the British withdrew and the Sudan became self-governing. Ever since then the majority Arabic Muslim Northerners had been applying increasing pressure against the minority animist and Christian populations in the South. The Sudan was theoretically a single political unit but, in reality, the Arabic North was (and still is) a world away from the pastoral life of the Nilotic South. 'I am afraid this business in Egypt will cause trouble with the Arabs. They are excitable. Khartoum is far from here, but the government can send soldiers against us. There are many soldiers here already. They despise us, and to them we are infidels. You have guns. Will you come with me and defend us against the Arabs?'

"After expressing sympathy, and having explained that the Queen would be unhappy if I acted without her orders, I promised to report his concerns but regretted that there was nothing I could do that day. I did not tell him that my platoon was unlikely to achieve much against the whole of the Sudanese army, nor did I mention that we had no radio, and only fifty rounds of ammunition between us. The difficulties of the situation were discussed for another hour or so, then he stood up, thanked me gravely for my time and departed. It is said that youth is callous and uncaring, but I could not resist the feeling of remorse that a once omnipotent Empire had abandoned this courteous old man and his people to their fate. All that he predicted came to pass.

"For a variety of reasons the Anglo-French expedition was soon withdrawn from Egypt and the Arab world rejoiced. Its moderate spokesmen were silenced. Militarism and militancy began to prevail and Southern Sudan fell under a brutal régime which continues to this day. In the months after our return to Jinja, several hundred Didinga crossed the Kidepo to seek refuge. Often I have wondered if my companion was among them, or whether his fears of disaster were, in his own case, too literally fulfilled."

Roger's colleague, 2Lt Paul Lewis, was commanding the mortar platoon and was first choice when unusual tasks came the battalion's way. Lt Col John Peddie detailed him to run a transit camp at Entebbe, for British service personnel whose aircraft were diverted to bypass the disputed air space of the Middle East. They had to spend a night at Entebbe airport while the crews rested at a local hotel and their aircraft were serviced. Paul's stories of his time as a catering manager, with modest resources such as a torch and a single Tilly lamp, would fill a book. Despite the difficulties, 4 KAR performed a valuable service in providing the facility. In a typical week, two air-trooping aircraft arrived eastbound and two westbound. Each carried a hundred or more passengers and Paul calculates that more than four thousand servicemen passed through his staging post before it was dismantled.

The process of preparation for independence involved training African leaders for greater responsibilities. Junior officer grades analogous to Viceroy's Commissioned Officers were introduced, and many RSMs and WOPCs became Effendis Class II initially, with consequent improvement to the promotion prospects of their juniors.

Some askari of 6 KAR took part in the birthday celebrations of HH the Sultan of Zanzibar in August, 1957. They travelled by the REAN vessels HMEASs *Rosalind* and *Mvita*, which sailed down from Mombasa for the occasion. At Dar es Salaam Major Rex de V. Carey MC, with Capt Davey and 2Lt Soaper, arrived on board with quantities of tentage, radios and two trailers. The aim was to arrive at Zanzibar at noon on Monday 19 August, so that they could disembark, move to Chakwa (twenty miles from the port) and set up camp before dark. In consequence the askari were embarked at 5.45 a.m. and the ships sailed at 6 a.m. They arrived at Zanzibar and were alongside at 12.30.

Naval, KAR and Police personnel began training for the ceremonial parade at 7.30 each morning, and a very satisfactory standard was achieved. There was a risk of clashes between the shirazui and Arab delegations at the official birthday celebrations, and plans were made to keep the parties apart. There were football matches, with the assistance of the Goan Sports Club; in one a combined Navy and Army team was badly beaten by a Police team. A rifle shooting competition involving a Navy and a Police team saw the home side the victors. They held a simple night amphibious landing exercise on 23 August, when HMEAS *Rosalind*, with a party of officers and NCOs of 6 KAR embarked, sailed to Kama beach, where they simulated an assault landing with the aid of the ship's motor boat and the sea boat. The Navy set up an outline Beachmaster's organization, with signals and beach control. The 6 KAR Company was back on 29 August, having gone on board at 6.45 a.m. They were back in Dar es Salaam by 2.15 p.m., but there was no berth available and they went ashore by a baggage lighter. *Rosalind* and *Mvita* returned to Mombasa on 6 September. (For more about the REAN, see Appendix C).

Alan Liddell (ex-23 KAR) was, in 1959, Divisional District Officer in the Kitui District of Ukamba, in the NFD. Many ex-KAR men were valuable public figures and great helps in the orderly running of the Division. Alan continues:-

"The whole of the Kitui District was great KAR territory. Probably more Kamba askari served in the Kenya battalions of the KAR than any other tribe, and these stocky, tough, humorous and rather bibulous tribesmen were steeped in the KAR lore, with several third generation men serving in the battalions by the time I was there. Large numbers of young men aspired to join the KAR, and on safari, which one was on for three weeks out of four, old men would appear from the bush in khaki drill and campaign medals, stamp to attention and salute and engage one in 'habari' and reminiscences. Bush telegraph had advertised the presence of an ex-KAR DO.

"In my Division I had eight Chiefs and four of these were former KAR WOs or NCOs of note. Senior Chief Kasina Ndoo MBE of Migwani had served in 3 KAR for eleven years, retiring as RSM in 1924. Chief Mwangangi Mwenga MM (Burma) of Katsee, a Sergeant Major in 5 KAR; Chief Kathuru Nyaja MM (Jambo Hill, Burma) of Tharaka, a Sergeant in 11 KAR, and Chief Mwangangi Syengo of Tseikuru, an 11 KAR Sergeant Major of more recent vintage. These men were excellent company in camp in the evenings, and two were marvellous raconteurs. Chief Kathuru regaled me with a particularly vivid and noisy exposition of the attack on Jambo Hill one night, with Tusker bottles illustrating KAR and Japanese positions. He concluded by leaning back, wiping beer froth from his lips and, with a dig in my ribs, saying 'The young today know nothing of what we went through. We were bulls in the KAR in those days.'

"Law was administered and justice dispensed on two levels in Kenya's districts. The DO held a Magistrate's Court, and at a more local level there were African Courts. The latter were experts in matters of local lore and customs, complex issues arising over disputes over bride price, land 'shauries', and so on, and also dealt with petty offences. African Courts were presided over by panels of dignified elders in robes. Of my two African Courts in Kitui's Northern Division, the President of one was Kuma Mukinga, who had also been awarded the MM in Burma, and who had retired from 5 KAR as a Sergeant.

"Each tribal district had a force of Tribal Police, or Dubas as they were known in the NFD. They were the eyes and ears of the Administration, and could be an invaluable body of men in a District such as Kitui, where they included numbers of ex-askari. The

Provincial Sergeant Major for Southern Province's TPs, and responsible for smartening up the TPs from Kenya's two Masai Districts, was ex-RSM Mulandi of 23 KAR (retired in 1959) and he made an impressive impact on our force when he arrived in early 1960. The core of my safari team included the TP Sergeant, Ndinga Kitonga (ex-Sergeant 11 KAR), and my safari cook, Kabubu Musanga (my former orderly in 23 KAR). These two, in a rapid and well drilled flurry on arrival in camp in the evening, had one in a camp chair with a whisky and water sundowner in hand, and the bath water warming up, before you could say Jack Robinson.

"Every other year Kitui District had a KAR recruiting safari, sometimes accompanied by the Corps of Drums, for evening entertainment. These drew miles-long queues of would-be recruits, watched keenly by the local old and bold in their starched khaki drill and medals. Keeping an eye on the latter, of those who had fallen on hard times, was the East African British Legion, run sensitively and efficiently by Lt Col Ninian Robertson-Glasgow, a welcome visitor at Mwingi. He had long KAR service, 2/4 KAR in Turkana in 1940, 1/6 KAR in Northern Abyssinia, and 3/6 KAR in Burma. I believe he commanded 1/6 as a major and 3/6 as a lieutenant colonel, and I doubt if his parent regiment saw much of him after the war broke out.

"The KAR influence on my Division was therefore considerable and beneficial in a variety of ways. Many retired askari relaxed, sent their wives out to work the shamba, patted their children and grand-children on the head, and lifted their elbows — always a favourite Kamba pastime. The more active of them played as distinguished a role in their home district as they had previously as KAR askari in wars and lesser skirmishes. They will always be to me the finest examples of servants of the Crown, and they always did it with some spirit and great good humour."

Mark Thomas, once of 23 KAR, became a District Officer in Tanganyika and soon became acquainted with the old soldiers in his district. One was known to all as Corporal Salehe, formerly of 3 KAR, who had been the village policeman at Mohoro, in the Rufiji District of Tanganyika, for many years. When he became destitute in 1959, the sub-chief wrote to the District Commissioner to see what could be done. With the letter he sent a tin embossed with the pictures of King George and Queen Mary, of the sort that held chocolate or sweets and was given to troops in World War I. In the tin were a Military Medal, the African General Service Medal with clasp (Nandi 1903), and the African Long Service and Good Conduct

Medal. As Mark was the District Officer, he went to see the old man in his home:-

"Salehe told me that he was awarded the MM for capturing a German machine gun at Narungombe in 1916. I wrote to the British Legion who gave him a small annual pension, and to CO 3 KAR, who sent a Benevolent Fund cheque and the information that the machine gun was displayed outside the officers' mess. We later bought the old man new medal ribbons and he was presented to the Governor, Sir Richard Turnbull, on his tour of Rufiji District in the following year."

The Northern Frontier of Kenya was always turbulent. In 1961 Major R.C.W. (Ray) Nightingale went with B Company, 3 KAR, to Wajir for three months, in the course of which he was asked to visit the border area from Saberia, west past the dry Lake Stephanis to Ileret on Lake Rudolph. There had been raiding by the Ethiopian Hamar Cocce and Boran against each other and into Kenya. The company's role was to deter them. He continues:-

"After a week at Ileret we moved to Buluk Wells for patrol training. The Kenya Police kindly provided four constables and hired eight camels and two handlers to carry our water and supplies. It took three days to become reasonably confident at loading, handling and moving the camels, and I decided to set out on a four-day patrol along the border where there had been incursions in recent months. It was during this first patrol that I learned the truth of the proverb 'The camel driver has his thoughts and the camel has his'. We marched at first light through scattered thorn scrub towards Lake Stephanis and the border. There were gazelle, topi, oryx, wildebeeste and zebra in abundance and we were all in cheerful mood at seeing new country. At midday, after a six-hour march, we closed up and unloaded the camels prior to turning them out to graze under armed guard. The radio operator reported that a police patrol had signalled about having found the tracks of an unknown number of men crossing into the area we were moving to. As the Government had moved the nomadic population back from the frontier in an attempt to control the murderous raiding, and as I knew the whereabouts of all the police, troops and administration officers in the District, the tracks could only be those of a raiding party. I left a guard with the camels and ordered them to move to a rendezvous to make camp and await my arrival. I then set out with twenty men, guided by two police constables who knew the area well.

"After marching fast for two hours over rough ground, we came upon the tracks and began to follow them. When we came to an open, grassy plain, the footprints were clearly visible in the soft sand. We estimated that there were about twelve men in the party, and the police concluded from the style of footprint that they were Boran. We came to where the party had rested under a low acacia tree, in a circle facing outwards, obviously to keep watch. There were clear impressions of the butts of their rifles. The Boran carry small wooden pillows to use when they sleep, to prevent damage to their elaborate hair-styles. Imprints from these were also found. We knew that several weeks previously the Hamar Cocce had raided the Boran, stolen several head of cattle, and had killed a number of women and children. A swift occupation of the tribal area by the Ethiopian authorities had merely driven the Hamar Cocce into their inaccessible mountains with their looted stock. It was possible that the Boran were only intending to recover their stolen cattle and were passing through British territory in order to approach their objective from the south. A more likely alternative was that the party were trying to make up some of their losses by raiding the softer Kenya tribes, who herded their stock in an area forty miles west of us, towards Lake Rudolph. The direction taken by the Boran indicated that if we continued on their tracks we would meet our baggage camels and escort on the way to the rendezvous. We hurried along the tracks and, about an hour before sunset, met the rest of our troops. Over the radio I instructed our base to warn the police post at Ileret, the nearest post to the Italian Keep, of a possible raid on the Merille tribesmen grazing their stock nearby. It was now nearly dark and because we had all been on the move since before dawn I decided to feed and rest, until three hours before first light, when we would march to the next waterhole, at Garba Merille, which was about seven miles to our west.

"Heavy storm clouds had been building up during the day, and by sunset the sky was blacked out by the approaching rain, which fell heavily as we tried to cook our meal. Askari are wonderful in such circumstances and we were all fed before it was completely dark. As we prepared for an uncomfortable night, the handlers brought in the camels from their grazing and hobbled them inside our perimeter. At ten o'clock the rain stopped and then we got no sleep at all. Two lion circled the camp and grunted in their attempts to stampede the camels. These beasts kept rising to their feet with roars and tried to stumble away from the danger. The shivering handlers would jump to their feet and beat their charges until, with sobs of complaint, they settled down once more. No sooner was it all quiet than the whole cycle would start again. From time to time the freezing drizzle would set us shivering. I tried huddling under the stinking, part-cured hide which was used to prevent our heavy water containers from chafing the backs of the camels. It did not take me long to decide that I preferred to be wet and cold than asphyxiated by the hides.

"At two o'clock in the morning I set off with twenty askari who towards Garba Merille. I told the baggage guard to return to our base camp as soon as the ground was dry enough for the camels to move without slipping. Garba is an excellent place for an ambush. We found that the Boran had watered there the previous evening and were twelve hours ahead of us, but they would have to return to water the stock before cutting across the border. I left men to ambush the water hole against the expected return of the raiders that night while I set off with two askari to walk back to our Buluk Wells base to organize the remainder of the company, and to a large rainwater pool in a dry river bed.

"At nine o'clock that night and before the moon arose, the raiders walked into the ambush. The next day the platoon commander told me he had heard the raiders approaching, but could not see them as the night was extremely dark. When the raiders were properly in the ambush, he ordered para illuminating to be fired to light the area. The first two failed to ignite. The alerted raiders fired in the direction of the askari and disappeared. The third bomb lit the countryside and the askari and the police were able to shoot at the disappearing Boran. The raiders left blood trails and blood-stained clothing as they abandoned their loot before crossing the border, only 200 yards from the waterhole. At dawn I drove with two trucks to help the ambush party bring in the cattle. When I arrived at the Garba Merille waterhole the platoon had just driven off a group of sixteen Gelubba who had followed up the original raiding party and had attempted to take the cattle from the platoon by force. The Boran had abandoned twenty-four steers which they had stolen from a Merille tribesman after killing and castrating him. The cattle were exhausted, as they had been driven hard for thirty miles. After resting and watering the weary cattle, we started back for our base, taking care to keep well out in the bushy plain and away from the rocky hills. Three days later we handed the cattle to a police party, who returned them to the relatives of the murdered man. B Company askari certainly enjoyed themselves, especially the beef from two steers which were far too weak for the police to drive back to their owners. The raiders had covered eighty miles in the twenty-four hours from when we first started after them."

The provision of medical services to KAR units involved close working with the Colonial Medical Services. Each KAR battalion had an establishment of one RAMC Medical Officer, five regimental Nursing Orderlies and a fully qualified civilian midwife. Colonel Tommy Pace OBE (late RAMC) describes how it functioned:-

"The medical services within the battalion were a Medical Centre, where sick parade was taken daily; next to it was the Medical Reception Station, which provided accommodation for patients requiring 'bed down' treatment for minor or uncomplicated conditions of relatively short duration. It had wards for askari (twelve beds) and a separate Families Wing made up of a General Ward (six adult beds and three infant cots) and a Labour Ward with one obstetric bed. Other elements of the MRS included a Minor Operating Theatre, Laboratory and Sluice Room. Under the RMO's supervision the civilian midwife conducted all normal deliveries; she also ran the Families Ward and assisted at the Battalion Families Welfare Clinic.

"Whenever the RMO considered it necessary patients were referred to the local Government Civil Hospital, either for direct admission or for consultancy out-patient care. Ancillary diagnostic services, (eg: X Rays, physiotherapy, elaborate laboratory investigations) required at MRS level were carried out at the local Government Hospital. This system worked very well, since the RMO was able to keep close contact with his civilian professional colleagues. The other great advantage of having a MRS staffed by battalion medical personnel was that it enabled the sick askari and their families to be treated and nursed within the familiar atmosphere of their own unit for as long as practicable, rather than in the comparatively strange atmosphere of a civil hospital. One of the most important duties of the RMO was in connection with the medical arrangements for recruiting. He was an indispensable member of the battalion team that went out on routine recruiting safaris, as his initial medical examinations enabled him to weed out on the spot those who would clearly never make the grade. He carried out a more detailed examination, of course, on return to barracks, where he continued to monitor all recruits very carefully through their training."

For a full account of life as RMO of 6 KAR, (as being typical of the situation in the KAR in the late 1960s) see an article in the *Journal* of the RAMC by Captain C.A. Veys MB ChB RAMC (now Dr C.A. Veys MD MB ChB FFOM DPH DIH), April, 1960 (Vol 106(2) pp 55–62).

In Kenya independence came on 31 December, 1963. Michael Price was Staff Captain at Headquarters 70 Brigade, at Nanyuki. He was with his wife at their home on Uhuru [freedom] Day. He recounts:-

"The night was worthy of the momentous occasion, absolutely clear and starlit. Nevertheless, one's thoughts turned to Robert Ruark's best seller *Uhuru* with its blood-curdling prognostications, as we saw off our house staff – Kimoto the cook and Geoffrey the garden boy – to the celebrations in the local stadium. And how might British officers fare in their vigil on Kenya's borders, along with African troops? From midnight onwards the night was lit up by fireworks, and the sound of revelry from the stadium and elsewhere wafted across to us. In due course Kimoto and Geoffrey returned, having imbibed a bit more pombe than was good for them. Further afield, in remote detachments, officers and askari together celebrated Uhuru and changed the badges of the KAR for those of the Kenya Army. In the Services Africanization was given the highest priority by the Kenya Government. When I reached Kenya in June, 1963, there were only about four dozen African officers in the KAR, when I left two years later the number had risen to 305."

Attachments of British units and individuals continued after independence, including 21 Squadron RAF, which operated Twin Pioneers in the NFD during the shifta operations just before and for a year or so after independence. The ugly "Twin Pin" could land and take off from an area not much larger than a tennis court, and was well suited to casualty evacuation and troop support roles. Flt Lt Tony Beswetherick RAF gives some experiences:-

"One of my most memorable flights took place on 7 December, 1963. Flt Lt Dave King and I were tasked to return several Somali chieftains and the DC, Hugh Walker (Somaliland Scouts, 1949–51), from a conference at Wajir to Mandera. About twenty minutes short of Mandera the weather forced us to abandon the mission and return to Wajir. However, the DC asked us to drop them off at El Wak. We were running out of daylight and there were no night landing facilities nearer than Nairobi, several hundred miles away. In the event we ran out of light ten miles short of Wajir and I spent the next ten minutes hanging my head out of the side window to follow the vague outline of the track that would lead us to Wajir. Finally it became so dark that we had to accept that we would not be able to find the strip without some assistance from the ground. On ETA we climbed to 1,000 feet and orbited the area firing red Very lights, and after a few anxious moments we saw the lights of a vehicle moving below us. We kept them in view and were relieved to see it halt and start to flash its lights. We guessed that the driver had positioned himself at the up-wind end of the landing strip, so we made a tight turn on this assumption and aimed for his lights. Dave King made an excellent landing in the circumstances and a relieved crew followed the land rover along the narrow taxi way to the KAR camp, where we secured our aircraft. It was fortunate for us that the company commander at the time was Major Ian Gordon, who had some flying experience and who had made an accurate assessment of our predicament."

The KAR had to dig out a Beverley whose nose wheel had dug into the soft earth when the plane overshot the runway. Another Beverley had a difficult landing when the wheels broke through the crust of the airstrip's surface, to the surprise and discomfort of twenty askari passengers who had undone their seat belts prematurely.

Tony Beswetherick was an RAF squash champion; in Wajir's open-topped court he stood still while those who played him continually ran round him in unproductive circles. Tony's recollections of those days end:-

"No report on air operations in the NFD would be complete without mention of the happy relationship that existed between the RAF crews on detachment and the KAR. We were always well looked after, and I particularly remember the kindness of Ian Gordon, Ben Dunkey, who was the last British company commander at Wajir before Africanization, and Richard Corkran, who was 2ic to both. We gained a permanent 'Air House' and even had running hot water after Richard learned a better use for the 'goose necks' than lighting the runway. In return I hope we made life a little more bearable when we flew in fresh food and crates of whatever we had space for on board. We ourselves were glad of the fresh meat, although the sight of our dinner, a reluctant goat being dragged past the mess early in the day, did nothing for our taste buds."

David Bowley and 67 Animal Transport Troop had been on Mount Kilimanjaro in support of 2 Coldstream Guards and were returning to Nanyuki. They moved the ponies in trucks, three to a truck, with askari and the equipment at the back of each vehicle. They set out before dawn; the road across the Amboseli Plain was deeply pot-holed, and progress was painfully slow. David continues:-

"Suddenly there was a shout from the rear and a frantic voice screamed

'Simba! Enda Hpesi!' Two big lionesses had caught wind of our cargo and were padding along behind us, within a few feet of the tail board. They could keep pace with us at our maximum speed, which was about ten mph. The ponies were also frantic, lashing out at all and sundry, their handlers terrified that at any time the lions would spring up into the vehicle.

"Immediate action was called for. I glanced across at Motoko, my driver, whose ebony features were now a light shade of grey. He turned off the road onto the sandy plain in the hope of gaining some speed. Alas, the wheels began to sink in the soft sand, and our worsening situation looked very bad indeed. However, by utilizing the four-wheel drive, we just made it to the dried-up river-bed and scrambled across. Looking back I could see to my great relief that the lions had come to a halt on the far bank and now stood watching us, an aloof expression on their faces. Needless to say there was much nervous laughter and ribald shouting from the askari behind, as we continued on our way with the magnificent African dawn slowly breaking behind us."

Chapter 13

THE KENYA REGIMENT

by Len Weaver Esq CBE

It was the most junior of the regiments on the Army List, and it was the shortest lived.
>Colonel Sir Guy Campbell Bt OBE MC
>(CO Kenya Regiment during the Mau Mau Emergency)

Editorial Note

The Kenya Regiment contributed to the successes of almost all East African units during World War II, particularly the KAR, but also the REAN and the East African Armoured Car Regiment. In the Mau Mau emergency they operated as a unit. They have a unique perspective on events and I am most grateful to Len Weaver CBE, a former member of the Regiment, who wrote this chapter.

Len Weaver writes:-

The regiment was formed in 1937 and disbanded in 1963; within this brief span it performed with flair and distinction. In World War II it provided hundreds of officers for the battalions of the KAR which served in Ethiopia, Madagascar and Burma. From 1952 until 1956 it operated with outstanding success against the Mau Mau, in addition to providing leaders for KAR and British battalions and Special Forces, as well as District Officers (Kikuyu Guard) and Field Intelligence Officers. It was a territorial force and possibly the only regiment in the British Army whose Colours bear no battle honours. Those who served in it cherish fond memories of the comradeship, humour and courage of that highly individualistic body of men.

The regiment was – for most of its existence – manned almost entirely by members of families who had settled in Kenya. The early days of the colony are described in Chapters 1 and 3, in sufficient detail for it to be appreciated that these were fiercely independent and highly resourceful men and women. It was hardly surprising that their descendants readily responded to the call to arms in 1939 and during the Mau Mau emergency.

The Italian conquest of Ethiopia by early 1936 highlighted that in Kenya the military forces seemed inadequate to provide any form of defence. The Governor, Sir Joseph Byrne, set up a Committee under the chairmanship of Colonel J.A. Campbell, DSO, Commander of the Northern Brigade KAR, to review the local defence forces and to make recommendations for their reorganization. They recommended the disbandment of the Kenya Defence Force and its replacement by a battalion-strong Volunteer Force, to be called the Kenya Regiment (Territorial Force), drawn from men aged 18 to 35, and up to 45 in exceptional cases. Permanent Staff Instructors (PSIs) were to come from the brigade of Guards, on a minimum scale of one per company, and one regular officer (staff officer, adjutant or quartermaster). The main recommendations were implemented in the Kenya Regiment Ordinance and Regulation 1937, which became effective on 29 March, 1937, and the regiment was formed on 1 June.

The first Commanding Officer was Lt Col Alfred Dunstan-Adams OBE MC and bar, TD, who had settled in Kenya in 1925, after service in Mesopotamia, on the Somme and at Ypres. The other officers gazetted on formation were Major O. Lennox-Brown, Captain C.J. Valentine and Captain J. Forrest. Captain the Lord Stratheden (Coldstream Guards) became Staff Officer, supported by the QM, Lt Cummins (Irish Guards), and CSMs Bobbitt (Welsh Guards) and Carter (Grenadier Guards). The response to recruiting was enthusiastic; 500 men joined out of the 2,000 eligible to do so. As a result, a third company was added; with Capt W.W. Mackinley in command and CSM Broomfield (Grenadier Guards) as the PSI.

At this time the CO was in London, representing the Regiment at the coronation of King George, and had the honour of sitting next to the King at a dinner for overseas officers. The Regiment's flash and badge appeared for the first time at the coronation. The colours of the flash represent brown for the askari, green for the young Europeans who would lead them and red for the support given by the regular army. The buffalo badge was modelled on the memorial in the Nairobi Club to the famous game hunter, Frederick Courteney Selous DSO (See Chapter 3).

In February, 1938, fourteen members of the regiment were granted commissions; Branston, Berkeley, Bompas, Buxton, Crawford Dorrington, Gledhill, Goldhawk, Hart, Lean, Luckham, Manning, Sweatman and Redhead. The first annual camp was held in March, 1938, on the slopes of the Ngong Hills. The programme was strenuous and included evening lectures by serving officers of the KAR. Every opportunity was given to test and develop leadership potential. The regiment was fortunate in the quality of the permanent staff; Lord Stratheden combined efficiency with considerable tact, while the Warrant Officers relished developing the latent military abilities of the enthusiastic young Kenyans.

In February, 1939, the fourth company was authorized, with Captain Redhead in command and CSM Allen (Scots Guards) as the PSI. Five new subalterns were commissioned; Furse, Garvey, Grant, Hopraft and Simpson. In May, 1939, the CO went to Uganda at the invitation of the Governor, Sir Philip Mitchell, to improve the state of military preparedness there. A month later thirty young men had been recruited into the Uganda Platoon of the Kenya Regiment, commanded by 2Lt F.H. Crittenden. In the same month a Reconnaissance Platoon was authorized, consisting mainly of white hunters.

The second annual camp was held in the Ngong Hills in August, 1939, attended by 534 men, and judged even more successful than the first; the progress made in training exceeded all expectations. Mobilization went smoothly a few days later. The boys' boarding block at the Nairobi Primary School served as the mobilization barracks. Groups of men earmarked for duty as junior officers and senior NCOs joined existing KAR battalions, at an average of forty to each of the six battalions, within ten days of mobilization. By the end of October, 1939, over 400 officers and men had been posted to KAR, Supplies and Transport, and other units.

The Reconnaissance Platoon was divided between 4 KAR and 5 KAR, but it was reunited later and brought up to strength from the regiment, to become the East Africa Reconnaissance Squadron, the "Recces", who were so successful in the dash for Addis Ababa in 1940. Later the Squadron was reformed as the first Armoured Car Regiment in East Africa Command.

In October, 1939, the formation of 1 (EA) Light Battery was authorized. Henry Shorman recalls; "The only artillery in East Africa were the Coast Defence guns at Mombasa. The 22 Indian Mountain Battery arrived shortly after the outbreak of war and were accommodated at M'bagathi Camp." (See Appendix D). "Towards the end of September, 1939, a notice was posted at the Kenya Regiment calling for forty volunteers to form a light battery, to be trained by the Mountain Battery. There was a bribe – immediate promotion to Bombardier and a consequent pay increase to Shs 6 per day, from Shs 3.99 [These were East African shillings, at twenty to the pound]. A few days later forty Kenya Regiment privates were deposited at Mbagathi Camp, under Major W. Mackinlay, Kenya Regiment, and the 1 (EA) Light Battery was born; it was equipped with a pneumatic-tyred version of the mountain gun and limbers, with vehicles capable of towing them."

At the beginning of 1940 the Regiment moved from Kampala to camp on the racecourse at Eldoret, where about 150 men were being trained. Another

130 were completing their training at the newly established OCTU at Nakuru. The Nakuru OCTU set high standards, but perhaps some of their judgements were rather harsh. Alistair McCalman relates: "I attended the Nakuru OCTU with my brother David, and Nigel Leakey was on the same course. My brother and I were given very low marks as 'lacking in aggressive spirit' and were not to serve with fighting troops. Nigel Leakey was sent back to 6 KAR as 'lacking the fighting spirit needed to become an officer'. Subsequently Alistair gained the Military Cross. So did David, who was also mentioned in despatches twice."

The first major engagements were in Italian Somaliland and Ethiopia, as described in Chapters 5 and 6. One of the most strenuous battles was at Colito, when 1/6 KAR was suddenly attacked by some medium tanks. The tide of battle was turned by the prompt action of Sergeant Nigel Leakey of the Kenya Regiment, seconded to 6 KAR, who was awarded a posthumous Victoria Cross. Leakey belonged to a distinguished family which has remained prominent in Kenya today. On 19 May, 1950, 6 KAR introduced the practice of observing Colito Day, in honour of Leakey and the battle; they also named their barracks after him.

By mid-1941 the supply of recruits was nearly exhausted and it was no longer economical to maintain the organization. Colonel Dunstan-Adams estimated that seventy-five percent of Kenyan and Ugandan men of eligible age had passed through their hands. Of the 3,500 men who joined the Kenya Regiment, more than 1,500 were commissioned as officers in the KAR battalions and the Northern Rhodesia Regiment. After Ethiopia they fought in Madagascar and Burma; their record of decorations speaks for itself:-

Victoria Cross	1	DFC	7
OBE	3	DCM	1
MBE	8	MM	7
MC	24	BEM	1

Mentioned in Despatches 40
150 men of the regiment were killed during World War II.

The Notice in the *Kenya Gazette* in 1941 only discontinued the existence of the first battalion. It did not suspend or repeal the Kenya Regiment Ordinance 1937, nor did it affect the service engagements of individuals enlisted and still serving as members of the regiment. In 1948 Colonel Dunstan-Adams, assisted by Cecil Valentine and John Garvey, together with some other pre-war officers, sought to clarify the position and, as part of their campaign, wrote to the Governor, Sir Philip Mitchell, urging the reformation of the first battalion. The Government agreed, and the post-war Regulations to the KR Ordinance 1937 were issued on 24 March, 1950.

Lt Col Valentine, who had been AA & QMG in Headquarters 11 (EA) Division in Burma, was appointed to command. The War Office regretted that the Household brigade could no longer provide Permanent Staff for the regiment, but instead the regiment benefited from a long and close association with The King's Royal Rifle Corps (60th), and The Rifle Brigade (95th). In March, 1950, the Foundation Stone for the Regimental Headquarters was laid by HRH The Duke of Gloucester.

In 1939 the Colours were subscribed for by the women of Kenya, through the East African Women's League, and by officers of the Regiment. The Colours arrived in Nairobi just before the outbreak of war and were immediately put into safe keeping. There was some doubt, just before their formal presentation in 1950, whether the King had, in fact, authorized the presentation. This was resolved by Sir Philip telephoning Buckingham Palace direct and securing the Monarch's personal authority. The Colours were presented by the Governor on 4 March, 1950, in an impressive ceremony at Nairobi West. On 20 November in the same year the Regiment was honoured with the Freedom of the City of Nairobi and, in accordance with its privilege, marched through the city with bayonets fixed, drums beating, band playing and Colours flying.

In January, 1952, the first call-up under the compulsory Military Training Ordinance of 100 young men led to their being flown to Southern Rhodesia for six months' training at the King George VI Barracks in Salisbury, pending the completion of the Kenya Regiment Training Centre at Lanet, near Nakuru. The Regimental Headquarters in Nairobi was officially opened on 2 February, 1952, by Princess Elizabeth. The Princess, wearing a pink and white polka-dot dress, looked absolutely radiant as she came along the lines. The whole parade of the CCF, the Old Comrades and the regiment was an astonishing success.

Lt Col Valentine relinquished command because of his business commitments and Major Guy Campbell, who had been his 2ic since 9 December, 1951, was appointed CO in 2 April, 1952. He had been commissioned into the King's Own Yorkshire Light Infantry in 1931, but transferred subsequently to the 60th Rifles, in which four generations of his family had served. He was awarded the MC while serving with the Sudan Defence Force and had soldiered in Libya, Eritrea and Palestine. Although he was the first regular officer to command the regiment, his appointment was inspired because he soon demonstrated an empathy with the young men of the regiment. These Kenyans were generally well educated, full of initiative, and most were natural leaders. Many were inclined to rebel against authority and some were incorrigible, even by Colonial standards. Yet Guy Campbell was welcomed by the Kenyans, who responded well to his robust approach to soldiering, his obvious dislike of bureaucracy, pomposity and phonies, and his humour. He was required to serve two masters; the GOCinC regulated the Regiment's military operations, but the Kenya Government was responsible for its financial backing. Guy Campbell and other astute members of the Regiment exploited this division of authority to achieve results and equipment that would not have been possible in a more conventional chain of command.

The Regiment was ready to serve as an operational unit for four years, during the Mau Mau emergency. At the beginning of the Emergency, in October, 1952, the Regiment consisted of the Battalion Headquarters and Headquarter Company in Nairobi and three companies on detachment. The Company Commanders were A – Capt "Boxer" Brown, B – Major David Gillett MC and C – Major Dick Josselyn. Staff seconded from KRRC and RB included the Adjutant, Capt Roly Guy; Training Officer, Capt Dick Cornell; Quartermaster, Major (QM) Frank Wakefield. The PSIs included RSM M. Pendry, CSM J. Holland and the ORQMS, W.G. Hutchinson. The Padre was Jimmy Gillett, who had been the regiment's chaplain since its foundation.

The three companies were mobilized immediately; as in the Second World War, many of the Regiment's personnel were quickly sent to other units. A substantial number went to be platoon and company commanders in KAR battalions, where some were able to renew comradeships with askari they had known in 1939–45. In addition the Security forces included up to six British infantry battalions. To help them adapt to the country, each British battalion had Kenya Regiment officers and NCOs attached, to help with language problems and the interrogation of prisoners.

The Kenya Regiment guarded Jomo Kenyatta and other Mau Mau leaders during their trial at Kapenguria. On one occasion Kenyatta agreed to come outside the building to have his photograph taken and to talk to members of the Kenya Regiment. Barry Jacob remembers:-
"He was most interesting and for that brief time we all got on very well. Little did we realize that he would lead Kenya to independence and become the President."

The activities of the Kenya Regiment during the early days of the Emergency were something of a paradox. On patrol they pursued and killed the enemy with single-minded efficiency, but elsewhere they were able to work well with the loyal Kikuyu and ex-Mau Mau. Some unusual units were created in the process. One of these was 'Ray Force', which distinguished itself in the early days of the emergency. Capt Ray Mayers commanded three groups of police guard posts, which were established throughout the Nyeri, Fort Hall and Kiambu reserves. Each of the groups was commanded by a temporary captain and had fifteen guard posts, with two members of the regiment in charge of a varying number of Home Guard. The Home Guard had been built up slowly and carefully from loyal members of the Kikuyu, Meru and Embu tribes.

On 20 April, 1953, The Home Guard was established as the Kikuyu Guard; Col Phillip Morcombe formed the KG, aided by young men from the Kenya Regiment as District Officers. The Guard was based on the Athigani, the traditional warriors and scouts of the Kikuyu. At first they were armed only with simis, spears and bows and arrows, but were later trained in the use of firearms. Each post also had a supply of grenades, Tilly lamps and alarm flares, and was linked by radio to other posts in the vicinity. Several of these posts were attacked by the Mau Mau; the best known example is the mass attack at Othayo, where there were four Kenya Regiment men, including Alan Wisdom and Ernest Day. The Mau Mau had been active in the area earlier in the day and in the evening a large force gathered on a nearby ridge. The Kenya Regiment men prepared carefully for the assault, which eventually started at thirty minutes after midnight. About 300 terrorists were held off, but the battle was fierce. Wave after fanatical wave, stimulated by the local drug Bhang [cannabis], attacked the guard post, but were repelled by well-disciplined fire and the steady lobbing of grenades. In the morning they left the battlefield strewn with over eighty casualties and a number of precious precision weapons. It was a major victory, news of which spread quickly across the guard posts and did much to bolster the morale of the KG.

Fifty-six members of the regiment served in the KG; their role was demanding. The Selection Board chose men who could lead Africans, and who could build up a fine team spirit. It was essential that they got on well with the District Officers and the Police, with whom they had to work closely. It was an exacting task to train and lead members of the KG, requiring cool heads and steady nerves. The KG eventually expanded to a strength of 4,500 – many of whom were armed with rifles – with efficiently run and effectively defended posts. By the end of 1955 they had accounted for a substantial number of terrorists. The young members of the Kenya Regiment and the Kikuyu from the villages meshed together very effectively in the difficult and dangerous work of severing the links between the terrorists and the supply lines in the reserves.

I Force was a mixed company of the Regiment, formed at Squiares Farm, near Mweiga, commanded by Capt Neville Cooper MBE MC GM, who was a platoon commander in B Company, assisted by Lt Tony Vetch of the

Kenya Police Reserve. They were an intelligence unit, with their numbers augmented by KAR askari, trackers and de-oathed Mau Mau. Each patrol consisted of about ten men, a mixture of Europeans and Africans, to which tracker dogs and their RAVC handlers were added when O Company became operational. Patrols took the battle into the enemy's own territory, the high altitude bamboo forests and woodlands of the Aberdares and Mount Kenya. Patrols were mentally and physically demanding, lasting up to fourteen days, and involving climbing up and down deep gullies and ravines, bitterly cold nights and with tropical rain drenching everything. Each man carried a sleeping bag, water, ammunition and rations, which was not easy at heights of 8–10,000 feet. I Force achieved some spectacular successes which were to have a significant effect on the way in which Kenya Regiment personnel were deployed subsequently.

A major development by the regiment, deriving from I Force, was what were later called 'pseudo-gangs'. Early in 1953 Capt Francis Erskine sought permission to carry out an operation with loyal Kikuyu disguised as Mau Mau. This was supported by Guy Campbell, and Erskine developed the method. Subsequently he was awarded a well-deserved MC. The very first pseudo-gang comprised Bill Woodley, Steve Bothma and Gibson Wanbugu.

By the end of 1953 all companies of the Kenya Regiment were operating pseudo-gangs, with the aim of eliminating the terrorists in their company areas. Their faces were darkened with various substances, including cocoa powder mixed with soot, black boot polish and black grease paint. Filthy cloth caps or hats were favoured as head cover; when pulled well down they would hide straight hair and blue eyes effectively. A coating of dirt and grease completed the exercise.

Later in the Emergency Superintendent Ian Henderson of Special Branch took the concept of the pseudo-terrorist even further, with the aid of the Kenya Regiment. By the end of 1955 an estimated 1,500 terrorists remained in the Aberdares, but only a handful were being killed or captured each week. To end the Emergency it was essential to kill or capture Dedan Kimathi. Henderson evolved a plan to use pseudo-terrorists to catch terrorists by sending them back into the forest, not to arrest or kill their quarry, but to rehabilitate them. By these means he hoped to penetrate the hard-core of Mau Mau surrounding Kimathi. Late in December Henderson placed letters to "The People in the Forest" in three separate locations, after which an aircraft fitted with a powerful loudspeaker flew over the forest shouting out where the letters were.

Early on Boxing Day morning, O Company was moving up the Kinangop/Fort Jerusalem track, when the leading man saw a typical Mau Mau letter in a cleft stick on the track. It was addressed to "Kinanjui", which both the Intelligence Officer, Robin "Dingo" Plenderleith, and the company commander, Ray Nightingale, knew was Henderson's Kikuyu name. It was from a terrorist who had once held high rank in Mau Mau. This gave Henderson the breakthrough that he needed in the hunt for Kimathi (Operation Blue Doctor); contact was established soon after. In early 1956 three men of the Kenya Regiment (Bill Eastbrook, Laurie Pearse and Jim Stephen) joined his team. They made several sorties into the forest accompanying newly converted hard-core Mau Mau; they were unarmed and relied on the strengths of their personalities to win the trust of the former terrorists. They had some close escapes when the teams brought out significant numbers of hard-core Mau Mau, before Kimathi was finally forced out of the forest to seek food; he was wounded and captured by a Kikuyu Guard ambush. Bill, Laurie and Jim made an immense contribution to the successful ending of the Emergency, through several months of cold, sustained courage, and brought in hundreds of dangerous, dedicated terrorists.

Early in 1945 the regiment was reorganized into patrol companies (modelled on I Force), augmented by trackers and KAR askari. These patrol companies worked closely with the Kenya Police Reserve Air Wing and the RAF Harvards which were based with the regiment near Nyeri. Between them they developed air strike and air resupply systems which became the norm in Kenya. The well-known and gallant pilot, "Punch" Bearcroft was an early member of the regiment who helped to develop the Air Wing. The pilots added a new dimension to Kenya Regiment patrols; they ensured that ground troops could be sustained by food drops and thus stay in the forest for long periods. They could also signal the positions of gangs by using smoke and flares. The successes of these patrols made the Mau Mau fear the Kenya Ngombe more than any other of the security forces.

After their successes in the Nyeri and Fort Hall reserves, the regiment moved to Naivasha, where it was reduced from seven companies to four (B, C, I and Support Company). This was necessary because of the continuous calls on them for manpower for the remainder of the Security Forces. There were some reservations about the reorganization, as many believed that the Emergency could have been ended earlier if the Regiment had remained at full strength.

Operation Anvil, in Nairobi on 29 April, 1954 involved four British battalions, one KAR battalion and the regiment, together with the police. Their sweep of the city detained thousands of suspects and did much to sever links between the terrorists in the forest and their supporters in the city.

Company commanders during the last two years included David Gillett MC, Dick Josselyn, Ray Mayers MBE, "Boxer" Brown, Neville Cooper

MBE MC GM, Peter Anderson MC, Peter Ragg, Wally Schuster, John Klynsmith, Tony Vetch and Oliver Waring. Further demands made on the regiment for more manpower denuded it to an extent that it had to be reduced to one company, designated O Company. It was commanded by Ray Nightingale and moved to several different operational areas, including Narok in Masailand, and back to the Aberdares. Reinforcements from the Kenya Regiment Training Centre (KRTC) near Nakuru received operational training and experience with O Company before secondment to any of the wide variety of tasks undertaken by members of the regiment.

In February, 1956, Col Guy Campbell handed over command of the regiment to Lt Col Charles Madden; his well-deserved farewell party was attended by over 400 people. His outstanding leadership had secured the respect and affection of his men; he also overcame opinions that opposed the Regiment. In 1956 the Queen approved the alliance between the 60th (Kings Royal Rifle Corps) and the regiment; in consequence the regiment adopted the green beret and patrol uniform, and all PSIs wore the green, red and black lanyard.

Early in 1956 O Company was at Ndaragua in the Northern Aberdares. From then until it was stood down on 10 November its operational commitments continued to vary; from the bamboo forests of the Southern Aberdares, to Mount Kenya, the Naivasha swamp, and some of the more remote areas of the Kikuyu reserves. In all of these they added to their considerable numbers of killed and captured.

Officers who had served in O Company included Bill Woodley MC, Brian Williamson, Jerry Adam, Simon Reynolds, Mike Tremlett, Nigel Bulley, Stan Bleazard, Henry Willemse, Boet de Bruin, Eddie Bristow, Jack Harnett, David Durrant, Francis Erskine MC, Mickey Wright, Freddy Seed, George Newby, Mike Higgins, Johny Jones, Scotty Meintjes, Denis Alexander (RMO), Tony Banister, Bob Muir, Clive Catania, Conway Plough, Don Rooken-Smith and Robin Plenderleith.

In October the regiment provided a Guard of Honour for HRH Princess Margaret at the Royal Show. By the end of December all full-time serving members had been released, and on 1 January, 1957, the unit reverted to Territorial Force status. At the farewell parade at RHQ, the GOCinC, General Lathbury, took the salute and made a speech in which he paid enormous tribute to the part played by the regiment in its many roles during the Emergency. There had been the unceasing demands for leaders for every KAR and British battalion, Brigade headquarters liaison, Field Intelligence Officers, the KPR Mounted Section, the Armoured Car Squadron, 156 Battery RA, the Kikuyu Guard, Interrogation Centres, the Jungle Warfare School, Battle School, Tracker Combat Teams and Special Forces. This immensely difficult task was superbly handled by the Adjutant, Roly Guy, and the Assistant Adjutant, Kenya-born Angus MacDonald. The Adjutant, who was to become General Sir Roly Guy GCB CBE DSO, Adjutant General, later recorded:-

"My posting as Adjutant to the Kenya Regiment gave me such education, experience and satisfaction that I never ceased to be grateful for my luck in getting the job." He was succeeded by Captain Roy Eve, whose sterling work in the last eighteen months of operations was followed by the difficult task of developing the regimental structure for the post-Mau Mau period and the run-up to independence.

The decorations and awards to members of the Kenya Regiment during the emergency were:-

OBE	1	MM	6
MBE	8	GM	5
MC	5	BEM	10
DCM	1	QPM(G)	3
Mentions in Despatches 33		CinC's Commendations 15	

Figures from the Military Secretary in the Ministry of Defence show that, in the period from April, 1954 to the reversion of the regiment to Territorial Force status, the Kenya Regiment represented 4.9% of the military forces in Kenya, yet they were awarded 30.77% of the decorations and 9.69% of the Mentions in Depatches.

During the last few months of 1956 the regiment began to re-form on a territorial basis and, by the beginning of 1957, seven companies were well established. A and B Companies were in Nairobi, C at Kitali, D at Nyeri, E at Mombasa, F at Kericho and I at Nakuru, with the Training Centre. The obligations on a recruit were six months at the Training Centre, followed by four years with the regiment. Each year involved attendance for three weekends and a two-week camp. Madden handled the transition to the peacetime structure skilfully and exercised a calming influence at a time of great political uncertainty in Kenya.

1958 saw many changes; most of the Regular officers who had been with the regiment during the later stages of the Emergency moved on. The Adjutant, Capt Roy Eve, was replaced by Capt Peter Welsh (later Maj Gen Peter Welsh OBE MC), Capt Colin Campbell was succeeded as Training Officer by Capt Gerald Carter, and Major Frank Wakefield, the Quatermaster was relieved by Lt George Blunden.

On 31 May and 1 June the regiment celebrated its twenty-first anniversary. On the Saturday morning, they were inspected by the Mayor, accompanied by the Honorary Colonel, Col Dunstan-Adams. They were drawn up in three companies under Lt Col Charles Madden, outside the Town Hall. Before they moved off the Mayor gave a short address; they then marched past with the KAR Band playing the Regimental March, after which they marched through the city to much applause from the crowd. In the evening the Birthday Ball was held in the City Hall, with the Governor, the GOC, the Mayor and a host of other VIPs among over 1,000 people who attended. A drumhead service on Sunday morning at the Drill Hall was conducted by the Padre, Rev John D'Aeth, before the Governor opened the Memorial Building.

In November, 1958, the regiment was reorganized into four rifle companies and HQ Company. A and B merged into one – O Company – in the Nairobi area, commanded first by Paddy Deacon and then by John Shaw. C Company, at Kitali was commanded by James McKillop and later by Jock Rutherford; D Company at Nyeri by Tony Vetch, who became 2ic later; he was succeeded by John Campbell. I Company was at Nakuru, under Bill Hindley; E Company in Mombasa became a platoon of O Company, under Ian Campbell first and then Sid Moscoff. HQ Company was commanded by Hammy O'Hara.

On 14 February, 1959, the regiment provided a Guard of Honour for Queen Elizabeth the Queen Mother, drawn from C and I Companies. It was commanded by Major Rutherford; the Queen's Colour was carried by Lt Don Rooken-Smith.

Lt Col Charles Madden handed over to Lt Col Dick Vernon, also of the 60th, who took a long-term view of the impending independence of Kenya. He and Tony Vetch reviewed the options at length, and concluded that:-

– The regiment was a fine institution, well worth preserving and it had a part to play in the new Kenya; but, whatever happened, standards must not be lowered.

– A purely European regiment, particularly one which had played a great part in the defeat of the Mau Mau, could not survive in an independent Kenya.

– The only chance lay in opening up recruitment to Africans and perhaps to Asians.

– If men of the three ethnic groups could live together, be treated exactly the same and "go through it" together at the KRTC and at annual camps, a truly multi-racial unit would emerge, able to be a role-model for the rest of Kenyan society.

The plan was prepared by Vernon and Vetch, who was succeeded as 2ic by Paddy Deacon, who was similarly minded. Their bold proposals were shown in turn to the company commanders, Colonel Dunstan-Adams, the Permanent Secretary at the Ministry of Defence, the GOC and finally to the Governor, all of whom gave their support.

In 1961 Vernon handed over to Lt Col Douglas Bright (Ox and Bucks Light Infantry), who skilfully handled affairs during the Independence period, with the help of Chris Adami as Adjutant and Carol Gurney as Training Officer. Seven Africans and six Asians, all very carefully selected – all with School Certificates and most of them good at sports – joined the training course at KRTC, where they were treated in exactly the same way as their European fellows. The experiment was a success, and other Africans and Asians joined subsequent courses. Several officers who later rose to senior ranks in the Kenya Defence Forces after independence were Africans who served with the Kenya Regiment.

The accelerating pace of political change defeated the Vernon/Vetch initiative. Africanization moved so quickly in the KAR that, within one year of independence, there were no seconded European officers. The decision to suspend the regiment was taken because no one in the Government wanted it to continue. In 1963 Colonel Dunstan-Adams and Paddy Deacon met President Kenyatta, who listened politely to their ideas on how the regiment could augment the regular army, but no action was taken. Nevertheless President Kenyatta, who had been guarded by the regiment some eleven years earlier, gave his assurance that the regiment would remain on the statute book, and it does to this day.

Colonel Dunstan-Adams, the Honorary Colonel and first Commanding Officer, who had guided the regiment from its earliest days in 1937, took the salute on 12 May, 1963, when the regiment marched through Nairobi with Colours flying, drums beating and bayonets fixed. Afterwards, with Lt Col Bright, the last CO, and Major Deacon, the 2ic, officiated at the laying up of the Colours in Nairobi Cathedral. In 1965 the Colours were moved to Winchester, where they were repaired and are displayed – under glass – in the entrance lobby of the Sir John Moore Barracks. Brigadier Dick Vernon arranged for a brief history and for the Roll of Honour to be framed and placed below the Colours.

For many years the Kenya Regiment has existed only in the memories of those who served in it; memories that span forty, and fifty and more years. The Kenya Regiment Association in Nairobi is supported by enthusiastic branches in the UK, Natal, Transvaal, Australia, New Zealand and Canada. The UK Branch holds an annual reunion dinner at the Headquarters of 4 (Volunteer) Battalion of the Royal Green Jackets. In the summer a curry lunch is held at the Sir John Moore Barracks at Winchester; 163 members and guests attended in 1996. The esprit de corps pervading the Association is almost tangible in its intensity. For many their service in the regiment was a demanding and exciting adventure which not only helped them to grow up, but stood them in good stead in their future careers. A great number would claim that the bonds forged in the regiment represent their most enduring and valued friendships.

Today the great majority of Association members have retired from full-time occupations, but still attach great importance to regimental reunions, which abound with good humour and nostalgia. Memories are shared of a very different, bygone era – of the final years of Kenya Colony and of the British Empire – of a dramatically beautiful country – of changing times and stirring events. The dominant theme still remains their unforgettable service with that remarkable and unique body of men, the Kenya Regiment.

EPILOGUE

People recall their experiences of Africa and Africans in a variety of ways. In December, 1961 David Bowley was in Tanganyika just before Uhuru. One of the events to mark Independence was to be the highest flag-raising ceremony in Africa, at the top of Mount Kilimanjaro (19,340 feet) by Lt Nyrenda. As David said, "Simultaneously we set off rockets that were intended to be seen in Dar es Salaam, the Nation's capital." The task of getting all the people and kit to the top of the mountain fell to Major Pat Stevens of the Signals Squadron at Buller Camp, Nairobi, with David to assist him. Dr Julius Nyerere, the President Designate, visited their base camp shortly before the expedition set out for the peak, to hand over the flag and the bronze plaque that they were to carry to the summit of Uhuru Peak. The plaque recorded the event and was to be set in cement at the top.

David looked after the animal transport. As he put it, "I was a platoon commander in charge of some rather scruffy pack ponies." The event was carried off as planned, and David was able to climb "Mount Kili" subsequently several times before leaving Africa. Thirty years later, living in Sonora, California, and in practice as a chiropractor, David decided that it was time to do it again, if only to ensure that the plaque was still there. He climbed in company with his daughter, her husband and a retired local school teacher. They set out from the Marangu Hotel, at the base of the mountain, in October, 1994, for their exhausting six-day trek. They went up in bounds, resting overnight at huts at 10,000, 12,500, and 15,000 feet before making the final assault. Things had changed somewhat; the huts were much more comfortable and the Tanzanian park service charged a $150 fee per climber, while the hire of porters and guides cost about $400 per climber. David had the same guide who had accompanied him in 1963. The plaque was still there, somewhat weathered. David's daughter Marianne, who had heard about the climb and the plaque since a child, burst into tears at the sight of it. David was more restrained in his reaction, noting that it was now festooned with flags and emblems left by scores of climbers. "It's held up pretty well, considering," he thought.

Back in Sonora he told his story to the local newspaper, the Union Democrat. The reporter did not give him the opportunity to check the text, and David was surprised to read a description of him and his "scruffy pack ponies" as "Bowley, who commanded a cavalry squadron of horses and soldiers".

The Burma Campaign Fellowship Group is committed to reconciliation between former enemies and regularly exchanges and visits with the All Burma Veterans' Association of Japan. BCFG learned of the admiration General Katagiri, then a battalion commander, had for the actions of a "gallant Royal officer", who was subsequently identified as Lt Grier of Ted Onslow's company in 36 KAR, when Ted was badly wounded and all three platoon commanders were killed, near Indainggyi. Katagiri described how Grier had got right up to a bunker position, shot one Japanese and was killed in turn. His askari were described as "well trained and obedient". A dossier describing Grier's brave action was handed to Tom King MP, then Secretary of State for Defence, at the KAR and EAF Officers' Club Dinner in 1991. Later, John Nunneley handed a similar dossier to ABVAJ in Japan. David Shirreff went with the BCFG party to Japan in November, 1993, and met General Katagiri. Among other things, they went to the Yasuknui Shrine, where two million Japanese war dead are commemorated. In David's words:-

"Here a tough old veteran of 31 Division, much scarred by British bullets, said prayers for peace and we all lined up and bowed".

In London in August, 1995, fifty years after the end of the Second World War, representatives of all the former Dominion and Empire countries that had fought on the British side met and paraded down the Mall on a very hot day; HM The Queen took the salute. A detachment of officers and one ex-RSM who had served in with East African troops, led by Maj Gen Rowley (Toto) Mans, marched with them. A contingent from Somaliland was joined by ex-RSM Farah Musa (formerly of the Somaliland Scouts), who had been on the Victory parade in 1946, had gained a Falklands medal subsequently, and who was to carry a replica of the banner of 71 KAR at the Albert Hall Festival of Remembrance on 11 November, 1995.

APPENDIX A

Lt Col H. Moyse-Barlett MBE MA PhD
A personal tribute by Professor Anthony Allott

My first contact with the renowned historian of the KAR was not with him in the flesh, but indirectly, through his omnipresence on the notice boards at the Signals Training Centre and Depot at Nanyuki.

When my battalion, 31 (N) Machine Gun Battalion KAR, returned to Africa in June, 1946, from its service as part of 11 (EA) Division at Ranchi, India, to be disbanded, I did not go with them. Instead, I was detached (by the War Office I assume) and posted to the Signals Training Centre at Nanyuki.

The chain of circumstances which led to this was complicated. I had been a temporary member of the Royal Corps of Signals before being commissioned in 1944 into the Royal Northumberland Fusiliers. I found myself – after an initial period assisting the post-D Day invasion of Northern Europe, but safely on the English side – put on a ship to East Africa to join the KAR.

With the 31st I went to India to fight the Japanese. This was a fairly safe posting, as we did not actually get to Burma, but stayed for further training in India, where there were at that time no Japanese.

With the passage of time, and thanks to my earlier experience with the Royal Signals, I was appointed Battalion Signals Officer. From there to Nanyuki was a logical move. The war was, of course, over and the posting was a congenial one without danger except for the night-time fusillades of small arms fire from jumpy settlers, who would fire their pistols out of their back doors at random into the darkness to put off armed robbers.

At the Signals Training Centre every notice on the Camp notice board seemed to have been signed by the erstwhile Commandant, who had recently left. Thus I became very familiar by proxy with the existence of the signatory, Lt Col H. Moyse-Bartlett.

Eventually, at the end of October, 1946, I secured a class B release to return to my studies in law at New College, Oxford. After graduating with a Bachelor's degree in law in 1948, and as a complement to my intended career at the Bar, I responded somewhat cheekily to an advertisement of a post at the School of Oriental and African Studies in the University of London. The post was for a lecturer in "African Law". Somewhat cheekily, because the ad said "Required: Retired Colonial Judge", which I was not. I did not know that there was such a thing as African Law, and anyhow knew nothing whatever about it.

I was called for a job interview at the School. So when the Director introduced the panel, and introduced the Secretary (the chief administrative officer) saying "This is Colonel Moyse-Bartlett," I nearly fell through the floor, and could not restrain myself from exclaiming (again, rather cheekily), "I know your name so well because it was on all the notices at the Signals Centre where I was".

Whether this connection influenced them to offer me the job I cannot say. Still, I took it. "MB", as we all called him, became a firm friend. The KAR connection between us was vital in this, creating a bond which lasted. From time to time he asked me to come as a guest to KAR dinners – I am ashamed to say that I never did, as I thought (that was mistake, as I now realize) that my war service was in the past.

MB enrolled for a PhD degree, taking as his thesis the history of the KAR. This was another enterprising and unusual (for an administrator) step to take. His researches were crowned with success, naturally; so that he could have called himself "Doctor Moyse-Bartlett", but he never did.

Modesty, as well as affability, was one of his main virtues. His style of management of the School and its sometimes difficult dons was a model of restraint. Ordering people about was not his way. Two personal features stand out in the memory. The first was that he had the reputation of picking not only the best lady secretaries, but the prettiest. The bachelor members of the teaching staff appreciated this accomplishment.

The other characteristic was that he had an involuntary twitch in one eye, which disconcerted those not familiar with him, since he would utter some profound or practical truth, but accompanied by a massive wink. In the more solemn academic meetings and occasions the result was particularly impressive.

Anthony Allott, February 1996.

APPENDIX B

'THEY WENT SINGING"
Songs of the King's African Rifles

by Professor George Shepperson, CBE
(formerly of 13 (N) KAR)

Appreciation of the songs of black soldiers, whether on the march or around the camp fire, goes back at least to 1869, when Thomas Wentworth Higginson, commanding officer of the first slave regiment to be mustered in the service of the United States during the American Civil War, published his classic book, *Army Life in a Black Regiment*. In a moving chapter on the songs of his black soldiers, Higginson commended their power, and declared, "It was a strange enjoyment to be brought suddenly into a world of unwritten songs". A World War I American officer, John J. Niles, in his *Singing Soldiers* (New York, 1927), devoted an entire volume to the songs of America's black troops: "natural-born singers, usually from rural districts, who, prompted by hunger, wounds, homesickness and the reaction of so many years of suppression, sang the legend of the black man to tunes and harmonies they made up as they went along".

Europeans who served with the King's African Rifles, whether from Nyasaland, Kenya, Uganda, Tanganyika or further afield, in peace or war, in Africa or overseas, often felt like Higginson or Niles about the songs of the askari. Like them, they were sometimes inclined to sentimentalize these singers or to interpret their songs in a spirit of negritude. But, once heard, these African airs were never forgotten and in later years echoes of them often came back to remind their hearers of service with African soldiers and of a comradeship between black and white which was rare in the history of Empire. When, for example, in the 1950s the film about ivory poaching in Kenya *Where No Vultures Fly* was shown, old KAR hands who saw it may have been surprised and then delighted to see an East African police detachment dancing to the tune of what is probably the best known of all KAR marching songs: "Tu funge safari" – "Let's get on with the journey". It must have reminded them of the start of many a safari at home or abroad, with the singing soldiers of the KAR.

Because of the power of these black singers, it was surprising that the historian of the KAR, Lt Col H. Moyse-Bartlett, in his magnum opus of 1956, ignored askari songs. His interest in music among the askari was limited to an essay on KAR bands, although he does make a reference to the making of one marching song which merits note because it indicates one of the two classes into which KAR marching songs may be divided, first those which were set initially by Europeans to well-known British or American tunes During the First World War, when the KAR was involved in the campaign in German East Africa, C.A. Harvey, the Bandmaster of 3 KAR, wrote Swahili words, representing the battalion at war, to the battalion march-past, Men of Harlech:-

"Haya! KAR askari,	"Get on with it, KAR soldiers
Sasa kazi ya safari.	Now it is the job of the journey.
Kazi yako kazi gani?	What is your work?
Vita kali leo!	The fierce work of today!
Amri ya Serikali!	The Government's orders!
KAR tayari . . ."	The KAR's ready . . ."

Harvey's simple but effective Swahili rhymes could be sung by African and European alike, and they lasted well into and beyond the Second World War. Other marching songs in this class included patriotic exhortations, often around the person of "Kingi Georgi", in simple Swahili, to such foreign melodies as "Marching through Georgia", "John Brown's Body", "Clementine" and "What a friend we have in Jesus". In studio recordings of KAR songs of this sort, made in India at the end of the Second World War, they sometimes seem rather childish. But, sung on the march, with African harmonies and improvisations added, they often lose their foreign character and take on the nature of true military ballads of no mean calibre.

The second class into which the KAR marching songs may be divided is that in which the African initiative is paramount and the European influence marginal – and often negligible. In this class it seems that the askari singers from Central Africa (centered on Nyasaland, but sometimes including African soldiers from Northern Rhodesia and Mozambique) were a major element. The 11 (EA) Division's correspondent in Burma in 1944, Gerald Hanley, in his book about the Division's campaign in the Kabaw valley and across the Chindwin, *Monsoon Victory*, stressed the importance of singing for the askari and had no hesitation in saying that "The Nyasas are the singers of East Africa, or at least, of the East African forces. Their songs have power and music in them". Some European witnesses of KAR balladry might dispute this assertion and award the palm to soldiers of other East African tribes. Notably among these were the Nyamwezi from Tanganyika, whose potentialities for development in many directions were observed as early as the mid-1870s by the explorer Stanley. The Nyamwezi were porters for Europeans, Arabs and local rulers and, in the growth of KAR songs, the heritage of stirring singing by African carriers is important.

However, from my own experience with the KAR in wartime, in Africa and in Asia, and from reading and research into East and Central African history since then, I would support Gerald Hanley's assertion; the Nyasas, from the origins of the KAR in the late nineteenth century to its incorporation in the 1960s into the armies of independent African states, whether singing in their military lingua franca, Chinyanja or in their tribal languages, were the outstanding singers of the KAR. In military service before the First World War, during the war, far from home, the Nyasas (a general term used by Europeans to cover congeries of tribes from the Lake Nyasa [now Lake Malawi] and Lower Zambezi regions) drew upon their own heritage for songs on the march or around the camp fire, when in the service of the colonial power.

James Stewart, a Scottish missionary on an expedition in 1879 to Lake Nyasa, noted their potential and something of the structure of their singing. "They have," he declared "indeed a good ear for music and many of them have fine voices. Over the campfire one of them will often lead in a recitative chant describing the events of the day, while the audience joins in the refrain or chorus, which is all the more appreciated if it contains a joke or a hit at any member of the party. For instance, one song they used to sing at their work in Livingstonia [a Scottish missionary station established in 1875], when Mr [E.D.] Young was there, ran:-

> "We bring chickens here for sale,
> And he makes us work so hard;
> We bring bananas here for sale,
> And yet he makes us work so hard."

"This song", commented James Stewart, in a notable missionary understatement, "must not be taken as indicating any grievance." But it certainly indicates one tendency of Nyasa singers, to give vent to complaints in a manner which makes the British soldier – often renowned for his moans on the march – seem by comparison a mere amateur in the art of complaining in song. To the influence on KAR balladry of Nyasaland porters' singing one must add the melodies, often with implicit social criticism, of the boatmen on Lake Nyasa and the Lower Zambezi. As one European traveller who went up the Zambezi in 1892 into British Central Africa observed, "Sometimes their song was a chorus which all of them could sing with full-throated assurance. But sometimes an improvisor would break forth with an impromptu version of his own. It might be a comment on the journey, but more likely it was a joke about one of the white passengers."

When Christian missions, especially from Scotland, were established in Nyasaland during the last three decades of the nineteenth century, Africans were introduced to hymn tunes which, in due course, they incorporated into their indigenous structure of singing. By the eve of the First World War the Nyasas in the KAR had no small repertoire of songs, combining indigenous and foreign elements, with which to boost their morale as they went off to war. They sang of their military burdens:-

    "Asikali – ee,   "The soldiers are going to war
    Ku nkhondo – ee ...(repeat) ...   They usually take a machine gun
    Amatenga chiwaya,   A knife,
    Mpeni,   And an entrenching tool behind
Khasu lili pambuyo."   them."

Above all, the Nyasa askari expressed their sorrow at leaving home through many an improvisation on the English word "sorry" which, in Bantu fashion, they rendered as "sole".

    "Sole, sole, sole, sole ...   "When they get to Kenya
    Ku Kenya kuli sole ..."   They'll be sorry."

This Nyasa "sole" song was taken to Burma in the Second World War and Gerald Hanley rightly called it "one of the best of all marching songs, with many variations of words . . . Sole also means trouble. The song is sung to the beat of marching feet, and when the Nyasa askari sing it, it is splendid to hear, for their sense of harmony is highly developed . . . It was sung by them when the Italians moved against the borders of Kenya in 1940. Now they march against Japan, and the words are the same." The African historian Dr O.E. Shiroya, in his book *Kenya and World War II* (Nairobi 1985) noted that this Nyasa "sole" song was "later sung by most East African soldiers in all theatres". In spite of the element of social criticism implicit in it, he sees it in the early days of the Second World War as basically a patriotic song. Later, he believes, African disillusion with the war effort set in, and he collected one song in Swahili which is expressed thus:-

    "Unaona tunachekwa na wazungu,   "See, the Europeans [must] be
    Wana wanaziri zao,   laughing at us

| Hawambii watu wengine." | They have their secrets Which they do not reveal to other peoples [races]." |

An element of disillusionment with the incursions of the European way of life into traditional societies and customs, however, certainly existed in Nyasa military singing, at least from the First World War onwards. I caught echoes of this in the remarkable singing of my orderly, Austin Chikapa of D Company, 13 (Nyasaland) Battalion as we marched back overnight in late December, 1944, after the capture and consolidation of Shwegyin in Burma. I had heard many African singers before we went to Burma, and had been impressed by their power, their skill in improvisation and the emotional nature of their harmonies. But I had never met a better balladeer on the march, whom Thomas Wentworth Higginson, had he been alive to hear him, would have compared him, as he did with his African American soldiers, to the Scottish border minstrels, singing songs "more uniformly plaintive, almost always more quaint, and often as essentially poetic."

I wrote earlier about Austin Chikapa and his fellow singers from Nyasaland before – "I can bear witness to the power and poetry of these songs. When D Company of 13 (N) KAR marched back out of Burma through the night, shortly before Christmas, 1944, after the completion of the last patrols by 11 (EA) Division, its askari sang almost continuously. The jungle roads were dusty, but the rains had gone; the Japanese were far away and Christmas lay just across the Chindwin, on the other side of the great Bailey bridge. Led by my stout-lunged orderly, a balladeer of almost superhuman force and endurance, they sang of joy to be leaving Burma alive; of sorrow at the thought of the dead they had left behind them; of their "dziko la Nyasaland... kwabwino kodi..." [the country of Nyasaland... wouldn't it be fine to be there...]; of old, unhappy, far-off things, and battles long ago; of the frailties and follies of the white bwanas who were responsible for their being in Burma; and of the prospects of peace. Into traditional songs they inserted anecdotes and emotions, joyful, mournful, and ribald, from their long "ulendo" [journey] between Zomba, Mombasa, Colombo, Chittagong, the Brahmaputra, Kalewa and the Chindwin. With excusable exaggeration, they attributed the Japanese retreat in the Kabaw valley to themselves alone; "Ajapani kundithawa chifukwa cha African" [the Japanese are running away because of the African]."

It is sad to think that many of these songs have disappeared from the military musical repertoire in Malawi, Nyasaland's successor. Visiting the Malawi Rifles barracks in 1974, I found that none of the young African officers knew many, if any, of these songs. Indeed, they prevailed upon me to sing selections for them! The transmigration of tunes is a curious business. A correspondent from Malawi, who went to a Christmas church service in 1995 in the Chiradzulu area, informed me that one of the hymns they sang was to the tune of an old KAR marching song.

The Nyasa element in the corpus of KAR marching songs was indicated at the Victory Searchlight Tattoo performed by 11 (EA) Division at Ranchi, Bihar, India from 23 to 27 November, 1945. (See Chapter 8). This unforgettable celebration began with a recital of six KAR songs. Two were in Kiswahili and four in Chinyanja. This ratio of two to one was a serviceable guide to the predominance and influence of songs from Nyasaland in the saga of KAR singing.

Sadly, the absence of adequate recording equipment and the lack of interest until recently in folk-lore and musicology among most historians, has destroyed or kept hidden – apparently – much of the evidence from which this story of African singing could be reconstructed. The limited edition of fifteen double-sided 78 rpm gramophone records made by the askari of 11 (EA) Division for the Colombia Gramophone Company Ltd in Calcutta in 1945, drew attention to the richness of this musical material. Gerald Hanley's book, published in the following year, carried this commendation further. Dr Anthony Clayton of the Royal Military Academy, Sandhurst, made a noble attempt, in his short book *Communications for New Loyalties: African Soldiers' Songs* (Athens, Ohio, 1978), to compare some aspects of KAR with West African singing. I gave a fifteen-minute broadcast on songs of the KAR for the BBC's Radio Scotland in 1979, and fourteen years later, the KAR and EA Forces Officers' Dinner Club issued for limited circulation to its members a cassette copy of the 1945 Calcutta records. However, this continuing interest in the KAR's heritage of song has not been enough to provide for posterity much more than an outline and a relatively small number of examples of the richness of this heritage.

It was a heritage which owed much to a large group of East and Central Africans who were not, strictly speaking, members of the KAR, but without whom, the KAR's efforts against von Lettow Vorbeck would have been impossible. They were the carriers of the East African Campaign, the tenga-tenga from Nyasaland and the wapagazi from Kenya. The lack of reasonable communications in that campaign, the inadequate mechanized transport, and often enforced labour in frequently harsh weather conditions pressed heavily on the underfed and overworked carriers. It is not surprising that, in satirical desperation, these African carriers sang:-

> "We are the porters who carry the food
> Of the porters who carry the food.
> Of the porters . . ."

and so on, ad absurdum. These African porters in the Great War in East Africa composed on the march and sang many songs, several of which became important parts of the KAR repertoire.

An anonymous author in the *Nyasaland Times* of 15 November, 1917, bore witness to the haunting power of the songs of these African porters in a poem entitled "They went Singing". I conclude with two verses from this poem, not only as evidence of the carriers' innate capacity for song, but also as a tribute to the askari and their fortitude in many a campaign far from home.

> "Quietly, unwilling to leave their simple lives,
> Tiny huts, tiny joys, little ones and wives,
> What if some reluctant met the white man's call,
> Counting life a precious thing, death the end of all?
> Deep, melodious voices drifted to us on the shore,
> We knew that many of these singers would return no more.
>   As they went singing.
>
> "Strong of body, strong of soul, knowing nothing of the goal,
> What should we and monstrous wars mean to them and theirs?
> Just a big relentless thing added to their cares.
>   Still they went singing."

They went singing . . . and for three wartime years I sang with them whenever I could. Even when I could not understand the language of their songs – often highly idiomatic and not always in the lingua franca – their melodies and harmonies helped to keep me going. Over half a century later, they still do.

Sources and Further Reading

T.W. Higginson, *Army Life in a Black Regiment*, ed John Hope Franklin (Boston, 1962)
J.J. Niles, *Singing Soldiers*, (New York, 1927)
H. Moyse-Bartlett, *The King's African Rifles* (Aldershot, 1956).
Gerald Hanley, *Monsoon Victory* (London, 1946)
Henry Morton Stanley, *Through the Dark Continent* (London, 1899)
Proceedings of the Royal Geographical Society (London) III, 1881
Emily B Langworthy, *This Africa was Mine* (Stirling, 1952)
O.E. Shiroya, *Kenya and World War II* (Nairobi 1985)
The Society of Malawi Journal (Blantyre) Vol 43 No2 1990

APPENDIX C

THE ROYAL EAST AFRICAN NAVY

By Lt Cdr B.B. Mitchell REAN (Rtd)
Formerly Commander of HMEAS *Rosalind*

At noon on 30 June, 1962, the White Ensign was lowered from the masthead outside Navy House, Telegraph Point, Liwatoni, Kilindini, on the disbandment of the Royal East African Navy, marking the end of a Colonial era as far as the navy was concerned. As a junior officer on loan service from the Royal Navy I was closely involved with this period. As both watches of the hands mustered at 8 a.m. on the parade ground adjacent to the colonial-style administration bungalow, there was time to study the three plaques displayed on the veranda, which provide a neat summary of the history of this naval force, as under:-

Royal Navy Volunteer Reserve – Mombasa
"These Headquarters have been established from funds most generously provided by the Honourable Sir Ali bin Salim KBE CMG in commemoration of the 25th Anniversary of the accession to the throne of His Majesty King George V."

East African Ship *Mvita*
"In commemoration of the inauguration of the East African Naval Force, this plaque was unveiled by His Excellency Sir Edward Twining KCMG MBE, Governor of Tanganyika and Chairman of the East Africa High Commission, on 7 July, 1950."

Royal East Africa Navy
"This plaque was unveiled by His Excellency Sir Evelyn Baring KCMG KCVO, Chairman of the East Africa High Commission and Governor of Kenya, to commemorate the granting of the title Royal East African Navy by Her Majesty Queen Elizabeth II on 13 May, 1952."

I have no precise details of the early days of the volunteer force, but I suppose that a few nautically minded people banded together in Mombasa late in 1933, possibly prompted by the presence of the Kenya Regiment "up country". Certainly the provision of a permanent base in May, 1935, marking the Silver Jubilee, must have given heart to the organization. None too soon, one would think with the war clouds gathering, to have the nucleus of a naval presence in Mombasa already established before 1939. The remarkable development of Mombasa as a major Royal Naval base, HMS *Tana*, during the war is another story in which the KNVR was involved in a small way.

Between 1939 and 1945 the complement of the KNVR grew to fifty-six European officers, 156 European ratings and 660 African ratings. They were primarily a mine-sweeping force, using two whale catchers brought from Durban, the *Oryx* and the *Gemsbok*. The harpoon guns were replaced by three-inchers, with two Lewis guns on the bridge wings and two racks of depth charges aft. These sweepers were on constant patrol in the Kilindini approaches and later one was deployed to the Gulf. After the East Indies Fleet arrived in 1942, the Kenyans manned the boom defence vessels *Barrier* and *Barform*, and crewed up the Isles class mine-sweeping trawlers *Shapinsay* and *Hildasay*, which replaced the two whalers later. On 21 June, 1945, *Hildasay* was wrecked on a reef twelve miles south of Mombasa and her bridge wheel house is a beach property gazebo to this day.

The end of the war saw the inevitable run-down, until the Royal East African Navy emerged in 1952. This involved a duality of responsibility for the Resident Naval Officer East Africa. He answered to the Admiralty wearing his RN hat, and to the East African High Commission and Common Services Organization wearing the hat of Commanding Officer, Royal East African Navy. He administered a force of two hundred African ratings, who were on five-year renewable engagements and drawn from all the East African territories, including Zanzibar. Numbers were in proportion to the territories' contributions to the annual vote of £120,000. Kenya's £56,000 entitled them to the majority, mostly Wakamba, surprisingly, not from the coastal tribes. On the whole the personnel took well to naval training and discipline; there were excellent longer-serving Petty Officers and Chief Petty Officers. The CO had a subordinate cadre of British officers with RN and RNR backgrounds, four of the executive branch, two from the supply and secretarial branch and one engineer. Training was done by seven superb retired RN Chief Petty Officers rated as CPOs (Instructor) REAN, of the W/T, yeoman, gunnery TAS, electrical and engineering branches.

In 1946 the Admiralty transferred, on a permanent loan basis, a minesweeper that had been deployed to East African waters for the Madagascar campaign. HMS *Rosalind* was a Shakespeare class trawler mine sweeper built by A & J Inglis in 1941, of 545 tons displacement, length overall of 164 feet, one cylindrical, coal-fired boiler driving triple expansion machinery, giving a top speed of twelve knots. She was armed with one Bofors 40 mm and two Oerlikon 22 mm guns, and had Oropesa wire mine-sweeping gear aft. Shakespeare's fair *Rosalind* she may have been, but a bit of a devil on the EA coast, and sheer hell for the stokers in the boiler room.

In 1958 the Ham Class inshore mine-sweeper HMS *Brassingham* was collected by an REAN delivery crew and redesignated HMEAS *Brassingham*. She had an epic voyage from Portsmouth, rounding Guarda Fui at the height of the monsoon; no mean feat for a small, 120 ton, 106-feet-long craft. Twin 550 hp diesels gave fourteen knots. Armament was one Bofors and one Oerlikon, with up to date mine-sweeping gear. HMEAS *Mvita* was a seventy-foot MFV (motor fishing boat); for sailing training there was a traditional thirty-foot cutter, three whalers and four RNSA fourteen-foot dinghies on establishment. The base supported miscellaneous motor cutters, a kitchen rubbish barge and a smart MFB (fast motor boat) as Captain's Barge.

My years in command of HMEAS *Rosalind*, from 1957, were never without interest. Shortly before my joining, she was involved in the up-lifting of Archbishop Makarios – in conjunction with HMS *Loch Fada*, to the Seychelles for banishment. Mau Mau detainees were ferried to the Lamu detention camps during the wet season, when the Prison Department lorries could not negotiate the road. The Game Department and Customs periodically requested patrols against the offshore dhows engaged in the endemic ivory-smuggling trade. With a coastal parish extending from Somalia in the north to the Rivuma River in the south, flag-showing cruises were particularly important. Each August the celebration of the Sultan of Zanzibar's birthday was always looked forward to. The crew of HMEAS *Rosalind* provided a Guard of Honour and we usually managed to have some sort of combined operation with the KAR from Colito Barracks, Dar es Salaam.

With the death of HH Seyyid Sir Kalifa bin Harub GBE GCMG, HMEAS *Rosalind* provided the Guard of Honour on the accession of the new Sultan of Zanzibar on 17 October, 1960. The fifty-year-old Sultan took the Oath of Allegiance to the Queen from the Throne in the Palace, Baraza Hall. A forty-one-gun salute then heralded the accession of the Tenth Sultan of the Said Dynasty. The Sultan appeared on the balcony with his three sons and received an ovation from thousands of his subjects. Within eight months the island was in conflagration.

A general election was held in Zanzibar on 1 June, 1961, with the Nationalist Party (mainly Arab) and the Afro Shirazi, (predominantly African) contending for power. Violence and intimidation, fanned by racial and political bitterness, started when the polling booths opened at 8 a.m.; sixty fatalities occurred, nearly all Arab, when fighting spread to all parts of the island. The British Resident, Sir George Mooring, declared a state of emergency. 5 KAR from Kenya and 6 KAR from Tanganyika were flown in by RAF Beverley aircraft, together with the Police General Service Unit. HMEAS *Rosalind* was ordered to the island for off-shore patrols and to assist in the sea transportation of military personnel. On arrival in Zanzibar harbour, Brig Chambers and Col Shorrocks conferred on board to arrange a programme that included the immediate movement of a company of 6 KAR from Wete Pemba to Dar es Salaam. This was confirmed at a policy meeting with Maj Gen Goodwin (GOC East Africa Command), Brig Fitzalan Howard and Col Cole at the Arab School, which had been taken over as military headquarters.

On 12 June Maj Flory, the Company Commander, with forty askari and eight tons of stores, were embarked by lighter at Wete for the voyage to Dar. The subsequent trooping trip to Mombasa with 5 KAR personnel was cancelled by Col Cook, as HMEAS *Rosalind* was required for coastal patrols around the islands of Zanzibar and Pemba until 19 June.

In earlier days the annual inspection of the REAN was carried out by the Commander in Chief, East Indies, during the flagship's May cruise of East African waters. Later, as Uhuru approached, Flag Officers' visits and inspections tied in with losing battles with the EA Defence Committee, in attempts to keep the navy intact. Lord Mountbatten was in Mombasa in 1960, with the declaration that the REAN had now changed rôle from mine-sweeping to patrol work, and that the navy must be maintained at minimum cost; but the financial position remained acute with the possibility of Tanganyika pulling out. Various admirals attempted to keep REAN intact, but the portents were clear – with the Federation coming to nothing, the promulgation of the disbandment of REAN was announced in December, 1961, to take effect from 30 June, 1962.

Tanganyika's independence coincided with the last cruise of HMEAS *Rosalind* to Dar es Salaam for their Uhuru celebrations. Rear Admiral Fitzroy Talbot flew his flag in HMS *Belfast* (Captain Morgan Giles), with HMS *Rhyl* and HMS *Loch Alvie* in company, and the Pakistani destroyer *Tughril* and HMEAS *Rosalind* completing the naval presence. It was a proud but sad moment to see the Union Jack lowered in the presence of HRH Prince Philip, Duke of Edinburgh, at the tattoo at midnight on 8 December, supported by very smart contingents from the REAN, RN, Royal Marines, the Coldstream Guards, Tanganyikan Rifles and the Pakistan Navy.

I took passage in HMS *Loch Fyne* to Malta, towing HMEAS *Brassingham* on her return to the RN at the end of 1961. My ship, HMEAS *Rosalind* was taken to the breakers' yard in Mombasa and the local auctioneer set about the ghoulish task of disposing of the naval assets. I remember that my favourite cutter went for £214. Dispersing the 200 personnel back to civilian life was not all that depressing, as many – with their excellent training – were much sought after to fill good jobs.

30 June, 1962, was the end of the Royal East African Navy; however two years later the Kenya Navy was established as a proud, independent force, nurtured in the best traditions of the Royal Navy, and today they continue to go from strength to strength.

APPENDIX D

EAST AFRICAN ARTILLERY

The following outline history of the East African Artillery is based mainly on notes provided by Brig K.A. Timbers of the Royal Artillery Historical Trust, and which were obtained through the good offices of Major George Correa.

In May, 1936, a Coast Defence Unit (KAR) was formed at Mombasa to man the coast defences at Kilindini, in the event of war. Initially it was a joint gunner/sapper combined organization and it survived, in one form or another, until 1949.

In September, 1939, 1 (EA) Light Battery was formed, and the first contingent reported for training to 22 Mountain Battery RA, near Nairobi. 22 Battery was an Indian Army unit that had left Quetta on 30 August and reached Nairobi on 11 September. It was very much the foster parent of the EA Artillery, as well as providing fire support to East African units through the Ethiopian campaign, until leaving them at Gondar to move to the Middle East in September, 1941. 22 Mountain Battery claim to have fired both the first and last rounds of the Ethiopian campaign.

When 22 Battery arrived in Kenya they set up camp at M'bagathi, about ten miles out of Nairobi. The Battery Captain (and subsequent Battery Commander) was Capt Lionel (Bulgy) Leach. Of the newly posted-in East African gunners, he wrote in his diary: "they were a pleasant lot". Among the names he noted were "Mackinley Mac", the Battery Commander designate, (Major W.W. Mackinley RA), Captain "Chalky" White, Lts "Buster" Powles and Eric Selby. He also mentions John Nazer and "Tubby" Block; the latter gained a MC in Burma. Soldiers came from a variety of sources; thirty-eight British bombardiers were drafted in from the Kenya Regiment (See Chapter 13), some askari were transferred from The Coastal Defence Battery KAR and some from 1 and 2 KAR.

Training proceeded rapidly, with the 22 Battery officers each concentrating on a specific subject. 1 (EA) Battery eventually received four 3.7 inch howitzers, but initially they had to use the Indian gunners' equipment for training. The achievements of 1 (EA) Battery when they first went into action, in Somaliland in August, 1940, are described in Chapter 5. The training and the practise camps run by 22 Battery more than proved their worth in that operation.

After their return from Somaliland the Battery was retitled 53 (EA) Battery. 54 (EA) Battery was formed and took part in the closing stages of the Ethiopian campaign.

By the end of 1941 an Artillery Training Centre, inevitably christened "Larkhill", had been established at Athi River, to the south-east of Nairobi. It was here that a total of five East African Artillery Regiments were formed. They were:-

– 301 (EA) Field Regiment, who formed in July 1942, and served in Madagascar, returning to Kenya in July 1943.

– 302 and 303 (EA) Field Regiments and 304 (EA) Anti Tank/LAA Regiment.

– 15 (EA) HAA Regiment.

Of these, the three field regiments and the Anti Tank/LAA regiment were to constitute the divisional artillery of 11 (EA) Division. Early in 1944 they all moved by sea to Ceylon, prior to going into action in Burma. Unfortunately, most of 301 Regiment was lost at sea when their troopship – the *Khedive Ismail* – was sunk by a Japanese submarine; see Chapter 8 for details. 15 (EA) HAA Regiment was at Chittagong, and later on Ramree Island.

By the end of 1947 the East African Artillery had been reduced to 303 (EA) Regiment, which comprised 53 (EA) Field Battery, 156 (EA) HAA Battery (all at Nanyuki) and a coast battery at Mombasa. 53 Battery was deployed on peace-keeping duties in Somalia in 1948. By mid-1949 303 (EA) Regiment had been reduced to 156 HAA Battery EAA, which survived until after the Mau Mau operations; it too was then disbanded.

Note:-
I am grateful to Capt Graham Seymour for his supplement to this information. 307 (EA) Field Regiment formed at Kijabe in 1943 and moved to Gilgil, where Graham joined it in early 1944. It moved to Naivasha, then finally to Nanyuki in April, 1946. In the interim it trained hard in the bamboo forest, at Isiolo and at the ranges at Naivasha, in preparation for a move to South-East Asia; but with the end of the war with Japan it remained in Kenya. It took part in the Army Exhibition at Nairobi in 1944 and the VJ celebrations – also at Nairobi – in the following year. It was absorbed into 303 (EA) Field Regiment in May, 1946.

MBP

APPENDIX E

THE ROYAL WAJIR YACHT CLUB

There are probably as many different versions as there were members about how this Club was established over 200 miles from the Indian Ocean, in the dry, barren and austere landscape of Kenya's Northern Frontier District. It is generally accepted that the founder was the then District Commissioner, Freddy Jennings, in 1932, who became the first Commodore. It is said by Robert Stanyon, a former Chief Inspector Kenya Police and a Purser of the Club (circa 1963–65) that it was formed "as a measure of self-defence against the plundering of his hospitality by safari parties wishing to experience the Beau Geste magic of the remote NFD". While this may be true, there is a variant that mentions an Ordinance that exempted bona fide clubs from payment of duty on imported alcohol; perhaps this was a factor.

David Hanson and John Garnett confirm that the Club was the creation of the officers of the Administration and the Kenya Police, but that KAR officers were invited to join – an offer which was usually accepted with enthusiasm. In the 1960s membership averaged six to eight, of whom two or three might have been KAR. During the shifta campaign, when the RAF Twin Pioneer crews were present, numbers rose accordingly. The Rules were as follows:-

1. The Club shall be styled the Royal Wajir Yacht Club.
2. The object of the Club shall be to encourage sailing before the wind, swinging the lead, profligacy on the high seas, and seeing the sun go down below the yard arm.
3. The Club shall consist of Ordinary Members, Extraordinary Members and Most Amazing Members. An Ordinary Member is deemed to have become an Extraordinary Member after three months in Wajir.
4. An Ordinary Member and an Extraordinary Member shall be one who is duly elected and does not pay his Entrance Fee or Annual Subscription.
5. A Member who pays his Entrance Fee or Annual Subscription shall be deemed a Most Amazing Member.
6. The amount of the subscription shall be optional. In the event of

it ever being paid, the whole amount shall be expended on liquid refreshment for the Commodore and the Officers.
7. Officers of His Majesty's Navy, Army and Air Force shall be considered "thirsty members" during their stay in Wajir.
8. The wives and lady friends ("sweeties") of members are welcomed to the Club at any time of the day or night at owner's risk.
9. The Club Flag shall be flown on Saints' Days, Public Holidays and Regatta Days.
10. Members are reminded that on Regatta days, craft temporarily out of control must be allowed right of way, whether luffing, hiccoughing, scudding before the wind or just heaving too. All assistance must be given to those coming alongside.
11. Any article found in or near the Club must be returned to the owners. This does not include wives or sweeties of members.
12. Any tanker or other vessel containing crude oil, raw spirit or pisco must fly the "Blue Peter" whilst at anchor in Club waters.

The Commodore's regalia came from various Royal Navy sources. The sword was donated by Lt Cdr Maurice Vernon, (who died in 1993, aged 93). Vernon had joined the KAR in 1936 or '37. Brig "Crew" Stoney recalls that when he was in Nairobi he lived in the 3 KAR mess and knew Capt "Phillipo" Phillips, who had been Vice Commodore when stationed at Wajir as a company commander. His Commodore was the DC, Dennis Wickham. The ceremonial sword was an infantry pattern one, with the blade twisted to look as much like a corkscrew as possible. He cannot remember how it was used on ceremonial occasions. There were two medals; one was Menelik dollar and the other a Maria Theresa, both suspended from "ribbons" – possibly braces elastic. The significance of these two were:-

The Menelik dollar – for long service in foreign parts.
The Maria Theresa – for retaining parts during long foreign service.

Robert Stanyon continues:-

"Visitors were expected to donate a hat to the Club. Occasionally they resisted and more than one visitor left complaining that his headgear had gone missing, (to reappear in the Club's collection in due course). It was the Purser's job to label and display these trophies, which included three or four Governors' hats, a couple of GOCs', about four from Members of Parliament and one from Kermit Roosevelt. Valerie Hobson donated an extravagant Ascot model when she visited with John Profumo."

Why "Royal"? It was the idea of the Prince of Wales (later King Edward VIII), although he did not visit the Club. He was due to do so in 1934, but his father's illness cut short his Kenya tour. His equerry sent a letter of regret and notified that HRH had authorized the "Royal". This gave rise to the distinctive tie – dark blue, with silver camels (as ships of the desert) each surmounted by a crown. The tie was the brainchild of David Hanson and Robin Dalgleash (DO). Robin's father, a retired architect, did the detailed design and arranged for its production by Lewins of Jermyn Street. The qualifying period for the tie is six months' residence at Wajir, either in the boma or in the KAR camp. Qualified members were, therefore, few; in the mid-sixties Robert believes that there were only forty-four of them.

The Club had a boat in 1961. The long and short rains merged and the Commodore's carpenter made a small flat-bottomed boat that could be rowed or punted. Big lakes lasted for six weeks or so, even the northern Uaso Nyira burst through the Lorian swamp and spread into Somalia south of Dif. There was also a sand yacht at one time, but its shattered remains littered the airfield on which it had once sailed proudly. Other sports were popular too. The World Series Liar Dice Championships were held at the Club in 1963. The winner by a mile was the Ship's Surgeon and Irish entrant, Jimmy Clearkin.

A visiting Sapper officer remembers that he had been sent to Wajir on a route reconnaissance, with the stated view of recommending (or not) the eventual tarmacking of the road from Nairobi. Arriving at Wajir:-

"After several days of struggling over the appalling track from Isiola via Garbatula, we found a bottle hoisted at the yardarm outside the mess, which, we were told, was to signify a "Regatta Night" and attract all the bwanas within range. That evening we assembled in the mess for dinner, at which the DC presided as Commodore of the Club, in full regalia."

The literature has many references to the pomp and dignified ceremony that marked these occasions. There are mentions of initiation ceremonies at which the novitiates are required to drink a glass of the Commodore's Cocktail; the main ingredient was Tabasco. Formality was all. The Sapper visitor saw things from a somewhat more detached standpoint:-

"Although the dinner started with dignity and correctness, it degenerated towards the end of an alcoholic evening, culminating with young Jefferies being sentenced by the Commodore to being keel-hauled. This involved him being dragged from one end to the other, under the table, thereby sweeping away all the trestles supporting it, in a chaos of broken glass and crockery. At the end of an unforgettable evening I tottered to bed, avoiding getting involved with two inebriated officers who were slugging it out by the light of a hurricane lamp hung on a bush in the mess garden."

Such a centre of social excellence attracted rivals. One was the Garissa Curling Club, of which Simon Combes was a member when serving there in 1963/64, when he was Intelligence Officer with what had become by then 3 Kenya Rifles. The RWYC had somehow acquired the cannon that was held sacred in Garissa, and plotting to recover it was a favourite topic, particularly late at night. Simon was there when it was recaptured and restored to its rightful place:-

"In 1964 the shifta's use of mines had seriously curtailed movement by road, so a cannon-recovery patrol, as mounted in previous years, was out of the question. Seeking perhaps to advance my military career, and also perhaps to demonstrate that 'Intelligence Officer' is not, in fact, a classic oxymoron, I conceived a plan to recover the cannon from Wajir.

"Together with that celebrated hooligan the late Chief Inspector Paddy Mair of Police Special Branch and Idris, the celebrated Welsh RAF Twin Pioneer pilot, we flew to Wajir one morning, carrying in the hold a packing case and a crowbar. As we taxied up to the camp perimeter, I pulled rank on the Regimental Police Sergeant and demanded a Land Rover to take us to the police station where we had to 'collect a generator'. He must have thought it strange that three officers should undertake such a mundane task, but complied willingly. I insisted on driving myself, and so, with crate and crowbar we set off for the RWYC, and dug the cannon from its concrete base, heaved it in the crate, returned to the airstrip, loaded it into the aircraft, thanked the RP sergeant for his kind assistance and flew back to Garissa.

"The next day we arranged a memorable celebration at the Curling Club, on the bank of the Tana River. The officers' mess cook baked a large number of his infamous, bullet-hard bread rolls uncannily of the same calibre as the cannon. A quantity of thunder flashes was withdrawn from the magazine 'for training purposes', and a fine 21-gun salute was fired to honour the cannon's return – or was it 24-gun? . . . maybe 29 gun . . . ?"

BIBLIOGRAPHY

Chapter 1 – How it All Began

The Scramble for Africa, Thomas Pakenham 1991, Weidenfeld and Nicolson.
Emin Pasha, A.J. Mountney-Jephson, Charles Scrivener's Sons.
Imperial Twilight, Maj Gen James Lunt, 1981, Macdonald.

Chapter 2 – The Mullah Campaign

Seventeen Trips to Somaliland and a Visit to Abyssinia, Major HGC Swayne RE FRGS, 1900, Roland Ward.
The Memoirs of Lord Ismay
The Mad Mullah of Somaliland, D.J. Jardine.
Imperial Sunset, Maj Gen James Lunt.
The Warrior Mullah, The Horn Aflame, Prof Ray Beachey, 1990, Bellow Publishing.
The Somali Dispute, J.G.S. Drysdale, 1964, Pall Mall Press.
Understanding Somalia, Prof Ioan Lewis, 1993, Haan Associates.

Chapter 3 – From German East Africa to Tanganyika, 1914–1918

The Carrier Corps 1914–1918, Geoffrey Hodges 1986, Greenwood Press.
The Battle of the Bundu, Charles Miller 1974, Purnell Book Services.
On to Kilimanjaro, Brian Gardner 1963. Macrae Smith and Co.
Oskar from Africa, Elizabeth Watkins 1995, Radcliffe Press.
My Reminiscences of East Africa, Maj Gen von Lettow Vorbeck 1920, Hurst and Blackett.
The East African Force 1915–1919, Brig Gen C.P. Fendall 1921, Battery Press, Nashville.

Chapters 5 and 6 Italian East African Empire, Parts 1 and 2

The Two Thousand Mile War, Lt Col W.E. Crosskill 1980, Robert Hale Ltd.
An Improvised War, Michael Glover 1987, Leo Cooper.
Abdul Mbele, John Pitt, published privately.

It's a long way to Addis, Carel Birkly 1942, Fredrick Muller.
Abyssinian Patchwork, Kenneth Gandar Down 1949, Frederick Muller.
War Journal of 5 KAR, Draffan and Lewin, published privately.
Bare Feet and Bandoliers, David Shirreff 1995, Radcliffe Press.
22 Mountain Battery, Lt Col Lionel Leach, published privately.

Chapter 8 – Burma

Defeat into Victory, FM Viscount Slim.
Slim the Standard Bearer, Ronald Lewin 1976, Leo Cooper.
Burma, the Longest War, Louis Allan 1984, Book Club Associates.
Burma, the Turning Point, Maj Gen Ian Lyall Grant 1993, Zampi Press.
Burma, a Miracle in Military Achievement, SEAC Press, Calcutta 1945.
Rhino Review, various editions, 1944/45, Statesman Press. Calcutta.

Chapter 9 – Malaya

War Since 1945, FM Lord Carver 1980, Weidenfeld and Nicolson.
The Jungle is Neutral, Lt Col F. Spencer Chapman 1949, Reprint Society.

Chapter 11 – Kenya and Mau Mau

Jomo's Jailer, Elizabeth Watkins 1992, Mulberry Books.
War Since 1945, FM Lord Carver 1980, Weidenfeld and Nicolson.
Jambo Effendi, Major Iain Graham 1966, J.A. Allen.
The Charging Buffalo, Col Sir Guy Campbell, Leo Cooper.

Chapter 12 – Imperial Twilight

Askari Ya Amri, Christopher C. Child, unpublished history of eighteen months with 4 KAR by a National Service Subaltern.
Askari Journal, various editions, Lt Col N.C. Robertson-Glasgow (Ed), Nairobi.

INDEX

Aberdare Mountains, Kenya, 201, 203, 205, 207, 213, 246, 248
Acholi (tribe and region), 148, 223, 226, 227
Adams Lt Col G.D.P., 159
Addis Ababa, Ethiopia, 10, 58, 65, 76, 78, 80, 90, 94, 95, 100, 103, 109, 111
Aden (now part of Yemen), 3, 10, 17, 56, 69, 95, 103, 109, 111, 113, 113, 156
Adler, Capt L.S., RAMC, 153
Adowa (battle, 1896, and town), 10, 65, 108
11 (African) Division, 78 and Ch 6 *passim*
12 (African) Division, 78 and Ch 6 *passim*
Afmadu, Somalia, 80, 82, 83, 85
70 Air Despatch Coy RASC, 220
Akyab, Burma, 116, 136, 163, 164
Alford, 2Lt J., 226
Allott, Prof Anthony, 255–256
An Chaung, Valley & Pass, 164–165
Anderson, Lt Gen Sir K. (later General, KCB MC), 111, 172, 176, 177
Anderson, Lt P.W.G., 148
Angus, Capt J.N., RA, 14–15
Annet, M., Governor of Madagascar, 119, 129

67 Animal Transport Coy, EAASC (later Troop), 219, 237
ANVIL (Operation), 204, 247
Aosta, Duke of (Prince Amedo), Viceroy and CinC, Italian East Africa, 66, 76, 91, 94, 97
Arakan, Burma, 113, 137, 141, 150, 158, 163–167, 174, 175
Archer, Sir Geoffrey, KCMG, Governor of Somaliland), 17 and Ch 2 *passim*
Archer's Post, Kenya, 57, 62
Argyll & Sutherland Highlanders, 104
XIV Army, 136 and Ch 8 *passim*
11 Army Group, 137 and Ch 8 *passim*
Army Kinema Corporation (AKC) 183
Ashley Cubitt, Lt Col T., RFA (later Maj Gen), 19, 20, 21
Ashley Hall, Sgt A., 182–183
Asmara, Eritrea, 78, 94, 95, 104
Aspinal, Major A.C.G., 148
Assam Regt (1 Bn), 149, 150
Auchinleck FM Sir Claude J.E., GCB, GCIE, CSI, DSO OBE, 174
Auster (aircraft) 194, 196
Awash River, bridge & battle, Ethiopia, 88, 98, 91, 95, 104

Badoglio, Marshal (It), 65, 75
Baring, Sir Evelyn, KCMG, KCVO (later Lord Howick, KG), 202
Bartlett, Lt Col J., 216
Bassett, Lt R. (later Capt), 111
Baxter, Lt Col G.L., DSO, 52
Bearcroft, A. Supt "Punch", 247
Bell, Pte C.R.V. (later Major, OBE), 59, 86
Bell, Lt E.W., 16
Bellfield, Sir Henry, Governor of Kenya, 27, 28
Berbera, Somaliland, 3, 11 and Ch 2 *passim*, 68 and Ch 5 *passim*, 75, 78, 86, 87, 95, 100, 104, 108, 109, 173
Bertello, Gen (It), 87, 95, 103
Beswetherick, Flt Lt A., RAF, 236, 237
Beverley (aircraft), 237, 267
Biggs, Major M.W. (later Brig, CBE), ix, 59, 84, 91, 107, 156, 172
Bihar Regt (1 Bn), 159
Bikineer Camel Corps, 15
Birkett, Capt A.J., 173
Birkbeck, Capt T.H. (later Maj Gen, CB CBE DSO & bar JP DL), 71, 143
Birru, Ethiopian Patriot leader, 106
Bisson, Gen (It), 102
Blackden, Lt Col C.F. (later Brig), 105
Black Watch (1 Bn), 69, 70, 72, 73
Blackie, Lt Col R.D., 163, 197
Block, Lt "Tubby" (later MC), 269
BLUE DOCTOR (Operation), 247

Blundell, Lt Col M. (later Sir Michael), 105, 203
Blunden Lt (QM) G., 249
Bombay Grenadiers, 15, 16, 17; 3/4 Bn, 151, 155
Bombo, Uganda, 9, 28, 53, 55, 61, 62
Bon Chaung, Burma, 152, 153, 155
BONUS (Operation), 115
Boran (tribe), 93, 232, 233, 234
Bowley, Capt D.J. (later Major), 237, 253, 254
Bowkeer's Horse, 30
Brake, Lt Col H.E.J. 3, 4
Brandram, Capt J., 226
Brassington, HMEAS (formerly HMS), 266, 267
Brenner, Sapper, SAEC, 106
Brick, Capt T.M. (later Major), 55
29 Brigade, 115, 116, 119, 120, 120, 123
Briggs, Sir Harold, 189, 190
Bright, Lt Col D., 251
Brink, Maj Gen G.E. (later Lt Gen, CB CBE DSO), 80
British South African Rifles, 3
Brits, Maj Gen C.J., 36
Brodie, Capt P.T., DSO, 45
Brooke, Gen Sir Alan (later FM Lord Alanbrooke), 175
Brooke, Capt O.G., (later Brig, CBE DSO), 74, 111, 113
Brown, Capt "Boxer", 224, 247
Bruce, Brig I.R.C., MBE, 110
Brunot, Commandant (Fr), 128
Buganda, nation & Kabaka, 6, 7, 222, 223
Buganda Rifles, 36
BULRUSH (Operation), 219

Burao, Somaliland, 13 and Ch 2 *passim*, 52, 112
Burgher Mounted Infantry, 15
Burma (now Myanmar), 60, 113, 115, 130, 133 & Ch 8 *passim*, 176, 239, 243, 261, 270
Burma Campaign Friendship Group (BCFG), 254
BURCORPS, 136, 146
Burma Military Police, 135
Burmese Rifles, 135
Byrne, Sir Joseph, 240

Cainey, Capt (QM) A., 216
Calvert, Brig M., DSO, 154
Camel Corps (later Somaliland Camel Corps), 18 and ch 2 *passim*, 51, 53, 56, 68, 69, 70, 71, 72, 74, 111, 112, 113
Campbell, Capt C., 248
Campbell, Capt G. (later Sir Guy, Bt OBE MC), 105, 239, 243, 244, 246, 248, 276
Campbell, Col J.A., DSO, 240
Campbell-Miles, Lt Col D "Milo" (later MBE), 159, 161
Cape Corps, 45
Caprioni (aircraft – It), 67
Carbonell, Major J.R. (later Lt Col), 161, 163
Carey, Major R. de Vic, MC, 229
Carne, Lt Col J.P. (later Col, VC DSO DL), 146, 176
Carter, Capt G., 229
Carton de Wiart, Capt A. (later Lt Gen Sir Adrian, VC CMG DSO), 10, 19, 20
Carver, FM Lord, GCB CBE DSO & bar, MC, 201
108 Casualty Clearing Section, EAAMC, 159

Casualty evacuation, 153
Central railway (German), 30 and Ch 3 *passim*
Ceres, HMS, 73
Cessna (aircraft), 220
Ceylon (now Sri Lanka), 115, 116, 137, 141, 142, 163, 270
Chapman, Lt Col S., OBE, 187
Chater, Lt Col A. RM (later Maj Gen, CB CVO DSO OBE), 68 & Ch 5 *passim*, 111, 112
Chiang Kai Shek, Generalissimo (Ch), 153, 137
Child, Lt C.C., 278
China, 133, 135, 136, 137
5 Chinese Army, 136
38 Chinese Division, 136
Chindwin River, Burma, 133, 137, 141, 142, 143, 145, 150, 155, 156, 157, 158, 159, 168, 169, 258, 261
1st Chin Hills Battalion, 159
Chin Peng, OBE, 187, 189
Christison, Lt Gen P. (later Gen Sir Philip), 136, 137
Churchill W.S. (later Sir Winston, KG), 10, 17, 18, 75, 115, 116, 187, 189
Church of Scotland, 201, 210
Clarkson, Capt J.E.S., 122
Clayton, Dr A., 262
Clearkin, Dr J., 273
Clemas, Major H., 216
Clio, HMS, 22
Coast(al) Irregulars (later EA Scouts), 60, 137
Coast Defence Battery, 60, 241, 269
Coast Defence Rifle Company, 60
Coates, 2Lt B., 224

Cobbe, Major A.S. (later Lt Col, VC), 3, 14
Cobbing, Capt R.A.A., 195
Colvile, Lt Col H. (later Maj Gen Sir Henry), 7
Coldstream Guards (2 Bn), 237
Colito, Ethiopia (battle & Barracks), 98, 99, 207, 242, 266
Collen, Lt Col K.H., 147
Collins, Capt H.G., 34
Collins, Lt Col R.G.T., 105, 117
Colonial Medical Services, 235
Colours, Regimental, 54, 176, 186, 223, 243, 250, 251
Columbia Gramophone Company Ltd, 262
Combes, Lt S. (later Major), 274
Comilla, Burma, 138, 141
Consett, Lt C. d'A.P. (later Lt Col, DSO, MC), 56, 70, 71, 74
Cooper, Capt N., MBE MC GM, 245
Corbet-Ward, 2Lt R.S., 126
Cordeaux, Capt H.E.S., 14
Corfield, Richard, 18, 19
Corkram, Capt R.S. (later Lt Col, OBE), 237
Cornell, Capt R., 244
4 Corps, 133, 158, 159, 163, 168
15 Corps, 133, 167, 161, 163, 164
33 Corps, 133, 141, 142, 158
Cossack, HMS, 14
Cresswell, Capt R.M., 97
Crewe-Read, Lt Col J.O. (later Col, OBE), 191–195, 196, 198
Crittenden, 2Lt F.H., 241
Crosskill, Lt W.E. (later Lt Col), 67, 275

Crow, 2Lt J., 210
Cummins, Lt (QM), 240
Cunningham, Lt Gen A.G. (later Gen Sir Alan, GCMG, KCB, DSO, MC), 76, 78, 79, 80, 81, 82, 86, 88, 90, 93, 94, 95, 103
Curtis, Capt D., 177
Curtis, Capt H.R.C., 153

D'Aeth, Rev J., CF, 25
Dagabur, Ethiopia, 86, 112
Dalgleash, R., 273
Damms, Capt V.R.S., RAMC, 170
DANTE (Operation), 205
Danakil (clan), 103, 110
Dar es Salaam, Tanzania, 25 & Ch 3 *passim*, 53, 55, 62, 229, 253, 266, 267
Darod (group of clans), 11 and Ch 2 *passim*
Dauntless, HMS, 118, 119
Davey, Capt, 22
Dawson, Major C. MacC Y., 120, 122
Day, Ernest, 245
Deacon, Major "Paddy", 250, 251
Dean, Lt Col D.J., VC TD, 131
Dedan Kimathi, Mau Mau leader, 203, 205, 206, 211, 246, 247
de Gaulle, Gen C. (Fr), later President, 115
Dervishes, 12 & Ch 2 *passim*
Delamere, Lord, 29
Dessie, Ethiopia, 104
Devonshire Regiment, 225
Dickinson, Lt Col H.C., 46, 48
Dickinson, Maj Gen D.P., 60
Didinga, Sudan (region and tribe), 53, 227, 228

Diego Suarez, Madagascar, 115 & Ch 7 *passim*
Dilwara, HMT, 196
Dimapur, India, 158, 171, 175
Dimoline, Brig W.A. (later Maj Gen, CB CMG CBE DSO MC), 104, 109, 113, 116, Ch 7 *passim*, 159-162, 171, 177
Diredawa, Ethiopia, 86, 87, 88, 109
2 Division (Brit), 158
5 Division (Brit), 115
26 Division (Brit), 137
36 Division (Brit), 137, 158
Dixon, Lt, EAE, 169
Djibouti, town and (now) Republic of, 12, 14, 17, 57, 65, 68, 73, 78, 88, 95, 103, 109, 110, 111, 113, 117, 221
Dobbs, Capt, 20
Docker, Lt Col P., 58
Dodoma, Tanzania, 37, 52, 186
Dolbahanta (clan), 11 & Ch 2 *passim*
Dowler, Maj Gen Sir Arthur, KBE (later KCB KBE DL), 191
Down, Rev Robert, CF, 173
Draffan, Major W.D. (later Lt Col), 150, 276
Drysdale, Capt J.G.S. (later Major, OBE), 178
Duke of Edinburgh's Regt (1 Bn, SA), 80-81
Dul Madobe, Somaliland (battle), 19
Dunera, HMT, 196
Dunkey, Major B.H., 237

Dunstan-Adams, Lt Col OBE, MC & bar, TD (later Col), 240, 242, 250, 251
Dwarha, SS., 4

1 (EA) Armoured Car Regt, 81, 91, 241
3 (EA) Armoured Car Regt, Depot, Squadron & Recce Squadron, 61, 104, 112, 130, 168, 230, 176, 248
East African Army Service Corps (EAASC), 55, 169-170, 176, 191, 237-238, 253
East African Artillery, 62, 69, 71, 72, 120, 142, 168-169, 176 & Appendix D
21 (EA) Brigade, 81, 92, 94, 95, 97, 104, 133, 142, 147, 149, 150, 155, 156, 158, 168, 169, 170
22 (EA) Brigade, 81, 82, 84, 86, 90, 93, 94, 95, 97, 100, 101, 103, 107 & Ch 7 *passim*, 133, 163-167, 168
25 (EA) Brigade, 80, 81, 93, 94, 104, 106, 107, 133, 142, 143, 146, 153, 154, 155, 167, 170
26 (EA) Brigade, 104, 106, 107, 133, 150, 157, 158, 168
28 (EA) Brigade, 109, 133, 158-163, 168
70 (EA) Brigade, 204, 236
East African British Legion, 231
East African Carrier Corps, 41-42, 49
EA Chaplain's Department, 171, 176
407 (EA) Command Workshop EAEME, 113

350 (EA) Composite Platoon EAASC, 173
11 (EA) Division, 133 & Ch 8 *passim*, 255, 261, 262, 270
East African Education Corps, 63, 191
East African Engineers (EAE), 63, 90, 104, 157, 169, 176
East African Electrical & Mechanical Engineers (EAEME), 63
2 (EA) Field Ambulance EAAMC, 107
10 (EA) Field Ambulance EAAMC, 171
53 (EA) Field Battery EAE, 270 (see also 1 (EA) Light Battery EAA)
54 (EA) Field Battery EAA, 270
54 (EA) Field Company EAE, 88, 101, 169
58 (EA) Field Company EAE, 169
59 (EA) Field Company EAE, 144, 167
63 (EA) Field Company EAE, 159
64 (EA) Field Company EAE, 169
62 (EA) Field Park Company EAE, 169
301 (EA) Field Regt EAA, 142, 270
302 (T) (EA) Field Regt EAA, 152, 168, 270
303 (EA) Field Regt EAA, 142, 151, 153, 270
304 (EA) Field Regt EAA (later 304 (EA) Anti-Tank/LAA Regt 149, 168, 270
307 (EA) Field Regt EAA, 270
156 (EA) Heavy Artillery Battery EAA, 270

15 (EA) Heavy Artillery Regt EAA, 270
East African High Commission, 264
21 (EA) Infantry Brigade Transport Company EAASC, 169
1 (EA) Light Battery EAA (later 53 (EA) Field Battery, 62, 69, 241, 269
EA Military Nursing Service, 176
East African Military Police (EAMP), 63, 171, 176, 182–183
East African Mounted Rifles (EAMR), 30, 31
EA Pioneer Battalion/Units EAPC, 63, 104–105, 110, 176, 179–182
East African Rifles, 5, 7
1 & 3 (EA) Reconnaissance Regt, 61, 67, 168, 176
East African Scouts, 133, 137–141
East African Army Service Corps (EAASC), 58, 169, 176, 177–178, 191, 255
East African Signals Corps (EASC), 58
Eastbrook, W., 247
Eastleigh Airport, Nairobi, 210, 218
Eaton Hall Officer Cadet School (OCS), 184, 186
Eaton, Lt T.F., 147, 149
Eden, Anthony MC (later Earl of Avon KG), 76, 109
Edinburgh, Duke of, Prince Philip, KG., 267
Edward, King VII, 4
Edward, King VIII, 54, as Prince of Wales, 273

Edwards, Brig-Gen W.S.F., 45, 48
Egerton, Maj Gen Sir Charles, 16
Eggers, Capt H., 214
El Doret, Kenya (later Eldoret), 59, 186, 241
Elizabeth, Queen (later Queen Mother), 177, 250
Elizabeth, Queen II, 54, 177, 213, 216, 218, 222, 223, 228, 243, 248, 254, 264, 266
El Wak, Kenya-Somalia border, 67, 79, 80, 82, 236
Embu (tribe), 203, 245
Emin Pasha, 1, 2, 5, 56
Entebbe, Uganda, 53, 225, 228
Erskine, Capt F. (later MC), 246
Erskine, Gen Sir George KBE DSO (later GCB), 203, 204, 205, 209
2 Ethiopian Battlion, 77, 78
Evans, 2 Lt (later Lt, MC), 96, 129
Eve, Capt R., 249
Everett, Lt, 15
Ewell, Major T., 195

Facey, Lt M., 125
Farrar, Lady Sidney (later MBE), 59
Fasken, Lt Col C.G.M., 16
Festival of Remembrance, Albert Hall, 254
Fiat CR 42 (aircraft) (It), 66
28 Field Battery RA, 122
1 Field Force Battalion (SA), 95, 97
9 Field Regt RA, 119, 120
347 Field Regt RA, 160
Field, Major SD (later Lt Col MC), 99, 159
Fike, Mount (battle), Ethiopia, 96

Findler, Capt A., 179
First Aid Nursing Yeomanry (FANY), 59
FIRST FLUTE, (Operation), 205, 219
Fissell, Lt Col H.S., 39
Fitzalan Howard, Brig M. (later Maj Gen The Duke of Norfolk KG KCVO CB CBE MC), 267
Fitzgerald, Capt T.O. (later Major), 33, 36
Fleet Air Arm, 116, 117
Ford, 2Lt M., 224
Forest Operating Companies, 205
Forrest, Capt J., 240
Fort Essex, Kenya, 211
Fort Gloucester, Kenya, 206, 219
Fort Hall, Kenya, (now Murang'a), 210, 247
Fort Jerusalem, Kenya, 246
Fort Jesus, Mombasa, Kenya, 5
Fort Winchester, Kenya, 211
Fowkes, Brig C.C., CBE DSO MC (later Maj Gen), 81, 84, 90, 91, 101–108, 142, 143, 144, 147, 156, 157, 162, 171, 176
FOWCOL, 85, 96, 100
Fraser, Lt R.K.J., 121
Free French Forces, 78, 109, 115, 131
French Indo-China (Laos), 133, 135
French, Lt Col H., 146
Friedrichs, Capt, 14
Frith, Major J.F., 151
Frost's Castle, 31
Fulton, Major R., 144

Gadabursi (clan), 16

Galla-Sidamo, Ethiopia, 80, 94, 103
Galletly, Lt Col T.H. (later Brig), 146, 153
Gambia Regt (1 Bn), (1 Gambia), 138–140
Gangaw Valley, Burma, 158, 159, 160
Garba, Kenya, 57, 234
Garnett, Major J.C.M. (later Lt Col), 271
Garissa, Kenya, 57, 78, 274
Gaynor, Lt J.A., 16
Gazzera, Gen (It), 97, 103
Gelib, Somalia, 80, 82, 85
"General China", Mau Mau leaders (Warahia Itotia), 203, 206, 214, 219
Gent, Sir Edward, 186
G(R) Force, 86
Germaine, Gen (Fr), 68
German East Africa Company, 85
George, King V, 54, 231, 264
George, King VI, 54, 144, 177, 180, 185, 240, 243
Gibb, Capt A. 22, 23
Gibraltar, 4, 179
Gideon Force, 77
Gidu River, Ethiopia, 96, 98
Giffard, Lt G. (later Gen Sir George, GCB DSO), 32, 35, 38, 39–40, 45, 46, 57, 60, 136, 137, 141, 158, 173–175
Gimma, Ethiopia, 94, 97, 102
Gillett, Major D., MC, 244
Gillet, Rev James, CF, 44
Giumbo, Somalia, 82, 84
Glanville, Capt R.C. (later Lt Col, OBE MC), 92–93
Gloucester, HRH Duke of, 184, 243
Gloucester Regt, 176, 219 (1Bn)
Gobwein, Somalia, 53, 82, 84
Godfrey, Lt G., 23
Godwin-Austen, Maj Gen A.R. (later Lt Gen Sir Alfred, KCSI, CB, OBE, MC), 73, 79, 81, 173
24 (Gold Coast) Brigade, 81, 84, 85, 93, 94, 95
53 Gold Coast Field Company, 81
2 Gold Coast Light Battery, 164
Gold Coast Regiment, 38, 39, 42–45
Gold Coast Regt, 1, 2 & 3 Bns, 81, 84, 85, 93, 95, 97
Gondar, Ethiopia, 77, 91, 104, battle, 103–107, 109, 117, 269
Gordon, Major A.F., 3
Goode, Lt Col G.H.W. (later Brig, CBE DSO), 165
Goodwin, Maj Gen (later Lt Gen Sir Richard, KCB, CBE, DSO, DL), 267
Gore-Browne, Major E.A., 46
Gordon, Major I., 237
Gordon, Major J. MBE, 210
Graham, Lt Col B.R., 28, 35
Graziani, Marshal (It), 76
Grier, Lt G.I.W., 152, 254
G(R) Force, 78
Guarda Fui, Cape, Somalia, 10, 69, 266
Guillmet, Gen (Fr), 119, 130
Gurkha troops, 187 & Ch 10 *passim*
Gurney, Capt C. (later Major), 251
Gurney, Sir Henry, 188

Guy, Capt R. (later Gen Sir Roland, GCB CBE DSO), 244, 249
Gwalor Rifles, 36

Haile Selassie, Emperor of Ethiopia, 65, 75, 77, 94, 102, 103, 109
Hamar Cocce (tribe), 232–233
HAMMER (Operation), 205, 219
Hanley, Gerald, 146, 259, 261, 262, 263
Hannyngton, Brig-Gen J.A., 36, 38, 44
Hanson, Major D. (later Col), 217
Happold, 2Lt D., 224–225
Harar, Ethiopia, 12, 86, 87, 91, 189, 203
Harding, Gen Sir John (later FM Lord), 189, 203
Harding, 2Lt P., 196
Hargeisa, Somaliland, 12, 52, 70, 87, 111, 113
Harley, Capt P., 209
Hartbeest (aircraft), 90
Harvard (aircraft), 204, 247
Harvey, Bandmaster C.A., 258
Hatch, Major G.P. (later Lt Col), 5
Haud, Ethiopia, 112, 113
Hawker Hart (aircraft), 67
Hawthorne, Col G.M.P., 54
Health in Burma and Ceylon, 145, 170
Heber-Percy, Brig A., 191
Henderson, Capt D., 67
Henderson, Supt J. GM (later & bar), 213, 246–247
Hendricks, Brig N., 143, 191
Hermione, HMS, 116

Henfry's Scouts (Ethiopian patriots), 97–98
Higginson, Thomas W., 257, 263
Hignett, Lt M.L., 120
Hinde, Brig R.W.M. (later Hon Maj Gen Sir William, KBE, CB, DSO & 2 bars), 203
Hindley, Major W., 250
Hitler, A., 61, 66, 115
Hlawaty, Major A. (later OBE), 216
Hobart HMAS, 70
Hobson, Valerie, (Mrs J. Profumo), 272
Hollyer, Major I.R.R., 167
Hopkinson, H., 110
Hopkins, Lt Col J.A.S., 86
Horner, Capt M.F.M., 219
Horton, 2Lt R.L., 210, 212–213
Hoskins, Col A.R. (later Maj Gen Sir Arthur), 22, 28, 36, 41, 42
Howard, Lt G.A. (later MC), 89, 90
Hurricanes & Hurribombers (aircraft), 79, 86, 151, 156, 165
Hurst, Lt Col R., 60
Hurt, Major R.A.F. (later Lt Col DSO), 84, 89, 96

I Force, 245–247
Illalos, 69, 72
Illig, Somalia, & Treaty of, 16, 17
Illustrious, HMS, 115
Imperial British East Africa Company, 4, 6, 27
Imphal, India (battle), 136, 137, 141, 159, 175, 141
Indainggyi, Burma, 153–155, 254
Indainggale, Burma, 153, 158, 168

29 Independent Brigade, 155–156, 119–120
4 (Ind) Brigade, 164–165
53 (Ind) Brigade, 164
5 (Ind) Division, 135, 141, 142, 146, 152, 168
7 (Ind) Division, 137, 159, 160, 161
17 (Ind) Division, 137, 141, 159
19 (Ind) Division, 158
23 (Ind) Division, 143
25 (Ind) Division, 133, 164
26 (Ind) Division, 133, 164
29 (Ind) Division, 141
71 (Ind) Field Ambulance, 164, 167
18 (Ind) Mountain Battery RA, 96
22 (Ind) Mountain Battery RA, 67, 81, 83, 84, 89, 99, 104, 241, 269
39 Infantry Brigade, 203, 204
49 Infantry Brigade, 204
21 Infantry Brigade Company, EAASC, 159
9 Infantry Brigade Workshops EAAEME, 159
Inspector-General KAR, 5, 19, 28, 53, 54, 57, 60, 174
International Geophysical Year, 219
International Red Cross, 108
IRONCLAD (Operation), 115
Irrawaddy River, Burma, 133, 158, 160, 163, 164
Irwin, Lt Gen N.M., 136
Isia Baidoa, Somalia, 80, 85, 92
Ismay, Capt H. (later Gen Lord), 20–24
Issaq (clan group), 10
Isiolo, Kenya, 61, 62, 270
Italian Eastern Army, 69

Ivato, Madagascar, 123, 128

Jackson Malengi, PSM (later Gen (K)), 195
Jacob, Barry, 244
Jambo Hill, Burma (battle), 144–145, 230
James, Brig, W.A.L., 104
Japan, 76, 112, 115, 135, & Ch 8 *passim*
Japanese submarines, 155, 142, 270
9 Jat Regt (1 Bn), 159
Jeffreys, Brig P.J. DSO OBE, 140
Jenkin, Sir William, 189
Jenkins, Lt Col H., 111
Jennings, F., DC, 271
Jigjiga, Ethiopia, 12, 86–87, 110
Jinja, Uganda, 53, 62, 143, 223, 225, 228
Johnson-Stewart, Capt J., 16
Johnstone, Brig R.F., 163, 167
Jomo Kenyatta (later President), 201, 202, 220, 244, 251
Jones, Capt R.I., 218
Jones, Major "Jonah", 226
Josselyn, Major R., 244
Juba River & Jubaland, Somalia, 5, 9, 10, 28, 51, 53, 80, 84, 85, 174

Kabaw Valley, Burma, 133, 141, 142, 150, 155, 157, 258, 261
Kaladan River, Burma, 138–140
Kaleba, Mau Mau leader, 231–235
Kalemyo, Burma, 142, 146, 152, 153, 159
Kalewa, Burma, 136, 146, 152, 154–157, 159, 170, 261

Kampala, Uganda, 7, 53, 182, 222–224, 226
Kapenguira, Kanya, 244
Karamajong (tribe), 226–227
Karatina, Kenya, 207, 214, 215–218
KAR Camel Battery, 15, 57
KAR Coastal Defence Unit/Battery, 57, 269
KAR March Past, 180, 218, 257
KAR Mounted Infantry, 31, 43, 46, 49
KAR Reserve of Officers, 54, 57
Karioker (see East African Carrier Corps)
Kashmir Rifles (2 Bn), 32, 174
Kasina Ndoo, MBE, Senior Chief (former RSM), 230
Katagiri, Gen (Jap), 254
Kathuru Nyaga, Chief, MM (former Sgt), 211, 230
Kemble, Major D.H.A., 125–126, 130
Kenya African Union, 201–202
Kenya Defence Force, 59, 240
Kenya, Mount, 192, 204, 205, 207, 214–215, 219, 224, 246, 248
Kenya Navy, 268
Kenya Navy Volunteer Reserve, 265
Kenya Police Force (including Special Branch, Police Reserve, Police Air Wing & General Service Unit), 202, 204, 205, 213–215, 218, 220, 232–234, 245, 246, 257, 271
Kenya Regt (Territorial Force), 57, 63, 176, 202, 204, 208 & Ch 13 *passim*

Kenyatta, Jomo (see Jomo Kenyatta)
Kenya-Uganda Railway, 29 & Ch 3 *passim*, 178, 186
Keren (battle) Eritrea, 75, 78
Khartoum, Sudan, 76, 77, 210, 228
Khedive of Egypt, 6, 10
Khedive Ismail, HMT, 142, 270
Kiambu & District, Kenya, 205
Kidd, Major, 197
Kidepo River & escarpment, Uganda, 226
Kikuyu (tribe), 5, 58, 201, Ch 11 *passim*, 245
Kikuyu Home Guard (later Kikuyu Guard), 202–204, 208, 239, 245
Kilimanjaro, Mount, Tanganyika, 29, Ch 3 *passim*, 237, 253
Kilindini, Mombasa, Kenya, 264, 265, 269
Kilwa, Tanganyika, 38, 39, 42
Kilwa Force (was 1 Division), 42–44
King, Flt Lt D., RAF, 236–237
King's Own Yorkshire Light Infantry, 243
King's Royal Rifle Corps, 243, 248
King, Tom, Rt Hon, PC, MP, Secretary of State for Defence, 254
King's African Rifles & East African Forces Dinner Club, xi, 254, 262
Kismayu, Somalia, 53, 76–79, 80 (Kismayu Command–It), 82, 84, 85
Kisumu, 30, 41
Kitali, Kenya, 249, 250

287

Kitchener, FM Lord, Secretary of State for War, 33
Kitui, Kenya, 229–231
Koehl, Capt (Ge), 45
Kohima, India (battle), 159
Königsberg, SMS, 27, Ch 3 *passim*
Kota Tinggi, Johore, Malaya, 192, 196, 197
Kraut, Major (Ge), 37, 43
Kuantan, Malaya, 194, 197, 198
Kul Kabir, Ethiopia, 106–107
Kuma Mukinga, MM, President of African Court (ex Sgt), 230
Kyauktaw, Burma, 139

Lakes, Battle of the, Ethiopia, 96–99
Lancashire Fusiliers (1 Bn), 202
Lancaster (aircraft), 204
Lancer Squadron (Lady Monica's Own), 30
Landridge, Lt R.A. (later Major, MC), 89–90, 172
Langworthy, Emily B., 263
Lango Field Force, 9
Lari massacre, Kenya, 203
"Larkhill" EAE Training Centre, Kenya, 270
Las Koreh, Somaliland, 21, 23
Lathbury, Gen Sir Gerald, GCB DSO MBE, 205, 248
Leach, Major L. "Bulgy" (later Lt Col), 84, 102, 269, 276
Leakey, Dr Gray, 214–215
Leakey, Sgt Nigel, VC, 99, 242
Leeming, 2Lt P.B.B., 196–199
Leese, Lt Gen Sir Oliver, Bt KCB CBE DSO, 158
Le Gentilhomme, Gen (Fr), 68, 73, 111, 131

Leik Hill, Burma (battle), 148–149, 176
Lennox-Brown, Major O., 240
Leopold, King of the Belgians, 5
Letpan, Burma, 164–165
Letse, Burma (battle), 161–163
Letsegan, Burma (battle), 149–150
Lewin, Capt T.C.C. "Chippy" (later Lt Col, OBE, MC), 84–90, 138–141, 149–150
Lewis, 2Lt P., 228
Liboi, Kenya, 82, 83
Liddell, Alan, Lt (later DC), 213–218, 229–231
145 Light Anti-Aircraft Battery RA, 120
7 Light Cavalry (C Sqn), 151
102 Light Regt, WAA, 165
Lindi, Tanganyika, 42, 93
Lindley, Lt P.A.N. (later Major), 138–141
Livingstone, Dr David, 1
Loch Alvie, HMS, 267
Loch Fada, HMS, 266
Loch Fyne, HMS, 267
Lockhart, Gen Sir Rob, KCB CIE MC, 176
Lokitaung, Uganda, 61, 62, 78, 80
Lomej, Uganda, 225–226
Looff, Capt (Ge), Imperial German Navy, 36
Lubwa's Fort, Uganda, 8
Lugard, Capt F.D. (later Lord), 2, 6–7
Lugh Ferrandi, Somalia, 30, 85, 92
Lunt, Maj Gen James, CBE, 133, 175
Lusaka, N. Rhodesia, 184, 186
Lushai Brigade, 141, 159–160

Lyall Grant, Maj Gen Ian, MC, 276
Lyttelton, Oliver, Rt Hon (later Lord Chandos), 189

Macdonald, Capt A., 249
MacDonald, Capt J.R.L. (later Major), 7, 8
MacDonald, Malcolm, Rt Hon, 188
MacGillivray, Sir Donald, 190
Mackerith, 2Lt N., 224
Mackinley, Capt W.W. (later Major), 240, 241, 269
Mackinnon & Mackinnon Road Project, 6, 181, 182, 221–222
Macnab, Major J.F. (later Brig, DSO), 84, 85, 117, 121–123, 147, 168
MacPherson Capt A.D. "Mac", 60
McCalman, 2Lt A. (later Capt MC), 242
McCalman, Capt D.H. (later MC), 242
McCreath, Capt (later MC), 73
McCormick, Lt G.A.C., 147
McKillop, Major J., 250
McKinnon, Capt L., 16
McMurtrie, 2Lt A., 183–186
McNeill, Capt M., 13
Machefaux, Commandant (Fr), 124
Mackenzie, Lt Col J.W.E., 164
Madagascar, 60, 96, 109, 110, Ch 7 *passim*, 239
Madden, Lt Col C., 248–250
Maguire, Capt C.M., 2
Mahitsey, Madagascar, 122–123
Mahiwa, Tanganyika (battle), 43
Maji, Ethiopia, 94–95

Majunga, Madagascar, 116, 119, 123
Makarios, Archbishop (later President), 266
Malaya (now Western Malaysia) & Malay Emergency, 60, 136, 187 & Ch 10 *passim*, 202, 208, 221
Malayan Communist Party and Communist Terrorists, 118 & Ch 10 *passim*
Malay Brigade (1) & Malay Bn (1), 193
Malgash, 123, 124, 125, 126, 129, 130
Manakara, Madagascar, 129, 130
Mandalay, Burma, 133, 158
Mandera, Kenya, 60, 62, 66, 92
Mandera, Somaliland, 18
Manders, Capt R., 217
Manning, Brig-Gen Sir William, 3, 15, 167
Mans, Capt R.S.N. "Toto", (later Maj Gen CBE), xi, 127, 131, 254
Mansergh, Maj Gen R., 171
Margaret, HRH Princess, 177, 248
Marindin, Brig P.C., 159
Marsabit, Kenya, 78, 79, 80, 82
Marshall, Capt J., 217
Martini, Gen (It), 107–108
Marventano, Col (It), 103
Masyuka Kivati, Pte, holder of the Margaret Wheatley Cross, 219
Massawa, Eritrea, 10, 75, 88, 94, 104, 108
Mather, 2Lt J., 196

289

Mathews, Lt L. RN (later Brig-Gen, Zanzibar & Sir Lloyd), 1
Masai, tribe & Plain, 5, 29, 36, 52, 184, 231
Mau Mau, 201, & Ch 11 *passim*, 221, 222, 239, 244, 245, 247, 249, 266, 270
Mauritius & Mauritian Regt, 3, 132, 131–134, 181, 262
Mawku, Burma, 147, 149
Mawlaik, Burma, 147, 149
Mayers, Capt R., 244
Mayotte Island, 118–119
M'bagathi Camp, Kenya, 58, 241, 269
Meiktila, Burma, 158, 159, 162
Menelike, Emperor of Ethiopia, 10, 65
Mercury, HMS, 29
Mega, Ethiopia, 80
Merille, tribe, 61, 80, 233–234
Mersa Matruh (battle), 76
Meru, tribe, 28, 36, 254
Messervy, Brig F. (later Lt Gen Sir Frank KCSI KBE CB DSO), 78
Metras, Col (Fr), 128
Meyer, Capt (Fr), 130
Midway (battle), 136
MILCOL, 160
Military Labour Bureau, 41
Military Training Ordinance, Kenya, 243
Mills, Lt H.M., 151
Minnery, Lt J. (later Col, MC), 23
Mirgo Pass, Somaliland, 71–72
Mission 101, 76–77
Mitchell, Maj Gen Sir Philip, GCMG MC, 202, 241, 242, 243

Mogadishu, Somalia, 78, 80, 85–86, 100, 111, 113, 179
Mohamedi, SS, 181
Molloy, Capt P.G. (later Lt Col, OBE MC), 61, 92–93, 106, 107–108
Mollison, 2Lt A.G. (later MC), 72
Mombasa, Kenya, 5, 29, 30, 32, 57, 58, 59, 60, 69, 75, 79, 95, 117, 177, 179, 181, 218, 221, 225, 229, 241, 245, 249, 250, 261, 264, 269, 270
Montgomery, Capt R.K. (later Lt Col, MC), 210
Mooring, Sir George, 267
Moraine (aircraft, Fr), 119, 124
Morcombe, Lt Col P.A. (later Col), 117, 125, 147, 149, 245
Morris, Capt H.H. de B, 16
Morton, Capt M., 197
Moscoff, Capt S., 250
Moshi, Tanganyika, 29, 30, 31, 60–61, 62
Mountbatten, Admiral Lord Louis (later Admiral of the Fleet Earl, of Burma), 137, 141, 144, 145, 175, 179, 267
27 Mountain Battery RA, 39, 81
Mountney-Jephson A.J., 6, 275
Moyale, Kenya, 52, 60, 66, 67, 76, 92
Moyse-Bartlett, Lt Col H. MBE MA PhD, xi, 13, 50, 141, Appendix A, 258, 263
Mozambique & Channel, 115, 118, 184, 221
Mulandi, RSM, BEM, 217, 231
Mulholland, Capt J., 122
Mullah (The), (Seyed Mohamed

Abdullahi Hassan), 9, 12 & Ch 2 *passim*
Mundy, Lt Col P.R.M. "Pat", DSO (later Col, DSO & bar), 61–62, 92–93
MUSKETEER, Operation, see Suez
Mussolini, 65, 66, 84, 103
Mvita, HMEAS, 229, 264–268
Mwanga, King, 6
Mwagangi Mwenga, Chief, M.M. (ex-Sgt Major), 230
Mweiga, Kenya, 208

Nairobi, Kenya, 52, 55, 58, 63, 67, 79, 108, 111, 174, 176, 179, 184, 186, 201, 218, 211, 236, 243, 247, 249, 250, 251, 269, 270
Naivasha, Lake & Swamp, Kenya, 219, 247, 248, 249, 270
Nakuru & OCTU, Kenya, 59, 60, 186, 222, 242, 243, 249, 250
Nam, Gen (It), 103
Nandi, tribe, 28, 172, 196, 231
Nandi Scouts, 36
Nanyuki, Kenya, 62, 104, 2190, 224, 237, 255, 270
Narungombe, Tanganyika, 207, 232
Nasi, Lt Gen G.B. (It) (later Vice Governor-General, Ethiopia), 69, 77, 103, 107, 108
Natal Mounted Rifles (1 Bn), 95, 96, 97
National Service, 186, 187, 188, 191, 206, 224, 225
Naumann, Capt (Ge), 43
Navy, Army & Air Force Institutes, 177, 194, 222
Nazer, Lt J., 269

Nderi, Senior Chief, 202
Ndinga Kitonga, T.P. Sgt (ex Sgt KAR), 231
Neghelli, Ethiopia, 92, 93, 95
Ngong Hills, Kenya, 240, 241
Nidd, Lt K.E., MC, 151
Nigerian Brigade, (1914–18), 38, 40, 42–43
23 Nigerian Brigade, 81, 82, 85, 86, 87, 88, 94, 96, 100, 101
Nigerian Regt; 1 Bn, 81, 88, 98, 139; 2 Bn, 81, 97, 100, 101; 3 Bn, 81
Nightingale, Major R.C.W. (later Col OBE), 232–234, 247, 248
Niles, John J., 237, 263
Norbury, Lt W.R., MC, 144
Northamptonshire Regt (2 Bn), 117, 118
Northbrook, HMS, 21
Northern Brigade, 55, 57
Northern Railway (Tanga-Moshi), 29, & Ch 3 *passim*
27 (Northern Rhodesia) Brigade, 119, 130
Northern Rhodesia Regiment, 56, 176, 242; 1 Bn, 69, 70, 71, 74, 81, 93, 142, 149, 150; 3 Bn, 163, 165, 167
Northey, Maj Gen Sir Edward, 40, 42, 43, 45, 47
Northern Frontier District, Kenya, 52, 53, 62, 66, 113, 219, 232, 236–237
Nott, Lt Col D. (later Brig, DSO), 224
Nunn, Lt C., 217
Nunneley, Capt J.H., 254
Nyamwezi, tribe, 258
Nyangao (battle), 174

Nyere, Dr Julius, (later President), 253
Nyeri, Kenya, 207, 214, 250
Nyrenda, Lt (Tan), 253
Nyvasha, Kenya, 7

Obbia, Somalia (including Sultan of), 13, 15, 17
O'Coffey, Capt G., 216
Odin, HMS, 22
Ogaden, clan, 11 & Ch 2 *passim*
Ogaden, Somali Region, Ethiopia, 12, 109, 111, 112, 113, 190, 191
O'Grady, Brig-Gen H. de C., 39, 43, 44, 174
O'Hara, Capt H., 250
O'Hare, CSM J., 151
Olivey, Capt H.E., 16
Omo River, Ethiopia, 100–102, 103
Onslow, Capt E. "Ted" MC (later Major, MC & bar), 100, 106, 124, 152, 178, 254
Operation Centres (Ethiopian Patriotic Movement), 59
Ormsby, Lt Col J., 107
O'shea, Mrs Eloise, 97
Otto, Capt Ernst (Ge), 39
Owen, Brig W., 81
Owoko Okumo, Sgt, 171

Pace, Col T.A., OBE, 235
Pahang, Sultan of, State of, 194–197, 198
Pagoda Hill, Burma (battle), 137–140
Palmer 2Lt A.P., 121
PAMFORCE, 45, 46
Parton, 2Lt B., 224
Patel, D.V. & R.V., tailors, 215

40th Pathan Regt, 39
Patriot Movement (Ethiopian), 60, 75, 76, 77–78, 94, 97–98, 100, 102, 103, 104, 105–106, 107
Payne, Lt D.J., 147
Payne-Gallwey, Lt Col L.P., 71–72
Pearl Harbor, 135
Pearse, L., 247
Peddie, Lt Col J.C.T., OBE MC (later DL), 228
Pegasus, HMS, 29
Peirse, Air Marshal Sir Richard, 137, 175
Penang Island, Malaya, 192
Perkins, 2Lt R., 225–228
Peters, 2Lt D., 206–207, 219
Peters, Karl (later von), 6
Phillips, Major G.E., 15
Phillips, Col G.F., 54
Phillips, Capt "Phillipo", 272
"Piano", Pte (nickname), 199
Piccinelli, Gen (It), 107–108
Pienaar, Brig D.H. (SA) (later Maj Gen), 81, 88, 91
Pienaar, Spr, SAEC, 106
Piper Pacer (aircraft), 220
Pitt, Lt John (later Capt), 102, 103, 107, 275
Platt, Lt Gen Sir William (later Gen GBE KCB DSO), 77, 78, 103, 108, 111, 116
Plenderlieth, Robin "Dingo", 247
Plunkett, Major A.W.V., 4, 12, 16
Pocock, Col A.H., 86
Poli, Gen (It), 107
Poppleton, Lt W., 156
Portal, Marshal of the RAF (later Lord), 175
Port Sudan, 78, 94, 108

Potez (aircraft) (Fr), 119
Powles, Lt "Buster", 269
Pownall, Lt Gen (later Sir Henry, KCB KBE DSO MC), 175
Prendergast, J., 204
Price, 2Lt M., 224
Price, Capt M.C.H. (later Major), 236
Prince of Wales, HMS, 135
Princess Royal, HRH, 177–178
Profumo, Brig J., Secretary of State for War (later CBE), 272
Pseudo-gangs, 204–205, 246
Punjab Mounted Infantry, 15
Punjab Regt; 29 Bn, 31; 33 Bn, 17; 4/14 Bn, 162, 1/2 Bn 3/15 Bn & Punjabi Ridge, 69, 70, 109; 1/2 Bn & 3/15 Bn & Punjabi Ridge
Purse, 2Lt J.F., 74

Quebec Conference, 136
Quetta & Staff College, now Pakistan, 136

Rajbir Singh, Col, 32–33
Rajput Regt (4/7 Bn), 154–155
Ramillies, HMS, 115, 116
Ramree Island, Burma, 163–164, 270
Ranchi, India, 171–173, 255, 262
Rangoon (now Yangon), Burma, 135, 136
RAYFORCE, 244
Raynal, Col (Fr), 110
Redhead, 2Lt, 240
Reid, AVM G.R.M., 78
Repulse, HMS, 135
Reserved Areas, Ethiopia, 111, 113

Rhino, "HMS", 145
Rhino Boys, 171
Rhino Review, 171
Rhodes, Cecil, 4
Rhodesian Native Regiment, 46
Rhodesian African Rifles; 1 Bn, 163, 165–167
Rhodesian Regiment; 2 Bn, 33, 35, 37, 38
Richie, Brig A. Mc D. DSO, 81
Ridley, Lt, 90
Rifle Brigade (95th), 243
Ringrose, Major, 104
Robathan, Major D.E., 58
Roberts, FM Lord, VC, 4, 16
Robertson, Capt J.D.I., 120
Robertson-Glasgow, Lt Col N.C., 104, 146, 231, 276
Robinson, Lt, 140
Robson, Major G.G., 127, 129
Rodd Line, 10, 11, 12
Roman, 2Lt R.T., 73
Rooken-Smith, Lt D., 250
Roosevelt, President Franklin D., 66, 115
Roosevelt, K., 252
Roosevelt, President Theodore, 33
Rosalind, HMEAS (formerly HMS), 229, 264–267
Rovuma River, 43, 44
Royal Air Force, 22–23, 56–57, 77, 104, 108, 112, 155, 194–195, 204, 236–237
Royal Army Veterinary Corps, 218, 246
Royal Artillery Historical Trust, 269
Royal Australian Air Force, 95
Royal East African Navy, 229, 239, 264–268
Royal Flying Corps, 45

Royal Fusiliers (25 Bn) (The Frontiersmen), 33, 43, 44
Royal Natal Carbineers (1 Bn), 81, 87, 91
Royal Navy Air Service, 35
Royal Scots Fusiliers, 117
Royal Wajir Yacht Club, 271–274
Ruck, Supt B. GM (later & bar), 213–215
Ruck, murdered Kenyan farmer, 202
Rudolph, Lake, Kenya border, 55, 80, 104, 232
Rufiji River & Delta, Tanganyika, 29, 39, 41, 231
Rusk, Major G.A. MC, 72
Rutherford, Major "Jock", 250
Ru-Ywa, Burma, 164–165

Sadler, Lt D. (later Capt), 111
Sale, Capt R.E.W. MC, 71
Salehe, "Cpl" MM., 231–232
Salisbury, Lord, Prime Minister, 1, 6
Salween River, Burma, 133, 171
Sandford, Brig D.A., DSO & bar, 76–77
Savoia (aircraft) (It), 67
Savoia Division (It), 75, 88
Scawin, Major A.L., 110–111
Schnee, Dr, 27 & Ch 3 *passim*
School of Oriental & African Studies, 255–256
Sciasciamanna, Ethiopia, 94, 96, 97, 103
Scot, Capt M., 224
Scott, Lt A.J., 152
Seaforth Highlanders (6 Bn), 117
Seikpyu, Burma, 160
Selika Walani, PSM DCM, 194
Sellar, Capt B.W., 152

Selous, Lt F.C. DSO, 33, 39, 240
Senegalese troops (Fr), 109–110, 119, 121, 124, 131
Severn, HMS, 29
Seymour, Sgt A.R. MM, 125
Seymour, Capt G., 270
Shackleton, Lt D., 169
Shaw, Major J., 250
Sheikh & Sheikh Pass, Somaliland, 69, 70
Shepperson, Prof G. CBE, 257–263
Shepperd, Brig-Gen S.H., 36
Sherman, Henry, 241
Shimber Beris, Somaliland (battle), 20–21
Shirreff, Lt D. (later Major MC), 83, 84, 85, 96, 97, 100, 118–119, 254, 276
Shorthose, Col W.J.T., 46
Shropshire, HMS, 85
Shwebo Plain, Burma, 158
Shwegyin, Burma, 133, 136, 156, 157, 158
Siam (Thailand), 133, 136
Sierra Leone Regt (1 Bn), 139–140
Sikh Regt (2 Bn), 15
Sikorski helicopters, 194
Sinclair, Major I.A., 219
Singapore, 135, 136, 192
Sittang River, Burma, 133, 171
Sittaung, Burma, 142, 145, 150, 158, 168
SKEECOL, 153–155
Slade, Humphrey, 203
Sladen, Capt, 138
Slim, Lt Gen W. (later FM Viscount), 136, 137, 138, 141, 144, 157, 158, 159, 174–175, 189, 276

Smallwood, Brig G.R. (later Maj Gen DSO MC), 88, 91, 108
Smith, Lt Gen Sir Arthur, 173
Smith, Lt N.D., 147
Smith-Dorrien, Gen Sir Horace, 34
Smuts, Lt Gen J.C. (later FM), 34–40, 75, 79, 90, 115, 116, 119
Soames, Major L.H., 32
Soaper, 2Lt, 229
Soddu, Ethiopia, 96, 97–100
Somalia Gendarmerie, 111–113
Somali Guard Companies, 110–111
Somaliland Scouts, 110–113, 176
Somali Hill, Burma, 162
Somaliland Signals & Somaliland Signals Squadron, 111
Somerville, V. Adm (later Adm of the Fleet Sir James), 117
Soroppa (battle), Ethiopia (incl Little Soroppa), 92–93, 95
SAAF, 82, 104
1 (SA) Brigade, 79, 81, 84, 85, 86, 88, 94, 95
2 (SA) Brigade, 80, 94, 95, 104
5 (SA) Brigade, 75, 80, 94
7 (SA) Brigade, 119, 130
1 (SA) Division, 75, 78, 80, 93
3 (SA) Field Company SAEC, 81
1 (SA) Light Tank Company, 81
Southern Brigade, 55
South-East Asia Command (SEAC), 136, 137, 174
Southforce, 104–105
South Lancashire Regiment (2 Bn), 163
Special Boat Section, 150
3 Special Service Brigade, 141
Spitfires (aircraft), 165, 167, 169

Spurway, Capt J.O. (later Major), 220
21 Squadron RAF, 236–237
Stanley, H. Morton, 5–6, 258, 263
Stanley Mathenge, Mau Mau leader, 203, 206
Stanyon, Robert, 271
Stephanis, Lake, Kenya/Ethiopian Border, 232
Stephen, J., 247
Stephens, Major P., 253
Sillitoe, Sir Percy, 202
St Lawrence, Lt Col (Fr), 129
Stalin, J., 137
Stewart, Brig Gen, 31
Stevenson, Capt, 140
Stilwell, Lt Gen J. (Vinegar Joe) (USA), 136, 137, 141, 158, 175
Stockwell, Major (later Lt Col), 191, 224
Stoneley, Major C.H. (Crew) (later Brig, CBE), 57, 58, 272
Stopford, Lt Gen M. (later Sir Monty, KBE), 141
Stratheden, Capt the Lord, 240–241
STREAM LINE JANE (Operation), 119 et seq
Sturges, Maj Gen R.G. (later Lt Gen Sir Robert, KBE CB DSO), 115
Sudanese Frontier Battalion, 77
Sudan, incl Sudanese Defence Force and SUDANCOL, 2, 12, 104, 105, 226–228, 243
Suez, Egypt, incl Canal & Canal Zone, 181–182, 226–229
Summers, Capt G.H. (later Col), 18–19, 22

37 Supply Depot EAASC, 220
Swallow, Major J.J.H. (later Lt Col, OBE), 58, 177–179
Swayne, Major H.G.C. (later Col, CMG FRGS FRZS), 10–11
Swayne, Capt E. (later Sir Eric, KCMG, Governor of Somaliland), 12–15
Swynnerton, 2Lt R., MC (later Sir Roger, CMG OBE MC), 100
Syrfret, Adm Sir Neville, 115

Tabora, Tanzania, 47, 52, 55, 60
Talbot, Rear Adm F., 267
Taleh, Somaliland, 21 & Ch 2 *passim*
Tana, HMS, 265
Tana River, Kenya, 53, 57, 78, 79, 82, 274
Tanga, Tanzania, 30, 31–32, 53
1 Tanganyika Field Ambulance, 81
255 Tank Brigade, 159
Tapp, Maj Gen N. (later Sir Nigel, KBE CB DSO DL), 225
Task Force T. (RN), 82
Taungup Valley, Chaung & Pass, Burma, 164–167
Taveta & Gap, 30, 35–36
Tawney, 2Lt T.J., 207–209
Temple-Borman, Capt E.W., 92
Templer, Gen Sir Gerald (later FM, KG), 189–190
Ternan, Major, 8
Thesiger, Col G.H., 28
Thomas, M.H., DO (former Capt), 231–232
Thorne, Lt MC, 100
Thornycroft, Capt E.G.M., 31
THROAT, Operation, 118

Thunderbolt (aircraft), 167
Tiddim & Valley, Burma, 141, 142–13, 146, 152, 154, 159
Tighe, Brig Gen M., (later Maj Gen Sir Michael), 35–36
Timbers, Brig K.A., 269
Times, The, 18
Townley, Capt, 150
Transvaal Scottish (1 Bn), 81, 88
Tree Tops Hotel, Kenya, 218
Tremlett, Capt J., 169–170
Trengganu State & Sultan, W Malaysia, 195
Tribal Police, Kenya, 202, 203, 205, 230–231
Tricore, Col (Fr), 129
Trimmer Major C.D. (Bombo) (later Lt Col, DSO), 106, 143
Triscott, Capt L.E.L., 34
TROJAN Teams, 205
Tufts, RSM H., 217
Tug Argan, Somaliland (battle), 69–74, 111
Tuna, SS, 56, 74
Tunku Abdul Rahman, 190
Turkana, tribe & region, 51, 52, 62, 80
Turnbull, Major J., 72
Turnbull, Sir Richard, GCMG, 232
Tutton, Lt Col J.T.S., 169
TWEEDCOL, 123, 128–129
Tweedy, Major H.D., 123, 126
Twining, Sir Edward, KCMG, MBE, 264
Twin Pioneer (aircraft), 236–237, 274

6 Uganda Field Ambulance, 81
56 Uganda Field Battery EAA, 120, 126, 130
Uganda Rifles, 8–9
U-GO (Plan C), 137, 141
Uhuru, 236, 253, 267
Urquart, Maj Gen, 189

Valencia (aircraft), 56
Valentine, Lt, 89–90
Valentine, Capt C.L. (later Lt Col), 240, 242, 243
van Deventer, Maj Gen J.L., 35 et seq, 174
Vernon, Lt Cdr M., 272
Vernon, Lt Col R. (later Brig), 250–251
Vetch, Lt A. (later Major), 254–256, 250–251
Veys, Capt C.A. (later Dr, MD, MB), 235
Viceroy of India, 8
Vichy French Government & Forces, 68, 76, 109–111, 115, & Ch 7 *passim*, 135
Vickers Vincent (aircraft), 56
Victoria, Queen, 1, 6
Victory Searchlight Tattoo, Ranchi, 172, 173
von Lettow Vorbeck, Lt Col (later Maj Gen) (Ge), 27 et seq, 275

Waganda (nation), 222–223
Wahle, Maj Gen Kurt (Ge), 30, 40, 43–44, 47
Wahehe (tribe), 25
Wajir, Kenya, 55, 61, 67, 68, 78, 82, 92, 236–237
Wajirati (clan), 110

Wakamba (tribe), 5, 36, 58, 144, 181, 256
Wakefield, Major (QM) F., 244, 249
Walker, Col H.A., 54
Walker, P.H. (DC) (formerly Lt), 236
Walsh, Capt P. (later Maj Gen OBE MC), 249
Wanyamwezi (tribe), 25
Wapshare, Maj Gen R., 32–33
Ward, Lt Col L.E.S., 32
Ward, Capt R. 179
War Dog Training School, 219
Warsengeli (clan & Sultan), 14 & Ch 2 *passim*
Warton, 2Lt W., 96
32 Water Supply Coy SAEC, 79
Watkins, Lt Col Oliver (later CBE DSO), 41–41, 49
Watson, Lt Col J.E.D., DSO, 147–149, 176–179
Watson, Lt, 129
Watson-Baker, Capt J. 168
Wavell, Maj Gen A.P. (later FM Earl), 56, 68, 75, 76, 78, 94, 109, 115, 135, 136
Weaver, Len CBE, 239 & Ch 13 *passim*
Wellesley (aircraft), 112
Wessel's Scouts, 30
4 (WA) Brigade, 165
5 (WA) Brigade, 138
6 (WA) Brigade, 38, 141
23 (WA) Brigade (later Nigerian), 79
81 (WA) Division, 133, 137–141, 164–167
82 (WA) Division, 133, 164–167
West African Frontier Force, 3
West, 2Lt J.M., 124

West, Sgt J.E., DCM, 93
West Indian Regiment, 4, 38, 44–45
Wetherall, Maj Gen H.E. de R, CB, DSO OBE MC, 81, 90, 91, 103, 107, 108
White, Capt 'Chalkey', 269
Whitworth Major G.B., ERD, 186
Wickham, D., DC, 272
Wigram, 2Lt P., 224
Wilkinson, Lt Col J.S., 22
Willey, Lt, 122
Williams, Sgt George, DCM, 31
Williams, Capt W.H., 6
Williamson, Lt W.H., 125
Willis, Lt J., 206
Wilson, Lt Bruce, 102
Wilson, Capt E.C.T. (later Hon Lt Col, VC), 72–73, 155
Winchester Castle, RMS, 117
Wingate, Lt Col O.C. (later Maj Gen DSO), 76, 77, 103, 137, 138, 154, 175
Winkley, Col., 58
Wintgens, Capt (Ge), 42–43
Wisdom, Alan, 225
Wise, Capt P.P., 169
Wisiki Bauleni, Cpl, DCM, 152

Women's Auxiliary Territorial Service (EA), 59–60, 142
Woodley, W., MC, 246, 248
Woolner, Maj Gen G.C., CB MC, 138–140

Yao (tribe), 3, 14, 15, 52, 54, 68, 74
Yeatman, Major, 107
Yeoman, Lt Guy (later Capt), 142
Yoke Har, CT, 198–199
Young, Sir Arthur, 190
Yunnan, China & Yunnan Armies, 137

Zanzibar, Sultan, Sultanate & Protectorate, 1, 4, 5, 10, 27, 51, 52, 172, 225, 229, 264, 265, 266, 267
Zanzibar African Rifles & Armed Constabulary, 9, 36
Zanzibari Field Ambulance, 81, 170
Zeila, Somaliland, 11, 70, 73, 110
Zeppelin, 44
Zomba, Malawi, 43, 52, 184–186, 196, 261